Studies in Eighteenth-Century Culture

VOLUME 14

Studies in

Eighteenth-Century

Culture VOLUME 14

EDITED BY O M Brack, Jr.
Arizona State University

PUBLISHED *for the*
AMERICAN SOCIETY FOR EIGHTEENTH-CENTURY STUDIES
by THE UNIVERSITY OF WISCONSIN PRESS

Published 1985

The University of Wisconsin Press
114 North Murray Street
Madison, Wisconsin 53715

The University of Wisconsin Press, Ltd.
1 Gower Street
London WC1E 6HA, England

First printing

Printed in the United States of America

LC 75–648277

ISBN 0–299–10040–5

Editorial Readers for Volume Fourteen

Contents

Preface

This is the 200th anniversary of Samuel Johnson's death. No other English author has written so perceptively about the life of writing and scholarship. Numerous passages come to mind, but perhaps his comments in *Adventurer* no. 85, written in late August 1753 in the midst of compiling his *Dictionary*, are most appropriate to our endeavors. As a starting point for the description of a scholar's activities, he borrows a passage from Bacon's essay "Of Study" that "reading makes a full man, conversation a ready man, and writing an exact man." "To read, write, and converse in due proportions," is the ideal, Johnson observes, but he realizes that "for all of these there is not equal opportunity." Nevertheless, it is "reasonable to have perfection in our eye; that we may always advance toward it, though we know it can never be reached." The danger of wearing out our days and nights in "perpetual research and solitary meditation" among our books and manuscripts is that whatever we gain in wisdom is likely to be lost by our inability to communicate our ideas. Happily for the members of the American Society for Eighteenth-Century Studies there are ample opportunities at the national and regional meetings to take the knowledge collected in solitude and learn its application by mixing with other scholars. But more important than the free exchange of ideas in conversation and discussion, is writing, for only by writing do we subject our ideas to careful examination and review and fix our thoughts. From among those scholars who filled their minds with ideas, readied themselves for discussion, and fixed their thoughts in writing, we have chosen the best.

O M BRACK, JR.

Arizona State University
December 13, 1984

Studies in Eighteenth-Century Culture

VOLUME 14

"The Complicated Plot of Piracy": Aspects of English Criminal Law and the Image of the Pirate in Defoe

JOEL H. BAER

The ocean is not only a place of venture, suffering, and achievement for Defoe, it is also a place of crime. Long before Pope, he had examined man's paradoxical nature and found in his actions at sea an emblem for his "dark" side:

> What strange, what inconsistent thing's a man!
> Who shall his nature search, his life explain?
> If in the ocean of his crimes we sail,
> Satire, our navigation all will fail;
> Shipwreck'd in dark absurdities of crime.[1]

He would have thought of a very specific set of crimes, knowledgeable as he was of merchant shipping, naval warfare, and colonial history. But throughout his lifetime, piracy, which flourished along all the European trade routes, was the most flagrant crime of all. Pirates suited him well as subjects, not only because they were in the news but also because their stories brought together so many of his favorite topics—travel, trade, crime, colonization, the national security, and

This essay won the ASECS James Clifford Essay Prize for 1983. It is reprinted with permission from *The Eighteenth Century: Theory and Interpretation*, ed. Robert M. Markley, Jeffrey R. Smitten, and Joel C. Weinsheimer (Lubbock: Texas Tech Press, 1982).

the isolation of the human soul. His stories of Singleton, Avery, Gow, and the others in the *General History of the Pyrates* (1724–28) may, in the widest sense, be motivated by the urge to see pirates as symbols of Satan's temptations and of our own spiritual weaknesses;[2] in the words of John Durant, "(O my soul) thou carryest petty pirates within thee, that will never fight for thee (flesh will not fight against the world and Satan) nay which war against thy soul. Look to it therefore to watch against those within, that thou mayest the better maintaine thy fight without."[3] Or, as the *Mariner's Divine Mate* exclaims, "The Sea hath strange Monsters, but mans heart far stranger then they."[4]

In *Popular Fiction Before Richardson*, John J. Richetti identifies the appeal of the pirate stories as that of the "daemonic" and concludes that the pirate embodied for the age that "radical individualism which summarizes the totally secular view of experience," or, in other words, "the uncommitted and disengaged modern personality."[5] But before we can fully understand the symbol, it will be helpful to know what sort of literal criminal Defoe took the pirate to be. In the legal literature and the reports of trials which he studied while compiling the *General History*, Defoe learned that the crime of piracy was unique, complex, and ambiguous as well as hateful. I would like to outline in this essay what he learned and how he used his knowledge in a variety of fictional and journalistic works. If this study does not rescue the unity of the novels, it may sharpen our awareness of the strange condition in which Defoe, his characters, and his age found the human heart and reveal the basis upon which Defoe and others were to erect the "imposing and terrifying heroic statuary" of the pirate.[6]

I

Defoe was justly proud of his knowledge of marine commerce and the legal terms relating to it. At times this pride appears as condescension to the gentlemen who will have nothing to do with the world of business, those who, reading his *Tour Thro' the Whole Island of Great Britain*, will have become confused by the discussion of Thames shipping practices: "But I must land, lest this part of the account seems to smell of the tarr, and I should tire the gentlemen with leading them out of their knowledge."[7] At other times, he seems genuinely disturbed by the ignorance of the "experts," especially Britain's lawyers, half of whose cases involved commercial law: "How do they mumble and chew the Sea Phrases, Merchants Language, and Terms of Foreign Negoce; like the Ass chewing of Thistles: When they come to Argue about Charter Parties, Protests against the Sea, Demorages, Avarages, Primage, Port-charges, Damages, Running Foul, Solvage, Prizage, Barratry, Piracies, Breaking Bulk, Delivering Ports, Taking a Hull, and a hundred such things needless here to report."[8] Defoe's own familiarity with the criminal law of the sea is demonstrated by his "Abstract of the Civil Law and Statute Law now in force in relation to Piracy,"[9] and, in a more creative form, by an episode from *Robinson Crusoe*.

In the early pages of *The Farther Adventures*, Crusoe asserts that he would be justified in hanging the three "pirate sailors" for their disruptive behavior on the island. Charles Gildon was quick to condemn Crusoe's notion and, by implication, the author who could give it to his chief character: "'So if I had hang'd them all, I had been much in the right, and should have been justified by the Laws of God and Man,' the contrary of which Assertion is directly true, viz., That if you had hang'd them all *you* had been guilty of downright Murther by all the Laws of God and Man; for pray, sweet Sir, what Authority had Robinson Crusoe so much as to fine, or inflict any Punishment upon any Man."[10] Divine Law to the contrary notwithstanding, it would seem by 11–12 Wm III, c. 7, that Crusoe is on solid ground. First, he properly identifies the mutineers as pirates, for "If any Commander or Master of a Ship, or Seaman or Mariner . . . combine to yield up, or run away from any Ship, or lay violent Hands on his Commander, or endeavour to make a Revolt in the Ship, he shall be adjudged a Pyrate" (*General History*, p. 379). Thus, even without the intent to run off and commit piracy, mutineers could be treated as confirmed pirates. Considering the frequency with which Crusoe calls the men "pirate Sailors" and the role that their piratical nature plays in the development of *The Farther Adventures*, it is mandatory that this rigor of English law be observed.

Once the sailors had been adjudged pirates—Crusoe would grant them a trial of sorts—the law sanctioned for them a procedure different than that for land-thieves. The following provision explains how Crusoe arrived at the belief that shocked Gildon: "If Pyracy be committed upon the Ocean, and the Pyrates in the Attempt be overcome, the Captors may, without any solemnity of Condemnation, hang them up at the Main-Yard; if they are brought to the next Port, and the Judge rejects the Tryal, or the Captors cannot wait for the Judge, without Peril or Loss, Justice may be done upon them by the Captors" (*General History,* pp. 377–78). Even though Crusoe's claim to be the duly commissioned governor of the island is mere pretense, the authority that this law granted to captors of pirates "taken in the fact" in regions remote from courts of Admiralty would probably have justified a summary execution of the English sailors.[11]

Pirates often experienced one-sided trials in courts more legitimate than the one Crusoe would have convened. The printed trial of Major Stede Bonnet gives an indication of the official behavior they could expect, especially in North America where courts tried to uphold the honor of the colonies against suspicions of profitable collusion with the pirates.[12] Chief Justice Trot's badgering questions and rejoinders made it clear that his was a hanging court. Whether critical of over-zealous authorities or in sympathy with the defendants' abused rights, Defoe created a lively scene in the *General History of the Pyrates* where Captain Anstis' crew parodies a trial before "His Honor George Bradley":

> *Judge.*—Hearkee me, Sirrah,—you lousy, pittiful, ill-look'd Dog; what have you to say why you should not be tuck'd up immediately, and set a Sundrying like a Scare-crow?—Are you guilty, or not guilty?
>
> *Pris.* Not guilty, an't please your Worship.
>
> *Judge.* Not guilty! say so again, Sirrah, and I'll have you hang'd without any Tryal.
>
> *Pris.* An't please your Worship's Honour, my Lord, I am as honest a poor Fellow as ever went between Stem and Stern of a Ship, and can hand, reef, steer, and clap two Ends of a Rope together, as well as e'er a He that ever cross'd salt Water; but I was taken by one *George Bradley* [the name of him that sat as Judge] a notorious Pyrate, a sad Rogue as ever was unhang'd, and he forc'd me, an't please your Honour.
>
> *Judge.* Answer me, Sirrah,—How will you be try'd?
>
> *Pris.* By G—and my Country.
>
> *Judge.* The Devil you will.—Why then, Gentlemen of the Jury, I think we have nothing to do but to proceed to Judgement.
>
> *Attor. Gen.* Right, my Lord; for if the Fellow should be suffer'd to speak, he may clear himself, and that's an Affront to the Court.
>
> *Pris.* Pray, my Lord, I hope your Lordship will consider—
>
> *Judge.* Consider!—How dare you talk of considering?—Sirrah, Sirrah, I never consider'd in all my Life.—I'll make it Treason to consider.
>
> *Pris.* But, I hope, your Lordship will hear some Reason.
>
> *Judge.* D'ye hear how the Scoundrel prates?—What have we to do with Reason?—I'd have you to know, Raskal, we don't sit here to hear Reason;—we go according to Law.—Is our Dinner ready? (p. 293)

The judge's threat to have the pirate "hang'd without any Tryal" is precisely what infuriated Gildon in his criticism of *The Farther Adventures;* but Bradley is within his rights, for where piracy was concerned, the authorities refused "to hear Reason;—we go according to Law."

Since the movement of *The Farther Adventures* is toward the rebirth of the sailors as repentant souls and good citizens, Defoe has quickly to establish their original wretched state. What better way than to remind us that their crimes had exposed them to an arbitrary and sudden form of justice? Crusoe will soon learn that the former pirates have become exemplary members of the little "colony," but his extraordinary power over them sets before us the kind of desperate wickedness the colonists have had to overcome.

Defoe's detailed knowledge of the pirate's standing before the law may not have been shared by all of his readers—certainly not by Gildon—but it was, nevertheless, widely understood that the pirate was a special order of thief, remarkable in his crime, his punishment, and, on occasion, his rehabilitation. The legal literature of eighteenth-century England reflects this attitude clearly in its definition and discussion of piracy.

In the *General History* a pirate is defined as "*Hostis humani generis,* a common Enemy, with whom neither Faith nor Oath is to be kept" (p. 377). More an expression of antipathy than a binding definition, the phrase *hostis humani generis* suggested the extent to which a pirate was thought beyond the pale of civilized society and hence the lawful prey of any who could destroy him by foul means or fair. The sense of the phrase was most directly treated by Matthew Tindal during a controversy over the power of James II to issue privateering commissions from his exile in France. When mariners acting under these commissions were apprehended, Dr. William Oldys, advocate of the Admiralty, refused to proceed against them, maintaining that since James's privateers restricted their depredations to "Hanoverian shipping," they were not "enemies of all mankind" and hence no pirates. Tindal is surely right, however, when he declares this an uninformed and narrow understanding of the term:

> *Hostis humani generis,* is neither a Definition, or as much as a Description of a Pirat, but a Rhetorical Invective to shew the Odiousness of that Crime. As a Man, who, tho he receives Protection from a Government, and has sworn to be true to it, yet acts against it as much as he dares, may be said to be an Enemy to all Governments, because he destroyeth, as far as in him lieth, all Goverment [*sic*] and

all Order, by breaking all those Ties and Bonds that unite People in
a Civil Society under any Government.[13]

The threat of these enemies to all government was frequently addressed in trials for piracy. It was pointed out, for example, that the
defendants' total denial of human values disabled them from claiming the protection of any established state and validated the severity
of their punishments. As they have willingly denied the social feelings that distinguish men from beasts, so mankind may deny to them
the benefits of distinctly human institutions, such as the civil law.[14]
This is the logic adopted by the Advocate General of Massachusetts
in an important trial of 1717. Mr. Smith learnedly notes that although
in classical Greek usage, *pirate* meant no more than "sea-faring person," a pirate is now the declared enemy of mankind: "And therefore
he can claim the Protection of no Prince, the privilege of no Country,
the benefit of no Law; He is denied common humanity and the very
rights of Nature, with whom no Faith, Promise nor Oath is to be
observed, nor is he to be otherwise dealt with, than as a wild & savage Beast, which every Man may lawfully destroy."[15] To impress upon
their auditors that this doctrine was not merely theoretical, attorneys
for the Crown would cite its most striking practical applications. "The
Civil Law," says Mr. Thomas Hepworth of Carolina, "terms the Pirates *Beasts of Prey*, with whom no Communication ought to be kept;
neither are Oaths or Promises made to them binding. And by the
Law-marine the Captors may execute such Beasts of Prey immediately, without any Solemnity of Condemnation, *they not deserving any
Benefit of the Law*."[16]

It is true that the term *hostis humani generis* could be applied to other
kinds of criminals. Swift's Ebenezor Elliston, for example, uses it in
his *Last Speech and Dying Words* (1722); instead of issuing the usual
whining recantation, he urges his listeners to treat his breed with the
severity that the law sanctioned against pirates. "We ought to be looked
upon as the common Enemies of Mankind; whose interest it is to root
us out like Wolves, and other mischievous Vermin, against which no
fair Play is required."[17] Nevertheless, the distinction between pirates
and other public enemies was insisted upon by the prosecution in
numerous trials; thus the Advocate General of Massachusetts finishes "the hateful character of this Monster" by observing, "He is
perhaps the only Criminal on Earth, whose crime cannot be absolutely pardoned, nor his punishment remitted by any Prince or State
whatever. For as a Pirate is equally an Enemy and dangerous to all
Societies, the bonds, which are to secure them from violence and

injury, being by him slighted and broken, every Power has equally a right to insist upon Reparation and his being Punished."[18]

The lonely and dangerous condition of being an enemy of all nations without the safeguards allowed to legitimate military personnel is expressed in a contemporary phrase meaning to become a pirate—"to declare war against all mankind." This phrase was so common by the 1720s that John Gay could use it in a humorous, proverbial way; Mr. Ducat of *Polly* scolds his wife for the immoderate use of her tongue in the following simile: "With that weapon, women, like pyrates, are at war with the whole world."[19] In the mouth of Captain Bellamy, one of Defoe's most zestful reprobates, the phrase is used to compare the pirate's villainy with that of the "lawful" plunderer. "I am a free Prince, and I have as much Authority to make War on the whole World, as he who has a hundred Sail of Ships at Sea, and an Army of 100,000 Men in the Field; and this my Conscience tells me" (*General History*, p. 587).

The bravado of declaring war against all mankind is no better illustrated than in Captain Avery's ballad inviting all brave boys to join him in his ship, the *Fancy:*

> Captain Every is in her, and calls her his own;
> He will box her about, boys, before he has done:
> French, Spaniard, and Portuguese, the heathen likewise,
> He had made a war with them until that he dies. . . .
>
> My commission is large, and I made it myself,
> And the capston shall stretch it full larger by half;
> It was dated in Corona, believe it, my friend,
> From the year ninety-three unto the world's end.
>
> I honour St. George, and his colours I were,
> Good quarters I give, but no nation I spare;
> The world must assist me with what I do want;
> I'll give them my bill when my money is scant.

Captain Avery could only grant himself his large commission by abandoning all thought of a home, and so he sings,

> Farwel, fair Plymouth, and Cat-Down be damn'd:
> I once was part-owner of most of that land;
> But as I am disown'd, so I'll abdicate
> My person from England to attend on my fate.[20]

Defoe's Bob Singleton, too, is excellently well fitted to declare war on the whole world by his sense of being a man without a nation; "it was not one farthing matter to me," he declares to his fellow mutineers, "whether we went or stayed [at Madagascar]; I had no home, and all the world was alike to me."[21]

Yet despite occasional levity or boastfulness, the feeling most often associated with the legal status of pirates was one of desolate estrangement from the human community. During a trial for piracy at Boston in 1723, the prosecutor delivered this striking portrayal of the pirates' self-incurred isolation: "they have no country, but by the nature of their guilt, separate themselves, renouncing the benefit of all lawful society, to commit these heinous offences, . . . and indeed they are enemies, and armed against themselves, a kind of *felons de se*, importing something more than a natural death."[22] The Advocate General probably means that pirates' hostility to all mankind betokens a kind of despair or self-hate which is spiritual suicide.

It is during moments of reflection upon this condition that the implications of *hostis humani generis* come home to us. The phrase is not a metaphor: it denotes a continual state of hostility, in feelings and actions, toward human life and, by consequence, toward the God in whose image man was created. For the eighteenth century it was no melodramatic hyperbole to liken the pirate to Satan, the prototype of self-hate and despair, who wages eternal war with God. Captain Avery in Defoe's *King of the Pirates* recognizes this likeness when he tells of his changing from a South Sea buccaneer into a full-fledged pirate. "When we came there we found they were a worse sort of wanderers than ourselves; for though we had been a kind of pirates, known and declared enemies to the Spaniards, yet it was to them only and to no other; for we never offered to rob any of our other European nations, either Dutch or French, much less English; but now we were listed in the service of the devil indeed, and, like him, were at war with all mankind."[23]

Perhaps it was their legal and spiritual isolation that made the biography of pirates especially interesting to Defoe. Upon reflection, the pirate knew himself to be as surely cut off from normal human intercourse as was Crusoe on his island. Solitude was both a punishment for his warfare against humanity and a goad to repentance. Defoe renders the beginning of Captain Singleton's spiritual awareness in a dialogue the old pirate has with his confessor, William the Quaker. When William suggests that the time has come to return home with their immense plunder, Singleton answers with feigned ease, "Why, man, I am at home; here is my habitation; I never had any other in my lifetime; I was kind of charity school boy; so that I can have no desire of going anywhere for being rich or poor, for I have nowhere to go."

> "Why," says William, looking a little confused, "art thou an Englishman?" "Yes, says I, "I think so: you see I speak English; but I came out of England a child, and never was in it but once since I was a man; and then I was cheated and imposed upon, and used so ill that I care not if I never see it more."
>
> "Why, hast thou no relations or friends there?" says he; "no acquaintance—none that thou hast any kindness or any remains of respect for?" "Not I, William," said I; "no more than I have in the court of the Great Mogul."
>
> "Nor any kindness for the country where thou wast born?" says William.
>
> "Not I, any more than for the island of Madagascar, nor so much neither; for that has been a fortunate island to me more than once, as thou knowest, William," says I.[24]

Singleton is not immediately repentant, but he does admit to disliking "this roving, cruising life" and asks William to propose some way of getting themselves "out of this *hellish* condition we are in."[25] Singleton's homelessness was probably suggested by the self-imposed exile of the legendary Captain Avery, even to the feeling in each of being cheated by their countrymen; in both cases we see the effects upon characterization of the pirates' legal status as an enemy to all, with "the Protection of no Prince, the privilege of no Country, the benefit of no Law."

II

In an age for which "sociability" and "human nature" were nearly synonymous, men who flagrantly and at times proudly cut themselves free of social bonds were dreadful creatures. *Criminal* and *robber* seemed pale words for this *lusus naturae*; hence, as the legal literature shows, pirates were often called *beasts of prey, savage beasts,* and the like. To Sir David Dalrymple, Queen's Solicitor in Scotland, even these terms fail to express the horror of their crimes: "They are worse than ravenous Beasts, in as far as their fatal Reason gives them a greater faculty and skill to do Evil; And whereas such Creatures follow the Bent of their Natures, and that promiscuously, Pirats extinguish Humanity in themselves, and prey upon Men only, especially upon Traders, who are most Innocent."[26] Attorney General Richard Allein of Carolina also finds the comparison with beasts inaccurate: piracy, he says, "is a Crime so odious and horrid in all its Circumstances, that those who have treated on that Subject have been at a loss for Words and Terms to Stamp a sufficient Ignominy upon it." *Sea wolves, beasts of prey, enemies of Mankind* are misleading because beasts kill only to ease their hunger; pirates, on the other hand, "are not content with taking from Merchants what Things they stand in need of, but throw their Goods over-board, burn their Ships, and sometimes bereave them of their Lives for Pastime and Diversion."[27] That such were the actions of creatures by nature rational and social was monstrous; and indeed, *monster* seemed the only term capable of expressing the age's revulsion for the pirate. Thus, Cotton Mather, in the fertility of his rhetoric, called the pirates that threatened New England a "Generation of Sea-Monsters," "Leviathans"; and he entitled his account of Captain Fly's apprehension, "A Remarkable Relation of a Cockatrice crush'd in the Egg."[28]

If the pirate's renunciation of national allegiance and common humanity established his notoriety, the special circumstances under which he acted further blackened his reputation. In eighteenth-century law, piracy entailed more than robbery on the high seas, for it was always aggravated by other, more hateful crimes; "The Crime of Piracy," charged Sir David Dalrymple, "is complex, and is made up of Oppression, Robbery and Murder committed in places far Remote and Solitary."[29] Dalrymple refers not only to the murder of those defending their ships from the pirates, but also of lawful officers by a mutinous crew who then go "on the account." Thus, when Captain Fly protested his innocence of murder, Cotton Mather asked incredulously, "Were the *Murders,* any other than one Article, in the *Complicated Plot* of *Piracy,* which you were now upon? Every step that any one of you all, took in the *Piracy* you have been prosecuting, involved you all in the *Murders,* which the *Piracy* begun withal."[30] (Captain Gulliver, of the *Adventure,* we recall, but for his immediate submission would have suffered the fate of Fly's commander.)

Dalrymple and Mather's understanding that piracy is not a single crime but a compound of offenses is generously supported in the legal literature and goes a long way toward explaining the symbolic force of the pirate in the eighteenth century. Dalrymple addresses another "article" in the complicated plot when he observes that piracy usually occurs "in Places far Remote and Solitary." In English legal practice crimes enacted far from the usual agencies of justice were termed "excepted cases," meaning that evidence of a conjectural nature might be admitted against the accused. Mr. Smith of Massachusetts also raised this point when he described the nature of piracy: "Now as Piracy is in itself a complication of Treason, Oppression, Murder, Assassination, Robbery and Theft, so it denotes the Crime to be perpetuated on the High Sea, or some part thereof, whereby it becomes more Atrocious." The sternest punishment ought to be meted out to persons convicted in "excepted cases" since by legal maxim, "Those Crimes ought to be punished with the utmost Severity, which cannot without the greatest difficulty be prevented."[31]

It appears from Mr. Smith's speech that the pirate—a prodigy of criminality—is also guilty of treason. Because of the ancient wartime practice of relying upon privateers outfitted by civilian investors, no clear distinction could be drawn between the Royal Navy and the merchant marine, the latter being considered a reserve of ships and seamen legally bound to serve His Majesty. Thus the frequent efforts to "encourage our navigation" and to support or establish trades that were "nurseries for our seamen" were as much patriotic as financial schemes.[32] It followed that an attack upon a merchant vessel was an attack upon England's security: "Masters of Ships," says Smith, "are Publick Officers, and therefore every Act of Violence and Spoliation committed on them or their Ships, may justly be accounted Treason, and so it was before the Statute of the 25th of *Edward* III."[33]

But pirates, mutineers, and their accomplices were not only treasonous in their own deeds; rumors of their fabulous wealth earned under easy working conditions encouraged others to treason or disaffection. Because the wars of the 1690–1728 period placed heavy demands upon the navy, piratical treason must have seemed more threatening than ever before.[34] Defoe, writing in 1728, ranked piracy among the four most important causes of the manpower shortage. In response to the King's address to Parliament on the need for more seamen, he viewed with alarm

> the tempting Profits of going upon the Account (so our Sailors call that wicked Trade of turning Pyrates), in which horrid Employment (however scandalous) many thousands of our Seamen have engaged since the late War, most of them being of the ablest Seamen and best Artists that were to be found among them; and by which, besides the Numbers that remain, abundance have been lost to their Country by Shipwreck, by Battles, by the Gallows, by Starving, and other Distresses natural to those desperate Adventures; so that this also has been a Great Cause of the Decrease in the Numbers of Seamen among us, and will continue to be so, unless some Remedy may be

found out to reduce them and restore them to the Service and Interest of their Country.[35]

The imputation of treason must have been strengthened by the suspicion that pirates were Jacobites. There are numerous accounts in which captives, under pain of pirate wrath, are forced to drink a health to the Pretender; and as we have already seen, the charge was upheld during the trial of Jacobite privateersmen in the 1690s. Moreover, pirates were supposed to have been employed in the '15 and subsequent Jacobite plots.[36]

The association of piracy with treason was further supported by the manner of punishing pirates: before 1352 they were executed as traitors, by being drawn and hanged, their lands and effects seized and their posterity disinherited. After that time, they were merely hanged and their property confiscated; but to demonstrate the odiousness of their crimes, their bodies were hung aloft in the port area. Convicted pirates rarely avoided this fate, for they were denied benefit of clergy and were not included in a general pardon.[37]

One reason for such enduring severity was that piracy often began with the violation of an oath of fidelity to superiors. As Judge Trot of Charleston, Carolina, put it in the trial of Stede Bonnet, piracy is an offense "done *contra Ligeanciae sua debitum.*"[38] Even as late as the eighteenth century, powerful emotions were stirred by crimes which destroyed the bonds between king and subject, husband and wife, master and servant, captain and mariner. Inherited from feudal thought, this aspect of English law troubled the observant young Swiss, César de Saussure; he had this to write in 1726 about English criminal justice:

> Women who have murdered their husbands are put to death in what I consider to be an unjust way; they are condemned to be burned alive. Men who murder their wives are only hanged, but the English say that any person guilty of treason, that is to say of murdering those to whom they owe faith and allegiance, must be punished in an exemplary and terrible fashion. Such would be the case of a woman murdering her husband, a slave or servant his master, a clerk his bishop, and, in short, any person who is guilty of the death of his lord and superior.[39]

The famous nineteenth-century print showing Captain Kidd hanging tidily in his chains at Wapping fails to do justice to the "exemplary and terrible fashion" in which piratical traitors were punished.[40]

Convicted of robbery, conspiracy, murder, savagery, treason and atheism, the pirate appeared to the eighteenth century as the complete criminal whose existence was a standing reproach to human nature and European civilization. Defoe was especially shocked that intelligent men, such as Edward England, should be guilty of the most comprehensive of crimes: "It is Surprizing that Men of good Understanding should engage in a Course of Life, that so much debases humane Nature, and sets them upon a Level with the wild Beasts of the Forest, who live and prey upon their weaker Fellow Creatures: A Crime so enormous! that it includes almost all others, as Murder, Rapine, Theft, Ingratitude, &c" (*General History*, p. 114). Ingratitude, which seems an odd cousin to murder, rapine, and theft, must be understood to include breaches of faith against superiors whose protection and favor one has enjoyed. The crew whose mutiny sets Captain Gulliver on his last, most revealing adventure are guilty of such ingratitude. It is clear from this episode that Swift, no less than Defoe, saw the pirate as an abstract of human viciousness.

Gulliver, it will be remembered, has difficulty explaining to his Houyhnhnm master the difference between piratical mutineers and Houyhnhnmland Yahoos: "He asked me, Who made the Ship, and how it was possible that the *Houyhnhnms* of my Country would leave it to the Management of Brutes?" In Europe, Gulliver informs him, horses are brutes and Yahoo-like creatures are their rational masters, but the whole manner of his arrival undermines this explanation. Gulliver's subsequent description of the mutineers introduces his master to the lexicon of human depravity:

> I said, they were Fellows of desperate Fortunes, forced to fly from the Places of their Birth, on Account of their Poverty or their Crimes. Some were undone by Law-suits; others spent all they had in Drinking, Whoring and Gaming; others fled for Treason; many for Murder, Theft, Poysoning, Robbery, Perjury, Forgery, Coining false Money; for committing Rapes or Sodomy; for flying from their Colours, or deserting to the Enemy; and most of them had broken Prison. None of these durst return to their native Countries for fear of being hanged, or of starving in a Jail; and therefore were under a Necessity of seeking a Livelihood in other Places.

The Houyhnhnm master finds it difficult to understand the "Use or Necessity of those Vices" so that Gulliver must endeavor "to give him some Ideas of the Desire of Power and Riches; of the terrible Effects of Lust, Intemperance, Malice, and Envy . . .[of] Power, Government, War, Law, Punishment, and a Thousand other Things" which the Houyhnhnm language could not express. By Gulliver's patient exercise of circumlocution, his master "at last arrived at a competent Knowledge of what human Nature in our Parts of the World is capable to perform."[41] From our study of the pirate's legal status and contemporary reputation, we see that Swift has found in him a felicitous symbol for the covetous and irrational life, the war of all against all. Perhaps it is no accident that *Gulliver's Travels* and the *General History of the Pyrates* were published in the same decade of European history.

Of a piece with Swift's image of the pirates are the atrocity stories often found in accounts of their careers. One recent commentator believes that Defoe introduced several of these stories to please the sadistic tastes of his audience.[42] It seems fairer to say that he—as his public—believed the "common enemies of mankind" to be extraordinarily brutal and that the historian's duty was to dramatize the nature of their crimes and the condition of their souls. Defoe as well as John Esquemeling, historian of the West Indian buccaneers, simply highlighted the depravity of criminals already notorious for barbarism.[43]

In the Cases of Lolonois, Blackbeard, Low, Fly, and Gow this resulted in a representation of "the evil pirate" which is now ludicrously theatrical. Lolonois the Cruel, for example, was supposed to have torn out and eaten the heart of a captive who refused to lead him to his treasure.[44] Edward Low's crew delighted in such jestbook pranks as burning a captured ship while its cook, "who, they said, being a greazy Fellow, would fry well in the Fire," was bound to the main mast (*General History*, p. 323). Blackbeard's very appearance was designed to throw terror into the hearts of his enemies; his great, black beard "like a frightful Meteor . . . frightened *America* more than any Comet. . . . In Time of Action, he wore a Sling over his Shoulders, with three Brace of Pistols, hanging in Holsters like Bandaliers; and stuck lighted Matches under his Hat, which appearing on each Side of his Face, his Eyes naturally looking fierce and wild, made him altogether such a Figure, that Imagination cannot form an Idea of a Fury, from Hell, to look more frightful" (*General History*, pp. 84–85).

The pirates' concern to keep up their reputation for cruelty appears to us absurd, but it was soundly motivated: the more terrible their image, the more quickly would their offer of quarter be accepted. On the other hand, if merchant crews were too fearful of falling into pirate hands, they might fight hotly on behalf of the owners. Perhaps this danger is implied by the speech Defoe gives to members of Low's infamous crew, who, moved by Captain Roberts' sermon on conscience, wish "some Humanity, were in more Practice among them;

which they believ'd, would be more to their Reputation, and cause a greater Esteem to be had for them, both from God and Man." Later even Low urges more humanity; against those who would set Roberts adrift without provisions, Low argues, "That tho' we are Pirates, yet we are Men, and tho' we are deem'd by some People dishonest, yet let us not wholly divest ourselves of Humanity, and make ourselves more Savage than Brutes."[45]

III

After what we have seen of the complex nature of piracy and of its standing before the law, it is odd to hear from a pirate concerned about his bad reputation. The admission that "we are deem'd by some People dishonest" only heightens our sense that an eighteenth-century W. S. Gilbert has been at work among the wretches of Newgate. Such a concern, however, was neither anomalous nor whimsical, for whatever the practical advantages of a bad or good reputation, these criminals possessed something that inspired self-respect and a degree of admiration from others. This was owing less to the myth of the Byronic outlaw at war with all mankind than to the fact that piracy had often been the prelude to "greatness." Unlike highwaymen, pickpockets, and other land-thieves, pirates could claim in their lineage personages like Raleigh and Drake—respected and successful in their own day and revered in later times. Moreover, the buccaneers had given fresh proof that piracy against the Spaniards of America was still to be rewarded with wealth, fame, and sometimes, as in the case of Henry Morgan, with political power. And the Barbary pirates continued to demonstrate throughout Defoe's lifetime that gangs of plunderers might be accorded the full rights of sovereign nations.

In order to disclose the roots of the affirmative, or at the least, pragmatic image of the pirates—as bold, resourceful warriors capable of self-discipline and imperial conquest—it will be helpful to reexamine the epithets by which they were known in the law.

In ancient Rome, pirates were characterized by phrases expressing their estrangement from the human community: "*piratis* etiam *omnium mortalium hostibus* transituros fama terrentibus" (Pliny, *Natural History,* 2.45.117); "nam pirata non est ex perduellium nemero definitus, sed *communis hostis omnium;* cum hoc nec fides debet nec ius iurandum commune" (Cicero, *De Officiis*, 3.29.107). Wishing to define a commonwealth as "an assemblage of people in large numbers associated in an agreement with respect to justice and a partnership for the common good," Cicero had to prohibit negotiations with pirates for the ransom of goods or persons. Such negotiations would raise criminals, who habitually behaved unjustly, to the power of a commonwealth and hence invalidate his first premise. His response to the record of corrupt nations was a denial that in such cases a commonwealth *per se* can be said to have existed at all.[46]

By Coke's time, Cicero's "*communis hostis omnium*" had been rendered more dramatic by the implied alienation of the pirate from the human race itself: "*Pirata est hostis humani generis*"; his crime was said to be "*contra ligeanciae suae debitum.*"[47] The feudal principle of allegiance to one's superiors had directed that this species of criminal—faithless to king, captain, and merchant—be consigned to another realm of being entirely: the Great Chain of Monsters.

Although Blackstone and a host of other commentators accepted Coke's phraseology, there had long been a body of opinion that allowed the negotiating and keeping of faith with thieves, under certain circumstances. Hobbes, for example, argued that an oath is binding, no matter how it was elicited, when the oath-taker receives some good by it. Grotius and Puffendorf opposed Hobbes's extreme position, but, on the authority of natural law, cautiously accepted oaths to thieves when made freely.[48] More significant was St. Augustine's rebuttal of Cicero's major premise, that only where justice guides the actions of a group can there be said to exist a commonweal, with the rights of legation and the power to conclude binding agreements. It is revealing that this challenge to the essence of Cicero's political thought should rest upon an example drawn from outlawry:

> AND SO if justice is left out, what are kingdoms except great robber bands? For what are robber bands except little kingdoms? The band also is a group of men governed by the orders of a leader, bound by a social compact, and its booty is divided according to a law agreed upon. If by repeatedly adding desperate men this plague grows to the point where it holds territory and establishes a fixed seat, seizes cities and subdues peoples, then it more conspicuously assumes the name of kingdom, and this name is now openly granted to it, not for any subtraction of cupidity, but by addition of impunity. For it was an elegant and true reply that was made to Alexander the Great by a certain pirate whom he had captured. When the king asked him what he was thinking of, that he should molest the sea, he said with defiant independence: "The same as you when you molest the world! Since I do this with a little ship I am called a pirate. You do it with a great fleet and are called an emperor."[49]

By the early eighteenth century, the pirate's answer to Alexander had become a commonplace in satire and Newgate literature. Gay's *Polly*, for example, sang the praises of Morano's pirate crew, "those brave spirits, those *Alexanders*, that shall soon by conquest be in possession of the *Indies*," and his Morano—a thinly veiled allusion to Sir Henry Morgan—went to execution with the disclaimer, "*Alexander* the great was more successful. That's all."[50] In his massive collection of criminal lives, Captain Alexander Smith referred derisively to the exploits of great princes: "What was *Nimrod* but a successful Freebooter? and what were all the Founders of Monarchies, but Encroachers on the Properties of their Brethren and Neighbours? *Alexander* was a Plunderer of the first Magnitude; and all his extraordinary Exploits, with which we have been so long amused, and which we have been taught to speak of with so much Admiration, were only Robberies commited upon Men every Way better than himself."[51] And Cotton Mather excoriated not only the pirates executed at Boston in 1717 but also the predatory Louis XIV: "And here it may be complained, That while the Laws reach the lesser *Pirates & Robbers*, there are, as one of them too truly told the Execrable *Alexander*, much *Greater Ones*, whom no Humane Laws Presume to meddle withal: *Monsters*, whom we dignify with the Title of *Hero's: Conquerors* and *Emperors*, but yet no other than a more splendid sort of *Highway-man*. Of these, *Many have done abominably*; But thou, the *Leviathan* lately at Versailles, hast excelled them all."[52]

In like manner Romulus and his band had also become a popular stereotype of roguish empire builders, cited sometimes satirically but more often with admiration. In Antoine Houdar de La Motte's *Romulus* (1724), for example, the hero is a plunderer turned lawgiver, proud of his historic role in organizing his vagabond followers and inspiring them with the thirst for glory. Defoe invoked this stereotype in the *Review* for yet another reason, to warn Europe that if the pirates of Madagascar are not immediately dealt with, they may become a major threat.[53] In his *King of the Pirates*, it appears as a clever exaggeration of the pirates' strength to discourage raids upon their settlement; Avery told his English captives that "the Romans themselves were at first no better than such a gang of rovers as we were; and who knew but our general, Captain Avery, might lay the foundation of as great an empire as they?"[54]

An amusing example of the pirates' imperial aspirations is found in the *General History* where an actor who joined Captain Bellamy's crew because "the stroling Business" had not satisfied "the Greatness of his Soul" (p. 588) attempts to stage a play called "the *Royale Pyr-*

ate," his version of Alexander's encounter with the bold pirate. After
the performance is aborted by a fight, he proposes the founding of a
pirate kingdom on the coast of Maine:

> I leave it to the mature Deliberation of your great Wisdom, whether
> it is not more eligible to found here an Empire, and make War by a
> lawful Authority derived from your Royal selves, than lye under the
> approbrious Appellations of Robbers, Thieves, profligate Rogues and
> Pyrates; for begging Pardon of your Majesties, for that Freedom of
> Speech, which my Zeal for your Royal Service, and the publick Good
> oblige me to; the World treats you and your loyal Subjects with no
> softer Terms. But, when you have once declared your selves lawful
> Monarchs, and that you have Strength enough to defend your Title,
> all the Universities in the World will declare you have a Right *Jure
> Divino;* and the Kings and Princes of the Earth, will send their Am-
> bassadors to court your Alliance. (*General History,* p. 591)

Here, satire is eclipsed by political speculation recalling the tone of
Jure Divino in which, two decades before, Defoe had labelled kings
"exalted thieves" and had wondered at the rise of great powers from
the collaborations of banditti.[55]

By the first quarter of the eighteenth century, it was, in fact, agreed
that whatever their taste for low diversions and petty cruelties, pirates were tormented by great ambitions. Their refusal to be content
with the position into which Providence had placed them—which
was also Crusoe's sin—did not entirely distinguish them from pickpockets and highwaymen; but it allowed a psychological and moral
explanation of their independence, self-exile, and territorial claims.
The cry of the English brutes in *The Farther Adventures*—"They shall
plant no colony in our dominions"—expresses what Defoe's age felt
to be the pirates' presumption and their challenge to lawful government. On the other hand, political romances such as Charles Johnson's *The Successful Pyrate* (1713) and Defoe's own tale of Captain Mis-
son (*General History,* pp. 383–439) went beyond the law's hatred for
the pirates to imagine what a state run by freedom-loving and mag-
nanimous outlaws might look like.

The potential evolution of pirate communities into legitimate states
was a deplored but accepted fact even in the law books Defoe consulted for the *General History.* In one standard work, *De Jure Maritimo
et Navali,* Charles Molloy distinguished between "nationalized" pirates and common plunderers, and insisted that English policy has
been to recognize the rights of pirates that have formed a government.[56] Molloy was supported by Sir Leoline Jenkins who cited a decision of Charles II's reign that Algerians "are to have the privileges

of enemies in an open war, and must be received to their ransom by exchange or otherwise."[57] In the words of Alexander Justice, "when a Company of them forming themselves into a Society, submit to Laws, and are acknowledg'd as a State, they cannot afterwards be treated as Pirates, but as Enemies; between whom and Pirates there is a great deal of difference."[58]

Even Matthew Tindal, who had called pirates the arch opponent of "all Goverment [*sic*] and all Order," agreed that, though robbers may act from "private Causes" when they are outside the law, when they achieve the status of a nation they "might have a Publick Cause, upon the account of that Nation, of making War." Moreover, Tindal granted that pirate "nations" might afford *justice* to its citizens and others: "the beginning of most of the great Empires were not much better: whatever any were at first, yet when they had formed themselves into Civil Societies, where Foreigners as well as Subjects might have Justice administered, then they were looked on as Nations and Civil Societies."[59]

That pirates could erect governments capable of dispensing justice and of securing the common safety was the most surprising revelation of their stories. Readers of John Esquemeling's *Bucaniers of America*, for example, learned of the organization and restraint achieved in buccaneer commonwealths. According to Esquemeling, honesty in sharing booty, the safety of property and person, swift arbitration of disputes, and democracy in the making of decisions were guaranteed on the pirate islands of Tortuga and Hispaniola. Buccaneer "articles" also made it clear that members of the commonwealth were expected to be civil to one another, to aid their fellows in time of want, to make provision for the wounded, and to preserve the booty of dead pirates for their "nearest relations" or their "lawful heirs."[60] Such commendable regulations drew the notice of Esquemeling's London editor who found it "very remarkable, that in such a lawless body as these buccaneers seem to be, in respect to all other, that yet there should be such an economy (if I may say so) kept, and regularity practised amongst themselves, so that everyone seemed to have his property as much secured to himself, as if he had been a member of the most civilized community in the world."[61]

Twenty-five years later, Defoe took advantage of the enduring interest in pirate "economy" by subtitling his *General History of the Pyrates*, "Their Policies, Discipline, and Government from their first rise . . . to the present year 1724." The first reviewer of this book, in fact, was struck chiefly by the remarkable system of laws in force among pirates, "as excellent for Policy as any Thing in *Plato's* Commonwealth."[62] The reviewer found in the pirates' lives ample confirmation of his belief that all government is the product of a covenant to curb "particular Appetites . . . for the Benefits of Society" and that man is by necessity a law-making and law-obeying animal, even in circumstances that undermine traditional systems of law. Government among pirates might be tyrannical or democratic, and it was certainly unstable; but it nourished the comforting idea that humanity would not sink below a certain level of rational organization. Blackstone may have believed that the pirate "has reduced himself afresh to the savage state of nature,"[63] but Defoe's and Esquemeling's readers knew that this regression did not always imply anarchic individualism but often a case of primitive social development with great potential for improvement.

The pirate, in short, was able to call forth diametrically opposed responses: he was to be hated and exterminated as loathesome monster—first among the Yahoos—or he was to be respected, even admired as pioneer of civil order in places remote and solitary. If gory atrocities by Lolonois, Blackbeard, and Low sustained the first response, romantic tales of utopian pirate republics on tropic islands presumed upon the second to the limits of credibility. Nor did the popular press scruple to call forth both responses in the same work, as is shown by the mixture of satire and heroics in Johnson's *The Successful Pyrate* and the anonymous *Life and Adventures of Captain John Avery* (1709).[64]

It is characteristic of Defoe to capitalize upon journalistic sensations but also to reconcile fact and fantasy.[65] This he achieves to a significant degree in *Captain Singleton*, in *The King of the Pirates*, and, above all, in the portrait of Will Atkins, one of the English sailors threatened with summary execution in *The Farther Adventures*. Defoe follows Atkins' maturation from destructive brute to civil leader in full and psychologically convincing detail; and, what is more, he suggests that Atkins' services to Crusoe's little commonwealth are expressions of the same qualities that made him a fearsome enemy. His boldness in combat with the cannibals, his skill in handicrafts, and his wisdom in supplying the colonists with wives and driving the cannibals into the hills (to prevent counterattack and provide a source of slave labor) witness that Atkins is, indeed, one of those "ablest Seamen and best Artists" Defoe feared lost to England through piracy. While at first a mortal danger, Atkins' turbulent and ambitious spirit proves a resource of the highest order, one that the better regulated Spaniards did not offer the community. The moral seems to be that if arbitrary self-assertion must be curbed, bold and sometimes ruthless action is often crucial to a colony's success.

At the beginning of this essay I argued that the law's revulsion for the pirate gave Defoe a means of quickly establishing his character's moral and psychological state. The conclusion of this episode from *The Farther Adventures* demonstrates his willingness to entertain another corollary of the law, the scandalous paradox that the opponents of all government, the common enemies of mankind, may be necessary to the spread of European civilization.[66] There is reason to believe that Atkins' story was intended to encourage a policy of pardoning and recruiting the West Indian pirates and to support the reclamation work of Captain Woodes Rogers, newly appointed governor of the Bahamas.[67] How different is this attitude from Swift's who describes the pirates' colonizing role in the following manner:

> A Crew of Pyrates are driven by a Storm they know not whither; at length a Boy discovers Land from the Top-mast; they go on Shore to rob and plunder; they see an harmless People, are entertained with Kindness, they give the Country a new Name, they take formal Possession of it for the King, they set up a rotten Plank or a Stone for a Memorial, they murder two or three Dozen of the Natives, bring away a Couple more by Force for a Sample, return home, and get their Pardon. Here commences a new Dominion acquired with a Title by *Divine Right*. Ships are sent with the first Opportunity; the Natives driven out or destroyed, their Princes tortured to discover their Gold; a free License given to all Acts of Inhumanity and Lust; the Earth reeking with the Blood of its Inhabitants: And this execrable Crew of Butchers employed in so pious an Expedition, is a *modern Colony* sent to convert and civilize an idolatrous and barbarous People.[68]

A devastating attack on church and state hypocrisy spoken with the hopelessness of one who has seen at first hand what a pirate "is capable to perform."

Defoe adopts a different mood in *The Farther Adventures* not because he was an ignorant or careless tool of colonialism—he knew well the pirates' double nature and has Crusoe warn of their potential reversion to barbarism. His optimism, however, is in keeping with his lifelong dream of a revitalized English economy and his faith in the potential conversion of the most hardened rogue. Even in the *General History of the Pyrates*, where destruction is the constant scene, he is interested "in every Thing, which may tend to the enriching or extending the Dominions of our glorious *Britain*" (*General History*, pp. 589–90) and cheerfully offers projects for the employment of seamen, the colonization of Maine and Madagascar, and the establishment of trade with Brazil. When in 1728 he completed work on the *General History,* he became buoyantly hopeful: "The World is wide: There are new Countries, and new Nations, who may be so planted, so improv'd, and the People so manag'd, as to create a new Commerce; and Millions of People shall call for our Manufacture, who never call'd for it before." To encourage the timorous, the prophets of commercial decline, and, perhaps, the overscrupulous, he predicted "that the Time will come, and is near at Hand, when the Improvement of the *British* Commerce shall no more appear in Project and Theory, but shew it self in a due and daily Progression."[69] Defoe was not one to shrink from the possibility that progress might come in the wake of England's bold, restless seamen whose crimes he had accurately chronicled.

Throughout his works Defoe exhibits a thorough knowledge of the pirate's contemporary reputation, but his fiction generally seeks to reconcile those stark contradictions we have traced in the popular and learned literature, the pirate as both cunning thief and generous lord of the sea, anarchist and nation builder, destructive demon and pioneer of commerce. The tensions and ironies of the pirate's image in Defoe are symbolically expressed by Captain Avery himself on the eve of his return to Europe: "We resolve . . . to separate in to three companies, as if we did not know one another; to dress ourselves as merchants, for now we look like hell-hounds and vagabonds; but when we are well dressed we expect to look as other men do."[70] Defoe's pirate chief emerges as a complex, recognizably human figure; but he retains nevertheless the aura of the legendary which assures his success as popular hero.

NOTES

1 *Jure Divino* (London, [1706]), in *The Works of Daniel De Foe,* ed. William Hazlitt (London: Clements, 1843), 3:1. Hereafter cited as *Works.*
2 For discussions of the process by which Defoe converted homiletic metaphors into the characters and events of his fiction, see G. A. Starr, *Defoe and Spiritual Autobiography* (Princeton: Princeton University Press, 1965), and J. Paul Hunter, *The Reluctant Pilgrim* (Baltimore: The Johns Hopkins University Press, 1966).
3 *The Spiritual Seaman: or, a Manual for Mariners* (London, 1655), pp. 73–74.
4 *The Mariner's Divine Mate* (London, 1670), p. 13.
5 John J. Richetti, *Popular Fiction Before Richardson* (Oxford: Clarendon Press, 1969), pp. 75, 87.
6 Ibid., p. 65.

7 *Tour thro' the Whole Island of Great Britain,* ed. G. D. H. Cole (London: Dent, [1927]), 1:348–49.

8 *A General History of Trade* [*June*] (London, 1713), p. 19.

9 In Defoe's *A General History of the Pyrates,* ed. Manuel Schonhorn (Columbia: University of South Carolina Press, 1972), pp. 377–79. All further references are to this edition, and will be cited parenthetically in the text.

10 Charles Gildon, *Robinson Crusoe, Examined and Criticiz'd,* ed. Paul Dottin (London: Dent, 1923), p. 116.

11 Before 1700 all pirates taken by colonial authorities had to be tried in England. After 1700 commissions were sent to the governors empowering them to try and punish pirates. This greatly facilitated the destruction of piracy in the West Indies.

12 See, in particular, *The Tryals of Major Stede Bonnet* . . . (London, 1719), pp. 20–44.

13 Matthew Tindal, *Essay on the Law of Nations* . . . (London, 1694), pp. 25–26. The phrase continued in legal usage until the 1930s when it was considered a hindrance to the advance of international agreements governing modern piracy. See *Research in International Law* . . . (Cambridge: Harvard Law School, 1932), pp. 739–886.

14 Pirates were quite literally denied the protections of the civil law due to the involved legal history of their crime. Piracy started as a felony at the common law and was once punished as *petit treason*. It was later made a felony at civil law (25 Ed III, stat. 5 c. 2), but since confession or eyewitnesses, required for conviction of capital offenses under the civil law, were hard to obtain in cases of piracy, its status was again altered. By 28 Hen VIII, c. 15, pirates were considered felons at common law for the purpose of their trial, but the crime itself was still considered felony at civil law. "It follows that this Offence remains as before, of a special Nature, and that it shall not be included in a General Pardon of all Felonies" (Matthew Bacon, *A New Abridgment of the Law,* 3rd ed. [London, 1768], 3:819).

15 *The Trials of Eight Persons Indited for Piracy* . . . (Boston, 1718), p. 6.

16 *Tryals of Bonnet,* pp. 10–11. My italics.

17 *The Prose Writings of Jonathan Swift,* ed. Herbert Davis (Oxford: Basil Blackwell, 1939–68), 9:41.

18 *Trials of Eight,* p. 6.

19 John Gay, *Polly, an Opera,* ed. Oswald Doughty (London: O'Connor, 1922), p. 26.

20 *Naval Songs and Ballads* . . . , ed. Charles Firth (London: Navy Records Society, 1908), pp. 131–32.

21 *Romances and Narratives by Daniel Defoe,* ed. George A. Aitken (London: Dent, 1895), 6:41.

22 *Tryals of Thirty-Six Persons for Piracy* . . . (Boston, 1723), rpt. Wilkins Updike, *Memoirs of The Rhode-Island Bar* (Boston: Webb, 1842), p. 265.

23 *Romances and Narratives,* 16:ii.

24 Ibid., 6:292–93.

25 Ibid., 6:293, 295. My italics.

26 *The Tryal of Captain Thomas Green and His Crew* . . . (Edinburgh, 1705), p. 48.

27 *Tryals of Bonnet,* p. 8.

28 Cotton Mather, *The Converted Sinner* (Boston, 1724), "The Occasion"; *The Vial Poured out upon the Sea* (Boston, 1726), pp. 5, 44.

29 *Tryal of Green,* p. 48.

30 Mather, *Vial,* p. 21.

31 *Trials of Eight,* pp. 7, 18.

32 For discussions of the relation between the merchant marine and the Royal Navy, see Christopher Lloyd, *The Nation and the Navy* (London: Cresset, 1961), and *Queen Anne's Navy* . . . , ed. R. D. Merriman (London: Navy Records Society, 1961), pp. 171–72, 176.

33 *Trials of Eight,* p. 7.

34 *Queen Anne's Navy,* p. 170. William and George II had called Parliament's attention to the manning of the Royal Navy.

35 *Some Considerations on the Reasonableness and Necessity of Encreasing and Encouraging the Seamen* (London, 1728), pp. 7–8. The pamphlet's occasion was George II's address to Parliament (23 Jan. 1727–28) urging measures to raise seamen without impressment.

36 Captain Bonnet's ship, for example, was renamed "The Royal James" in July, 1718 (*General History,* p. 99). Captain Vane was reported to have drunk damnation to King George (*Calendar of State Papers, America and the West Indies,* 25 [1717–18], 263). In 1723 a pirate named Tookerman, it was reported, fired his guns to celebrate the birthday of the Pretender (*Acts of the Privy Council of England, Colonial Series,* 3 [1720–45], 43–44). In the same year a scheme to pardon the Madagascar pirates and engage them in the founding of a Swedish colony on Madagascar was unmasked as cover for the preparation of a Jacobite fleet to bring the Duke of Ormond to England; see *The Historical Register* (London, 1729), 8:291–94 and J. S. Bromley, "The Jacobite Privateers in the Nine Years War," in *Statesmen, Scholars and Merchants,* ed. Anne Whiteman, J. S. Bromley, and P. G. M. Dickson (Oxford: Clarendon Press, 1973), pp. 17–43.

37 For the complex legal history of piracy, see note 14 above.

38 *Tryals of Bonnet,* pp. 4–5.

39 César de Saussure, *A Foreign View of England in the Reigns of George I and George II,* trans. Madame Van Muyden (New York: Dutton 1902), p. 127.

40 The print is reproduced in Douglas Botting's *The Pirates* (Alexandria, Va.: Time-Life, 1978), p. 127.

41 Swift, *Prose Writings,* 11:238, 243–44.

42 Patrick Pringle, *Jolly Roger* (London: Museum Press, 1953), p. 14.

43 Alexander Olivier Exquemelin's *De Americaeneche Zee-Roovers* (Amsterdam, 1678) was first published in English in London, 1684–85, by W. Crooke. A convenient modern edition of this translation (bearing the anglicised name John Esquemeling and the title *Bucaniers of America*) is that edited by H. Powell (London: Sonnenschein, 1893) reprinted by George Allen & Unwin (London, 1951).

44 Esquemeling, *Bucaniers*, p. 104 [2:iii].

45 Defoe, *The Four Years Voyages of Captain George Roberts* (London, 1726), pp. 67, 88.

46 Cicero, *De Re Publica*, trans. Clinton Walker Keyes (London: Heinemann, 1928), pp. 65 [1:xxv], 219 [3:xxxi].

47 Edward Coke, *The Third Part of the Institutes of the Laws of England . . .* (London, 1644), 3:113. Defoe (*General History*, p. 377) erroneously attributes Coke's phrase to Cicero.

48 Thomas Hobbes, *"De Cive" or The Citizen*, ed. Sterling P. Lamprecht (New York: Appleton-Century Crofts, 1949), pp. 38–39; Hugo Grotius, *De Jure Belli et Pacis*, ed. William Whewell (Cambridge: Cambridge University Press, 1853), 2:203 and 3:56–58, 302–308; Samuel Puffendorf, *De Jure Naturae et Gentium Libri Octo*, trans. C. H. Oldfather and W. A. Oldfather (Oxford: Clarendon Press, 1934), pp. 419–22.

49 St. Augustine, *The City of God against the Pagans*, trans. William M. Green (Cambridge: Harvard University Press, 1963), 2:17. Augustine wittily draws the anecdote from Cicero, *De Re Publica* (3.14), and follows it with an even more damaging allusion to the "sort of men Romulus brought together" (2:17–19). Augustine implies that if Rome, Cicero's exemplary "commonwealth," rests upon such rotten foundations, it is vain to deny that robbers and pirates may form a commonwealth and to insist that justice is an indispensable condition of the earthly city. In place of Cicero's impractical and self-righteous definition, Augustine offers one that would comprehend just and unjust communities, violent as well as peaceful republics: "A people is a large gathering of rational beings united in fellowship by their agreement about the objects of their love." This definition allows us to judge a people by observing what it loves: "the better the objects of its united love, the better the people, and the worse the objects of its love, the worse the people" (*City of God*, 6:231–33). For Augustine, the focus of historical study ought to be the changing loves of a people, which reveal its character and health.

50 Gay, *Polly*, pp. 53, 104.

51 Alexander Smith, *A General History of the Lives and Adventures of the Most Famous Highwaymen . . . To Which is Added, a Genuine Account of the Most Notorious Pyrates* (London, 1734), "Introduction."

52 Cotton Mather, *Instructions to the Living, from the Condition of the Dead* (Boston, 1717), p. 44.

53 *Defoe's Review*, ed. Arthur W. Second (New York: Columbia University Press, 1938), 10:425–28.

54 *Romances and Narratives*, 16:77.

55 *Works*, 3:12b–13a, 33a.

56 Charles Molloy, *De Jure Maritimo et Navali*, 3rd ed. (London, 1682), pp. 53–54.

57 Cited in *A New Abridgment of the Law* by Matthew Bacon, ed. Sir Henry Groyllim, C. E. Dodd, B. Wilson, J. Bonvier (Philadelphia: Johnson, 1852), 7:441.

58 Alexander Justice, *A General Treatise of the Dominion of the Sea: and a Compleat Body of Sea-Laws*, 3rd ed. (London, 1724), p. 476.
59 Tindal, *Law of Nations*, pp. 19, 17.
60 Esquemeling, *Bucaniers*, pp. 59–60 [1:vii].
61 Reprinted in *The History of the Buccaneers of America* (Boston: Mussey, 1853), "Preface."
62 *Mist's Weekly Journal*, May 23, 1724. J. R. Moore believes that Defoe wrote this review (*A Checklist of the Writings of Daniel Defoe* [Bloomington: Indiana University Press, 1960], p. 187).
63 Sir William Blackstone, *Commentaries on the Laws of England*, ed. William Draper Lewis (Philadelphia: Welsh, 1902), 4:1478.
64 For a discussion of the Avery legend, see my "Introduction" to *"The Life and Adventures of Capt. John Avery" and "The Successful Pyrate,"* Augustan Reprint Society, nos. 203–4 (1980).
65 For a more thorough treatment of Defoe's "revision of popular legend," see John J. Richetti, *Defoe's Narratives: Situations and Structures* (Oxford: Clarendon Press, 1975), pp. 63–93. Richetti's contention that the pirate was "a demonic folk hero, . . . the satanically attractive figure who separates himself from any existing human community and creates his own world by declaring unconditional war on all mankind" (p. 69), belies the extent to which pirates were found to support the myth of the social contract and to imitate the practices of respectable society. Maurice Wehrung goes to the opposite extreme in concluding that for Defoe's age, the pirate "lived and fought according to certain rules and standards of morality, which enabled him to keep a passably respectable idea of himself as a man" ("The Literature of Privateering and Piracy as a Source of the Defoean Hero's Personality," in *Tradition et Innovation Littérature et Paralittérature* [Paris: Didier, 1975], p. 179).
66 My interpretation complements that of Maximillian Novak, *Defoe and the Nature of Man* (Oxford: Oxford University Press, 1963), pp. 51–63; Novak finds a parallel between the development of Crusoe's colony and the early history of Bermuda designed "to show how laws arose in the state of nature both because and in spite of the 'Nature of Man.'"
67 See my unpublished dissertation "Piracy Examined: A Study of Daniel Defoe's *General History of the Pirates* and its Milieu" (Princeton, 1970), pp. 228–38. For an account of schemes to colonize the Madagascar pirate communities, see pp. 120–37.
68 Swift, *Prose Writings*, 11:294.
69 *A Plan of the English Commerce* (London, 1728), pp. ix–x, xvi.
70 *Romances and Narratives*, 16:78.

Concepts of Revolution in England and France in the Eighteenth Century

PETER MATHIAS

It is a well-tried fact that foreign observers bring perceptions and insight to the understanding of countries other than their own which defy indigenous commentators. James Bryce sought to explain the American Commonwealth for European readers—and found the book's reception in the United States "equally gratifying and unexpected." There was Denis Brogan more recently, interpreting us both to each other. Such perceptions by the external eye have not been sharpened by the salt spray of the Atlantic voyage alone: the Channel has always offered a fascinating series of such alternative perspectives between England and France. Voltaire and Burke projected visions of their own political hopes and fears through the commentaries they made upon their neighbours. Faujas de St. Fond reported more perceptively upon the stirrings of the factory system in Lancashire in the 1780s than any local English traveller. Arthur Young's travels in France (in the same decade) produced descriptions unmatched by contemporary French observers. The list continues through de Saussure, Gabriel Jars (in that splendidly titled journal of a tour *Voyages Métallurgiques*), Tocqueville, Taine, and Faucher—to take only the most celebrated before the mid-nineteenth century; and on the whole the French travellers to England observed rather better (or wrote and published rather more effectively) than the equivalent English travellers in France.

So it has also proved with observations and insight mediated through historical scholarship. Elie Halévy is still honored as one of the most profound political and intellectual historians of the nineteenth-century English scene in his own generation. Paul Mantoux enjoys equivalent status in the historiography of the British Industrial Revolution. Sir Denis Brogan, in his second mediation, and Sir John Clapham maintained this tradition on the English side. In our own generation—it would be invidious to seek a definitive list—there are such French scholars as François Crouzet and François Bedarida and such British scholars as Richard Cobb, Theodore Zeldin, Olwen Hufton, John McManners and Patrick O'Brien.

Most travellers, if not the historians, compare, either more or less explicitly and with greater or lesser self-consciousness, the subject of their observations to their own country, often using the comparison to create a critique of their own institutions, their own government's policy, or their own cultural values. Their native country provides the reference point. Comparisons are made to point a moral for their own countrymen. We often learn, through the reflecting mirror of these observations, as much about their own country and their own values as about the ostensible object of their descriptions in a value-neutral way. Thus are our neighbors made the stalking-horses for a self-critique.

From such mirror images of each other, the stereotypes of historical interpretation concerning France and Britain in the eighteenth century were born and have enjoyed astonishing survival powers, despite, and in a few cases because of, the perceptions of the greatest of contemporary observers and latter-day historians. This text considers some of these interlocking views, which have conditioned so much historiography, not only at the more popular and textbook levels of academic sophistication. Such reciprocities, multi-faceted, interlocking, mutually dependent in many subtle ways, demand much more intricate exploration than can be offered in a short article. However, many interpretations converge upon the images of national strength projected by the two nations in the eighteenth century and consolidated subsequently in the aspic of historiography; and such views about national strength combine, and sometimes confuse, the political with the economic, the public and the private weal. Images of the strengths and weaknesses of the French *ancien régime* are closely related to interpretations of the French Revolution; those of the British state to interpretations of the Industrial Revolution. This provides a pretext, if not a justification, for entitling such an exploration of comparisons: concepts of revolution in the eighteenth century.

The first antithesis to be considered is the general presumption that, as a state, in the essential matter of deploying governmental power and authority, France in the eighteenth century was strong and England weak. The stereotype has it that France had the massive strength afforded by autocracy. The King, heading the apparatus of central government administration,[1] suffered no constitutional restraints, so that the ability of the state to increase taxation was not shackled by the need for an annual parliamentary vote of supply. The resources of the richest and much the largest single realm in western Europe could be exploited effectively for public purposes. Considerable lands still remained in the royal demesne, with the King drawing income and resources from them essentially as private landlord as well as monarch. Although such royal and public demesne was not nearly as significant relative to total state income as in the case of Prussia or Sweden (for parts, at least, of the eighteenth century) it compared favorably with an impoverished Hanoverian monarchy in England, long since denuded of almost all royal lands (the duchy of Cornwall and one or two much smaller estates apart). The British monarchy, living as a pensionary upon a Parliamentary grant, was relatively modest even in terms of personal wealth compared with the greatest of the landed magnates of the realm, the dukes and earls, whose great mansions standing in the midst of thousands of rural acres with prestigious town houses in London could not be matched by any of the Georges. Government itself in England had no significant discretionary financial resources to draw upon at all.

For visiting Englishmen and subsequent historians the manifestations of a powerful French state were plain to see from the moment the coaches set out along the high road from Calais or Boulogne. Splendid trunk routes were taken by such as Arthur Young as symbols of an efficient autocratic state, both because they were created by the hated *corvée* and were needed to deploy troops effectively. Characteristically he thought most of the French inns were execrable compared with their English equivalents—but that, like the unfavorable comparison about French agriculture relative to English standards, was as symbolic in its own way as the disparity between the standards of French and English roads.[2] An efficient trunk road system, like the great Canal du Midi, on a scale and with a century's precedence over any significant still-water navigation in England, was the visible sign of an institutional structure, supporting an administrative system supposedly wholly absent on the British side of the Channel. The *corps des ponts et chaussées*, the finest national civil engineering organization in Europe, was but one manifestation of this. Comparable British official civil engineering was principally limited to General Wade's mapping activities, roads, bridges, and barracks in

Scotland (confirming English prejudices that the real political purposes of such a highway network was to allow the rapid deployment
of a standing army against a recalcitrant citizenry). The mapping activities of the British Army's "ordnance" survey throughout the island after 1765, which complemented the justly famous Admiralty
charts, remained little known.[3] England also had nothing comparable
to the *École des Mines* in France.

Other contrasts are well known: the royal manufactures of France
had no rivals in England. The British surrogate was to be the warrant
of Royal Patronage to selected private manufacturers and suppliers—
which absorbed no public resources at all. Equally the Royal Academy in France was lavishly funded and was intended to play a major
public role in the state; whereas Charles II gave the Royal Society in
England only a charter, a mace, and his good wishes.[4] Departments
of State in France promoted new technology in a systematic way
throughout the eighteenth century, mobilizing the whole range of
Colbertian interventionist measures: monopolies, subsidies, concessions, privileged conditions and reward for entrepreneurs and skilled
workmen, guaranteed purchasing of output at fancy prices. All this
was evidence of intention (if not of result) by a progressive, strong
state, staffed by efficient bureaucrats, determined to modernize, and
had evolved long before the establishment of the *école polytechnique,*
the *conservatoire des arts et métiers* and other forward-looking institutions of the Revolutionary and Napoleonic regimes.

Above all, the strength and power of the French state was expressed in terms of a large standing army and navy—extant in much
larger degree in peacetime than were the armed services in Britain
where constitutional priorities (given that the King remained in person Commander in Chief), no less than financial exigence determined that there should be no significant standing army of regular
troops and only a minimum navy in time of peace.[5] Just over 10,000
seamen, for example, were on the muster rolls of the British Royal
Navy in 1792, compared with over 190,000 in 1797. All the formidable
apparatus of state in France, more particularly the costs of the army
and navy which accounted for more than half of total public sector
spending in the eighteenth century, depended upon very high levels
of taxation. This was the essential financial base upon which the whole
superstructure rested. It was at once the symbol and the embodiment
of a powerful autocracy. Not accidentally taxation—levels of taxation,
the range of taxes, and the social incidence of taxation—has assumed
a prominent place in the historiography of eighteenth-century France,
in particular the historiography of the causes of the French Revolu-

tion. The revolution of the peasants, at least—if not the occasion for a disaffected aristocracy—has been explained in large measure as a product of high and socially regressive taxation, coupled with the political oppression embodied in its administration by ruthless and all-powerful administrative cadres.

Against all this, stood the mirror image of England's supposed weakness as a state: a minimum state in interventionist economic roles, as we have seen; a minimum state (in peacetime at least) in relation to military spending; a minimum state in financial terms with state power shackled by constitutional constraints. Parliament refused to accept poll taxes or hearth taxes after 1697. Widespread popular and parliamentary hostility blocked the administration's proposal for a general excise (in fact only an extension to tobacco and wine) in 1733.[6] This was, moreover, a failure by the century's most astute, experienced, and effective political manager—Robert Walpole. The country gentlemen in Parliament declined to allow the land tax to rise above 2s in the pound (10 percent) in time of peace; or 4s in the pound (20 percent) in wartime—and that in a context of steadily declining assessments in terms of the real value of agricultural land (particularly in the more remote counties of the West and North) and the land tax's failure to embrace effectively any form of property other than agricultural land. Before 1841 an income tax was politically tolerable only in the extraordinary emergencies of war, being instituted in 1799 in the aftermath of the greatest wartime crisis the nation had known in 1797, and promptly abolished for a brief period of peace between 1801 and 1803 and then again in 1816, as soon as hostilities ceased. And such was the fear of a professional bureaucracy that the income tax had to be assessed by amateur committees of J.P.s in the counties—gentlemen passing judgment upon fellow gentlemen—with an amateur system of local receivers of tax, following the precedent of the land tax.[7] Low-profile government thus had its base in low-profile taxation, runs the common assumption. And if the political revolution of 1789 in France owed much to high and oppressive taxation, the Industrial Revolution in England was encouraged by low taxation allowing the surpluses of the nation to fructify in private hands and be deployed for productive investment.

If this is the myth what of the reality? Highlighting in this way certain of the political and administrative realities of both countries has kept the other half of their profiles in darkness; and those hidden perspectives show as great a contrast as the public face of the comparison—but in the opposite sense. For Great Britain was a very strong state in the eighteenth century: limited in the range of government action but powerfully based and financially secure. Moreover the indigenous financial base of British state power and public authority was administratively modernized in a sense which made the French public finances seem medieval in comparison.

Consider first the ability of the British state to extract resources from its population and the economy. In absolute terms Great Britain was a much smaller nation than France, with a population of perhaps 6 million at the opening of the eighteenth century in comparison with the 20 million in France. By the century's end 27.3 million people in France faced 10.2 in Great Britain. Thus in the aggregate, with the natural resources of a land almost three times the area of Britain, tax revenues in France were always greater than in Britain but not by as much as might be supposed.[8] In terms of wheat equivalent (designated in order to establish a common standard of comparison), the French state had a total tax income 15 percent higher than Britain's in 1715 and 30 percent higher than Britain's in 1785. At the height of the Napoleonic Wars in 1807–8, however, total British tax revenue actually exceeded that of France. If this is the story in aggregate, relative to their respective populations and to the size of their respective national incomes, the contrast falls predictably, very strongly the other way. During the eighteenth century as a whole, in Britain real tax incomes of central government were twice as high per capita as in France—for most of the century more than twice as high—and at the peak of the Napoleonic Wars the real British tax burden per capita (for central government finances) was almost three times higher than that in France. The real tax burden on the average Briton almost doubled between 1700 and 1790; and then almost doubled again during the Napoleonic Wars. The ratio of taxation to national income rose from 9 percent to 24 percent in the same period.

In terms of social incidence (a concept which requires much elaboration), a much higher proportion of the taxes levied by central government in France were direct taxes falling upon income and wealth than in Britain. The proportion of such direct taxes in England declined in the course of the eighteenth century from 27–28 percent of total revenue from taxation to 18 percent in the 1780s; in France the proportion ranged from 61 percent to 48 percent. Of course, the social distribution of wealth and income was different in France than in England. The privileged orders in sections of France were exempt from some taxation. Feudal dues and local taxation further skew the picture. But even so, the contrast is remarkable.

This should not be surprising given the fact that the British waged war during the eighteenth and early nineteenth century on a scale and with an effect comparable with France. Efficient taxation, plus the great British seventeenth-century invention of a permanent funded debt, itself secured on the annual produce of specific taxes, provided the foundation of this primary expression of state power. Public credit remained secure throughout the eighteenth century and the British government was always able to borrow money. In turn effective taxation was the product of administrative efficiency applied to the fiscal possibilities consequent upon a particular form of economic structure.

Taxation of imports and more important, the excise taxation of home-produced goods together normally provided three-quarters of total revenue from taxation in peacetime (of which the excise yielded twice the amount of customs). With such a structure British taxation in the eighteenth century was inevitably regressive: only commodities in mass demand, such as beer (with associated excises on malt and hops), gin, salt, tea, sugar, tobacco, bricks, and the like could produce large revenues—commodities for which demand was not only more widely based but also less elastic than for the luxuries of the rich. As Lord North remarked: "where great sums have to be obtained the burden must lie upon the bulk of the people."

The English customs were directly administered by state authority from the late seventeenth century with customs officials in direct, salaried public employment, even though some of the debris of the medieval system of places and patronage (particularly at the upper levels of posts in the outports) survived into a world of job hierarchies, internal promotion ladders, age limits, formal instruction and training, certification, and even pension funds. The excise in England sprang newly-armed into existence with Cromwellian efficiency in a post-medieval administrative world of formal organization, hierarchical structure, salaried, full-time employment with graded salary scales, and sanctions against receiving fees or accepting other employments. Max Weber would have recognized the English excise establishment of the eighteenth century as meeting most of his criteria for an efficient public bureaucracy. For example over 3,000 full-time, salaried officials, in an elaborately graded organization were surveying the English brewing industry in the provinces in 1781–82, with an additional 237 full-time officers in London.

Compared with this, the French system of tax administration was medieval, even if extortionate, in its traditional farming methods and in the absence of a unitary national structure.[9] Effective direct administration in France was also hampered in many other spheres by the survival of medieval franchises and ancient jurisdictions, which created a sort of "administrative feudalism." In practice, aristocratic privilege, some surviving ecclesiastical powers, and entrenched regionalism severely handicapped the direct administrative authority of central government in France,—despite the theoretical omnipotence of the King and officials acting on his authority.[10] In England administrative efficiencies, most completely exemplified by the excise establishment, were also developing in such diverse areas as the Admiralty and the naval dockyards, in the Royal ordnance arsenals and gunpowder factories, in the Post Office, and in the Treasury.[11] In other departments, such as the Exchequer and the Court of Chancery, medievalism resisted modern administrative standards much more successfully until the nineteenth century. The flagrant corruption and inefficiencies of the British electoral and parliamentary scene masked the growth of these administrative efficiencies from unobservant visitors and historians. Westminster has been overemphasized and Whitehall underemphasized in these comparisons.

The economic base for the British tax system reflected important structural differences between the British and French economies in the eighteenth century. England's heavy reliance on customs revenue was possible only where foreign trade was significant in relation to the national market (import values were between 20 percent and 25 percent of national income in the period 1780–1800) and where some of the major imported commodities, such as tea, sugar, and tobacco had passed down the social scale in the course of the century to become mass-traded "necessities" of the poor.[12] Equally, excise taxation on products in mass demand implied very little local self-subsistence, important levels of urban demand, and highly articulated basic commodity markets. Most families and individuals, for example, bought most of their beer and gin in shops, from commercial manufacturers rather than making it for themselves (more than half the excise revenue came from the production of alcoholic drink). Such pervasive commodity markets at the local level of provincial life in England, where even most of the agricultural labor force was a rural proletariat of farm laborers working for money wages, had become a precondition for the effective taxation of the laboring masses. They remained for the most part without savings, but working for wages formed the basis of their ability to consume, and hence the ability of government to levy effective taxation on the mass of the nation. Not accidentally the only other country in Europe where such high per capita taxation prevailed was Holland, where excises on basic foodstuffs (in the Dutch case, unlike England, including bread grains) were also the staple of the fiscal system, and where the commercialization of family consumption, the spread of money wages, commitment to the market by

all groups in society, urban demand, and the consequential development of commodity markets were even more advanced than in England.[13]

It would be pushing paradox too far to seek to entirely reverse the
normal caricature portraits of a strong French state and a weak British
one. The ability of both to wage war on a rising scale throughout the
century, culminating in the generation of conflict between 1792 and
1815, when hostilities were conducted at an unprecedented level, is
sufficient evidence that the public apparatus of both countries was
effective in extracting and transferring resources on a massive scale.
It cost Great Britain £1,000 million in direct military costs alone to
defeat the French, with £500 million added to the permanent funded
debt as a cross for succeeding generations to bear. To put this vast
sum into perspective it may be compared with the entire capital of
the British canal network, which, when roughly complete in 1820,
had absorbed only about £20 million—and had been accumulated
much more gradually since the mid-eighteenth century. This contrast
in the order of financial magnitude needs no gloss. Equally there are
lessons to be drawn from the same military experience faced by France
after 1792. A traditional state apparatus, financially and politically
bankrupt by 1789, faced administrative chaos in the immediate aftermath, a loss of public credit and disruption of the fiscal base of the
regime. Yet such was the essential economic strength of France, when
translated into mobilized resources, that her armies could conquer
Europe and hold the embattled nations at bay for a generation.

To return to the original point of departure: given the important
explanatory role which taxation has played in the French Revolution
and the Industrial Revolution, now that the quantitative record reveals that the level of taxation was so much higher in Britain than in
France, and that the fiscal regime of central government in Britain
was so much more regressive than that in France, might we not argue
that, if contemporaries in the eighteenth century had been generally
aware of these truths, we might have expected a political revolution
in England and an industrial revolution in France? One side of this
conundrum, at least, deserves an answer, when the question is posed
less provocatively. Why did such an extraordinary tax burden in England—even if denounced by Tom Paine and a sequence of radicals,
not to mention the sequence of equally vociferous critics from the
extreme right and most points in between—not provoke political opposition nearly as deeply structured as in France?

Added point is given to the question by the distribution of public
spending. The expenditure side of the public accounts in Britain, it

should be remembered, was as regressive in its social effects as the income side. In peacetime the largest single financial commitment of government was the payment of annual interest on the national debt, which was absorbing over half of total receipts from taxation by the latter decades of the century, with military costs making up most of the remainder. Thus most taxes were paid by poorer working people and most payments received by richer savers: a massive transfer from poor to rich. Doubtless the representative nature of parliamentary government had something to do with this minimal public reaction to high and inequitable taxation, even if most of those paying most of the indirect taxes on outlay remained unenfranchised. The principal reason, however, is that taxes on outlay remained largely invisible politically, or were certainly of a much lower political profile, raising much less resentment than direct taxation falling on modest incomes—as they still do. Import duties were paid, for the most part, by a relatively small group of wealthy import merchants concentrated in a few ports. Many thought that such import taxes were, in fact, paid by the foreign merchants selling the goods, and that such exotic commodities, in any case, were proper subjects for such levies, benefitting home producers of identical or substitute products. Excise taxation was levied on commercial manufacturers of indigenous products and paid at the time and point of production. Both forms of taxation thus enjoyed the administrative advantage of not requiring the presence of the tax official at the houses of the families who were actually paying the levies or even at the shops of their local merchants: the taxes were absorbed into the final selling price of the articles in question.[14] The highly visible extraction of the *taille* or the *gabelle* from French peasants, by contrast, produced a much greater awareness of taxation. The political consequences varied accordingly.

The stereotype of views about the relative strengths of the French and British state in the eighteenth century has a mirror image in some of the older stereotyped interpretations of the French Revolution and the Industrial Revolution—the two images are not unconnected. A weak state in England, with a minimum presence in the economy and making minimum claims on resources for nonproductive purposes, was a factor in encouraging the Industrial Revolution to develop. Spontaneous momentum for change, for the most part, was not blocked by the heavy hand of governmental interference, which through corruption and inefficiency diminished the functional efficiency of all state institutions under such patronage and control. Great Britain was the largest free-trade area in Europe; all citizens enjoyed free access to all careers. Local monopolies consecrated by Royal Charter or Letters Patent had been dissolved by judges independent of the Crown and government after 1660 and 1689. Judge-made law, with the enhancement of the common law, confirmed and extended private property rights. Most extensions of economic activity demanding corporate legal forms (whether public utility investment, land and urban improvement, transport, some mining and insurance enterprise) were accommodated by private acts of Parliament authorizing local bodies with powers limited to the act or by the device of the equitable trust without benefit of Parliamentary sanction, rather than by extending the public sector, with all that might bring in its wake through the dysfunctional imperatives of patronage and corruption. This makes basic assumptions that the path to economic growth and industrialization, at least in contemporary circumstances of the *ancien régime* in France and the unreformed political regime of patronage in England, could only arise from the free market and the free play of economic, social, and cultural forces.

Few historians would be so bold as to argue that this line of argument holds no degree of truth. The state and the legal processes in England did institutionalize, more than in most countries in Europe, such underlying forces. The political process in England reflected the impetus of new wealth just as the English social matrix accredited new sources of wealth with status. This complex process of accommodation was subject to less inertia than in more autocratic and legitimist forms of government. But the methodology of explanation is more general than this. Put crudely the argument runs that Britain experienced an industrial revolution in the eighteenth century (Scots object, rightly, to the assertion that England experienced an industrial revolution): therefore, any major country worth the name *ought* to have experienced an industrial revolution. France did not (continues the assertion). Therefore some particular reason must have prevented it, and, by comparing the two countries, we can identify the missing component.

Perhaps the nature of the state, as already instanced, was the problem. Setting up the model in this way, however, invites a single-cause explanation, or at least suggests that a single critical variable might exist, which can be identified by means of a comparison of the variables present in the two case histories under investigation. This is, of course, a simplistic and pseudoscientific analogue; but by such expedients has comparative historical analysis been pursued.

The candidates for the missing critical variable in France have been many. It was fashionable in the nineteenth century to give great weight to natural resources, in particular to the plenitude and cheapness of coal in England. (This is much less popular as an explanation today—the vicarious implications of the oil crises since 1973 not having worked their way through into a retrospective historical consciousness—but this will come.) Colonial trade and the profits of empire were difficult to work up into a credible unique English variable (more particularly after Britain's defeat in the American War of Independence) because France was not devoid of such attributes. Perhaps the most favored choice for the British secret weapon was the Protestant nonconformists: the Quaker ironmasters, bankers and brewers; the Unitarian cotton spinners; the Presbyterian Scots. France, after all, had forfeited this asset with the expulsion of the Huguenots following the Revocation of the Edict of Nantes in 1685. This explanation that entrepreneurship was the key variable, and that the nonconformists gave Britain a unique advantage, was particularly prominent in the 1950s under the influence of Schumpeterian concepts. In Schumpeter's *Theory of Economic Development* the entrepreneur was the "unmoved mover," the *primum mobile*, of progress, forcing the economy out of a "steady state," circular flow. The achievement motivations of minority groups, reacting against and excluded from traditional established social elites, fitted neatly into this schema, when subsequently elaborated.

The relative truth of these assertions cannot be argued here. The explanatory apparatus of the Industrial Revolution is, in any case, much more complex than the identification of any single factor as a model inviting the specification of one critical variable implies. And subsequent quantification of French rates of growth, expansion of foreign trade, productivity levels in industry, and various other indices of economic change suggest that—at least up to the 1780s—there was no great gap to be explained between French and British economic performance, judged in quantitative terms.[15] In any case the basic historical question to be argued out, on its own intrinsic terms, is the actual phenomenon of why Britain experienced an industrial revolution rather than the hypothetical issue of why France did not and therefore what must have prevented it. However the tradition of explanation was set in terms of *la révolution manqué* in France, and this has exerted immense influence over the historiography of European industrialization (not alone that of France) in the eighteenth and early nineteenth centuries. The term *la révolution manqué* is customarily applied, of course, not to the missing industrial revolution in France but to the absent political revolution in England.[16] The analogue, however, is conceptually identical. France had a political revolution in 1789. It is therefore to be presumed that England was also in a revolutionary situation and ought to have had a political revolution. This did not happen, and the absence of revolution demands special explanation.[17]

We are concerned here with the debate focussing upon the 1790s, but *la révolution manqué* has a wider span, making assumptions about the reaction of the British working class to industrialization in the longer term, particularly in the 1840s, when Frederick Engels' famous predictions about immediately impending revolution were published in *The Condition of the Working Class in England* (1845).[18] Modern Marxist and radical scholarship in British historiography, led by Dr. Edward Thompson, Professor E. J. Hobsbawm, and Dr. John Foster, gives greater prominence to the perverse reluctance of the British working classes to revolt, let alone to revolt successfully, in the early decades of the nineteenth century, particularly the 1840s, than to their confused response to the French Revolution in the 1790s, where patriotism in a nation at war soon muffled most radical protest. According to Marxist dogma, claiming scientific truth for its interpretation of the dynamics of the historical process, revolution stood at the end of the road of capitalist development. Given the subsequent record of non-revolution, clearly, the revolution was thwarted, or indefinitely postponed, by a variety of special explanations: effective repression and counterrevolution (despite the extraordinary ineffectiveness of local police forces in Britain and the extreme reticence in the use of troops); embourgeoisement of the working class after the 1840s; tactical retreats by government at moments of crisis (particularly in 1832); the buying off of the middle classes by the ruling class which prevented the necessary alliance with the working class from being consolidated. The English working classes themselves, runs the argument, showed irrational restraint, had too much faith in legal processes and constitutionality, were deluded by the belief in a "moral economy," were supine or stupid, were let down by their leaders, were duped by religion and false consciousness about the possibility of improving their lot by peaceful, legitimate means.

It is well known that Elie Halévy, although no Marxist, attributed the—for him—surprising quiescence of the English working classes to the influence of evangelicalism in general and to Methodism in particular. "We shall attempt to find here," he wrote, "the key to the problem whose solution has hitherto escaped us; for we shall explain by this movement [Methodism] the extraordinary stability which English society was destined to enjoy throughout a period of revolutions and crises; what we may truly term the miracle of modern England. . . ."[19] Does this provide a common theme—the Methodists—in this canon of explanation for industrial revolution and the absence of political revolution in eighteenth-century England? Scarcely in Methodism itself, for Methodists were conspicuously absent from the ranks of the entrepreneurs in late eighteenth-century Britain—but, perhaps, in Protestant nonconformity in general.

To follow these speculations is to accept the original assumptions of the methodology. Without the original hypothetical assumption that there *ought* to have been a revolution, a whole range of collateral hypothetical assumptions can be abandoned, or at least sharply downgraded in importance if they are no longer to be construed as potential necessary explanations according to the terms of a pre-accepted theory. England was, on many occasions, a locally turbulent society—that is quite clear from the evidence.[20] Blood letting and many corpses were not characteristic of these local eruptions of social protest in England, however, and a locally turbulent society was a quite different phenomenon from incipient revolution overthrowing the political regime and system of government. In any case social turbulence characterized English society on such occasions long before the example of the French Revolution was available to inspire English radicals and long before the emergence of those structural transformations which the Industrial Revolution brought in its wake.

Ex ante, both revolutions need to be analysed in their own terms, in the first instance at least as unique phenomena, subject to external influences, of course, but without the presumption that they characterized a general condition or a universal dynamic of history operating, or predestined to operate, in the same way, unless specifically prevented from doing so, across all nations. We need to elaborate much more fully, that is to say, our concepts of political time and economic time, and to be much more reluctant about construing them in matching terms.

NOTES

1 M. Antoine, *Le Conseil du Roi sous la règne de Louis XV* (Geneva, 1970).
2 A. Young, *Travels in France during the years 1787, 1788 and 1789*, ed. C. Maxwell (Cambridge, 1950), passim (see, for example pp. 17, 19, 22, 30–

31, 37, etc.). Similar views about inns were expressed by Smollett and most other English travellers in France, for example, T. Smollett, *Travels through France and Italy* [in 1763] (Oxford, 1979), pp. 8, 42–43. Local roads in the French countryside were a different matter (P. Goubert, *L'Ancien Régime* [Paris, 1973], 1:61–62).

3 C. Close, *The Early Years of the Ordnance Survey,* ed. J. B. Hartley (Newton Abbot, 1969).

4 R. Hahn, *The Anatomy of a Scientific Institution: The Paris Academy of Sciences 1666–1803* (Berkeley, 1971); C. C. Gillispie, *Science and Polity in France at the End of the Old Regime* (Princeton, 1980); S. T. McCloy, *Government Assistance in Eighteenth-Century France* (Durham, N.C., 1946). For the British side of the issue see P. Mathias, *The Transformation of England* (London, 1979), chs. 2–4, and authorities cited there.

5 E. G. Léonard, *L'Armée et ses problèmes au XVIIIᵉ siècle* (Paris, 1958); A. Corvisier, *Les Français et l'armée sous Louis XIV* (Vincennes, 1975); *Armées et sociétés en l'Europe de 1494 à 1789* (Paris, 1976). For Anglo-French comparisons in the 1760s see A. Young, *Letters Concerning the Present State of the French Nation* (London, 1769), pp. 120–34, 432–35. The French standing army in time of peace was approximately 150,000–200,000 men; the British approximately 17,000. Although the disparity in numbers of seamen was not as great, numbers on the muster rolls of the British Navy in the 1760s after the peace of 1763 were limited to 16,000.

6 P. Langford, *The Excise Crisis: Society and Politics in the Age of Walpole* (Oxford, 1975); J. M. Price, "The Excise Crisis revisited," in *England's Rise to Greatness, 1660–1763,* ed. S. B. Baxter (Berkeley, Cal., 1983).

7 W. R. Ward, *The English Land Tax in the Eighteenth Century* (London, 1953); A. Hope-Jones, *Income Tax in the Napoleonic Wars* (Cambridge, 1939).

8 The following data are taken from P. Mathias and P. K. O'Brien, "Taxation in England and France, 1715–1810," *Journal of European Economic History* (1976); P. Mathias, *The Transformation of England* (London, 1979), ch. 6. The broad facts were appreciated by some contemporaries: for example, A. Smith, *An Inquiry into the Nature and Causes of the Wealth of Nations,* 8th ed. (London, 1796), 3:392; A. Young, *Letters Concerning the French Nation* (London, 1769), pp. 429–32. They acknowledged that the political perception of taxation in the two countries was in inverse ratio to its real incidence.

9 J. F. Bosher, *French Finances, 1770–95: from Business to Bureaucracy,* (Cambridge, 1970); M. Marion, *Histoire financière de la France depuis 1715* (Paris, 1914); M. Marion, *L'impôt sur le revenu* (Geneva, 1976; Toulouse, 1901); J. Bouvier and H. Germain-Martin, *Finances et financiers de l'Ancien Régime* (Paris, 1964); G. T. Matthews, *The Royal General Farms in Eighteenth Century France* (New York, 1958); M. Morineau, "Budgets de l'Etat et gestion des finances royales en France au 18ᵉ siècle," *Review Historique* 264, no. 2.

10 C. B. A. Behrens, *The Ancien Régime* (London, 1967), pp. 85–118; "Nobles, Privileges and Taxes in France at the end of the *Ancien Régime,*" *Economic History Review* (1962–63).

11 G. S. Holmes, *Augustan England: Professions, State and Society, 1680–1730* (London, 1982); J. Brewer and J. Styles, eds. *An Ungovernable People: the English and their Law in the 17th and 18th Centuries* (London, 1980).

12 R. Davis, *The Industrial Revolution and British Overseas Trade* (Leicester, 1979), p. 86.

13 J. de Vries, *The Dutch Rural Economy in the Golden Age* (New Haven, Conn., 1974).

14 This makes major assumptions about who "really" paid the tax. Complex elasticities of demand and other factors could mean that such taxes affected the costs, profits, and margins of manufacturers and distributors instead of being completely passed down the chain of transactions to rest fully with the ultimate purchaser. In general, however, it seems that the customer paid. The question is discussed in more detail in the exchange between D. N. McCloskey and P. Mathias and P. K. O'Brien in the *Journal of European Economic History* 7 (1978).

15 There is now a flourishing revisionist literature (much of it based upon systematic quantification of data and hence the availability of new time series). See, for example, P. K. O'Brien and C. Keyder, *Economic Growth in Britain and France, 1780–1914* (London, 1978); M. Levy-Leboyer, "La Croissance Economique en France au XIXᵉ siècle," *Annales* (1968); F. Crouzet, "Essai de construction d'un indice annuel de la production industrielle française au XIXᵉ siècle," *Annales* (1970); F. Crouzet, "England and France in the eighteenth century: a comparative analysis of two economic growths," in R. M. Hartwell, ed., *The Causes of the Industrial Revolution* (London, 1967); F. Crouzet, "Bordeaux au XVIIIᵉ siècle" in *Histoire de Bordeaux*, vol. 5 (Bordeaux, 1968), ch. 2; R. Cameron and C. E. Freeman, "French Economic Growth: a Radical Revision," *Social Science History* 7 (1983). The relatively slow rate of economic growth in Britain has also been much stressed. See data in R. Floud and D. McCloskey, *The Economic History of Britain since 1700* (Cambridge, 1981); R. C. O. Matthews, C. H. Feinstein and J. C. Odling-Smee, *British Economic Growth 1856–1973* (Oxford, 1982), with new assessment by N. F. R. Crafts in *Economic History Review* 36 (1983).

16 There is an active Italian counterpart debate dating from Gramsci's use of the term in 1949. See A. W. Salamone, "The Political Myth of *rivoluzione mancata*," *American Historical Review* (1962), p. 47n.

17 This historiographical tradition is discussed at length by R. M. Hartwell, "La Révolution Manqué" in *Essays in Honour of Charles Wilson*, ed. D. C. Coleman and P. Mathias (Cambridge: Cambridge University Press, forthcoming). The following passage owes much to Dr. Hartwell's text.

18 This edition was in German, an English edition not being published in England until 1892.

19 E. Halévy, *A History of the English People in the Nineteenth Century*, vol. 1, *England in 1815*, rev. ed. (London, 1949), Prologue to Part 3, p. 387.

20 M. I. Thomis, *The Luddites* (Newton Abbot, 1970); W. J. Shelton, *English Hunger and Industrial Disorder* (London, 1973); E. P. Thompson, "The Moral

Economy of the English Crowd," *Past and Present* (1971); W. G. Hoskins, "Harvest Fluctuations and English Economic History, 1620–1759," *Agricultural History Review* 16 (1968); P. Clark and P. Slack, eds., *Crisis and Order in English Towns, 1500–1700* (London, 1972); J. Stevenson, *Popular Disturbances in England, 1700–1870* (London, 1979).

Pin Money

SUSAN STAVES

In the fifth act of Vanbrugh's comedy, *The Relapse* (1696), Miss Hoyden, the simple-minded daughter of an almost equally simple-minded country gentleman, eagerly anticipates her approaching marriage to Lord Foppington and all the concomitant delights of fashionable London life. Attempting to rebut some of her old nurse's doubts about the marital happiness to be expected with fashionable lords, who have been known to give their money "to their sluts and their trulls" instead of to their wives, Miss Hoyden declares that Lord Foppington, at least, is "as free as an open house at Christmas": "For this very morning he told me I should have two hundred a year to buy pins. Now, nurse, if he gives me two hundred a year to buy pins, what do you think he will give me to buy fine petticoats?" The nurse enlightens her: "Ah, my dearest, he deceives thee faully, and he's no better than a rogue for his pains. These Londoners have got a gibberidge with 'em, would confound a gipsy. That which they call pin-money is to buy their wives every thing in the varsal world, down to their very shoe-ties: nay, I have heard folks say that some ladies, if they will have gallants, as they call 'em, are forced to find them out of their pin-money too."[1] As the nurse suggests, pin money was paid by husbands to wives, so much per year, and was supposed to be spent on clothes, amusements, charities, and such other out-of-pocket expenses as a wife incurred—not, of course, including the maintenance of a lover. In 1696 even a girl more worldly-wise than Miss Hoyden might have found "pin money" a puzzling term, since it seems to have been a relatively new social phenomenon in the late Restoration and early eighteenth century.[2] Though the term was used more loosely, for my purposes here, it will be convenient to define pin money as payments under a contract by a husband to a wife during coverture of a set annual sum. Usually the contract was the marriage settlement, but sometimes husbands entered into other pre- and postnuptial agreements to pay pin money. Sheridan in *The School for Scandal* (1777) realistically enough makes Sir Peter Teazle's failure to settle any pin money or separate estate on Lady Teazle a bone of contention between them, then, in the famous screen scene of Act 4, has Sir Peter appear with the drafts of two deeds, one giving Lady Teazle property after his death, the other giving her "eight hundred a year independent" while he lives.[3]

Pin money was thus one species of married women's separate property, that is, one species of property which women could be said to own despite the coverture which under common law made the wife's property belong to her husband. In the eighteenth-century lawyer's mind, the paradigmatic form of married women's separate property was the wife's separate estate put in trust for her at the time of the prenuptial marriage settlement, an estate which the wife was to possess "for her sole and separate use," not subject to the control of her husband and not available to her husband's creditors. One aim in creating the married woman's separate estate was to increase the security of the wife and the minor children should her husband prove feckless or unlucky. Another was to secure some of the wife's father's property for his grandchildren without risking its being swallowed up in the husband's estate; thus, the wife's separate estate was likely to be settled on her for life with remainders to the children of her body. Most lawyers preferred to have the property which was to be the wife's separate estate conveyed to trustees "for her use," apparently both because they supposed male trustees would manage it better and because the contract could then be thought of as between the husband and the trustees with the wife as a sort of third-party beneficiary, thus softening the common law objection to contracts between husbands and wives. But by 1725 in *Bennet* v. *Davis* the courts had permitted a wife to possess separate property without trustees.[4] In the early nineteenth century an attempt was made to distinguish pin money clearly from the married woman's separate estate, yet though such a distinction would make my exposition here easier, no such clear distinction was made in the eighteenth century.

The eighteenth-century idea of pin money, while in some ways simple enough, was, in other ways almost hopelessly tortuous and contradictory. On the one hand, pin money reflected a tendency to construe marriage as contractual and imported into the matrimonial relationship elements of the eighteenth-century ideology of contract. On the other hand, neither the legal establishment nor polite society generally was prepared to see all the traditional status incidents of marriage become the subjects of purely private negotiation, to allow those rights and duties of the matrimonial relationship thought to be fundamental to social order to be bargained over as individual whim might dictate. A crucial status incident of marriage was the husband's obligation to support the wife and to provide her with necessaries appropriate to their rank. Insofar as pin money was supposed to contribute to the wife's maintenance, it was by no means clear that a contract for the performance of what was, prior to any contract, a common law duty could have any validity. Moreover, time was required to work through the consequences of construing either marriage or marriage settlements as contractual, and what turned out to seem logical corollaries of this construction sometimes proved disturbing. For example, in the 1760s when the judges reasoned that a female minor's consent to a marriage settlement could not bind her, since a minor's consent to a contract could not bind him, the social consequences of this were found intolerable and the decision overturned in the House of Lords.[5]

Throughout the eighteenth century the legal system had two general problems with women and property which I will venture to state here with brutal simplicity. New forms of women's property had supposedly been created in part to provide greater security for women and children, forms of property secured by contract, and consequently to assure that one man's women and children did not become public charges to other men. But the first general problem was that these new forms of property, under contract logic, did not seem to provide the social control over women that had been part of the customary and other earlier systems of maintaining women and children. For example, under some customary tenures a widow's freebench was forfeited by her unchastity and under the Statute of Westminster the Second (1285) dower was forfeited by elopement and adultery, but a widow's jointure in the eighteenth century was secured by contract and not so subject to forfeit for sexual misconduct. The second general problem was that, although according to liberal political theory a wife who had separate property legally secured to her ought to have gained power and although male contemporaries certainly complained enough that married women with separate property were entirely too powerful and too independent, it frequently happened that, despite separate property being secured to them, women were unwilling or unable even to hang on to it, being, as contemporaries said, "kissed or kicked," "bullied or coaxed" out of it by husbands who had physical or emotional power that rendered their wives' legal powers nugatory.

The history of the legal thought concerning pin money from about 1690 to 1834, I will argue, shows the legal system responding to these two perceived problems by developing a set of special rules to maximize the probabilities that married women's separate property would provide secure maintenance for the women and children upon whom it was settled and to minimize the possibilities that women could take property intended for maintenance and use it as capital. In order to do this, it was necessary to develop different rules for women's property and for men's property and to have idiosyncratic protective rules that restricted the powers attendant upon ownership when the owners were married women. Some of the earliest late seventeenth- and very early eighteenth-century cases involving pin money doubt that a husband's agreement to pay his wife can have legal consequence.[6] In the eighteenth century, however, the validity of these contracts was recognized, and the consequences of treating pin money as a contract debt were developed—up to a point. From the Restoration through the early nineteenth century, as we shall see, the history of pin money reflects a variety of contradictions. First, pin money is construed as a contract debt, but an idiosyncratic rule of no arrears beyond a year was developed, based on the assumption that if the husband and wife cohabit the husband has maintained the wife. Second, the actual purposes of paying pin money could not be fully acknowledged either in official discourse or in legal theory, and this contributed substantially to the incoherence of the legal theory. Third, pin money came to the wife as cash payments which were her separate property, but if she bought certain things other than clothes with that money, she might discover that the traditional law of baron and feme had gone into effect and that the things she had bought were subject to rules different from those normally governing married women's separate property or had become her husband's property. Fourth, marriage settlements frequently gave the wife a fund "for such uses and purposes as she shall direct or appoint," which might seem to imply that the wife could do anything she wished with the fund, but when experience showed that some wives elected to mortgage or alienate the capital, to "sink the fund," as contemporaries said, ways were found to prohibit such alienation.

Although I shall here be concerned principally with the development of the legal theory of pin money from about 1690 to 1834, it will make the subsequent discussion of cases easier to follow and may be of general use to historians and biographers who encounter such documents among family papers first to consider briefly the forms in which agreements to pay pin money were usually made. It was usual to settle some property as the capital fund which was to support the annual payments. The property so settled might be land or it might be in another form, long leases or stock or consols, for instance. In the forms of conveyances most approved by lawyers, the capital fund was conveyed to trustees who became responsible for managing the fund and paying the wife, customarily in quarterly installments. A marriage settlement or other instrument (for example, a bond) might make it clear either that an annual sum was denominated "pin money" or that an annual sum was to be spent for such items as the wife's clothes. Other agreements, it is important to realize, made provisions for similar payments without denominating them "pin money" or specifying the purposes for which expenditures from the fund were to be made.

Gilbert Horsman's *Precedents in Conveyancing* prints a sample marriage settlement dated 1729 providing for a jointure and also for pin money. In this particular settlement the bride has brought a portion of £6,000 and is to have a jointure from lands the yearly value of which is £500 "or thereabouts"; the pin money payments are to be £120 a year in the first three years of the marriage and £250 a year thereafter (glosses mine):

And this Indenture further witnesseth, that in Consideration of the said intended Marriage and Marriage Portion, and of the great Love and Affection which he the said *Aaron Assley* hath and beareth unto the said *Frances Eave* his intended Wife, and of the sum of 10s. . . . to him in Hand paid by the said *Charles Castor* and *Daniel Darby*, at and before the Ensealing and Delivery of these Presents, the Receipt whereof is hereby acknowledged, he the said *Aaron Assley* hath granted, bargained, sold and demised, and by these Presents doth grant, bargain, sell and demise unto the said *Charles Castor* and *Daniel Darby*, their Executors, Administrators and Assigns, all and every the said Messuages, Farms, Lands, Tenements, Tithes, Hereditaments and Premises herein before granted, settled, limited and ap-

the groom, A.A., sells specific land, described earlier in the settlement, to the trustees, C.C. and D.D., for the nominal sum of 10s.

the trustees to hold the land to the use of the wife, i.e., in trust for the wife, to be a capital fund from which will issue her jointure payments after her husband's death raises a 99-year trust term on the same land for the same trustees to pay pin money to the wife during the coverture, i.e., these payments to be made only during the joint lives of husband and wife

trustees to pay out of rents and profits of this land, annually, in quarterly installments, payable on days stipulated

£120 a year until St. Michael's Day in 1733, and £250 a year thereafter

pointed, unto and upon the said *Frances Eave* for her Life, for her Jointure as aforesaid, with their and every of their Appurtenances, and the Reversion and Reversions, Remainder and Remainders, yearly and other Rents, Issues and Profits thereof, and of every Part and Parcel thereof; To have and to hold the said Messuages, Farms, Lands, Tenements, Tithes, Hereditaments . . . unto the said *Charles Castor* and *Daniel Darby*, their Executors, Administrators and Assigns, from the Day next before the Day of the Date of these Presents, for and during the full Time and Term, and unto the full End and Term of ninety-nine Years from thence next ensuing, and fully to be compleat and ended, if they the said *Aaron Assley* and *Frances* his intended Wife shall both of them so long jointly live, upon the Trusts, and to and for the Intents and Purposes, and under and subject to the Proviso and Agreements herein after mentioned, expressed and declared of and concerning the same Term, (that is to say) . . . upon Trust, and to the Intent and Purpose, that they the said *Charles Castor* and *Daniel Darby*, and the Survivor of them, his Executors, Administrators and Assigns, shall and do yearly and every Year, by and out of the Rents, Issues and Profits of the said Messuages, Farms, Lands, Tenements, Tithes, Hereditaments and Premisses so demised . . . pay, or cause to be paid by four equal quarterly Payments, on the four most usual Feasts or Days of Payment in the Year (that is to say) the Feasts of the Birth of our Lord *Christ*, the Annunciation of the blessed Virgin *Mary*, the Nativity of Saint *John* Baptist, and Saint *Michael* the Archangel, by even and equal Portions, free of all Taxes and Deductions whatsoever, the several yearly Sums of Money, . . . the yearly Sum of 120 l . . . until the Feast-day of Saint *Michael* the Archangel which shall be in the Year of our Lord 1732, (if they the said *Aaron As-sley* and *Frances* his intended Wife shall both of them so long jointly live) and then and from thenceforth, and from and after the said Feast-day of Saint *Michael* the Archangel 1732 the yearly Sum of 250 l . . . , for and during the Joint Lives of them the said *Aaron Assley* and *Frances* his in-tended Wife; both the said yearly Sums to be paid unto the proper Hands of her the said *Frances Eave*, or to such Person or Persons, and for such Uses and Purposes as she, without the said *Aaron Assley*, by any Note or Writing under her Hand, shall from Time to Time, notwithstanding her Coverture, direct or appoint; the same to be for her own sole and separate Use and Benefit, exclusive of the said *Aaron Assley*, and not to be liable or subject to his Con-troul, Debts or Incumbrances, but to be disposed of by her for her Cloaths, and such other Uses and Purposes as she shall think fit; and her Receipt, or the Receipts of the Person or Persons to whom she shall appoint the said Monies to be paid as aforesaid, under her or their respective Hand or Hands, shall from Time to Time, notwithstanding her Coverture, be suffi-cient Discharges to the Person or Persons who shall so pay the same, for so much of the said several yearly Sums for which such Receipts shall be given. . . .[7]

pin money not subject to the husband's control or liable for his debts

only the wife's receipts or the receipts of her as-signee to be a discharge of the trustees' obligation to pay the pin money

The somewhat casual status of the term "pin money" is indicated, for example, by Horsman's describing one precedent as containing a "term for pin money" in the table of contents, then printing a text which speaks only of raising a term for 99 years for the wife, describ-ing this in the marginal gloss as a sum "for her separate use."[8] Most settlements and similar documents providing payments under a con-tract by a husband to a wife of a set annual sum—as I have defined pin money here—probably did not use the term "pin money" or even a descriptive phrase like "for her Cloaths" in the body of the docu-ment and many probably did not use it in a descriptive title on the document either. Such practices caused difficulty for the courts at the beginning of the nineteenth century when an attempt was made to develop different rules for "pin money" and for "the wife's separate estate." Moreover, not every agreement was so well-drawn as Horsman's sample precedents. Since all these agreements were private contracts, in practice they could be drawn in an infinite variety of ways, with or without trustees, and with the payments dependent upon more or less well-secured capital funds, or, indeed, not secured by any fund.

Once these agreements were drawn, it remained to be seen what legal effect the courts would give them. Since married women's separate property was a new species of property, basic questions arose of whether or to what extent it should be treated by analogy to men's property or, alternatively, whether idiosyncratic rules were required for it alone. These questions, of course, occurred in the context of a system of property law where there were special rules for many categories of property. On the one hand, cases could be decided by simple analogy, the property constituting a married woman's separate estate being treated as though she acquired it by contract and as though it were the property of a man or a feme sole. For example, in *Milles* and *Wikes* (1694) it was said that a woman who "by Management or good House-wifry" saved money out of her pin money or separate maintenance allowance might "dispose of such Money so saved by her or of any Jewels bought with it" by "Writing in Nature of a Will" if she died before her husband or, if her husband predeceased her, might retain such savings against her husband's creditors or heirs.[9] On the other hand, cases could be decided by emphasizing the peculiar status of married women's separate property as a "creature of equity" and stressing its ostensible special purposes, including the maintenance of wives and children and the preservation of some property for children no matter what the financial fate of the husband. This peculiar status and these special purposes were invoked to justify the development of special rules.

Among the earlier pin money cases decided by the invocation of contract logic and by analogy to men's property was *Moore* v. *Moore* (1737).[10] The marriage settlement of 1707 between Sir Richard Francis Moore and his wife put certain land in trust for a term of 99 years to secure £100 out of the rents payable to Lady Moore for her separate use. In 1728, "some differences and disputes arising between the husband and wife," Lady Moore went to live in France and subsequently sued Sir Richard for several years' arrears of the payments of her allowance. Sir Richard's counsel argued that the wife's behavior should forfeit her entitlement and, moreover, "that this allowance was only to promote harmony between the plaintiff and the defendant, and to enable her to do acts of bounty in her family, therefore, when the reason for it ceases, the allowance ought to cease likewise. . . ." Lady Moore's counsel, however, relied on the express words of the contract, arguing that "according to the words and legal operation of the deed, there is a provision at all events for the defendant of £100 a year, and *quoad hoc,* she is to be considered as a feme sole, and as a stranger to the plaintiff. . . ." Lord Chancellor Hardwicke rejected both the husband's social policy arguments and his offer to take his wife back instead of paying her, finding for the wife on the explicit language of the contract, which gave her property in the allowance and was silent about forfeiture for elopement.[11]

Idiosyncratic rules for married women's separate property, on the contrary, were derived in part from analysis of the purposes such property was intended to serve and are, consequently, revelatory of those purposes. Our first important idiosyncratic rule developed in the pin money cases is that arrears of pin money are not to be paid beyond one year. Normally, of course, contract creditors could sue for their debts under a contract over the full term of the contract. In *Powell* v. *Hankey and Cox* (1722), a case of a widow suing her husband's executors for the arrears of her pin money, Lord Chancellor Macclesfield determined to construe the wife's not having demanded the pin money "for several years together" as her consent that her husband "should receive it."[12] He invoked three ideas to justify this construction. First, he said that since married women's separate property is "against common right" "all reasonable intendments and presumptions were to be admitted against the wife." Second, he invoked a social policy argument that sudden demands for many years' arrears of pin money might ruin husbands, or, if the husband were dead, cause substantial injury to his heirs. Third, he assumed that the wife, living with her husband, had in any case shared in the enjoyment of her presumed gift of the pin money to him. Rejecting the wife's contention that she had feared to press for payment during her husband's life "by reason of the husband's passionate temper," the Lord Chancellor replied that she might have applied to her trustees, "whom she must be supposed to have had a confidence in, as persons who would have protected her against any resentment of her husband, had there been occasion. . . ." Despite the conventionality of such clauses as the one in the Horsman settlement I quoted earlier that only the wife's receipts or the receipts of her assigns were to be discharges of the trustees' obligation to pay pin money, the rule in *Powell* implying the wife's consent that the husband should receive her money was regularly applied in subsequent cases in the obvious absence of any such receipts. Under special circumstances, this presumption of the wife's consent to make her husband a gift of the arrears of her pin money could be rebutted, as, for example, in *Ridout* v. *Lewis* (1738), where a widow succeeded in collecting the arrears of her pin money from her husband's executors because he had made partial payments, explicitly referred to as such, and had accompanied these partial payments with promises to pay the rest later.[13]

This rule of no arrears beyond one year meant that a wife whose husband did not pay her by the usual quarterly dates would normally have had to sue him at least each year for the debt or lose her entitlement; if she sued him and he lacked the will or the resources to pay her, she would also have to have been prepared to see him imprisoned for the debt. While there was considerable quarreling over pin money, I know of no case of a husband imprisoned for failure to pay—nor is it easy to imagine that a gentlewoman who had had her husband imprisoned for failure to pay her pin money would have been warmly received in polite society.[14]

There has been a long and not entirely unreasonable prejudice against interspousal suits in either contract or tort. Relations within the family are said to be too intimate to be made the subject of contract. In contract, there is the idea that "within the closely-knit family demands for a contractual spelling out of obligations will seem to imply an inappropriate distrust."[15] Moreover, relations, rights, and obligations within the family—the wife's obligation to provide her husband with service and consortium, for instance—are to a considerable extent already determined by law in ways which contract is not permitted to alter. Courts have also disliked invading the supposedly private sphere of the family and are likely to despair of successful fact-finding there. Furthermore, if spouses are going to continue living together after the suit, success for one and defeat for the other has been thought likely to poison the matrimonial relationship. Indeed, when only very recently interspousal tort suits have been allowed, the old rule was abandoned partly on the ground that many tort claims are now actually against insurance companies, so that one spouse who injures another by his act or negligence could ordinarily be presumed to be relieved and happy to see insurance pay for the injury.[16] In contract, anxieties similar to those in tort made judges worry that they might have to listen to litigation about private trivia, to decide, for instance, a question of whether a husband was entitled to make a deduction from his wife's allowance if she spent an afternoon "visiting her mother, instead of making jellies."[17] This general prejudice against interspousal suits certainly also affected the results in pin money, the courts finding it more bearable to inquire into recent events within a family than to try to uncover more remote and more tangled family history.

But the establishment of the rule in *Powell* raised a fundamental problem concerning the nature of pin money: was pin money for the ordinary maintenance of the wife or was it for expenses other than ordinary maintenance? To justify the rule of no arrears beyond a year as a special case of laches grounded on hostility to interspousal suits and on fear of the disruptiveness of claims for large lump sums when smaller periodic payments had been intended is at least intelligible, though the interval of one year is startlingly short. However, to justify the rule by assuming that so long as the wife has lived with her husband she has shared in the enjoyment of her presumed gift is trickier because this strand of the argument comes perilously close to assuming that pin money is for the wife's maintenance and that if she has lived with her husband she has been maintained. In *Thomas* v. *Bennet* (1725), shortly after *Powell*, where the executors of a wife demanded ten years' arrears of her pin money and there was no proof that she had demanded it herself, the court ruled that if husband and wife cohabit and the husband maintain, arrears of pin money are not recoverable.[18] In *Moore*, after both *Powell* and *Thomas*, where the spouses were living apart and the husband not maintaining the wife, the court did not invoke its no-arrears rule.

When we confront the question of whether pin money was for maintenance, I believe, we confront the problem that the actual social purposes of paying pin money were not and could not be fully acknowledged either in official discourse or in legal theory. The actual social purposes of paying pin money are probably fairly described by saying that—beyond the general purposes of creating the wife's separate estate, which I mentioned earlier—pin money was normally paid for partial maintenance (clothes and tips to servants, but not food or house rent), for some extras above maintenance (though upper-class women were entitled to some frills as maintenance), and for "insurance" for the wife should the husband prove so stingy as to be unwilling to support her at an appropriate level or should the husband lose his assets or should the marriage prove so unhappy the couple separated. Let us consider the partial maintenance and the insurance functions. That partial maintenance was one intention is suggested not only by explicit provisions for clothes in some settlements and by the general understanding that clothes were to be bought with pin money, but also by the fact that the annual sums specified for pin money, usually enough to outfit the woman appropriately, were commonly although not invariably less than the annual sums specified for jointure for the same woman, the woman having to provide housing and food as well as clothes out of her jointure money. The Horsman settlement giving £120 to £250 for pin money and £500 for jointure is a good example. Lord Chancellor Brougham, after consulting his own experience and that of other peers, reported, "it is . . . clear that no nobleman or person of however high and honourable degree, being in ever so wealthy circumstances, would ever dream of making an allowance to his wife for pin-money, if he were at the same time to be paying all her bills year after year, her milliner's bills and others, over and above her pin-money."[19] With respect to the insurance function of pin money, in theory the wife should not have needed such insurance unless her husband lost his assets, in which case her separate property would be shielded from his creditors. At common law her remedy against a stingy or cruel husband was simply to charge her purchases of the necessaries appropriate to her rank, leaving merchants to recover from her husband, who had a duty to provide his wife with such necessaries. However, there seems to have been some appreciable practical gap between a wife's common law right to such necessaries and a wife's ability to obtain credit for them. Moreover, the wife lost her right to the husband's support if she left him without what the courts considered sufficient legal justification. There was, therefore, an impulse to offer secure support to the wife by the method of pin money. Addison reported that women had defended pin money to him as "a necessary Provision they make for themselves, in case their Husband proves a Churl or a Miser; so they consider this Allowance as a kind of Alimony, which they may lay their Claim to, without actually separating from their Husbands."[20] Such motives, I suspect, were even more likely to inspire the fathers of brides than young brides themselves. Lord Hardwicke observed, "possibly this agreement before marriage might be designed to provide for the wife, if such dissention should happen between the parties, as would be a just inducement for them to separate, though their quarrels should be of such a nature as are not proper to be laid before a court."[21]

Yet although contemporaries paid pin money with these intentions of partial maintenance and insurance in mind, to justify either of these intentions in terms of legal theory posed significant difficulties. If pin money is to be understood as intended for maintenance and if the husband's maintenance of the wife is to bar claims for arrears, then it would seem that the husband has contracted to perform what was in any case his legal obligation to maintain his wife, an obligation which existed independent of any marriage settlement, and thus, that agreements to pay pin money were invalid in the first place. In other words, the husband could be seen as attempting to make one of the status incidents of marriage the subject of contract, which has traditionally been impermissible. Given the support/service reciprocity which is supposed to constitute the marriage relationship (the husband's obligation to support the wife and the wife's obligation to provide him with service), a husband's attempt to make his obligation to support or maintain his wife the subject of contract should be like a wife's attempt to make her obligation to provide her husband with service the subject of contract—which has been repeatedly disallowed.[22] To say that partial rather than full maintenance was intended would not improve the situation because contracts for partial maintenance are still contracts for maintenance. With respect to the insurance function, to admit openly that pin money was to provide such insurance not only seemed to denigrate the effectiveness of the wife's common law right to necessaries, but, what was worse, it looked like approving a contract for future separation. As separate maintenance contracts grew more common, there was increasing temptation to plan ahead and to provide in prenuptial agreements for possible future separations, but eighteenth-century courts disliked doing anything to facilitate separations and such agreements for future separations were eventually found to be void as against public policy.[23] Even in *Moore,* where Lord Hardwicke at one point referred to the wife's allowance secured by the marriage settlement as a "separate maintenance," he also insisted, "These separate maintenances are not to incourage a wife to leave her husband, whatever his behaviour may be; for, was this the construction, it would destroy the very end of the marriage contract, and be a public detriment."[24] Only if the agreement to pay pin money were understood to be an agreement to pay for expenses "above and beyond the call of duty" or for extra "frills and furbelows" would it seem to have constituted a valid agreement. But the social reality was, as the sums contracted for suggest and as Lord Brougham's statement indicates, that men did not bind themselves to pay such sums merely for extras. During the eighteenth century these contradictions about the purposes of pin money were not squarely faced or resolved, and this theoretical problem remained, as we shall see, to erupt in a spectacular early nineteenth-century case involving the executors of the Duke and Duchess of Norfolk.

In addition to the anomalies of the no-arrears rule and the difficulties of reconciling the social purposes of paying pin money with any legal justification of those purposes, a third kind of problem arose around what might be described as the "categories" of women's property. To what extent were various kinds of chattel or real property bought with pin money or with the savings from or interest on pin money to be considered as falling into the category of pin money and thus as "owned" by the wife? In the simple world of a medieval village, a husband might maintain his wife by letting her lie in his bed under his roof, eat the produce of his land, and clothe herself with wool from his sheep or cloth made from his flax. But an eighteenth-century wife's pin money came in the form of cash, and cash could be spent to acquire property in any form. Clearly a wife could buy a dress with her pin money, but was she equally entitled to buy bank stock or to save her pin money and buy a cottage? (After all, it might not take a frugal woman who was getting £300 a year very long to save enough to buy a cottage.) If she did buy bank stock or a cottage, what rules should be applied to such property? Was the new property as much hers as the pin money had been or was pin money more or less like the later "household allowance" in the sense that any savings from it and any property bought with it "*prima facie* remained the husband's property"?[25]

It is probably true that at the deepest level the development of the legal theory of pin money in the eighteenth century was confused by a conflict between the older sense of the naturalness of having particular rules pertaining to the ownership of particular kinds of things (for example, forests, wife's clothes, etc.), on the one hand, and, on the other, the development of a more modern, general, abstract category of "property" and stress on alienability or the right to exchange one kind of property for another as the fundamental sign of ownership. Older rules tend to provide for the appropriate present enjoyment of a particular kind of thing rather than to allow for the exercise of individual will to determine the future use of the thing or to exchange it for another kind of thing. Thus, in the fourteenth century a tenant of a forest can cut branches to repair his house but he cannot turn the forest into a meadow for grazing without incurring penalties for waste; in the fourteenth century, also, the "owner" of land cannot make a will determining how it will descend.[26]

In the realm of married women's property, there is the old category, paraphernalia, describing a particular kind of thing, namely, the wife's clothes and personal ornaments, such as jewels. Such things are appropriately usable by a woman and not by a man and are "owned" by the wife in a particular sense. Pollock and Maitland observe that "very ancient Germanic law knows special rules for the transmission of female attire; it passes from female to female."[27] At common law, while the wife's paraphernalia may be alienated by the husband during coverture (as her other chattels may), the husband cannot bequeath them to another, and, if he predeceases her, unlike her other chattels, which go to his representatives, her paraphernalia goes to her, subject to rights of his creditors. Although in the thirteenth century some wives made wills disposing of their own clothes and ornaments, it later came to be common law that a wife could only devise her paraphernalia with the consent of her husband; if she predeceased her husband without having secured his consent to such a testamentary devise, her paraphernalia were his. Thus, questions arose as to whether paraphernalia-like objects bought with pin money should be treated according to paraphernalia rules.

Some settlements gave the wife explicit testamentary power over her separate property, and some cases suggest that a wife was to be considered as the absolute owner of the savings or other proceeds of her pin money. In *Milles* and *Wikes* (1694), as we have seen, it was decided that the wife could devise the savings from her pin money if she predeceased her husband or alienate them if she survived. Similarly, in *Gore* v. *Knight* (1705), equity ruled that if a wife had reserved the power of disposing of her separate estate, "all that she dies possessed of is to be taken her separate Estate, and the Produce of it, unless the contrary can be made appear, and as she has Power over the Principal, so she may dispose of the Produce or Interest."[28] Also, in *Wilson* v. *Pack* (1710), it was decided that "where the Wife has a *separate* Allowance *made before marriage*, and *buys Jewels with the Money* arising thereout, *they will not be Assets liable to the Husband's debts.*"[29] Results like these weaken the contention that pin money is for current maintenance.

However, in *Peacock* v. *Monk* (1750–51), Mrs. Lestock, an admiral's wife, having a prenuptial agreement providing for pin money and giving her the right to devise her own real estate, used some of her money to buy a house.[30] She devised this real estate to a person of her choice and died. After her death and her husband's death a dispute arose over whether this house should go to her heir or to her devisee. The court decided that while the prenuptial agreement permitted her to devise property specified in that agreement, the husband's "bare agreement" concerning real estate she acquired after the marriage could not deprive the heir of his rights: "for though in respect of the husband, money to be laid out in land will be considered as part of her separate estate, yet it is going a great way to say, that it shall be considered as personal [that is, as personal property] as between her heir and executor; for she having made it realty, the court would say, it was in that manner [that is, it was real property, not personal property]; and she has purchased it so as to go to the heir. . . ." In other words, by turning what was personal property into real estate, Mrs. Lestock had lost her right to devise it. A similar case, discussed in *Peacock*, in which a married woman with real estate to her separate use was found not to have the power to devise it was said to have provoked "a good deal of discourse"; "it seeming extraordinary that she should not have this [the power to devise] in equity as incident to her ownership" and that she "should not be in equity considered as the absolute owner of it."

Such results might seem extraordinary if one thinks in terms of a certain modern idea of "absolute ownership," but the more traditionally minded might find it equally extraordinary that in *Milles* the wife could treat jewels—paraphernalia—bought with her pin money as though she were the absolute owner of them. Logic would seem to decree that to make *Milles* and *Peacock* symmetrical, the court in *Milles* should have said of the wife, "she having made her pin money paraphernalia, the court would say that it was paraphernalia, not her separate estate, and she has purchased it so as to go to her husband's creditors." Indeed, in *Lady Tyrell's Case* (1674), where Lady Tyrell said she had bought jewels with her pin money and attempted to retain them as her paraphernalia, Lord Keeper Finch ruled that they must go to her husband's creditors:

> And as to the point of buying them with her own money, that should make no difference, so long as the husband and wife do cohabit; for if the wife out of her good housewifery do save any thing out of it, this will be the husband's estate, and he shall reap the benefit of his wife's frugality; and he said, the reason of it is, because when the husband agrees to allow his wife a certain sum yearly, the end of this agreement is, that she may be provided with clothes and other necessaries, and whatsoever is saved out of this redounds to the husband.[31]

One can only speculate as to why symmetrical results were not reached in *Milles* and *Peacock*; it is unlikely that equity felt significantly more concern for heirs than for creditors, but it is quite possible that equity was inclined to be more conservative with respect to real property than with respect to chattel property.

The rule of no arrears beyond a year from *Powell* and a result like that in *Peacock*, which resists the conversion of pin money into real property, help to maximize the probabilities that such property would provide maintenance for the women upon whom it was settled and to minimize the possibilities that women could take property intended for maintenance and use it as capital. An additional key issue was whether a wife could alienate the capital fund, or a substantial part of the capital fund, from which her yearly payments were to come. In the usual language of the settlements, the wife was to have her money, in the words of the Horsman settlement quoted earlier, "for such Uses and Purposes as she . . . shall from Time to Time, notwithstanding her Coverture, direct or appoint . . . for her own sole and separate Use and Benefit, exclusive of [her husband], and not to be liable or subject to his Controul, Debts or Incumbrances." But suppose the use the wife wished to appoint was to pledge her entire interest in the fund as security for a large loan to herself for some present expenditure? Or suppose, though the separate estate was established as not subject to her husband's control or debts, she wished to make him a gift of it? It was natural enough that some wives would wish to use their assets to advance their husbands in their careers or businesses, as the wife in *Tate* v. *Austen* (1714) raised £400 out of her separate estate to equip her husband as an officer in the army.[32] But for a wife to "sink the fund" from which her maintenance was to come in such a way defeated her father's attempt to provide her and her children with a kind of insurance against her husband's fecklessness or ill luck, and, moreover, tempted greedy or unscrupulous husbands to coerce wives to make such gifts. As one contemporary song recommended to a man with a troublesome wife possessed of a "separate Fortune" which she refused to pay him, such a wife might be locked up alone in a room:

> There a while let her dance,
> Without Cordial or Nantz,
> Til sober and penitent grown,
> She submits to your Will,
> Consent, Sign, and Seal,
> And make all her Fortune you're own.[33]

A number of cases contain rather sweeping dicta that a married woman is to be considered as a feme sole with respect to her separate estate, thus implying that she is free to "sink the fund." For example, in *Grigby* v. *Cox* (1750) a wife sold part of her separate estate, then complained that she had executed the deeds "by compulsion of her husband" and that her trustees should have been consulted. Lord

Chancellor Hardwicke ruled in favor of the purchaser and said, "the rule of the court is, that where any thing is settled to the wife's separate use, she is considered as a feme sole; may appoint in what manner she pleases; and unless the joining of her trustees with her is made necessary [which would have been very uncommon], there is no occasion for that."[34] In *Fettiplace* v. *Gorges* (1789), Sophia Charlotte Fettiplace during her life had been entitled to £200 pin money a year, had after marriage acquired £1,000 in bank annuities as separate property bequeathed to her by an aunt, and with savings and gifts had had £1,900 in consols purchased for her separate estate with a female relative as trustee. Sophia Charlotte bequeathed all her personal estate to her niece, who was sued by Mr. Fettiplace on the ground that he had never assented to his wife's having such separate property and that, therefore, it belonged to him. Lord Chancellor Thurlow found for the niece, declaring, "All the cases shew that the personal property, where it can be enjoyed separately, must be so with all its incidents, and the *jus disponendi* is one of them."[35] In *Pybus* v. *Smith* (1791), Thomas Vernon, a trader, eloped to Scotland with a ward of Chancery, married her, then agreed to a postnuptial settlement giving her separate property. Shortly after the marriage, he persuaded her to pledge this property as security for his debts, then went bankrupt three years later. Despite some apparent temptation to find that the words "from Time to Time" in the settlement prohibited an appointment of the capital fund, Lord Chancellor Thurlow felt compelled to rule in favor of the husband's creditors, on the principle that "a *feme covert* had been considered by the Court, with respect to her separate property, as a *feme sole*. . . ."[36]

But by the end of the eighteenth century allowing married women such powers of alienation with respect to their separate estates was found to be intolerable. Some earlier cases offered support to this effort, for example, *Caverly* v. *Dudley and Bisco* (1747), in which Lord Hardwicke decided Lady Dudley's purchase of an annuity from her separate estate was "too large an anticipation," and gave her leave to redeem what was supposed to have been an irredeemable annuity.[37] Great frustration was expressed over *Pybus* v. *Smith*, and very late eighteenth-century cases contain lamentations that wives have the power to defeat provisions intended for their protection.[38] Out of such frustration over the difficulty of providing married women with inalienable security for their maintenance, Lord Thurlow invented the "restraint on anticipation" by inserting into a settlement words positively restricting alienation of the capital fund.[39]

By 1839 in *Tullet* v. *Armstrong* restraints on anticipation were well established, and Lord Chancellor Cottenham was able to decide that, though admittedly "inconsistent with the ordinary rules of property," these restraints might come and go with coverture, allowing a father to give his daughter a separate estate before her marriage, with the assurance that, once married, the daughter would be unable to alienate the fund, but that if she happened to be single or widowed, she could deal with the property as though a feme sole. Lord Cottenham in the course of this decision gave a rather candid history of the problem making the social policy considerations clear:

> When this Court first established the separate estate, it violated the laws of property as between husband and wife; but it was thought beneficial, and it prevailed. It being once settled that a wife might enjoy separate estate as a *feme sole*, the laws of property attached to this new estate; and it was found, as part of such law, that the power of alienation belonged to the wife, and was destructive of the security intended for it. Equity again interfered, and by another violation of the laws of property supported the validity of the prohibition against alienation. . . . Why then should not equity in this case also interfere; and if it cannot protect the wife consistently with the ordinary rules of property, extend its own rules with respect to the separate estate, so as to secure to her the enjoyment of that estate which has been so invented for her benefit?[40]

In my earlier discussion of the rule of no arrears of pin money, I noted that under special circumstances the wife's presumed relinquishment of her entitlement to the arrears could be rebutted. One such special circumstance seemed to be the insanity of the wife; an insane person cannot waive his right to payment under a contract. The most elaborate pin money case ever was produced when the executors of the Duchess of Norfolk, who had been certified a lunatic, sued the executors of the Duke of Norfolk for arrears of her pin money. This case provoked a serious reconsideration of the legal theory of pin money.

Since Charles Howard, later Duke of Norfolk, and Francis Fitzroy Scudamore had married in 1771 with suitably elaborate and lavish settlements, and since she was a certified lunatic for decades, the arrears of her pin money arguably amounted to £33,000 and Vice-Chancellor Shadwell decreed payment of that sum. Considerable confusion arose around the issue of whether pin money was supposed to be for a wife's maintenance or whether it was supposed to be for expenses, perhaps "fanciful and luxurious," over and above the maintenance appropriate to the wife's station. The Duke in this case had provided the Duchess with clothes, carriages, and even for many years a separate establishment, and, as we have seen, there were some earlier cases where the husband's having maintained his wife was apparently added to her failure to demand payment to reach a result of no arrears due. But Vice-Chancellor Shadwell in *Howard* v. *Digby* (1831) refused even to let the Duke's executors set his account of expenses he incurred on her behalf off against the arrears on the principle that the Duke was liable to maintain the Duchess "notwithstanding the income which was provided for her separate use."[41] Shadwell considered that pin money "never could be intended to be applied to the necessary maintenance of the duchess" but could only be for extras, and that, consequently, the justification of the no-arrears rule in *Powell* could only be the wife's implied consent to her husband's receipt of the money. Since a lunatic could not have so consented, the no-arrears rule could not apply to the Duchess.

Shadwell's decision in *Digby*, however, was overturned on appeal to the Lords in 1834 in an opinion of Lord Chancellor Brougham, who reported that he had been driven not only to a careful examination of the earlier cases but also to introspection and to interviewing various peers on the question of what they considered the purposes of pin money to be. This unusual bit of empirical research by the Whig chancellor contributed to his insistence that pin money was to go toward maintenance. He reported, as I noted earlier, that no man, however wealthy, would pay pin money if he were also expected to pay bills for dresses and hats, and he decided that "the general opinion of all those who give pin-money" "is a very material fact."[42] Not surprisingly, Lord Brougham did not think to interview a sample of those who "receive pin money." Indeed, since it would seem more ordinary to speak of "paying" someone to whom you are indebted under a contract than to speak of "giving him money," his phrase, "give pin-money" suggests how far he was from thinking of wives with pin money allowances as contract creditors.

Lord Chancellor Brougham's decision depended upon making a distinction between pin money and the married woman's separate estate, a distinction which he was honest enough to admit "is very obscure" and does not seem to have been made with any regularity earlier. Commenting on his researches in the books, he noted, "you cannot trace the line which divides it [pin money] from the separate property of the wife, with any distinctness. . . ."[43] This is quite true and supports the Duchess's executors' claim that there were not two separate sets of rules for pin money and for married women's separate property in the earlier cases. Moreover, though the Lord Chancellor in *Howard* encountered a settlement which actually used the term "pin money," as I observed in my earlier discussion of convey-ancing practice, many settlements conveying what even Lord Brougham would have wished to consider pin money, did not use the term. (Lord Brougham, among other aims, wished to use his distinc-tion between pin money and separate property to say that while there is a rule of no arrears of pin money, there is no such rule for separate property, and that, further, though the wife's personal representa-tives after her death have no claim to arrears of her pin money, ob-viously the personal representatives of a wife with a separate estate have a claim to that.)

Pin money, as opposed to the wife's separate property, Lord Brougham determined, was to pay "the ordinary expenses" of the wife. It was a modern "refinement" to relieve the wife of "the some-what humiliating necessity" of asking her husband's consent every time she wishes to "go to the milliner's shop." However: "the money is meant to dress the wife so as to keep up the dignity of the husband, not for the mere accumulation of the fund; and as it is meant that the money should be expended for the husband's honour, to support his and her rank in society, if the *femme* [sic] did not chose to pay away the money to the *baron's* honour, she would in vain come to the Court of Chancery and pray, 'order payment of £9000 into my banker's, for 10 years; for I only spent £1000, when it was meant that I should spend £10,000.'"[44] Lord Brougham even fancifully hypothesizes, ab-sent any cases for authority, that if a nobleman's wife "chose to dress herself like a mechanic's housewife, or a farmer's dame," spending only £25 of her £1000 a year for dress, she would appeal in vain to Chancery for the savings. Later he insists: "The purpose [of pin money] is not the purpose of the wife alone; it is for the establishment, it is for the joint concern, it is for the maintenance of the common dignity; it is for the support of that family whose brightest ornament very probably is the wife; whose support and strength is the husband, but whose ornament is the wife."[45] Thus, without having reference to the waiver of consent argument, the Lord Chancellor was able to justify denying arrears on the ground that pin money is for present expend-iture, and, the Duchess being dead, there can be no call for orna-menting her and no point in paying money intended for such a pur-pose to her personal representative.

Moreover, rejecting Shadwell's idea that pin money was for ex-penditure over and above maintenance, the Lord Chancellor argued that since pin money was for the normal expenses of maintaining a wife and the Duke was liable for tradesmen's bills for maintenance, it would be inequitable to make him liable also to the Duchess's personal representatives for the same expenses. A lunatic could not release a debt, but he could receive payment of a debt and thereby make himself or his executors liable in discharge for what he has received, as the Duchess's enjoyment of the maintenance provided by the Duke can be considered in discharge of his pin money debt to her. On Lord Brougham's theory of pin money as intended for maintenance, he was struck by the apparent unfairness of a husband's being doubly liable for the same expenses, once under common law if sued for his wife's debts for necessaries by tradesmen who had supplied her and again under contract for payments to his wife to cover these same expenses. Although in separate maintenance cases, there was for a time a rule that a husband who paid his wife a separate maintenance allowance was not liable to tradesmen for his wife's bills, no similar rule was developed in pin money. On Lord Brougham's logic, it might have made sense to delineate which maintenance expenses pin money was to cover (for example, milliner's bills but not house rent) and then let husbands who paid pin money avoid direct liability for tradesmen's bills for those expenses. But Lord Brougham took it that a husband, so long as he and his wife lived together, had another, presumably better, protection from double liability: "he has an opportunity of controlling her, so that she shall not go and game, for example, with her pin-money, and leave him to pay her milliners' bills."[46]

The self-conscious airing of some of the contradictions in the theory of pin money in *Howard* was probably provoked by a number of factors beyond the obvious importance of the Norfolk estate. Of some significance, I would suggest, was the progressive improvement in law reporting and in the availability of fuller reports over the course of the eighteenth century, which seems to have promoted more awareness of competing cases. Also of significance, no doubt, was a changed and rationalized style of treatise writing and the growing number of treatises on baron and feme and on contract. Whereas R. S. Donnison Roper in 1800 in *A Treatise on the Revocations and Republication of Wills and Testaments: Together with Tracts Upon the Law Concerning Baron and Feme* has no separate discussion of pin money and describes a no-arrears rule pertaining to "the produce" of the wife's "separate estate," his 1820 *Treatise on the Law of Property Arising from the Relation between Husband and Wife* devotes a chapter to "Gifts and Allowances by Husband to Wife" and establishes three different categories for pin money, household allowances, and paraphernalia.[47] Roper there attempts to reconcile the cases and to articulate an integrated set of rules. Brougham's retreat from contract logic to the logic of protection and publicly controlled maintenance in *Howard* is also congruent with a similar retreat I have described elsewhere in writing about separate maintenance contract cases, where contract logic is given some play in the mid-eighteenth century, then cut back in the very late eighteenth century and early nineteenth century.

Lawrence Stone in *The Family, Sex and Marriage in England, 1500–1800* has argued that "the hardest evidence for a decline in the near-absolute authority of the husband over the wife among the proper-tied classes is an admittedly limited series of changes in the power of the former to control the latter's estate and income," adding that "the introduction of the practice of inserting into the marriage contract a clause about pin money now guaranteed the wife an independent fixed income at her exclusive disposal."[48] It is true that under certain circumstances wives with pin money did attain some increased autonomy in spending and even that some women could use pin money to support themselves if they separated from unsatisfactory husbands.[49] Yet there was not much self-congratulation over the institution of pin money in the eighteenth century. Indeed, that the law and modern fashion allowed pin money was a subject of satire and a fact almost universally lamented by gentlemen moralists. Agreements requiring the husband to pay pin money, it was said, gave the husband and wife separate interests (the wife could sue the husband on the contract), allowed the wife to make independent judgments about expenditure, and, what was perhaps worst, made the husband's payments to the wife seem to depend on her right rather than on his generosity, thus, it was feared, not inspiring appropriate wifely gratitude. Addison, writing as a "professed Advocate for the Fair Sex" in *The Spectator*, lamented the introduction of pin money and explained: "Separate Purses, between Man and Wife, are, in my Opinion, as unnatural as separate Beds. A Marriage cannot be happy, where the Pleasures, Inclinations and Interests of both Parties are not the same. There is no greater Incitement to Love in the Mind of Man, than the Sense of a Person's depending upon him for her Ease and Happiness; as a Woman uses all her Endeavours to please the Person whom she looks upon as her Honour, her Comfort, and her Support."[50] Similarly, Samuel Richardson, who might also reasonably have described himself as a professed advocate for the fair sex, in an essay written for Johnson's *Rambler* complained that in the mid-eighteenth century, "settlements are expected, that often, to a mercantile man especially, sink a fortune into uselessness; and pin-money is stipulated for, which makes a wife independent, and destroys love, by putting it out of a man's power to lay obligation upon her, that might engage gratitude, and kindle affection. . . ."[51] Propaganda against pin money reached a nearly melodramatic climax in Mrs. Catherine Gore's novel, *Pin Money* (1831). Her basically good heroine spends her allowance on progressively disastrous things, beginning with a white marble fountain for their garden, progressing through a subscription to the opera which exposes her to the attentions of a peer who thinks nothing of trying to seduce married women, and finally ending by incurring, before she is aware of it, a debt of £280 at the écarté table. Distressing experience leads her to understand the moral: "Had I found it necessary to have recourse to [my husband] for the detailed payments of my debts,—had full and entire confidence been established between us in the defrayment of my personal expenses,—never, never should I have been plunged into the excesses which embitter [my] destiny. . . .when by referring [to my husband] for the immediate payment of my bills, I expose myself to reprehension for any prodigal or frivolous action, I shall be insured from all danger of further extravagance."[52]

The contemporary complaint that modern women demanded pin money payments as matters of right instead of trusting to their husbands and being grateful for the allowances they chose to dispense is actually quite a peculiar complaint. Although usually presented as a longing for the good old days before marriage settlements, the complaint is oddly reflective of a demand for an even greater privatization of the family than is represented by negotiated and legally enforceable marriage settlements. The complaint manages to ignore the husband's common law duty to maintain his wife and to provide her with necessaries appropriate to their rank, an obligation which means that the wife has a corresponding right to that support. It is quite unlikely that women's "demands" had much to do with the existence or the forms of upper-class marriage settlements. The reasons for these settlements were not to bestow new rights on wives or to increase the autonomy of wives. On the contrary, marriage settlements providing jointure were needed by husbands and husbands' families in order to deny wives their common law rights to dower. Eighteenth-century theories of "equitable jointure" permitted jointures of considerably less value than the corresponding estates in dower to bar dower. The husband's family's desire for a marriage settlement with jointure and other features advantageous to their side gave the wife's family some bargaining power when they wished to preserve some property free of the husband's control as the wife's separate estate. Contemporary complaint about settlements which make "a wife independent" displaces responsibility onto women's "demands" and masks the dynastic motives and the interests of husbands' families in these settlements. The complaint itself seeks to substitute for the publicly enforceable wife's right to support a private exchange of the husband's "gift" for the wife's gratitude.

There is evidence that such propaganda had an effect and that even among those upper-class women who were allowed and who allowed themselves to participate in discussions of their marriage settlements some were reluctant to ask for or even to accept pin money. Lady Mary Pierrepont, who was capable of reminding Edward Montagu that she could have £300 a year pin money from another suitor and of asking Edward for a jointure, also wrote to Edward: "I say nothing of pin money etc. I don't understand the meaning of any divided interest from a Man I willingly give my selfe to."[53] The less famous Mrs. Peach, widow of a former governor of Calcutta, who brought a fortune of £20,000 to her second marriage, persisted in refusing to have any pin money settled on her despite the best efforts of the groom's father, Lord Lyndhurst, to persuade her. According to Lord Lyndhurst, "she persevered in her resolution, thinking that my son's love and her happiness would depend on her putting this trust in him. . . ."[54] In the event, in the first year of the marriage, son Thomas deserted his wife to run off to Paris with a barmaid. Furthermore, as our cases have suggested, even when wives did have pin money settled on them, the extralegal powers of husbands, including various sorts of physical and psychological intimidation, could keep wives from enjoying those allowances.

Moreover, the development of the legal doctrines concerning pin money between the Restoration and the early nineteenth century shows that the law, having created a potentially threatening source of women's power in the married woman's separate estate, soon appreciated that threat and responded by creating idiosyncratic rules for pin money and other forms of married women's separate property which minimized the possibility that such property could become a source of women's power or the material basis for equality between men and women. These legal rules helped insure that women's property was for the maintenance of the woman and the family, and, as Lord Brougham said, "expended for the husband's honour."

Though the development of these idiosyncratic rules occured within conveyancing practice and equity opinions without the influence of new statutes, it was a cultural and political choice, not an inevitable development decreed by abstract legal logic. Indeed, legal logic alone could also have justified a more liberal reliance on the argument by analogy to men's property which I noted here in *Moore*. It could even have justified the leap made in *Slanning* v. *Style* (1734), a creative case in which, despite the absence of any written contract providing for pin money payments, the court decided to construe a husband's statements that his wife should have the proceeds from the sale of eggs and such on their farm as an implied contract for pin money.[55] The eighteenth-century courts might have ignored the political pressures of patriarchy and elected to build on the logic of *Slanning* instead of on that of *Powell*. But they did not, and the alternative historical development of idiosyncratic rules for pin money and other forms of married women's separate property was one reason why married women's property did not then lead to married women's power.

NOTES

1 John Vanbrugh, "The Relapse," in *British Dramatists from Dryden to Sheridan*, ed. George H. Nettleton, Arthur E. Case, and George Winchester Stone, Jr. (Carbondale: Southern Illinois University Press, 1969), pp. 301–2.

2 *The Oxford English Dictionary*, at "pin-money," gives as its first citation, "1542. *Test. Ebor.* (Surtees) VI. 160, I give my said doughter Margarett my lease of the parsonadge of Kirkdall Churche . . . to buy her pynnes withal." Also cited there is Addison's comment, "The Doctrine of Pin-money is of very late Date, unknown to our Great Grandmothers, and not yet received by many of our Modern Ladies" (*Spectator* no. 295, 1712). For speculation on the origin of the term, see Sir Edward Sugden, *A Treatise on the Law of Property as Administered by the House of Lords* (London, 1849), p. 165, n. 1.

3 Richard Brinsley Sheridan, "The School for Scandal," in *British Dramatists*, p. 863.

4 Bennet v. Davis (1725), 2 P. Wms. 316. The wife's father had devised land to her separate use without establishing a trust. Especially since the husband had not consented to her having a separate estate in this property acquired after their marriage, it might well have been considered simply his property. But equity ruled that the husband's assignees in bankruptcy had no claim on the wife's property and construed the husband as the wife's trustee.

5 Buckingham (Earl of) v. Drury (1762), 3 Bro. P.C. 492.

6 Thus, in the briefly reported case of Cornwall and Earl of Mountague (1701), 1 Eq. Ca. Abr. 66:

> The Plaintiff's Relation (to whom he was Heir) allowed his Wife Pin-Money, which being in Arrear, he gave her a Note to this Purpose; I am indebted to my Wife £100, which became due to her such a Day; after, by his Will, he makes Provision

out of his Lands for Payment of all his Debts, and all Monies which he owed to any Person in Trust for his Wife; and the Question was whether the £100 was to be paid within this Trust; and Ld. K. decreed not, because in Point of Law, it was no Debt, because a Man cannot be indebted to his Wife; and it was not Money due to any Trust for her.

Cf. Lady Tyrell's Case (1674), discussed infra.

7 Gilbert Horsman, Esq., *Precedents in Conveyancing, Settled and Approved by Gilbert Horsman*, 2nd ed., 2 vols. (Savoy, 1757), 1:33–39. For a form showing pin money secured to the wife by a penal bond, the payments to come directly from the husband with no mention of trustees, see, "Condition of a Bond, made by an intended Husband to the Women's Father, to pay her Pin-Money," Horsman, 1:199.

8 Horsman, *Precedents in Conveyancing*, 1:557.

9 Milles and Wikes (1694), 1 Eq. Ca. Abr. 66.

10 Moore v. Moore (1737), 1 Atk. 272. Cf. Sidney v. Sidney (1734), 3 P. Wms. 276, in which Lord Chancellor Talbot decreed specific performance of marriage articles providing for jointure and pin money, despite the husband's contention that his wife had eloped with an adulterer and that he, as presumptive heir to a peerage, particularly dreaded the introduction of a bastard as his heir: "But the articles being, that the husband shall settle such and such lands in certainty on his wife the plaintiff, for her jointure, this is pretty much in the nature of an actual and vested jointure; in regard what is convenanted for good consideration to be done is considered in equity in most respects as done; consequently, this is a jointure, and not forfeitable either by adultery or an elopement."

11 In an earlier case, More v. Earl of Scarborough, 2 Eq. Ca. Abr. 156 (no date, but the only Earl of Scarborough who married was created Earl in 1690 and died in 1721), trustees were not permitted to recover pin money for a wife who eloped and lived in adultery; "for *Pin-Money was never designed to make Women independant of their Husbands, and support them in Vice.* But if *she left him by ill Usage,* or other reasonable Grounds, or the *Husband acquiesed in her Departure,* Equity won't interpose." After Lord Hardwicke's term as Lord Chancellor, Lord Keeper Henley decided Lee v. Lee (1758), Dickens 321, 806, a case similar to Moore, differently, declining to give a separated wife an injunction against her husband's receiving the rents of her separate estate and basing his decision on the kind of arguments used by the losing side in Moore. A treatise writer might attempt to reconcile these cases by stressing Lord Hardwicke's sense that the husband in Moore had not made timely or convincing appeals to his wife to return and that the husband's early payments to his separated wife created a "presumption that he thought at least she was excusable in separating herself from him." In Blount v. Winter (1781), specific performance of marriage articles was decreed despite the husband's proof that his wife was living apart from him in adultery.

12 Powell v. Hankey and Cox (1722), 2 P. Wms. 82. Cf. Offley and Offley (1691), 1 Eq. Ca. Abr. 66.

13 Ridout v. Lewis (1738), 1 Atk. 269. Cf. Countess of Warwick and Edwards

(1728), 1 Eq. Ca. Abr. 140, where one and three-quarter years' arrears of pin money were allowed to the widow as a debt against her husband's estate.

14 Addison in *Spectator* no. 295 has a presumably fictitious correspondent, Josiah Fribble, complain that his pin money payments have furthered his wife's adultery and the birth of children to her not his own. When he asks her to permit him to use the pin money to make provision for these children, "This Proposal makes her noble Blood swell in her Veins, insomuch that finding me a little tardy in her last Quarter's Payment, she threatens me every Day to arrest me; and proceeds so far as to tell me, that if I do not do her Justice, I shall die in a Jayl." *The Spectator,* ed. Donald F. Bond, 5 vols. (Oxford: Clarendon Press, 1965), 3:51.

15 Lon F. Fuller and Melvin Aron Eisenberg, *Basic Contract Law,* 3rd ed. (St. Paul, Minn.: West Publishing Co., 1972), p. 101.

16 In England, the restrictions on interspousal tort claims were altered by statute. See O. M. Stone, "Ninth Report of the Law Reform Commission (Liability in Tort between Husband and Wife)," *Modern Law Review* 24 (1961): 481–86; O. Kahn-Freund, "Law Reform (Husband and Wife) Act, 1962," *Modern Law Review* 25 (1962): 695–97. For America, where the rules vary from state to state, see William L. Prosser, *Handbook of the Law of Torts,* 4th ed. (St. Paul, Minn.: West Publishing Co., 1971), pp. 554–55, 860–64, 868.

17 Miller v. Miller (Iowa, 1887), in Fuller and Eisenberg, *Basic Contract Law,* p. 106.

18 Thomas v. Bennet (1725), 2 P. Wms. 341.

19 Howard v. Digby (1834), 2 Clark & Finnelly 655.

20 Addison, *Spectator,* Bond ed., 3:53.

21 Moore v. Moore, 1 Atk. 277.

22 Barbara Allen Babcock, Ann E. Freedman, Eleanor Holmes Norton, Susan C. Ross, *Sex Discrimination and the Law: Causes and Remedies* (Boston: Little, Brown & Co., 1975), pp. 619–46; Banks McDowell, "Contracts in the Family," *Boston University Law Review* 45 (1965): 43–62.

23 Durant v. Titley (1819), 7 Price 577.

24 Moore v. Moore, 1 Atk. 276.

25 P. M. Bromley, *Family Law,* 5th ed. (London: Butterworth's, 1976), p. 445. This rule was changed by the Married Women's Property Act, 1964, which provided that any property "derived from any allowance made by the husband for the expenses of the matrimonial home or for similar purposes" which came into dispute should "be treated as belonging to the husband and wife in equal shares." Cf. O. Kahn-Freund, "Inconsistencies and Injustices in the Law of Husband and Wife," *Modern Law Review* 16 (1953): 34–49, 148–73; O. M. Stone, "Married Women's Property Act, 1964," *Modern Law Review* 27 (1964): 576–80. In America the older rule has not been the subject of such sweeping statutory change. Comment, however, has been provoked by the case of a wife who, unbeknownst to her husband, saved enough money from her household allowance to create a portfolio of securities in her own name, securities which the court ruled

belonged to her husband (Hardy v. Hardy, D.D.C., 1964), 235 F. Supp. 208, in Babcock, *Sex Discrimination*, pp. 626–27: "The court recognizes that such household allowances generally comprehend expenditures by the wife for personal needs such as clothes, entertainment and transportation. Such expenses are within the obligation of the husband to support and maintain his wife. Acquiescence in these expenditures does not indicate an acquiescence in the use of such funds for the creation of a portfolio of securities for the wife's sole account. To hold otherwise would be to invite disruptive influences in the home."

26 Sir Frederick Pollock and Frederic William Maitland, *The History of English Law Before the Time of Edward I*, ed. S. F. C. Milsom, 2 vols. (Cambridge: Cambridge University Press, 1968), 2:26–27, 325–30; cf. J. H. Baker, *An Introduction to English Legal History* (London: Butterworth's, 1979), pp. 209–13.

27 Pollock and Maitland, *History of English Law*, 2:430.

28 Gore v. Knight (1705), 1 Eq. Ca. Abr. 66. Cf. the briefly reported Mangey and Hungerford, 2 Eq. Ca. Abr. 156, where Lord Chancellor King (Ch. 1725–35) allowed a wife "a considerable Sum of Money out of Housekeeping."

29 Wilson v. Pack (1710), 2 Eq. Ca. Abr. 155.

30 Peacock v. Monk (1750–51), 2 Ves. Sen. 190; it may not have been a whole house, the case refers to "real estate in a house."

31 Lady Tyrell's Case (1674), 1 Freem. 304. In Graham v. Londonderry (1746), 3 Atk. 393, Lord Chancellor Hardwicke decided that diamonds given to the wife by the husband's father on her marriage and subsequently pledged as security for her husband's debt were to be considered "a gift to her separate use," though as the husband's personal estate in this case had assets sufficient to redeem the diamonds, Hardwicke merely had to rule that she was entitled to reimbursement rather than to decide if her claim were to be satisfied in the absence of sufficient personal property in the husband's estate.

32 Tate v. Austen (1714), 2 Vern. 689. She is owed a debt from her husband's estate, "but all other debts shall be first paid."

33 "A Song. *The Tune*, Ye Commons and Peers," in *Love a la Mode: or, The Amours of Florella and Phillis, Being the Memoirs of two celebrated Ladies under those Names: In which the Whole Circle of modern Gallantry is display'd* (London, 1732), p. [58].

34 Grigby v. Cox (1750), 1 Ves. Sen. 518.

35 Fettiplace v. Gorges (1789), 3 Bro. C.C. 8, 10.

36 Pybus v. Smith (1791), 3 Bro. C.C. 340, 346.

37 Caverly v. Dudley and Bisco (1747), 3 Atk. 541, 542.

38 For example, Whistler v. Newman (1798), 4 Ves. Jun. 129. Lord Loughborough was confronted with a wife who had had £1,300 in bank annuities settled on her, had then sold them after marriage to provide her husband with capital for his trade, and then, when her husband died insolvent, was left a widow with six children to support. Mrs. Whistler, he observed,

"was prevailed upon in the common manner, in which things bad in themselves are done, partly by being coaxed, partly by being bullied." Happily for Mrs. Whistler, Lord Loughborough found himself able to distinguish her case from the ones he regretted on the ground that her trustees had made themselves party to the husband's act and had taken a bond of indemnity from him against any claims of her children, so the husband becoming insolvent, it was incumbent upon them to make up the fund. In a similar vein, Sir Richard Arden in Sockett v. Wray (1794), 4 Bro. C.C. 483, found for the trustees of a wife's separate estate who refused to permit her to dispose of her capital by deciding that the language of her marriage settlement allowing her to dispose of her estate "by any note or notes, instrument or instruments, writing or writings" had significantly and purposefully omitted reference to a power to dispose of the property by any "deed or deeds," thus showing that she was to dispose of it only by "a revocable act."

39 Pybus v. Smith, n. 1; Walter G. Hart, "The Origin of the Restraint upon Anticipation," *Law Quarterly Review* 40 (1924): 221–26. Lord Chancellor Thurlow inserted the phrase "not to be paid by anticipation" into a settlement he drew up for one "Miss Watson" and equity subsequently allowed such language to prohibit alienation of capital.

40 Tullet v. Armstrong (1839), 4 My. & Cr. 394, 405–6.

41 Earl Digby v. Howard (1831), 4 Sim. 588, 605. Cf. Brodie v. Barry (1813), 2 V. & B. 37, an earlier case involving a lunatic wife.

42 Howard v. Digby (1834), 2 Clark & Finnelley 634.

43 2 Clark & Finnelley 670.

44 2 Clark & Finnelley 655, 657.

45 2 Clark & Finnelley 677.

46 2 Clark & Finnelley 679. Later Lord St. Leonards, who himself was said to have "as nearly as possible realized the ideal of an infallible oracle of the law" (*Dictionary of National Biography* at "Sugden") and who did not have the highest opinion of Brougham's legal learning, took a most critical view of Brougham's opinion in Howard, believing that though Shadwell should have allowed some account of the Duke's actual expenditure insofar as it was made for things the Duchess would presumably have bought with the pin money if sane, still her insanity might well have resulted in significant savings to which her personal representatives were entitled. Sugden, *A Treatise on the Law of Property*, p. 170.

47 R. S. Donnison Roper, Esq., *A Treatise on the Revocation and Republication of Wills and Testaments: Together with Tracts Upon the Law Concerning Baron and Feme* (London, 1800), p. 200; Roper, *A Treatise on the Law of Property Arising from the Relation between Husband and Wife*, 2 vols. (London, 1820), ch. 17. Cf. *Baron and Feme. A Treatise of Law and Equity*, 3rd ed. (Savoy, 1758), which offers no discussion of pin money, and Charles Viner, Esq., *A General Abridgment of Law and Equity*, 2nd ed., 23 vols. (London, 1791–95), 4:133–34, which uses the term "pin money" and briefly reports several cases without attempting to derive any coherent doctrine.

48 Lawrence Stone, *The Family, Sex and Marriage in England, 1500–1800* (New York: Harper & Row, 1977), p. 330.

49 Frequently, separated women with pin money settled on them must have had those pin money allowances replaced by separate maintenance allowances because it would have been in the husband's interest to have a separate maintenance contract with a clause indemnifying him from his wife's debts. In such circumstances, the pin money would be a bargaining chip in discussions over how much the separate maintenance should be.

50 *The Spectator*, Bond ed., 3:51, 53.

51 Samuel Johnson, *Rambler* no. 97, *The Yale Edition of the Works of Samuel Johnson: The Rambler*, ed. W. J. Bate and Albrecht Strauss, 3 vols. (New Haven: Yale University Press, 1969), 2:158.

52 [Mrs. Catherine Gore], *Pin Money; a Novel*, 3 vols. (London, 1831), 3:224, 293.

53 Lady Mary Wortley Montagu, *The Complete Letters of Lady Mary Wortley Montagu*, ed. Robert Halsband, 3 vols. (Oxford: Clarendon Press, 1965–67), 1:141.

54 Reginald Blunt, *Thomas Lord Lyttleton. The Portrait of a Rake, with a Brief Memoir of his Sister Lucy Valentia* (London: Hutchinson & Co., 1936), p. 92. I thank Edith Larson for calling Lord Lyndhurst's letter of 22 July 1772 to my attention. The MS is part of the Montagu Collection at the Huntington Library, MO 1370.

55 Slanning v. Style (1734), 3 P. Wms. 334.

Evil in The Magic Flute

JANE PERRY-CAMP

The plot of *The Magic Flute* obstinately defies simplification. Certain ambiguities exist in the narrative and with the identification of characters as good or evil (indeed, some scholars insist that there was a fundamental change made in the direction of the story mid-stream); yet a dramatic, even homiletic, effect springs from those ambiguities, serving as a foil for an ultimate clarity of knowledge. One point emerges: that the basic struggle within the opera centers on the age-old contest between good and evil, right and wrong, light and darkness, no matter which symbols are used in the allegorical representation of that struggle. Ultimately, while Schikaneder's libretto does offer much direction towards a deeper understanding of the plot, it is Mozart's music which provides full expression of the drama and the necessary cohesion and unification, just as the music provides us, the listeners, insight into Mozart's own credo, into his intimate beliefs.

First and foremost, certain tenets of Christian faith underlie some strategic conflicts set in motion within *The Magic Flute*. In the larger order of things, evil as a force has to be reckoned with through divine principle, not simply accepted. The presuppositions behind *The Magic Flute* stem from the Judeo-Christian belief that the world "exists for the sake of man,"[1] the evolution of which belief brought the early Church fathers face to face with the problem of a perfect God's having created a world containing imperfection, even evil. The resulting justification of evil as non-Being, that is, privative evil, returned a sense of order to God's universe. God's creations remained only good; thus, Being is, by definition, good.[2] Insofar as evil is contrary to God's cre-

ation and to Being, evil is confirmed as non-Being. The familiar analogy follows that darkness (evil) is but the absence of light (good).
Evil's destruction is ultimately self-destruction, summarized in the
Boethian paradox in which the aggrandizement of evil's apparent power
is merely the approach of evil's self-destruction, thus making evil's
apparent power nothing other than actual impotence.

Several seminal ideas from this theological argument point directly
to *The Magic Flute*. Most fundamental of all is the discovery of the
concept of privative evil, for it is precisely the notion of non-Being,
hence impotence, which resolves the pervasive dilemma in Mozart's
masterpiece. This analysis is confirmed musically towards the close
of the concluding act's finale when E-flat major, the opera's key of
truth and of Being in this Christian sense, ultimately triumphs over
C major, the temporarily dominating opposing tonality, as that conflicting tonal center is first converted to C minor and then subsumed
within the more powerful force of E flat. Thus the opposing force is
reckoned with, not simply accepted; and the overriding dissonance
resolved by negating the "alien" key, by banishing it into nothing-
ness, into non-Being, into non-identity as a tonal center, by means of
its absorption into all-encompassing E flat and through the satisfying
revelation of the omnipotence of E flat. In the process, C major becomes merely a chromatic inflection with no power to control the
momentum and direction of the hierarchical harmonic scheme. In
such a musical scheme, if personified, any self-destruction comes from
a secondary tonality's encroaching too boldly on the primary tonality's harmonies. Or, in a larger structural sense, a counterpart of evil
might be the subsidiary key's pretense at primacy, disguising or ob-
scuring the main key's true unifying function, hence deceiving the
auditor.[3]

Against the dramatic and life-giving background of the harmonic
structure of the opera and its metaphysical extensions, details enliven
the foreground and further draw our attention to the theological argument. We are offered an assortment of wickednesses: obedience
and disobedience whether of good or of evil; evil's relation to suffering; a Dantean selection of iniquity ranging from human frailty to
willful deception; and, closely related to deception, an analogy of evil
to darkness, hence to disguise. Lastly, in *The Magic Flute*, two more
facets of evil remain to entice us: its capacity for comedy and its faculty, paradoxically, to cause good.

Obedience, for example, is requisite for Tamino's and Papageno's
passing their trials to become eligible for membership in the enlightened Brotherhood (II, 3):

Papageno: "Worin besteht diese Prüfung?" ["Of what do these trials consist?"]

Second Priest: "Dich allen unseren Gesetzen zu unterwerfen, selbst den Tod nicht zu scheuen." ["You must subject yourself to all our laws, and not even fear death."][4]

On the other hand, evil, when demanding obedience, is turned upon itself, as when the Queen of Night's command to Tamino to save Pamina, to "free her from bonds of slavery"[5] is obeyed in the larger sense, but, of course, not to the same end as the Queen had expected (I, 6: Aria, no. 4, "O zitt're nicht, mein lieber Sohn"). The powerlessness of evil is evident in this ironic twist of the plot.

As to Dante's classification of evil, both moral sins and physical sins are to be found, the former representing the greater degrees of deprivation (privative evil). The bestial acts of lust, violence, gluttony, that is, sins against the physical being, are exercised willingly by the likes of Monostatos whom we see as prone to lusting after an innocent maiden when we first meet him (I, 11: Trio, no. 6, "Du feines Täubchen, nur herein!").

That the Three Ladies favor violence is readily illustrated by their reaction to the serpent as Act I opens. They smite it (I, 1: Introduction, no. 1). As to gormandizing, we turn to lovable Papageno (I, 2; II, 15, 17, 18, 19, 22, 23, and 24).

Moral evil, "diabolic[,] . . . [involving] perversion of the intellect [and] distortion of . . . 'right reason' by directing it to wrong ends,"[6] characterizes a quintet of evildoers in *The Magic Flute*: the Queen of Night, who corrupts her own claims to matrilinear succession;[7] the Three Ladies, the Queen's accomplices; and Monostatos whose duplicity debases the trust placed in him by Sarastro's Brotherhood.

The figure representing the greatest evil, the Queen of Night, is motivated—in an almost Iago-like manner—by an appetite for power (a metaphorical gluttony) and an obsession with vengeance. As with Iago, "ultimately [her] assault is upon unity and order and the piety of love in all its forms."[8] The Queen's frenzied demand that Pamina kill Sarastro, "Du wirst ihn töten" ["You will kill him"], sets in motion her cutthroat aria with its Italianate artifice that dissects the Germanic character of the opera (II, 8 and Aria, no. 14, "Der Hölle Rache kocht in meinem Herzen").

Sarastro's attitude toward vengeance, expectedly, differs from the Queen's (II, 12 and Aria, no. 15, "In diesen heil'gen Hallen"):

> Within these holy portals,
> Revenge remains unknown,

> And to all erring mortals,
> Their way by love is shown.
>
> . . . .
>
> Of hatred is no telling
> For man his foe forgives.[9]

Mozart's straightforward setting of this sentiment ratifies its meaning. As the glittering Italian *opera seria* style marks the Queen of Night,[10] so the direct and rich sound of hymnlike strophic aria, chorale, and chorus represents Sarastro's realm.

An apparent logical conflict arising here can be bothersome, for Sarastro's eventual banishment of evil from the realm of good, thus from evil's source of nourishment (according to the Boethian definition of privative evil)—such banishment seems to be forgiveness of a rather diabolical sort. However, in view of the fact that each of the evil characters chose to consume good rather than to produce it, the irony of their fate seems justifiably clever.

Eventually, the intricacies of the plot fall into place and the allegory of good and evil unfolds: Pamina's father, the late husband of the Queen of Night, had been Sarastro's predecessor as leader of the Brotherhood of Enlightenment, symbolized by the sun and encompassing the entire world. The crisis arises upon the death of Pamina's father, whereupon the world is divided into the realms of his appointed successor, the goodly Sarastro, and of his widow, the wicked Iago-like Queen of Night—a schism analogous to that following the Fall of Man.[11] The reunion of those realms can be effected only by the joining of Tamino, once he is initiated into Sarastro's Brotherhood (thereby having proved his worthiness) and Pamina, the epitome of innocence, goodness, and idealized womanhood and likewise proved worthy, the daughter of the Queen of Night and of Sarastro's forerunner.[12] Sings the chorus in concluding the first act, words later echoed by the Three Boys (I, 19: Finale, no. 8; and II, 26: Finale, no. 21):

> Let virtue and integrity
> Throughout our life the mentors be.
> Then doomed are evil, sin and vice,
> And earth becomes a paradise.[13]

The utopia sung of is not the paradise of pre-Fall innocence when neither good nor evil was known, but that of the banishment of evil into eternal darkness, thereby denying that unilluminated force any eventual enlightenment.[14]

The notion of privative and impotent evil, in *The Magic Flute*, pre-vails within the context of suffering which seems to come in two va-rieties: that caused by punishment and that caused by vengeance. A census of planned (or threatened) suffering and of actual suffering yields the pattern that those persons associated with good cause ac-tual suffering (punishment), although usually of a relatively mild character, while those associated with evil merely threaten to cause suffering (vengeance), although of a relatively drastic nature. On the one hand, for example, Sarastro does have seventy-seven lashes ad-ministered to Monostatos for his self-motivated lechery (I, 19: Finale, no. 8); and Sarastro does send the Queen of Night, her Three Ladies, and Monostatos into exile (II, 30: Finale, no. 21). Sarastro's kidnap-ping of Pamina does seem to cause suffering in Pamina's mind, but only temporarily, and merely a pretense of suffering in her mother's mind.

On the other hand, the Queen of Night only threatens murder and total destruction (II, 8 and Aria, no. 14, "Der Hölle Rache kocht in meinem Herzen"); II, 27 and 30: Finale, no. 21; see also II, 1); and Monostatos only attempts seduction and sexual harassment (I, 11: Trio, no. 6, "Du feines Täubchen, nur herein!"; II, 7 and Aria, no. 13, "Alles fühlt der Liebe Freunden"; II, 8 and 10). Neither character has any real power. Yet there is an important and telling anomaly in the pattern: the actions of the Three Ladies. At the outset, they do kill the serpent, an act variously interpreted;[15] and they do, on the Queen's order, place a padlock on Papageno's mouth for talking too much and too falsely (I, 3). But in the latter part of the plot, their attempted waylaying of Tamino and Papageno falls short (II, 5: Quintet, no. 12, "Wie? wie? wie? Ihr an diesem Schreckensort?").

Significantly, to whatever extent an ambivalent nature may be as-signed to the Three Ladies' earlier deeds, the temptation of Tamino and Papageno to break their sacred oaths of silence is an unmitigat-edly evil act. The Queen's accomplices not merely threaten but phys-ically initiate their iniquitous scheme; and they fail, their failure in-delibly identifying them with evil. The become powerless, without Being, and they are summarily dismissed from the stage.

In *The Magic Flute*, disguise and concealment arouse a metaphorical awareness of falsity.[16] Literally, the faces of the Queen of Night and her Three Ladies are veiled as Tamino first meets them, suggesting a certain lack of verity within the Queen's own territory (I, 1: Introduc-tion, no. 1; I, 2).[17] Later, in turn, the heads of Tamino and Papageno are covered during the initial stage of their tenure in Sarastro's realm, symbolizing their limited knowledge of truth (II, 2). Always in costume, Papageno and Papagena, while quite well aware of their own natures, remain very much unaware of the highest level of enlightenment, a level never to be attained by the feather-clad pair (II, 3 and 23; II, 29: Finale, no. 21).

Not to be overlooked is the less tangible disguise worn by evil during the Queen of Night's first aria when her claims of a mother's helplessness and violated rights mask her darker instincts which drive her to wallow in self-pity over her daughter's disappearance rather than provoke her to be concerned for her child's welfare. In Jungian terms, it is the illusion of the Queen's being good that makes her so dangerous (I, 6: Aria, no. 4, "O zitt're nicht, mein lieber Sohn!").

The pivotal importance of deceit and the discovery of deceit is underscored both musically and dramatically by Tamino in his dialogue with the Priest when the young Prince comes to the Temple for the first time, the scene which forms the turning point of the entire opera. Simultaneously, here in the first act finale, a new tonality is confirmed, a tonality dissonant with the fundamental key of the opera. Hence, the opera's internal dramatic and musical contradiction is actuated (I, 15: Finale, no. 8).

In accompanied recitative, vindictive and angry Tamino is calmly told, "Den wirst du wohl bei uns nicht finden" ["My son, you are ensnared in error"], then "Dich täuschet ein Betrug" ["You have been told a lie"]. Torn by confusion at the discrepancies between his expectations and his experiences, Tamino finally cries, "Wann also wird die Decke schwinden?" ["When will this veil of dark be lifted?"]. Immediately, the lengthy recitative section is broken; the Priest responds in exalted *arioso* style: "Sobald dich führt der Freundschaft Hand / Ins Heiligtum zum ew'gen Band" ["As soon as friendship's guiding hand / Will lead you to the holy band"]. Tamino's repeated question once more is answered, now by the Priests together, accompanied by the *arioso* melody: "Bald, Jüngling, oder nie!" ["Soon, soon, stranger, or no more"] (I, 15: Finale, no. 8).[18]

Much of the effectiveness of the accompanied recitative results from the fact that throughout *The Magic Flute* the majority of the dialogue is, of course, spoken. And much of the spoken dialogue, as appropriate to the *Singspiel* tradition, is comic. Within the context of a monumental struggle, the universal battle between good and evil, comedy holds a special and forceful place. It is an absurd irony that, when evil, parasitic by nature, is at its strongest, it is actually closest to its own destruction because it attempts to deplete good, its host and its means of sustenance. One's inevitable feeling of superiority under these circumstances brings laughter.[19] The humorous villain, then, is an especially useful device because, in our laughing, he makes us feel *good*.

Among *The Magic Flute*'s comic characters, Papageno comes to mind first. But is he villainous, in addition to being a bit untruthful, somewhat cowardly, and unabashedly gluttonous?[20] A direct descendent of Hans Wurst, Papageno's merriment often almost does him in. But in truth his comedy is so harmless as to be helpful: it makes us appreciate our own foibles and laugh at and with them.

Monostatos presents quite a different picture. In many ways, he is the stereotype of the evil character. Profane, vulgar, and coarse, Monostatos, much like Shakespeare's Caliban, resides in a realm where reverence and good manners reign.[21] Unlike Caliban, who cannot be educated, Monostatos learns very well ways that he can put information to his own distorted use.[22] Yet there is a kind of comedy in this despicable character, a kind of preposterous incongruity when his boastfulness of bravery and his cruel enchaining of Pamina are juxtaposed against his irrational terror upon seeing a bird-man (Papageno) for the first time (I, 11: Trio, no. 6, "Du feines Täubchen, nur herein!").

Comparably ridiculous, and comparably belittling in a contest with Papageno, is Monostatos's involuntary dance induced by Papageno's magic bells only seconds after the Moor had mocked Papageno and Pamina's attempted escape and had threatened them with chains, ropes, and lions (I, 17: Finale, no. 8, "Werviel wagt, gewinnt oft viel! Komm, du schönes Glockenspiel").

The charm of Mozart's setting of Monostatos's lecherous advances towards the sleeping Pamina masks with impotence the Moor's intentions; the inconsistency between the lightness of the music and the weight of the threat slits open that threat and reveals emptiness (II, 7–8: Aria, no. 13, "Alles fühlt der Liebe Freunden").

One must note that, had Pamina succeeded in escaping from the imprisonment Sarastro had ordered and entrusted to Monostatos, she would have returned to her mother's wicked grasp. So it is that Monostatos, in his evil deed of recapturing Pamina, saves her from worse evil (I, 9 and 10). In this context, the practical result of his action is good, just as good occasionally results from the Three Ladies' evil activities. The mischief and naughtiness of fundamentally good characters is thus balanced by the unwitting goodness in basically evil characters, in much the same manner that Pamina, identified with good, comes from the realm of the evil while Monostatos, identified with evil, comes from the realm of the good.

Students of philosophy might recognize in the suggestion that evil could serve a beneficial function a certain hint of Leibnitzian thought.[23] Similarly, Tamino's crucial dialogue with the Priest smacks of Leibnitz's position that an early experience of evil is mandatory to one's self-realization later and so to one's awareness that "[w]hat was previously right, now appears to be wrong,"[24] an argument applicable to the Three Ladies' seeming transformation as well. It is significant that, if one accepts Leibnitz's view of evil as necessary and useful in its capacity to deceive, the so-called break in the plot of The Magic Flute is reduced to an irrelevancy.

Traditionally, the platform of the Singspiel was not one for arguing subtle theological and philosophical distinctions. Instead, its boards customarily supported points made indisputably and vigorously evident. Although Boethius might have predicted The Magic Flute's conclusion ("the enlargement of evil produces its 'imminent diminution and ultimate disappearance'"),[25] making the ending a stock one, the audience had to be provoked into a sense of joy and of superiority through the inevitable triumph of good over the characters which seemed to have been a genuine threat: the Queen of Night, with her deception even of us; Monostatos, with his dishonorable filthiness both in his intentions towards Pamina and in his traitorous behavior towards the ideals of Sarastro; and the Three Ladies, the henchpersons of this sickeningly sinister consort. It is not that these five had not been given a chance to be enlightened; after all, the Queen had been the wife of Sarastro's predecessor, Monostatos was associated with the Brotherhood, and the Three Ladies had stood for honesty, on a small scale, at the start of the opera.

Evil's final fall commences, embedded in Pink-Panther-like stealth as the unwholesome quintet intends to sneak up on and destroy all-wise and all-knowing Sarastro and his Temple (II, 30: Finale, no. 21). Even as the conspirators proceed, Monostatos is consummating a deal with the Queen: that he be given Pamina. Within earshot of the thunderous power of Sarastro's realm, the Queen's company offers her a parody of the holy liturgy of the Priests. Blasphemed are the Priests' sacred chorales and hallowed dotted rhythms as the invocation to the Queen, seemingly now a goddess, is intoned: "Dir, grosse Königen der Nacht" ["Thou great and mighty Queen of Night"].[26] This culmination of accumulated evil is greeted by thunder, lightning, and storm, as evil plunges into the earth, forever banished from light.

The diminished seventh chord, down whose thirds evil is thus bumped, is the most unstable harmony of the late eighteenth-century musical vocabulary and is perfectly suited to its dramatic task. Fully diminished seventh chords have already marked two strategic moments in the course of the unfolding drama: in the first act finale when Tamino cries out against the falsity he believes he finds (I, 15: Finale, no. 8, "So ist denn alles Heuchelei!"); and in the second act after the crucial failure of the Three Ladies to cause Tamino and Papageno to break their oath of silence, when the chord escorts the horrified Ladies off stage to the accompaniment of thunder and lightning—and inflicts on Papageno a healthy amount of respect (II, 5: Quintet, no. 12, "Wie? wie? wie?" ending "O weh, o weh!").

Each appearance of the harmony intensifies the effect of its predecessor. The chord's final appearance not only justly forces evil to its deserved "reward" but equally leads the harmonic movement, indirectly at first, then directly to the sanctified key of E-flat major, the tonality of final stability and final resolution for *The Magic Flute*, a key of special significance for Mozart. As the harmonic dissonance resolves, the entire theater is bathed in light. Sarastro appears; his short utterance in recitative introduces the chorus' announcement of good's ultimate triumph over evil (II, 30: Finale, no. 21).

If good is omnipotent, then the forces of heaven can make full use of the forces of the nether world. In *The Magic Flute*, the dissonance, harmonic and metaphoric, associated with evil makes possible the recognition of consonance. Evil's eventual usefulness, in this large sense, becomes predictable when the opera's presumed plot is rendered absurd: when prima facie evidence of Sarastro's nature is introduced.

Dissonance, by definition, creates a sense of relative instability. A jolt to reality, while good in and of itself, then, is of necessity dissonant; in the process falsity is cast off and left behind as merely part of a past that had appeared to be stable. It is fitting that, in *The Magic Flute*, the therapeutic blow is delivered by Sarastro; evil's veil is rent asunder.

Were the exposure of a sham all that was required of life's drama, then life's metaphor, *The Magic Flute*, could end with the first act finale. That the debunking of evil does not suffice here is evident in Mozart's harmonic scheme. E-flat major is the key of large-scale consonance, but, after the opera's overture, it is stated only twice in the first act, each appearance propounding love and the joy love brings. C major is here the key of dissonance; its disruptive arrival, brought in by Sarastro's altruistic forces, produces a strong sense of dissonance—by analogy, evil. Thus, harmonically, the arrival of good seems evil. At the same time, C major is presented in such a way as to suggest, temporarily, a sense of harmonic stability. In this light, the same dissonance now seems good. That all conflicts are not resolved in the first act finale is patently evident.

Only through the exposure of various kinds and examples of evil is the positive force of good revealed, as only through various kinds and examples of harmonic dissonance is C major eventually embraced by E flat. The gradual absorption of large-scale dissonant harmonies into consonant ones ironically complies with Boethian logic: it is not good's, but evil's energy which is consumed, with that very consumption simultaneously propelling the forces of good into victory.

The earthly paradise, for which Mozart so yearned yet which was denied him in his everyday world, was fully realized in the harmonic justice of his poetry.

NOTES

1 Karl Löwith, "The Philosophical Concepts of Good and Evil," in *Evil*, ed. The Curatorium of the C. G. Jung Institute, Zürich (Evanston: Northwestern University Press, 1967), p. 208. A fuller discussion of the nature-centered and the man-centered views of the world may be found on pp. 205 and 209; in Carl Kerenyi, "The Problem of Evil in Mythology," in the same collection of essays, pp. 12, 14; and, in reference to St. Paul, in Charlotte Spivack, *The Comedy of Evil on Shakespeare's Stage* (Rutherford, N. J.: Fairleigh Dickinson University Press, 1978), p. 56.

2 The line of reasoning, then, held that evil is the absence of good, brought on by man's voluntary act of disobedience to God. The association of evil with mankind is vividly described by Kerenyi, "The Problem of Evil," pp. 6–8, which passage includes a hair-raising description of Iago, by Carl J. Burckhardt, from his *Bildnisse*. See also Charlotte Spivack, *The Comedy of Evil*, pp. 17–18. Marie-Louise von Franz, in "The Problem of Evil in Fairy Tales," in *Evil*, ed. The Curatorium of the C. G. Jung Institute, Zürich, p. 107, cites a similar concept of privative evil in the Chinese *I-Ching* or *Book of Changes:* "Evil, which lives on negation, is not destructive to the good alone, but inevitably destroys itself as well in the end." See also Bernard Spivack, *Shakespeare and the Allegory of Evil* (New York: Columbia University Press, 1958), p. 45.

3 It is proposed that the analogy can be expanded, historically, to include the evolution of nineteenth-century harmonic practice, wherein the secondary harmonies increasingly tend to usurp the sovereignty of the primary harmonies. The evaluation of such an expanded sense of harmony as being evil, however, imposes a moral judgment upon a historical fact;

we like to think our present-day musical criticism to be free of such inappropriate bias.

4 All translations of the libretto cited here are taken from the translation by Ruth and Thomas Martin. See "The Magic Flute," English version by Ruth and Thomas Martin (1941; rpt. in Nathan Broder, *The Great Operas of Mozart* [1962; rpt. New York: W.W. Norton, 1964]). The excerpt quoted may be found on p. 361.

5 Ibid., p. 341.

6 Charlotte Spivack, *The Comedy of Evil*, p. 25.

7 See William Mann, *The Operas of Mozart* (New York: Oxford University Press, 1977), p. 612.

8 Bernard Spivack, *The Allegory of Evil*, p. 45.

9 Ruth and Thomas Martin, trans., *The Magic Flute* p. 367.

10 The cadenza originally intended for the Queen's Three Ladies (for no. 1, Introduction), but deleted by Mozart, would have further emphasized their allegiance to their Queen.

11 Eve, not Adam, is given the credit for the post-Fall difficulties of mankind, just as the Queen of Night, not Sarastro, is considered responsible for the schism here. Both females are associated with a snake; see n. 15, below, for an alternative interpretation of the serpent in *The Magic Flute*.

12 Details of the history of Pamina's father are summarized in Jacques Chailley, *The Magic Flute, Masonic Opera*, trans. Herbert Weinstock (1971; rpt. New York: Da Capo Press, 1982), esp. pp. 93, 96, 124.

13 Ruth and Thomas Martin, trans., *The Magic Flute*, p. 357.

14 Prior to the Fall of Man, in Christian doctrine, innocence prevailed, whereas after the Fall, division ran rampant. But since "neither good nor evil can be known without the other, . . . the simple goodness of creation before the fall was pre-human and pre-ethical, in contrast to the good and evil (inseparable and mutually determinant) which have now entered the world" (Löwith, "The Concept of Good and Evil," p. 209).

15 E. M. Batley contends that a myth from India, "which reported the common . . . belief that a wealthy man [Pamino's father, in this case] who died without [male] heir would return to guard his wealth in the form of a serpent" was "in Schikaneder's mind" during the writing of the libretto (E. M. Batley, *A Preface to The Magic Flute* [London: Dennis Dobson, 1969], p. 124). On the basis of this myth, one's evaluation of the Three Ladies' act and one's affection towards the snake might be shifted drastically.

16 "[T]he evil man [has] a trait that lends evil a hidden permanence: the trait of falsity" (Kerenyi, "The Problem of Evil," p. 8).

17 The reference to the Queen of Night's veil, often omitted in performances, is contained in Papageno's question, "Welches Menschen Auge würde durch ihren schwarzdurchwebten Schleier blicken können?" ["What human sight could see through her veil woven from darkness?"] (*The Magic Flute, Wolfgang Amadeus Mozart*, lyrics trans. Michael Geliot, dialogue trans. Anthony Besch, *English National Opera Guides*, ed. Nicholas John [London: John Calder, 1980], p. 66).

18 Ruth and Thomas Martin, trans., *The Magic Flute*, pp. 350–53.

19 For a discussion of theories of comedy, see Leonard Feinberg, *Introduction to Satire* (Ames, Iowa: Iowa State University Press, 1967).

20 Papageno's lying about his bravery and claiming victory over the serpent comes early in the plot. Confronted with other situations involving fear (with or without reason), Papageno can be counted on to wish he were a mouse (I, 17: Finale, no. 8), or a girl or to come down with a fever (II, 2), or to muster a convenient faint (II, 6). His recurring pangs of hunger and thirst (II, 15; II, 22; II, 23; II, 16) even provoke the arrival of a heavenly picnic basket (II, 16: Trio, no. 16), just as their power over him prompts him to accept the Old Woman's marriage proposal upon the threat of a future with only bread and water (II, 24). These paroxysms requiring more than ample sustenance are matched only by an absence of attacks of conscience in the face of self-denial—self-denial, that is, of opportunities to enlarge his horizons, physical or mental. Examples abound: his preferring [1] not to carry out his order to accompany Tamino to Sarastro's dwelling (the time at which his indenture was turned over from the Queen and the Three Ladies to Tamino); [2] not to face Sarastro for the first time (I, Finale, no. 8); [3] not to accept the invitation for initiation and subsequent trials; and [4] not to accede to the Old Woman's request for faithfulness (until she threatened him with the bread-and-water diet).

21 Typically, the evil character is one of "physical vulgarity [and] vain boasting" (Charlotte Spivack, *The Comedy of Evil*, p. 46). Mrs. Spivack's description of Shakespeare's Caliban and Cloten, likewise suits Monostatos: "Both play negative roles, opposing the values of their particular societies. Both are boorish in a world that treasures civility, both lustful in a world that puts a high moral and poetic premium on chastity, both with delusions of grandeur about conquering those worlds in which their very presence is so alien" (ibid., p. 166). For comparisons of *The Magic Flute* with *The Tempest* see also Janos Liebner, *Mozart on the Stage* (Budapest, 1961; London: Calder & Boyars, 1972), pp. 227 ff.; and Daniel Heartz, "La clemenza di Sarastro: Masonic benevolence in Mozart's last operas," *The Musical Times* 124 (1983): 156.

22 For example, Monostatos, having eavesdropped on the conversation between Pamina and her mother (II, 9, 10, and 11), tries to use the information so gained to force Pamina to yield to his wishes; or Monostatos, knowing the subterranean passageways below the Temple, employs this intelligence in leading the Queen and the Three Ladies to the Temple with plans to destroy it (II, 30).

23 It is hardly farfetched to suggest that the authors of *The Magic Flute* were sensitive to eighteenth-century thought, if through no other channel than that of Baron Ignaz von Born, a distinguished scientist, a student of law and philosophy, and a close Masonic associate.

24 Liliane Frey-Rohn, "Evil from the Psychological Point of View," in *Evil*, ed. The Curatorium of the C. G. Jung Institute, Zürich, p. 186.

25 Charlotte Spivack, *The Comedy of Evil*, p. 17, who continues, "And when

in the Antichrist plays the devil is unveiled as an imposter, the lesson of deficient evil is most explicit. Actually powerless, though falsely commanding in appearance and manner, the figure is whisked off to hell 'by the toppe' and 'by the tayle'" (p. 48).

26 Ruth and Thomas Martin, trans., *The Magic Flute*, p. 383.

Jean-Baptiste Greuze's Italian Sojourn 1755–57

HEATHER McPHERSON

After his triumph at the Salon of 1755, Jean-Baptiste Greuze set off for Rome in the company of the abbé Gougenot and remained in Italy until April 1757. A trip to Italy was still practically de rigueur for a young artist who wished to succeed, and Greuze did not lack ambition. However, most scholars from Mariette to Brookner have discounted the importance of Greuze's Italian sojourn. In the words of the noted connoisseur Mariette, "Il a fait le voyage d'Italie en 1756, voyage qui lui était assez inutile, et où la vanité dut avoir la principale part."[1] Brookner's denial of the utility of Greuze's Italian trip is even more categorical.

> It is generally recognized that the journey to Italy, which took place in 1755–57, did nothing for Greuze's art. It might almost be true to say that it wasted two years which he might otherwise have employed in following up the Dutch models which he had set himself and to which he returned in the late 1750s.[2]

Only Sauerländer, in his 1965 article entitled "Pathosfiguren im Oeuvre des Jean-Baptiste Greuze," recognized an early and lasting Italian influence on Greuze's art.[3] Edgar Munhall, in his 1976 exhibition catalogue, *Jean-Baptiste Greuze 1725–1805*, emphasized the importance of the four paintings in Italian costume which Greuze exhibited at the 1757 Salon.[4]

In this author's view, Greuze's Italian sojourn was more significant in the development of his unique moralizing genre than has generally been realized. The impact of the Italian trip was both immediate and lasting. Italian influence surfaced in the paintings shown in 1757 and continued to affect Greuze's art during the rest of his career. This paper will focus on the four Italian paintings which figured at the 1757 Salon: *La Paresseuse italienne, Un Oiseleur, Les Oeufs cassés,* and *Le Geste napolitain.*[5] In addition, Greuze exhibited the following works: *Le Matelot napolitain, Un Ecolier qui étudie sa leçon,* two portraits, two heads, and a sketch representing *Des Italiens qui jouent à la More.*[6]

The four Italian paintings draw upon different aspects of the Italian heritage from antique statuary to contemporary genre painting. Greuze's early and continuing appreciation of Italian art sheds light upon his subsequent artistic development, his history painting ambitions, and his precocious neoclassical tendencies. In addition, the Italian link contributes to our understanding of the evolution of genre painting in France. The ascendancy of Netherlandish painting has long been recognized, but Italian influence has received little attention from scholars. However, it was in Italy that many young French artists came of age and began experimenting with genre subjects.

French artists, like Greuze, who travelled to eighteenth-century Rome encountered a sort of "moveable feast" where antiquity coexisted with Renaissance and baroque art and the picturesqueness of Roman street life. The genre tradition was alive and well in Italy, especially outside Rome. Eighteenth-century Italian genre artists such as Crespi, Ceruti, and Longhi enjoyed considerable reknown at midcentury. Two parallel genre painting currents existed: the costume study and the anecdotal realistic scene or *bambochade.* Greuze's Italian works drew upon both these currents, but were also indebted to Renaissance and Baroque history painting and classical antiquity. This is hardly surprising for an ambitious artist like Greuze who aspired to the title of history painter.

On the way to Rome, Greuze visited the major Italian cities and copied diverse works ranging from the *Dying Gladiator* to the paintings of Michelangelo and Titian. In 1755, he designed a series of costume studies for Gougenot's *Album de voyage en Italie* which were engraved by the Moitte family in 1768. These illustrations fall within the tradition of picturesque costume studies which were in vogue in eighteenth-century France.

Relatively little is known about Greuze's Italian sojourn.[7] We do know the itinerary Greuze and Gougenot followed but frustratingly little about Greuze's social and artistic contacts, especially in Rome. Greuze and Gougenot passed through Turin, Genoa, Modena, Bologna, Florence, and Naples, finally arriving in Rome on 28 January 1756.[8] In May of the same year, Greuze opted to remain in Rome rather than returning to France with his patron Gougenot as anticipated. The official reasons for Greuze's extended stay are discussed in a letter from the abbé Barthélémy to Caylus, dated 12 May 1756:

> Greuze reste à Rome; l'abbé Gougenot vouloit le ramener. Il a répondu que, l'académie lui ayant fait l'honneur de l'agréér, il devoit reconnoître ses bontés par de nouveaux efforts; qu'en se renfermant dans son genre, il trouveroit, dans les sites et dans les ruines de Rome, des richesses piquantes pour ses compositions: et qui sait si la vue et l'étendue des tableaux de Raphaël ne l'élèveront pas au-dessus de lui-même? . . .[9]

However, Greuze's desire to remain in Rome may have had an ulterior motive. Fragonard referred to Greuze as the "chérubin amoureux" and Madame de Valori recounted Greuze's tragic love affair in a notice on the artist.[10] The statement attributed to Greuze is uncharacteristically modest and diplomatic. If it was a calculated ploy to gain more time in Rome, it served its purpose. However, in light of Greuze's history painting ambitions, the statement should perhaps be accepted at face value. The young artist may have hoped to elevate his genre painting through the study of past masters, although Raphael does not seem the most likely candidate. The reference to the sites of Rome is less credible since no Italian landscape subjects by Greuze are known. The outdoor setting of the *Geste napolitain* is unique among the artist's genre compositions.

Greuze's trip to Italy and prolonged stay in Rome were facilitated by exceptional marks of official favor. In 1756 the abbé Gougenot was elected an *associé libre* of the Académie as a recompense for taking Greuze to Italy.[11] The young artist was apparently regarded as a valuable national asset. Although Greuze's trip was undertaken independently, he was given lodgings at the Palazzo Mancini in 1756 at Marigny's request. The artist also received a prestigious commission for two oval paintings for the royal favorite, Madame de Pompadour.[12] In addition, Greuze painted the portraits of the French ambassador Monsieur de Stainville and his wife during his stay in Rome. In the official correspondence between Rome and Paris, Greuze is rarely mentioned since his stay in Rome was not officially sponsored by the Académie. The abbé Barthélémy refers to the artist twice in his letters to Caylus. Due to the scanty documentation, Greuze's sojourn remains something of a mystery. It is the four paintings in Italian costume which provide the most striking evidence regarding the Italian contribution to Greuze's genre painting.

The Italian paintings of 1756–57 already illustrate the interest in narrative structure, moralizing subject matter, and intense, conflicting emotional reactions which characterize Greuze's mature *peinture morale*. Before leaving for Italy, Greuze had exhibited several genre works at the 1755 Salon, including the sensationally popular *La Lecture de la Bible*. This Netherlandish-inspired subject shows Greuze's capacity for creating genre scenes of unusual emotional concentration. The nostalgic, moralizing subject, the picturesque lower-class interior, and the emotional intensity of the family members set this work apart from the genre compositions of other French artists like Chardin and Jeaurat who were active during the 1740s and 1750s. *La Lecture de la Bible* also attests to the widespread *goût néerlandais* which influenced art collecting and printmaking and contributed to the rise of genre painting in France. The four Italian paintings are more ambitious than Greuze's previous works. Human figures play a more prominent, active role. The artist's large-scale figures and emphatic emotional states are already symptomatic of an attempt to abolish the distinction between genre and history painting. Although the subjects are ordinary, Greuze has portrayed them in the *grande manière*.

Since the Italian paintings were conceived as pendants, they should be considered as pairs. Both the *Paresseuse italienne* (fig. 1) and the *Oiseleur* (fig. 2) are single figure compositions. Both portray large, full-length figures in untidy, rustic interiors. The powerful single figures set close to the picture plane fill most of the available space. This closeup format is striking since figures are often somewhat subordinated to setting in genre painting. In examining the two works, it becomes clear that they are intimately linked both stylistically and iconographically.

In the *Paresseuse*, Greuze represents an indolent young woman in a cluttered interior stacked with crockery and chianti bottles. The virtuoso handling of the still life objects may reflect Chardin's influence as Munhall suggests, but the objects also contribute to the emblematic meaning of the picture.[13] The young woman illustrates indolence or sloth, one of the seven deadly sins.[14] Greuze may have been acquainted with Netherlandish prototypes of lazy servants, but Crespi's famous *Chercheuse de puces* in the Uffizi is another possible source, especially for the setting.[15] Crespi's interior, like Greuze's, is cluttered with a picturesque array of pots and pans and features a scantily clad buxom young woman. However, the mood is quite different and Crespi portrays an actual flea hunt. Much of the impact of Greuze's power-

Figure 1: Jean-Baptiste Greuze, *La Paresseuse italienne*. Wadsworth Atheneum, Hartford, The Ella Gallup Sumner and Mary Catlin Sumner Collection. Photo courtesy of the Wadsworth Atheneum.

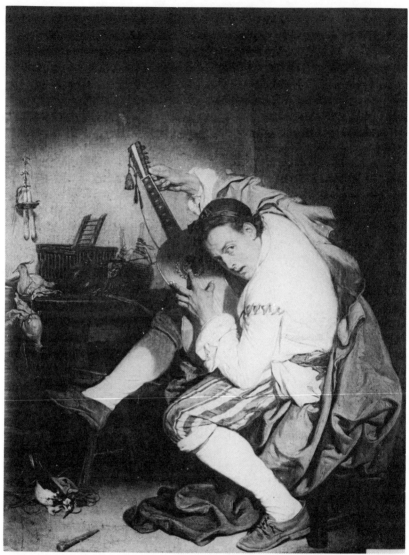

Figure 2: Jean-Baptiste Greuze, *L'Oiseleur*. Muzeum Narodowe, Warsaw. Photo courtesy of the Muzeum Narodowe.

ful, contemplative figure derives from the disparity between the slovenliness of the setting and her dress and the nobility of her pose. In fact the pose of the *Paresseuse* recalls that of Caravaggio's *Magdalene* (fig. 3) from the Palazzo Doria.[16] Greuze has synthesized the Northern emblematic tradition of sloth and the nobler attitude of the penitent Magdalen, her head bent in sorrow, her hands crossed in her

Figure 3: Caravaggio, *Magdalene*. Palazzo Doria, Rome. Photo courtesy of Alinari Art Resource, Inc.

lap. The meaning of the *Paresseuse* is further illuminated by that of its pendant, the *Oiseleur.*

Greuze's *Oiseleur* is precariously perched on a chair in a tense, contorted attitude recalling that of Michelangelo's *ignudi* from the Sistine ceiling.[17] The array of traps, cages, limp dead birds, and bottles gives the interior a sinister ambiance. Birds and cages, which figure prominently in Greuze's oeuvre, had definite sexual overtones for the eighteenth-century viewer. The birdcatcher's contorted pose and anguished expression may also indicate his failure to tune his guitar and achieve musical harmony. As Munhall points out, the nervous, suppressed energy of the birdcatcher contrasts vividly with the lassitude of the young woman.[18] Hal Opperman has suggested that the birdcatcher represents *luxuria,* another of the seven deadly sins.[19] In this reading, he is the seducer and the young woman is the seduced. Moitte's 1768 engraving after the painting was entitled the *Donneur de sérénade* which evokes the notion of the musician/seducer. If the *Oiseleur* does represent lust, Greuze has departed from iconographical norms where *luxuria* is most often personified by a woman.

The *Oiseleur* is a disturbing painting because of its sinister psychological dimension. Although the birdcatcher's pose is Michelangelesque, his leering expression is more akin to Caravaggio's representations of John the Baptist. The strong, raking light and spotlighting and the diagonal emphasis also recall Caravaggio. The *Oiseleur* is an early example of Greuze's fascination with extremes of expression. In the young man's face, he combines tense concentration with watchful expectancy. Throughout his career, Greuze painted numerous *têtes d'expression,* especially of wanton young girls. These works, like Greuze's genre paintings, explore the extremes of human passion, the traditional domain of history painting.

The *Oiseleur* and the *Paresseuse* present a number of dichotomies: male as opposed to female, active versus passive, and so on. The *Oiseleur* and the *Paresseuse* also represent two of the deadly sins, *luxuria* and *desidia* which are directly linked. The sexual connotations of the paintings are reinforced by the still life arrangements which are suggestive in the same way that Chardin's pendants, the *Garçon Cabaretier* and the *Ecureuse* are. The *Paresseuse* with her echoes of the Magdalen combines the idea of sloth with that of the fallen woman. Greuze's interest in contrasting psychological and emotional states, which characterizes later works such as the *Accordée de village* (1761), is already evident in these two paintings.

The *Oeufs cassés* (fig. 4) and the *Geste napolitain* (fig. 5) are more theatrical multi-figure paintings which share the same cast of char-

Figure 4: Jean-Baptiste Greuze, *Les Oeufs cassés*. The Metropolitan Museum of Art, New York, Bequest of William K. Vanderbilt, 1920. All rights reserved, The Metropolitan Museum of Art.

acters. Both works include an old woman, a brash young man, a seductive young girl, and one or more infants. Their long, descriptive titles in the 1757 Salon *livret* are indicative of their narrative complexity. The *Oeufs cassés* is set in a rustic interior, more spacious and less cluttered than those of the *Paresseuse* and the *Oiseleur*. In a letter to Caylus, Barthélémy briefly describes the painting's action: the mother furiously scolds the young man and points to the basket of broken eggs; the abashed young girl sits with her head bowed; at the right, a child tries to mend a broken egg. Barthélémy adds, "Tout çela me paroît très-joli; et la figure de la fille a une position si noble, qu'elle pourroit orner un tableau d'histoire. . . ."[20] Barthélémy was right about the young girl's nobility. Her attitude is reminiscent of Caravaggio's *Magdalene* from the Palazzo Doria. In his *Voyage en Italie* first published in 1769, De La Lande describes Caravaggio's *Magdalene* as fol-

Figure 5: Jean-Baptiste Greuze, *Le Geste napolitain*. Worcester Art Museum, Worcester, Massachusetts. Photo courtesy of the Worcester Art Museum.

lows: ". . . elle est fort jolie, mais elle a l'air d'une fille du commun. L'attitude en est naïve et la couleur belle et claire, ce qui n'étoit pas familier à ce maître."[21] Greuze reverses Caravaggio's process and makes the ordinary noble. The naïve quality which De La Lande noticed in the *Magdalene* is one of the aspects of Greuze's art which was most admired by eighteenth-century critics.

Greuze's sources for the *Oeufs cassés* are eclectic. Moitte's engraving after van Mieris' *Broken Eggs* has been cited by various scholars, but the Dutch girl is vulgar and awkward in comparison to Greuze's figure. Greuze's young girl possesses the same innocence and self-absorption as Caravaggio's *Magdalene*. Although the subject may be indebted to van Mieris, Greuze's figures belong to a higher realm.

In the *Oeufs cassés*, the noble poses and attitudes of the figures belie their humble setting. Sauerländer has suggested that the young man's ambivalent pose may be derived from the Farnese *Hercules*.[22] The child's pose parodies that of the young man. The child, an innocent by-stander who does not comprehend the scene, attempts to repair a broken egg. He exemplifies the naïveté so prized by the eighteenth century. Greuze often includes children in his moralizing genre subjects as a means of indicating different levels of understanding. He also exploits opposites: youth versus old age; experience versus innocence; silence versus accusation. Scenes such as the *Oeufs cassés* cannot and should not be taken absolutely seriously. Subtle visual puns, sexual innuendos, and humor enhance the painting's appeal.

The companion piece, *Le Geste napolitain*, depicts an outdoor setting. This is Greuze's only known landscape from the Italian years. According to Barthélémy, Greuze painted the composition to show-case the so-called *geste napolitain* which was popular in Naples and Rome during the eighteenth century.[23] In a letter to Caylus, the abbé was somewhat critical of the figures' expressions, and noted that the young woman lacked vivacity. However, Barthélémy added, "Dans un tableau d'histoire, ce seroit la plus belle créature du monde. . . ."[24] Conversely, he found that the young Portuguese nobleman looked too much like a *marchand d'allumettes*. Barthélémy's remarks are perceptive. The work, although beautifully painted, is somewhat incongruous. The nobility and poses of the figures are at odds with the humble setting. The scene represents a young gentleman disguised as a merchant who has just been unveiled by the duenna. A young woman mockingly dismisses him with the *geste napolitain* while two children look on innocently. Even the moral signification of the scene is ambiguous. Is the basic idea that imposters will be unveiled? Or is the painting simply intended as a picturesque foreign costume piece featuring a typically Italian gesture? The contrived, artificial aspect of the painting results from its inconsistencies and lack of clear purpose.

In the *Geste napolitain*, Greuze portrays a broken ionic capital with almost microscopic precision. This is the only painting by the artist which contains classical architectural elements. Ruins frequently grace eighteenth-century landscapes, often injecting a melancholy note. Ruins evoke the past, the destruction of man's proudest endeavors, and the inevitable passage of time. Is the ionic capital merely a picturesque prop in the *Geste napolitain*? Or does it contribute to the meaning of the painting? Greuze has purposely contrasted the pure, graceful profile of the young girl with that of the old woman. The presence of children suggests that the painting may allude to the different ages of man. The capital also, of course, evokes the Italian campagna.

The artistic sources for the *Geste napolitain* are surprisingly varied.

Sauerländer has suggested that the furtive figure of the young man may be based upon the *Fleeing Niobide* in the Uffizi.[25] The young man has more in common, however, with the images of merchants and tradesmen which were popularized by the Carracci and remained in vogue during the eighteenth century. The young girl demonstrates a contemporary gesture which Greuze and other visitors found extremely charming. Munhall notes that the old woman is one of the earliest examples of a type which fascinated Greuze throughout his career.[26] Her dramatic forward-leaning pose with both arms outstretched is especially noteworthy. The young woman leans against her shoulder. This configuration echoes that of the principal mourning figures from Caravaggio's famous *Entombment* (fig. 6) in the Vatican. The Virgin's head is lowered and at a slightly different angle, but her outstretched arms possess the same almost electrical tension. In Greuze's composition, the exaggerated diagonals, the intensity of the old woman's expression, and the interweaving of the figures recall Caravaggio. The superb preparatory study of the old woman with her arms outstretched is even closer to Caravaggio in mood. The *Entombment* has always been one of Caravaggio's most admired paintings. Its popularity is attested to by numerous copies, variants, and prints. From Rubens to Fragonard, visiting artists in Rome copied and adapted it. The *Entombment*'s special appeal is due to its underlying classicism. The powerful emotions conveyed by Caravaggio's mourning figures would also have appealed to Greuze.

The *Geste napolitain* and the *Oeufs cassés*, like the *Paresseuse* and the *Oiseleur*, were intended as pendants, but their connection is less evident. Although they share the same cast of characters, the roles change. Munhall has noted that both works feature children as innocent, uncomprehending witnesses.[27] Another common theme is love: simple and direct in the *Oeufs cassés*, indirect and deceitful in the *Geste napolitain*. The young man's degree of success is also vividly contrasted: in the *Geste napolitain*, he is mockingly rejected; in the *Oeufs cassés*, he must pay the consequences of his conquest. Although Greuze was greatly admired for the moralizing content of his genre compositions, the moral message contained in these two works is dubious at best. Ultimately they are more successful as picturesque costume pieces.

Greuze's Italian sojourn played a crucial role in his development as a genre painter. The four Italian subjects represent a critical juncture in his artistic development. Although Greuze turned to French and Netherlandish-inspired genre subjects on his return to Paris, he continued to assimilate the lessons of Italian art. It was in Rome that Greuze first synthesized classical, Renaissance, and baroque artistic

Figure 6: Caravaggio, *The Entombment*. The Vatican Museums, Rome. Photo courtesy of Alinari Art Resource, Inc.

influences with contemporary genre painting. In the process, he forged
a new, exalted genre style which exploited traditional history painting devices and concentrated on the study of human passions. Greuze
was not seduced by classical antiquity to the extent that the neoclas-
sicists were. Instead what interested him most were realism of setting
and costume, intensity of emotion and gesture, and human interaction. Greuze absorbed the lessons of earlier history painting, but it
was Caravaggio, the greatest of Italian realists, who provided a precedent for his hybrid ideal of painting. However, Greuze reversed Caravaggio's procedure—instead of selecting ordinary models for lofty
religious subjects, Greuze attempted to ennoble ordinary subjects.

The flattened space, friezelike composition, and intensity of emotion and gesture of the *Oeufs cassés* and the *Geste napolitain* anticipate
the stylistic features of French neoclassicism of the 1770s and 1780s.
Greuze's Italian paintings also prepared the way for his classicizing
Septime Sévère of 1769. Greuze hoped to gain admission to the Académie as a history painter with the *Septime Sévère*. The painting contains the same mixture of the noble and the base found in the Italian
works. However, this was considered highly inappropriate for a history painting. Greuze's invention of a new genre, *peinture morale*, which
could compete with history painting on moral grounds was recognized and widely approved by contemporary critics including Diderot. Greuze almost succeeded in bridging the gap between history
and genre painting. The Italian paintings are early examples of Greuze's
genre subjects painted in the *grande manière*. They form an essential
link in Greuze's genre production and exemplify both his eclecticism
and his unbridled ambition.

NOTES

1 P. J. Mariette, *Abecedario*, reprinted in *Archives de l'art français*, 4: (1853–
   54): 329 ff.
2 Anita Brookner, *Greuze: The Rise and Fall of an Eighteenth-Century Phenomenon* (Greenwich: New York Graphic Society, 1972), pp. 95–96.
3 Willibald Sauerländer, "Pathosfiguren im Oeuvre des Jean-Baptiste Greuze,"
   in *Walter Friedlaender zum 90. Geburtstag* (Berlin, 1965), pp. 146–50.
4 Edgar Munhall, *Jean-Baptiste Greuze 1725–1805* (Hartford: Wadsworth Atheneum, 1976), pp. 10–11. The page numbers given are those of the French
   edition, translated by Evelyne Mornat.
5 Munhall, *Jean-Baptiste Greuze*, p. 20. The 1757 Salon *livret* listed the four
   Italian paintings as follows:

112 Une Mère grondant un jeune homme pour avoir renversé un panier d'oeufs que la servante apportoit du marché. Un enfant tente de raccommoder un oeuf cassé (*Les Oeufs cassés*)

113 Une Jeune italienne congédiant (avec le geste napolitain) un cavalier portugais travesti, et reconnu par sa suivante: deux enfans ornent ce sujet, l'un retient un chien qui abboye (*Le Geste napolitain*)

114 *La Paresseuse italienne*

115 Un Oiseleur qui, au retour de la chasse, accorde sa guitarre. (*L'Oiseleur*)

6 Munhall, *Jean-Baptiste Greuze*, p. 20.
7 The most complete account is R. Michéa, "Quelques détails inédits sur le voyage en Italie de Greuze et de Gougenot," *Etudes italiennes* 4, no. 2 (Apr.–June 1934): 136–54. Munhall complains that Gougenot's manuscript *Album de voyage en Italie* is inaccessible, but later cites it.
8 Munhall, *Jean-Baptiste Greuze*, p. 19. Munhall cites Gougenot and enumerates the cities that Greuze and the abbé visited.
9 L'abbé Barthélémy, *Voyage en Italie* (1802; rpt. Geneva, 1972), Letter XXII, p. 137.
10 See Madame de Valori, "Notice sur Greuze et sur ses ouvrages," reprinted in *Revue universelle des arts* 11 (1860): 248–61, 362–77. Madame de Valori's account of Greuze's love affair is probably somewhat embroidered.
11 Munhall, *Jean-Baptiste Greuze*, p. 19.
12 Ibid., p. 68. The subjects were left to Greuze's discretion. The two paintings commissioned by Marigny for Madame de Pompadour's appartment at Versailles are *La Simplicité* (England, private collection) and *Jeune Berger tenant une fleur* (Paris, Petit Palais).
13 Munhall, *Jean-Baptiste Greuze*, p. 42.
14 See Hal N. Opperman, review of *Jean-Baptiste Greuze 1725–1805*, by Edgar Munhall, *Eighteenth-Century Studies* 12 (Spring 1979): 411.
15 Munhall, *Jean-Baptiste Greuze*, p. 42.
16 Ibid.
17 Sauerländer, "Pathosfiguren," p. 148.
18 Munhall, *Jean-Baptiste Greuze*, p. 46.
19 Opperman, review of *Jean-Baptiste Greuze*, p. 411.
20 Barthélémy, *Voyage en Italie*, Letter XXII, p. 138.
21 Jérôme le Français de La Lande, *Voyage en Italie* (Paris, 1786), vol. 4.
22 Sauerländer, "Pathosfiguren," p. 149.
23 Barthélémy, *Voyage en Italie*, Letter XLVI, p. 219. See also Munhall, *Jean-Baptiste Greuze*, p. 50. Both the *Geste napolitain* and the *Oeufs cassés* belonged to Gougenot.
24 Barthélémy, *Voyage en Italie*, p. 219.
25 Sauerländer, "Pathosfiguren," p. 149.
26 Munhall, *Jean-Baptiste Greuze*, p. 48.
27 Ibid., p. 50.

Fellow Travellers: Eighteenth-Century Englishwomen and German Literature

SYNDY McMILLEN CONGER

Generous attention has been paid to the efforts of the few cosmopolitan Englishmen in the eighteenth century who introduced their countrymen to an emerging German literature: the pioneer Henry Mackenzie, the astute critic and translator William Taylor of Norwich, the popularizer Matthew G. Lewis, their mutual protégé Sir Walter Scott, and the enthusiastic travellers Henry Crabb Robinson and Thomas Holcroft. What remains unnoticed is that these mediators had female counterparts: fellow readers, translators, essayists, imitators, and fellow travellers. As individuals, these women writers have not been all or altogether neglected, but they have not been generally recognized as students of German culture or literature.

Perhaps in this instance Jane Austen has encouraged some neglect, for she introduces the subject of female Germanophilia in *Northanger Abbey* only to ridicule it. Of the seven novels that Isabella Thorpe has in mind for Catherine Morland to read once she finishes *The Mysteries of Udolpho*, six are linked, in subtitle if not in subject matter, to Germany.[1] Actually, none of the real eighteenth-century Englishwomen investigating Germany or German literature were, like Isabella and Catherine, silly young ladies in quest of shallow diversion. As a group they were intelligent, mature, and diverse. Their lives nearly spanned the century, as their attitudes did the political spectrum, and their interest was hardly frivolous. They include the Augustan Lady Mary Wortley Montagu and the Romantic Dorothy

Wordsworth; the relatively conservative Hester Thrale Piozzi, Elizabeth Inchbald, and Ann Radcliffe; and radicals of varying degrees: Mary Wollstonecraft, Anne Plumptre, Anna Seward, and Anna Laetitia Barbauld.

The measurable effects of this feminine cosmopolitanism were modest. To be sure, most of these women writers enjoyed alliances with the male literati of the day which gave them some indirect influence on major literary developments. In addition to the well-known connections of Dorothy Wordsworth, Mrs. Thrale, and Wollstonecraft, Inchbald was a friend of Holcroft and William Godwin and was quite respected in theatrical circles; Barbauld is known to have inspired, in addition to William Taylor, who dubbed her the "mother of my mind," Blake, Coleridge, Wordsworth, Hazlitt, Lamb, and Scott; and Radcliffe received tributes of various kinds from Ireland (Charles Robert Maturin) and Scotland (Scott) as well as from her own native England (Lewis, Austen, the Shelleys, Coleridge).[2] Their story, however, finally has much more to do with reception[3] than it does with influence. German culture did not, through these few women mediators, effect the larger shifts in the English literary scene that it would in the nineteenth century. What it did do was serve as a catalyst to feminine self-consciousness.

An emerging sense of a women's literary community was perhaps the most visible sign of this new consciousness. Piozzi read Montagu's travels; Seward and Radcliffe read Piozzi's; Mary Shelley, of course, read the works of her mother, Wollstonecraft; and Austen and Mary Shelley absorbed Radcliffe.[4] Even firmer than the women's sense of belonging to a group was the unity attributed to their efforts by literary journals of the day. They were, for better or worse, often discussed under the general heading, "The German School."[5] The real or imagined communality of their literary enterprise, however, should not be exaggerated, for from the beginning their Germanophilia was noticeably extra-literary and self-absorbed.

Their preference was for the German literature of sensibility, the literature of *Empfindsamkeit* with its extra-literary concern for realms of experience felt to be underprivileged—the individual, the emotional, the feminine—often at the expense of the classical unities or precise generic identity. They were, moreover, indiscriminately persistent about that preference. Even well into the volatile 90s when the quality of imported German literature had sunk demonstrably and when most Englishmen involved in literary pursuits had polarized and then grown weary of the debate about it (the anti-Jacobin reviewers condemning it as dangerous to family, church, and state, and the

remaining radicals tempering or disguising their youthful enthusiasm[6]),
women persevered in its translation and its imitation.

Of the commentaries that often accompanied their work, finally,
the single most persistent feature was self-referentiality. From the study
of German literature and culture these women extracted private lessons: a clearer sense of themselves and their position in society and
a clarification of values, most particularly a clarification of the value
of sensibility.[7] The defense of German literature became, to some, a
matter of self-defense. Its use to others, notably to Radcliffe, became
a matter of course. The present essay explores this range of eighteenth-century feminine bonds with German culture by beginning
with the most accidental and ending with the more deliberate. The
figures chosen for discussion are necessarily representative: beyond
them stand the nameless, faceless, numberless devotees of the cir-
culating libraries and the London stage, the Isabellas and Catherines
of the age.

The prologue to this story has to do with two travel books which,
for all their distance from one another in time and tone, made their
women readers irrevocably knowledgeable about Germany: Lady Mary
Wortley Montagu's *Letters from the Levant*, written in 1716–17, published in 1763, and Mrs. Hester Thrale Piozzi's *Observations and Reflections Made in the Course of a Journey Through France, Italy, and Germany,*[8]
which appeared in 1789 just a few years after her continental tour.
Germany was not the main goal of either of these two female travellers, who were both accompanying their husbands to other places,
but what makes their travel accounts significant in the present context is their occasional use of Germany to call attention to restrictions
on Englishwomen.

Both travellers include much information which aimed at delight-
ing their women readers: Lady Mary's generous praise of the beauties
in Hanover, for example, or her sad tale of the death of an empress's
son or of the mystery of a beautiful nun in Vienna; Mrs. Piozzi's tale
of the Viennese Emperor's rescue of a woman in danger of drowning,
her praise of the lustre of the German complexion, or her obvious
and repeated delight with the brightness and cleanliness of German
interiors.[9] With a touch of characteristic wit, Lady Mary notes distinctive manners and mores in the Viennese drawing room and under
the ladies' canopy at the open-air theater; she also draws a caricature
of Viennese hairstyles for ladies: "They build certain fabrics of gauze
on their heads, about a yard high, consisting of three or four stories,
fortified with numberless yards of heavy ribbon . . . about four times
as big as those rolls our prudent milkmaids make use of to fix their

pails upon. . . ."[10] Mrs. Piozzi's account is often tinged with melancholy, but she does seem to smile as she wonders that the women she sees in Innsbruck can "take the nearest way to be warm . . . and wear a sort of rug cap grossly unbecoming . . . these German girls . . . plainly proclaim their resolution not to sacrifice a grain of personal comfort for the pleasure of pleasing all the men alive."[11] The possibility that Mrs. Piozzi's remark evinces grudging admiration brings up a second, and, for present purposes, an important point: both Lady Mary and Mrs. Piozzi seem willing to encourage their women readers to view Germany, in some respects, as an attractive alternative culture for women.

The fact that neither traveller praises Germany or the Germans indiscriminately only makes their approval in this one area the more remarkable. Neither appreciates the signs of superstition, intolerance, aristocratic snobbery, and absolutism she believes that she encounters there. One of Lady Mary's first impressions on entering Germany is the shabby appearance of the towns, and this she attributes to their political system: ". . . under the government of absolute princes . . . you see a sort of shabby finery, a number of dirty people of quality, tawdered out; narrow nasty streets out of repair, wretchedly thin of inhabitants, and above half of the common sort asking alms." Later she pokes fun at the "farce of relics" she is forced to see in "Romish churches" and at the obsessive preoccupation of the residents of Ratisbon (Regensburg) with rank: "The foundation of these everlasting disputes turns entirely upon rank, place, and title of Excellency, which they all pretend to; and, what is very hard, will give it to nobody."[12] Piozzi is much more indiscriminately enthusiastic about her experiences on the continent ("I have now walked over the oldest and the youngest cities in all Europe, and have left each with sincere admiration of their contents"), but she is dismayed by the martial atmosphere in both Vienna and Berlin: "the quantity and disposition of the cannon, bombs, and mortars . . . shook my nerves."[13]

Despite such reservations, both stop to take note of little freedoms they see German women enjoying that Englishwomen do not. These feminine, and in Katharine Rogers' extension of the term, feminist,[14] footnotes are, not surprisingly, more frequent in Lady Mary's letters. She describes with playful approval, and possibly a little chagrin, for example, a game of marksmanship she witnesses between the Viennese Empress and her ladies-in-waiting: "I had . . . the pleasure," she begins her account, "of seeing a diversion wholly new to me, but which is the common amusement of this court." A vignette follows of the Empress Amelia and her ladies-in-waiting, their targets, and the sumptuous trophies. What Lady Mary chooses to emphasize in the final third of her narrative, however, is the feminine exclusivity of this courtly pastime:

> All the men of quality at Vienna were spectators; but *the ladies only* had permission to shoot, and the Archduchess Amelia carried off the first prize. I was very well pleased with having seen this entertainment, and I do not know but it might make as good a figure as the prize-shooting in the Æneid, if I could write as well as Virgil. This is the favourite pleasure of the emperor, and there is rarely a week without some feast of this kind, which makes the *young ladies skilful enough to defend a fort. They laughed very much to see me afraid to handle a gun.*[15]

The sentence with which the account ends adds more than self-irony to the passage; it points to a considerable gap in the education of the English gentlewoman.

The Viennese appreciation of older women Lady Mary finds even more attractive, and this time she contrasts it explicitly to her own country's callous usage. These remarks are apparently occasioned by some news Lady Mary received from Lady Rich concerning a mutual friend of theirs: "I have compassion for the mortifications that you tell me befel our little friend; and I pity her much more, since I know that they are only owing to the barbarous customs of our country." Age in Vienna, Lady Mary continues, is not an obstacle but rather an advantage:

> Upon my word, if she were here, she would have no other fault but that of being something too young for the fashion, and she has nothing to do but to transplant herself hither about seven years hence, to be again a young and blooming beauty. I can assure you that wrinkles, or a small stoop in the shoulders, nay, even gray hairs are no objection to the making new conquests. I know you cannot easily figure to yourself a young fellow of five-and-twenty ogling my Lady Suffolk with passion, or pressing to hand the Countess of Oxford from an opera. But such are the sights I see every day, and I do not perceive any body surprised at them but myself. A woman, till five-and-thirty, is only looked upon as a raw girl; and can possibly make no noise in the world till about forty.

This state of affairs inspires Lady Mary to a memorable epithet and a playful resolution, and then to some final remarks about "the barbarous customs" of England: "I do not know what your ladyship may think of this matter; but it is a considerable comfort to me to know that there is upon earth such a *paradise for old women;* and I am content to be insignificant at present, in the design of returning when I am fit to appear nowhere else. I cannot help lamenting, on this occasion, the pitiful case of too many good English ladies, long since retired to prudery and ratafia, whom, if their stars had luckily conducted hither, would shine in the first rank of beauties."[16] Not only do women in Vienna enjoy attention longer, Lady Mary continues, they are free to have more of it, both from husbands and lovers; and although she does not endorse the idea of lovers, she does indicate the absence in Vienna, in this context, of two undesirable "sects that divide our whole nation of petticoats. . . . Here are neither coquettes nor prudes."[17]

Mrs. Piozzi, who is less preoccupied by a feminist perspective, even in the broader sense of that term, nevertheless remarks twice in her travels, once in Vienna and once in Dresden, on the intellectual freedom that women seem to enjoy in Germany: "The society here is charming. . . . The ladies . . . seem very highly accomplished, and speak a great variety of languages with facility, studying to adorn the conversation with every ornament that literature can bestow; nor do they appear terrified as in London, lest pedantry should be imputed to them, for venturing sometimes to use in company that knowledge they have acquired in private by diligent application."[18]

To say that these two travel books were responsible for the surge of interest in German literature among Englishwomen in the last decade of the century would be, of course, to oversimplify drastically. Above all else, the economic and political complications of the French Revolution accelerated the turning of English intellectual attention to Germany that marks this period. At the same time, both Lady Mary and Mrs. Piozzi were too well known to be ignored by their sisters. In her "Preface" to Lady Mary's *Letters,* Mary Aston praises it quite pointedly as a travel book with a refreshingly new woman's perspective: "I confess I am malicious enough," she begins, to rejoice "that, whilst it [the world] is surfeited with *male* travels, all in the same tone, and stuffed with the same trifles, a lady has the skill to strike out a new path, and to embellish a worn-out subject with a variety of fresh and elegant entertainment. . . . the reader will find a more true and accurate account of the customs and manners of the several nations with whom this lady conversed, than he can in any other author."[19]

Anna Seward speaks with comparable if somewhat more qualified approval of Mrs. Piozzi's travels in a letter to her (21 December 1789), her disappointment with the book's style simply underlining the care with which she read it and the importance she imputed to it:

> Suffer me now to speak to you of your highly ingenious, instruc-
> tive, and entertaining publication . . . with the sincerity of friend-
> ship. . . . No work of the sort I ever read possesses, in an equal
> degree, the power of placing the reader in the scenes, and amongst
> the people it describes. Wit, knowledge, and imagination illuminate
> its pages—but the infinite inequality of the style!— . . . those strange
> *dids*, and *does*, and *thoughs*, and *toos*, which produce jerking angles,
> and stop-short abruptness, fatal at once to the grace and ease of the
> sentence. . . . With what pleasure should I see this your cluster of
> intellectual jewels, appearing through future editions, in cloudless
> brilliance! That done, and The Travels of Mrs. Piozzi will be one of
> the first ornaments of that class of reading.[20]

Clearly, the two travel accounts had drawn attention to a land that
had long been remote to the English.

Unlike Austen's Catherine Morland, whose literary taste was exclusively for perfectly "horrid" Gothic novels, the women actually reading or translating German literature in the 1780s and 90s show interest in a variety of genres.[21] What distinguishes them from their male
counterparts is their preference for the literature of sentiment rather
than that of rebellion, for the so-called literature of *Empfindsamkeit*
rather than that of the *Sturm und Drang*. While their male contemporaries revelled in the irreverent derring-do of Schiller's robbers or rebels or the bold adventure stories of Flammenberg or Grosse, they
seemed to prefer the introspective and sometimes luxuriant emotionality of Goethe's *Sorrows of Werther* (*Die Leiden des jungen Werthers*);
Gessner's pastorals or his *Death of Abel* (*Der Tod Abels*); Gellert's *Life of
the Countess of G——(Das Leben der schwedischen Gräfin von G——)*;
Bürger's *Lenore*; Kotzebue's *The Stranger* (*Menschenhass und Reue*); or
Lavater's *Essays on Physiognomy* (*Physiognomische Fragmente*).

No less than sixteen of the early literary responses to Werther were
written by women; several others were active in the translation of
Kotzebue's works. None of the several translations of *Lenore* was done
by a woman, but Lady Beauclerk did provide her nephew's version
with universally admired illustrations; and Anna Seward and Mrs.
Barbauld offered numerous public readings of it. A notable exception
in taste seems, at first, to be Mary Wollstonecraft, whose single commissioned translation from the German was of a didactic work by the
clergyman C. G. Salzmann titled *Elements of Morality* (*Moralisches Ele-
mentarbuch*), which she praises in her advertisement as a "very rational book." Her elaboration of that point, however, suggests that
she, too, had an eye to the heart as well as the head as she judged

the lessons the book tried to inculcate: "I was pleased to find that chance had thrown in my way a very rational book and that the writer coincided with me in opinion respecting the method which ought to be pursued to join the heart and temper. . . ."[22]

Although many of these literary works were designed to elicit tears from the reader, it is a mistake to assume that they were incapable of doing anything else. Even the milder German documents of sensibility, permeated with the cultural pessimism of Rousseau, were potentially revolutionary, both aesthetically and morally. They not only disregarded neoclassical standards, especially of decorum and reason, which inhibited the flow of emotion, but also, as Henry Mackenzie had noted in 1788,[23] they often cut the English tether between morality and sensibility, opting instead for the ethos of the heart. They presented the English reader with a cluster of male and female character types outside the familiar English exemplary model of the good-natured man, whose sensibility expressed itself almost exclusively in sympathy for others, making it a social asset. The German characters were not Harleys or My Uncle Tobys or Vicars of Wakefield; they were instead characters markedly estranged from others or the norms or values of their society: the defiant man of feeling, the pitiable suicide or parricide, the sympathetic skeptic, insubordinate lovers, or the reclaimed adulteress and her forgiving husband.

By the end of the century, this new German literature had been condemned by various male critics; for example, William Preston, whose vitriolic "Reflections on the Peculiarities of Style and Manner in the late German Writers, and on the Tendency of their Productions" is often cited as representative. He links the German disregard for neoclassical literary standards with a disregard for *all* standards of politics, religion, and society; and he forecasts general anarchy, should their popularity continue. The characters he finds especially objectionable, as they exalt "a morbid and absurd sensibility, into the perfection of human nature": "The favourite characters, most frequently displayed on the German stage, are frantic lovers, parricides, highwaymen, ministers, mistresses, melancholy and raving persons of all sorts. . . . They represent the force of passion as irresistible. . . . They even justify it, as meritorious, as an act of obedience to the supreme decrees of Heaven. . . . These writings sap and unnerve the soundness of the intellect. . . ."[24]

Curiously, comments from Englishwomen reading the same literature suggest that, although they, too, saw its aesthetic, moral, and social unorthodoxy, they did not find it nearly so disturbing. On the contrary, in a guarded way, they defended the new trends.

The first example is Anna Seward's response to *Werther*, significant both because it anticipates her later and better-known comments on Bürger's ballad *Lenore* and because it epitomizes those of her fellow mediators. Her verses "Written in the blank page of the Sorrows of Werther"[25] reveal her awareness of the controversy surrounding Goethe's hero, a character whom male critics had deplored as unmanly and immoral (in the words of Thomas Love Peacock, "a puling driveler"). Seward urges her reader not to remain frozen in "relentless prejudice." She admits the hero's faults but insists that he and his story's merits outweigh the demerits. He is an "ill-starred" Romeo, "a martyr to love with a bleeding brow," and his story can teach how to *pity* as well as how to *love*. Surely readers can remember, she concludes, to love, "but not to mourn, like him!"

The privileging of the affective in art and life also characterizes Seward's remarks on Bürger's poem, although her letters of late 1796 suggest that she had an additional reason for her enthusiasm. She tells Miss Arden on 17 December that she has been asked to read *Lenore* aloud, "to exhibit the equestrian ghost," as she puts it, "not less than 50 times," and to a diversified audience. On one occasion, "Mrs. Powys of Berwick engaged me to read it to a party at her house, Lady Scarborough, Colonel Lumley and his sisters, Lady Louisa, and Lady Sophia." On another, "Lady Lawley desired I would bring it to her rooms. . . . There I found Lady Harewood, her intelligent friend, Mrs. Wood of York, and engaging Miss Garth of Carleton household with Lady and Miss Lawley." "Then," she continues:

> one party after another petitioned to hear it, till there was scarce a morning in which a knot of eight or ten did not flock to my apartments, to be poetically frightened: Mr. Erskine, Mr. Wilberforce— every thing that was every thing and every thing that was nothing, flocked to Leonora. . . . Its terrible graces grapple minds and tastes of every complexion.[26]

Seward's preference for the "crude" and "obvious" *Lenore* over Coleridge's "Ancient Mariner" has been seen as a sign of her reactionary aesthetic stance. Samuel Monk believes that Seward is trapped in the earlier eighteenth-century audience-oriented aesthetic, an aesthetic of didactics and sensation that prevents her from appreciating the new subtle demands of Coleridge's poetry of imagination.[27] If the eighteenth century is seen diachronically, primarily as a movement from one major aesthetic to another, from Augustan to Romantic, then this conclusion is nearly inescapable. If, however, Seward's pref-

erence is considered in the context of other struggles of the 90s—
between Jacobins and anti-Jacobins, Gothic writers and periodical reviewers, or women and men—then it is no longer simply "anomalous" or "reactionary." Seward was an ardent supporter of the French
Revolution, and she is predictably fascinated by the ballad's universal
appeal. Aristocrats and cits, men and women, literati and nonliterati,
all respond to its "terrible graces." In an era characterized by a growing split between the elite and the popular readership (and the male
and female readership), then, this poem's virtue for Seward is that it
unites that readership. It levels them by reducing them *all* to the same
state of poetic fright. Seward is drifting, whether consciously or not,
towards the formulation of a new aesthetic, essentially radical and
feminist in its time, one that demands of literature that it be affective,
androgynous, and democratic in its appeal.

Anna Laetitia Barbauld also read *Lenore* aloud in Edinburgh in 1794,
a reading remembered because Sir Walter Scott claimed that hearing
about it from friends (women friends) turned him into a poet.[28] Mrs.
Barbauld, unfortunately, recorded no response to the poem; but her
own political allegiance with the opponents of Pitt, the enthusiasti-
cally pro-German attitudes of her well-known pupil, William Taylor
of Norwich, and especially her eloquent defense of romances, written in 1773, all indicate that she shared Seward's aesthetic interests.
Romances are beneficial, she claims, even though they are not intellectually challenging in the conventional way. They can "exhilirate,"
"smooth," or "relieve" boredom and loneliness and can teach, by representing affecting scenes of sorrow, such virtues as patience and
compassion. Moreover, they appeal to a wider readership: "for few
can reason, but all can feel; and many who cannot enter into an argument, may yet listen to a tale."[29]

The actress, novelist, and playwright Elizabeth Inchbald was herself neither Jacobin nor Germanophile, but she nevertheless added
her voice to the small chorus of women in the 90s defending German
literature. Asked by the director of the Covent Garden Theatre to
adapt two of Kotzebue's plays for the English stage, she wrote a preface in defense of *Lovers' Vows* (*Das Kind der Liebe*) that indicates that
she was sensitive to, but not terribly bothered by, a potential clash
between the social expectations of English critics and those of the
German dramatist.[30] She explains that she has moderated the characters' emotionality slightly but stopped short of changing the ending, which, like the controversial ending in *The Stranger* (*Menschenhass
und Reue*), includes a reconciliation with, essentially the forgiveness
of, a "fallen female."

Inchbald insists that the play should not be viewed as an apology for adultery. "There is a punishment called *conscience*," she writes, "that causes both the fallen female and her libertine seducer" to suffer for years; and she concludes with a question: "Where is the immorality? . . . Not that a worldly man would class it amongst the prosperous events of life to be . . . compelled to marry his cast-off mistress, after twenty years' absence."[31] Her comment is subtle but has an unmistakable edge: it is at once a criticism of things as they are between the sexes, and tacit approval of things as Kotzebue would have them. It is a tactful defense of the rights of seduced women. Katharine Rogers has recently gathered evidence to suggest that late eighteenth-century women authors like Inchbald had come to view the early English literary model consigned to them, the Richardsonian novel of manners with its conservative moral code, as a "set of constrictions," and the later English models of sensibility as liberating.[32] In just such a way, Kotzebue's alternative code, with forgiveness as its keystone, clearly gave Inchbald intimations of freedom.

If Inchbald's defense of Kotzebue, who had been branded a Jacobin in 1798,[33] is in part accidental, Anne Plumptre's most decidedly is not. A self-proclaimed Jacobin, later "an extravagant worshipper of Napoleon," she trained herself in foreign languages and devoted most of her life to translating from the French and the German. By the end of 1800, she had produced English versions of Matthison's *Letters from the Continent (Briefe)*, Musäus's *Physiognomical Travels (Physiognomische Reisen)*, and Kotzebue's autobiography as well as at least six of his plays including *The Natural Son (Das Kind der Liebe); The Spaniards in Peru (Die Spanier in Peru)*; and *Virgin of the Sun (Die Sonnen-Jungfrau)*.[34] In her critical prefaces and editorial notes, Kotzebue finds an unequivocal English apologist, and the alternative feminist stance on the German literature of sensibility gains its fullest expression. To Plumptre, Kotzebue is "unrivalled" because of his mastery of appeal to the heart; and she, like Inchbald, champions his depiction of male-female relationships. She assures her readers that his *Stranger*, notwithstanding objections that have been made to its morality, "was the means of reclaiming a wife who had eloped from her husband." She even defends Kotzebue's controversial flight from home, children, and other responsibilities after his wife's sudden death: "They must have very little heart themselves who could thus arraign Kotzebue's conduct. Who among us shall pretend to dictate to another the exact measure of affliction proper to be felt on the loss of a tenderly-beloved friend, or the manner in which that affliction should operate upon the heart? . . ."[35] This is a question that Inchbald, too, might have asked, and it emphasizes what the two had in common: an interest in elevating the concerns of the individual heart over the rigid codes of sexual behavior they had sensed in English life and art. It was an interest that this German literature of sensibility allowed them to articulate.

The Jacobin controversy of the mid-90s temporarily endangered this quiet commerce between Englishwomen authors and German literature. Cautious authors like Fanny Burney and Hannah More felt obliged to avoid German novels and dramas,[36] and women who persisted in emulating other continental models were publicly denounced in 1798 for their "gallic mania" in a poem entitled "The Unsex'd Females."[37] Such social pressures may, in part, account for the relatively cool responses to Germany of two prominent late eighteenth-century female travellers there, who provide an instructive contrast to the earlier travellers Lady Mary and Mrs. Piozzi: Ann Radcliffe, who took a Rhine trip with her husband in 1794; and Dorothy Wordsworth, who accompanied her brother to Germany in 1798.

Radcliffe was dismayed with the Germans' "etiquette of sullenness," "idleness," and "prison-like houses." Although she enjoyed stays in several cities along the Rhine, including Frankfort and Manheim, Bonn and Friburg (her spellings), the existence of such attractive cities seemed to her "little less than a phenomenon," rare exceptions to "the mental and physical desolation otherwise spread over the country." She recommends to the English "as little political intercourse as possible, either of friendship, or of enmity, between the blessings of their Island and the wretchedness of the Continent."[38] Dorothy Wordsworth was equally disappointed by the lack of hospitality and cleanliness she experienced in several of the towns in Saxony during her year-long stay there with William. In Goslar they found "no society. . . . it is a lifeless town"; in Nordhausen the peasants were "rude and barbarous"; and in Osterode "people . . . looked dirty, impudent and vulgar. . . . we were stared completely out of countenance."[39]

Their disappointment, however, should not be allowed to obscure the fact that for both women, unlike their two predecessors Lady Mary and Mrs. Piozzi, Germany had been a conscious goal, a place worthy of a sentimental journey. Dorothy and her brother (and Coleridge as well) were on a linguistic and literary pilgrimage, and in that respect felt that they had accomplished their aim;[40] and Radcliffe's journey was a holiday and an aesthetic pilgrimage. As always, here she was susceptible to the natural sublime, something she first glimpsed at Cologne: "Over the wild and gigantic features of the Seven Mountains dark thunder mists soon spread an awful obscurity, and heightened the expectation. . . . The air above is crowded with the towers and spires of churches and convents. . . . the cathedral, with its huge, unfinished mass, has a striking appearance."[41]

Even though Radcliffe seems to have consciously struggled to resist German influence, to her contemporaries she became, with the publication of her last great novel, *The Italian* (1797), the most prominent representative of a growing group of women admirers and imitators of the so-called German Gothic school. She did not, it is true, advertise her affiliation with them as did Eliza Parsons in *The Castle of Wolfenbach: A German Story* (1793) or Harriet Lee in her *The German's Tale: Kruitzner* (1801). Rather she deliberately set her novels elsewhere—in Italy or in France—and her headnotes constantly refer the reader to the English literary heritage from Shakespeare through Milton to Horace Walpole and William Collins. Nevertheless, as both her contemporaries and later critics have recognized,[42] she had assimilated German motifs and character types, to some extent directly from Schiller's *Ghostseer (Der Geisterseher)* and *Robbers (Die Räuber)*, to some extent indirectly from the Gothic novels of Lewis and Parsons: most frequently mentioned are the banditti, the mysterious monks, the blood-chilling convents, and the inquisition and abduction scenes.

What has gone unnoticed is Radcliffe's profound assimilation, by whatever means and however indirectly, of the radical sentimentalism and cultural pessimism especially prevalent in the German literature of sensibility, attitudes sometimes at odds with the endorsement of propriety and property that dominates her stories. The first of these are the allied notions that a true touchstone of merit is not one's pedigree but one's physiognomy (or pathognomy), not one's reasonableness but one's sensibility. These were certainly far from new ideas at the time, but only in the wake of the popularity of Lavater's *Essays on Physiognomy* in the 80s and early 90s were they adopted unreservedly by some authors in England.[43] To a degree unmatched by her less credulous English predecessors Fielding, Mackenzie, and Sterne, Radcliffe simply assumes that physiognomy allows a trustworthy moral test for beholder and beheld at the same instant.

Ellena immediately sees in Spalatro "a man, who had 'villain' engraved in every line on his face,"[44] thereby demonstrating her own sensitivity while she verifies his depravity. Schedoni, on the other hand, misreads even Ellena's "expressive countenance" (p. 288); his sensitivities have clearly become fixed, as deadened as his own remarkable face, one he inherited, it should be added here, from Schiller's Armenian in *The Ghostseer*:[45] "There was something in his [Schedoni's] physiognomy extremely singular, and that can not easily be defined. It bore the traces of many passions, which seemed to have fixed the features they no longer animated. An habitual gloom and severity prevailed over the deep lines of his countenance; and his eyes were so piercing that they seemed to penetrate, at a single glance, into the hearts of men, and to read their most secret thoughts . . ." (p. 35).

Another notion that surfaces frequently in *The Italian*, and one that Radcliffe shares with *Sturm und Drang* authors, is that the older generation and its society is corrupt—or corruptible—and insensitive to the needs of the younger. Schedoni is, of course, the elder archvillain of the tale, and his actions amply illustrate the idea, but Vivaldi's mother shares Schedoni's self-serving motives of ambition and revenge. Besides, both churchman and noblewoman cultivate ties with unscrupulous people inside and outside Naples—Nicola de Zampari, a monk whose crass ambition leads him to do whatever Schedoni bids; Spalatro, the wicked, self-exiled assassin; and the cruel abbess who imprisons Ellena against her will, and on hearsay evidence—and together they suggest an adult society sadly compromised by criminal activity.

Those not wicked themselves often become credulous gulls, victims of the sophisticated hypocrites around them. As Schedoni and the Marchesa plot the punishment of Vivaldi, they give us a sampling of their duplicity: even in conversation with each other, they cloak their dark desires in the language of injured virtue. "Love" becomes "disgrace," and "justice" demands Ellena's death (pp. 168–69). The Marchese is no match for such duplicity, such seeming moral impeccability; and he believes the tales he is told about his son and Ellena. Cold, peremptory, inflexible, as the misinformed Marchese admonishes his son, he is remarkably reminiscent of the father in Schiller's *Cabal and Love*, one of Germany's most memorable *Sturm und Drang* portraits of a decadent and gullible aristocratic father. And as Vivaldi defends the propriety of his attachment to Ellena, he strikes an impassioned, rebellious tone much like that of the son Ferdinand in *Cabal and Love*, who, in the last two scenes of Act 2, must witness his father accusing his beloved Luise of being a whore.

"'Signora Rosalba has, my Lord, exalted me to the honour of being her suitor,'" begins Vivaldi, "unable longer to command his feelings." But the Marchese, like Ferdinand's father, rebukes the son for his "arrogance and romantic enthusiasm." He enjoins him to "acknowledge your error, instantly dismiss this new favourite" and offers, with a calculated cynicism matching that of Ferdinand's father, "to allow her a small annuity as some reparation for the depravity, into which you have assisted to sink her." Vivaldi's reaction to his father's insinuations stops short of threatening murder—Ferdinand's recourse; but although Vivaldi dissolves in tender tears, he still does not abandon completely Ferdinand's language of accusation: "'My Lord!' exclaimed Vivaldi aghast, and scarcely daring to trust his voice, 'my lord!—depravity?' struggling for breath. 'Who has dared to pollute her spotless fame by insulting your ears with such infamous falsehood? . . . O Ellena! Ellena!' As he pronounced her name tears of tenderness mingled with those of indignation" (p. 29).

Along with the generational conflict in this scene, of course, Radcliffe dramatizes the central ideological conflict of the literature of the *Sturm und Drang* period: reason versus passion. Radcliffe's parental characters, like the father in *Cabal and Love* and the mothers in *Werther* and *Lenore*, are relics from the rationalist past. They seem to exist to remind their children and their readers of the dangers of unbridling the emotions, of the virtues of filial duty, moderation, piety. Ironically, they themselves often suffer from the ravages of such passions.

St. Aubert in *The Mysteries of Udolpho* (1792) has some such incompatible traits, but Schedoni is the best Radcliffean example of this composite construct. His past career is *passion-driven* like those of the fratricidal brothers Franz Moor (from Schiller's *Robbers*) or Rhodophil (from Parsons' *The Mysterious Warning*); but his comportment is that of Schiller's mysterious, calculating, *passionless* Armenian: "He would sometimes abstract himself from the society for whole days together, or when with such a disposition he was compelled to mingle with it, he seemed unconscious where he was, and continued shrouded in meditation and silence till he was again alone."(p. 34). Although he is haunted by passion, he hates a display of emotion; indeed, he finds it a ready reason to denigrate woman: "Behold, what is woman!" he scoffs at the Marchesa after she has compunctions about murdering Ellena, "The slave of her passion. . . . Assail but her senses . . . and lo! all her perceptions change: she shrinks from the act she had but an instant before believed meritorious, yields to some new emotion, and sinks. . . . O, weak and contemptible being!" (pp. 177–78).

Vivaldi and Ellena, in sharp contrast, are depicted not only as equals in courage and intelligence but also in sensibility. On this latter subject, moreover, they are Rousseau-like rebels, firm defenders of the rights of the individual heart in a world where they see that institutional corruption and parental tyranny have tarnished older codes: "It is unnecessary," Ellena says to the wicked abbess who gives her the choice of either marrying against her will or taking the veil, "that

I should withdraw for the purposes of . . . deciding. My resolution is already taken, and *I reject each of the offered alternatives.* . . . Having said this, I am prepared to meet whatever suffering you shall inflict upon me. . . . The sanctuary is prophaned . . . it is become a prison. It is only *when the Superior ceases to respect . . . religion . . . that she herself is no longer respected"* (p. 84, italics mine). Ellena's mild and dignified manner clearly cannot altogether mask the rebellion in her message, and the abbess's reprimand takes the form of a question which helps us to measure the newness of this late eighteenth-century heroine: "Where is it that you have learned these heroics! . . ." From the Germans? Not entirely or directly, perhaps. But Ellena's words, and Vivaldi's to his father as well, do echo those of a series of German rebels of sensibility, and they lend new force to Clara McIntyre's remark that Schiller's *Robbers* was one of Radcliffe's favorite books.[46]

In Radcliffe's novels, obviously, the preferences of both men and women Germanophiles come together successfully for the first time in the century—*Sturm und Drang* joins *Empfindsamkeit*, rebellion joins sensibility. In addition, the goals of the women discussed in this essay come to fruition. Radcliffe created a literature with less constricting models for young heroes and heroines and with a much greater respect for that "unmanly" virtue of sensibility; yet she managed to do so without alarming her male readers or reviewers. Through Radcliffe, moreover, these new attitudes fan out to touch a number of major nineteenth-century authors under her spell from Scott to Henry James. This tale of triumph ends as quietly as it does perhaps because it was never so much a story of feminist revolt and backlash as it was a story of women authors in search of new literary and social models. They had encountered, as Ellen Moers has said, "an order of reality perhaps more intractable than social fact—the literary";[47] and throughout the century they sought ways to modify that literary reality to better reflect women's needs. Margaret Anne Doody has argued that the period between Richardson and Scott is too often misconstrued as "a dead period, a dull blank" when, in fact, eighteenth-century women writers were developing "the paradigm for women's fiction of the nineteenth century."[48] I would add to that, "in part, by importing subversive literature."

NOTES

1 Of the famed Northanger Seven, three—*The Castle of Wolfenbach* (Eliza Parsons), *The Mysterious Warning* (also Mrs. Parsons), and *The Midnight Bell* (F. Lathom)—are identified by subtitle as "German tales"; *Necromancer of the Black Forest* (Ludwig Flammenberg) and *Orphan of the Rhine* (Mrs. Eleanor Sleath) both announce their geographical affiliation in their titles; and *Horrid Mysteries* was written by a German, Carl von Grosse. Only *Clermont* by Regina Maria Roche is free from association with things German. Daniel V. Hegeman, "Three English Bluestockings Visit Germany," *Kentucky Foreign Language Quarterly* 4, no. 2 (1957): 57–73, is the sole general article to date on eighteenth-century Englishwomen and Germany.

2 In addition to the entry in the *Dictionary of National Biography* on Mrs. Barbauld, see Betsey Rodgers, *Georgian Chronicle: Mrs. Barbauld and her Family* (London: Methuen, 1958) and two articles: Porter Williams, Jr., "The Influence of Mrs. Barbauld's *Hymns in Prose for Children* on Blake's *Songs of Innocence and Experience*," in *A Fair Day in the Affections*, ed. Jack D. Durant and M. Thomas Hester (Rawleigh: Winston, 1980); and Sam Pickering, "Mrs. Barbauld's *Hymns in Prose*: 'An Air Blown Particle of Romanticism'?" *Southern Humanities Review* 9 (1975): 259–68. On the Holcroft-Godwin-Inchbald connections, see S. R. Littlewood, *Elizabeth Inchbald and Her Circle, 1753–1821* (London: O'Connor, 1921). The references to Radcliffe need not be detailed here; but briefly, Maturin's discussion occurs in a review he wrote in 1818 of Maria Edgeworth's *Harrington and Ormond, Tales* for *British Review*; Scott's in his comments on Radcliffe in his *Lives*; Lewis's in a letter to his mother from the continent (see his biography by Louis Peck); Austen's in ch. 6 of *Northanger Abbey*. The Shelleys reread Radcliffe's later novels just before Mary wrote *Frankenstein*.

3 I share the presuppositions of Hans-Robert Jauss of the University of Constance that reception studies constitute a crucial part of the work of a student of literary history, as they provide ready access both to the dominant aesthetic attitudes of a particular moment in history and to the eventual value assigned to certain texts by literary historians. Jauss's approach is more inclusive than that of traditional influence studies (indeed, it includes the idea of influence), especially because it welcomes the investigation of all levels of readers, writers, and texts (popular as well as high literature). In the case of women writers, who felt themselves under scrutiny and often, as a result, expressed their concerns indirectly, investigating *what* they read and *how* they read may be richly rewarding. Jauss first outlined his position in his *Literaturgeschichte als Provokation* (Frankfurt: Suhrkamp, 1970).

4 This information was gleaned for the most part from primary sources: Hester Lynch Piozzi, *Observations and Reflections Made in the Course of a Journey Through France, Italy, and Germany*, ed. Herbert Barrows (Ann Arbor: University of Michigan Press, 1967), p. 386; Hasketh Pearson, ed.,

The Swan of Lichfield (New York: Oxford University Press, 1937), pp. 126–27; but helpful on Radcliffe's reading is also still Clara Frances McIntyre, *Ann Radcliffe in Relation to her Time* (1920; rpt. New York: Archon, 1970).

5 Journals of the day speak with increasing frequency after 1790 of the German school (especially, of course, *The Anti-Jacobin Review*, but also the more sympathetic *Monthly Review*). They tend to mean by this the dramatists and novelists of Gothic and sentimental tales, but the term is never carefully defined and is, essentially, an English invention. For further examples, see nn. 6, 23, 24, 41.

6 This controversy is often documented, most thoroughly and recently by John Boening, ed., *The Reception of Classical German Literature in England, 1760–1860: A Documentary History From Contemporary Periodicals*, 10 vols. (New York: Garland, 1977).

7 A similar point is made about the value of the *English* literature of sensibility by Katharine Rogers in her *Feminism in Eighteenth-Century England* (Urbana: University of Illinois Press, 1982); see esp. ch. 4, "The Liberating Effect of Sentimentalism."

8 Lady Mary Wortley Montagu, *Letters from the Levant During the Embassy to Constantinople 1716–18*, ed. Harry Schwartz (1838; rpt. New York: Arno, 1971); Piozzi, *Observations*.

9 Montagu, *Letters*, pp. 65–66, 67, 52; Piozzi, *Observations*, pp. 372–73, 363, 358–59.

10 Montagu, *Letters*, pp. 35–36.

11 Piozzi, *Observations*, p. 360

12 Montagu, *Letters*, pp. 15–16, 17, 19.

13 Piozzi, *Observations*, pp. 404, 368–69.

14 Rogers, *Feminism*, p. 4.

15 Montagu, *Letters*, pp. 40–41. Italics are mine.

16 Ibid., pp. 42–43. Italics are mine. See also the following items by Robert Halsband on Lady Mary: "Lady Mary Wortley Montagu as a Friend of Continental Writers," *Bulletin of the John Rylands Library* 39 (1956–57): 57–74; "Lady Mary Wortley Montagu as a Letter Writer," *PMLA* 80 (1965): 155–63; and *The Life of Lady Mary Wortley Montagu* (Oxford: Clarendon, 1956).

17 Montagu, *Letters*, pp. 41–43.

18 Piozzi, *Observations*, pp. 373–74.

19 Montagu, *Letters*, p. 4. Italics are Aston's.

20 Pearson, ed., *Swan*, pp. 126–27. Italics are Seward's.

21 Places to begin gleaning such information are the translation checklists of Violet M. M. Stockley, *German Literature as Known in England, 1750–1830* (London: G. Routledge & Sons, 1929) and Frank Woodyer Stokoe, *German Influence in the English Romantic Period, 1788–1818* (1926; rpt. New York: Russell and Russell, 1963). All German works listed or later discussed here were available in English translations, before 1800.

For an overview of Bürger's mediators, O. F. Emerson's article is still useful, "The Earliest English Translations of Bürger's *Lenore*," *Western Reserve University Bulletin* 18 (May 1915): 1–120; for Gessner, Bertha Reed's "The Influence of Salomon Gessner upon English Literature," *German American Annals* 3 (1905): 67–80, 99–112, 131–47, 380–88; and for Goethe's *Werther*, see esp. Stuart Pratt Atkins, *The Testament of Werther in Poetry and Drama* (Cambridge, Mass.: Harvard University Press, 1949).

22 C. G. Salzmann, *Elements of Morality*, trans. Mary Wollstonecraft (London: J. Crowder, 1791), pp. 1–2.

23 Henry Mackenzie, "An Account of the German Theatre," read in 1788, published in *Transactions of the Royal Society of Edinburgh* 2 (1790): 154–92.

24 *Edinburgh Magazine* 21 (January 1803): 10–11.

25 Anna Seward, *Poetical Works*, ed. Walter Scott (Edinburgh: Ballantyne, 1810), 2:130–32.

26 Pearson, ed., *Swan*, pp. 205–6.

27 Samuel H. Monk, "Anna Seward and the Romantic Poets: A Study in Taste," on pp. 118–34 of *Wordsworth and Coleridge*, ed. Earl Leslie Griggs (Princeton: Princeton University Press, 1939). See esp. pp. 131, 134.

28 See Stokoe, *German Influence*, pp. 64–66 and especially Appendix 2, "The Date of the *Lenore*-reading by Mrs. Barbauld."

29 "On Romances," from *Miscellaneous Pieces in Prose*, vol. 2 of *The Works of Anna Laetitia Barbauld* (London: Longman, Hurst, Rees, Orme, Brown, and Green, 1825), pp. 172, 173–74.

30 Parts of this story are told in *Memoirs of Mrs. Inchbald*, ed. James Boaden (London: Bentley, 1833), 2:20–28 and in S. R. Littlewood, *Elizabeth Inchbald*, pp. 108–9.

31 Littlewood, *Elizabeth Inchbald*, pp. 108–9. Inchbald defends Kotzebue's *Stranger* in a preface to the translation of Benjamin Thompson on nearly identical grounds (London: Longman, n.d.): "can this be holding out temptation, as alleged, for women to be false to their husbands? Sure it would rather act as a preservative" (p. 5).

32 Katharine M. Rogers, "Inhibitions on Eighteenth-Century Women Novelists: Elizabeth Inchbald and Charlotte Smith," *Eighteenth-Century Studies* 11 (1977): 64.

33 The play *Lovers' Vows* was performed in late October of 1798. In June and July of that year *The Anti-Jacobin; or Weekly Examiner* had published its political and literary satire "The Rovers" with Kotzebue as a central target.

34 Other plays translated were: *The Count of Burgundy (Der Graf von Burgund); The Widow and the Riding Horse (Die Witwe und das Reitpferd);* and *The Force of Calumny (Die Verleumder). The Natural Son* was Plumptre's title for *Das Kind der Liebe.*

35 Anne Plumptre, editorial remarks in *Sketch of the Life and Literary Career of Augustus von Kotzebue; with the Journal of his Tour to Paris, at the Close of the Year 1790* (London: H. D. Symonds, 1800), pp. 107–8, 92–148.

36 Fanny Burney avoided *Werther*; Hannah More criticized the modern German theater.

37 *The Unsex'd Females: A Poem, Addressed to the Author of "The Pursuits of Literature"* (1798, rpt. New York: Garland, 1974), p. 18.

38 Ann Radcliffe, *A Journey Made in the Summer of 1794, through Holland and the Western Frontier of Germany* (1795; rpt. Hildesheim: Georg Olms, 1975), pp. 97, 219, 102, 226, 108.

39 Hegeman, "Three English Bluestockings," pp. 70–71.

40 Ibid., p. 69.

41 Radcliffe, *Journey*, p. 100.

42 Review of *The Italian* in *The Anti-Jacobin Review* 7 (1800): 28—even they are relatively positive in their assessment of Radcliffe's novels. Cf. J. M. S. Tompkins' discussion of Radcliffe's possible debts to German literature in *The Popular Novel in England 1700–1800* (1932; rpt. Lincoln: University of Nebraska Press, 1961), pp. 247–48, 278–81, 285, 375–77. Though there is no direct evidence for this, Radcliffe and her fellow Gothic romancers probably knew at least some of the popular German Gothic thrillers (in English translation at the time) by Carl von Grosse, Ludwig Flammenberg, Benedikte Naubert, and Veit Weber. The tone of the typical female Gothic tale of the day, however, is markedly less sensational than that of these authors, all of whom were read and drawn upon by Matthew G. Lewis for *The Monk*.

43 Graeme Tytler, *Physiognomy in the European Novel: Faces and Fortunes* (Princeton: Princeton University Press, 1982), pp. 164–65.

44 Ann Radcliffe, *The Italian or the Confessional of the Black Penitents. A Romance*, ed. Frederick Garber (London: Oxford University Press, 1968), p. 211. Hereafter cited parenthetically in text.

45 J. M. S. Tompkins first noted this resemblance, *The Popular Novel*, Appendix 3, pp. 376–77.

46 McIntyre, *Ann Radcliffe*, p. 67, does not mention *Cabal and Love*, but the play was available in English from 1795 on, as was *The Ghostseer*. Matthew G. Lewis added his translation of *Kabale und Liebe* in 1797, titled *The Minister*.

47 Ellen Moers, *Literary Women* (Garden City, N.Y.: Anchor/Doubleday, 1977), p. 187.

48 Margaret Anne Doody, "George Eliot and the Eighteenth-Century Novel," *Nineteenth-Century Fiction* 35 (1980): 267–68.

Edmund Burke and Economical Reform, 1779–83

E. A. REITAN

Although there is an enormous scholarly literature dealing with Edmund Burke, the four years when he stood forward as the leader of "economical reform" and, for the only time in his long political career held office, have been strangely neglected.[1] Perhaps scholars have been discouraged by the complexities of public finance and administration; perhaps the role of reformer seems an anomaly to those whose interest in Burke is based on his role as a theorist of conservatism. Yet it seems clear that these years were a watershed in Burke's political career and political thought. The death of Rockingham, the breakup of the Rockingham ministry, and the decline of the issues which had characterized the Rockingham party obviously changed Burke's life. His experience of public office under the Rockingham and Coalition ministries gave him a perspective different from that developed in the long years of opposition. The challenges, flawed achievements, and disappointments of the period strengthened his conservative instincts and diminished the zest for problem solving characteristic of the younger Burke. Until the French Revolution gave him a new role in British politics Burke saw this period as the high point of his career, and his reflections upon those exciting years were an important influence on his later conservative thought.

Early in his political career Burke developed a theory of reform consistent with his essential conservatism. In his *Thoughts on the Causes of the Present Discontents* (1770) he identified "the influence of the crown" as the principal threat to the constitution, and he gave special attention to the civil list as the major source of the political corruption which he saw as the foundation of Britain's troubles.[2] Despite the dangers which he saw in Britain's disordered state, Burke advocated caution in reform: "Every project of a material change in a government so complicated as ours, combined at the same time with external complications still more complicated, is a matter full of difficulties; in which a considerate man will not be too ready to decide; a prudent man too ready to undertake; or an honest man too ready to promise."[3] A year earlier he defined the criteria by which sensible men would judge proposals for reform:

> They must see the object to be of proper magnitude to engage them; they must see the means of compassing it to be next to certain; the mischiefs not to balance the profit; they will examine how a proposed imposition or regulation agrees with the opinion of those who are likely to be affected by it; they will not despise the consideration even of their habitudes or prejudices.[4]

Reform, Burke added, must be in accord with popular wishes, and might need to be promoted by popular appeals. "I like a clamor," he said in 1771, "wherever there is an abuse" and when it was combined with an effort to provide redress.[5] As a practical politician he wrote to Rockingham in 1775: "But speaking of the prudential consideration, we know that all opposition is absolutely crippled, if it can obtain no kind of support without Doors."[6]

In the autumn, 1779, Burke sensed the emergence of conditions needed for a successful attack on "the influence of the crown." The war in America was going badly, the French and Spanish navies sailed the Channel with impunity, the North ministry was crumbling internally, and public discontent was growing. "The Blisters begin to rise," he wrote to Rockingham, "and there are signs of life in the body." Rockingham replied that the problem was "the corrupt *Influence of the Crown*" which "must soon submit to be *shorn*." He added: "NB I must prefer the shears to the Hatchets."[7] It was Yorkshire and the leadership of the Rev. Christopher Wyvill which gave the opposition the groundswell of popular support it needed. In the last week of November, Wyvill sent a circular letter to the gentlemen of Yorkshire, inviting them to attend a meeting which would prepare a petition for presentation to the House of Commons, requesting economy in government, an inquiry into the civil list, and abolition of "all sinecure places, exorbitant salaries to efficient places, and pensions unmerited by public service." He proposed that the meeting form an association to support its petition and hinted that "once the fund of corruption was reduced, it would be an easy matter to carry other regulations which are thought necessary to restore the freedom of Parliament."[8] The Yorkshire meeting was a great success and led to a petitioning movement which in the winter of 1779–80 spread throughout England.[9]

When Parliament met in November the Rockingham party identified "the influence of the crown" as the issue upon which it would base its attack, giving special attention to the civil list.[10] On 15 December Burke announced his intention to introduce a plan of "economical reform" after the Christmas recess. He defined his objective as primarily political: "the whole of our grievances," he stated, "are owing to the fatal and overgrown influence of the crown; and that influence itself to our enormous prodigality." He proposed parliamentary reform of the "civil executive government" which would abolish fifty offices normally used for support of the ministry, resulting in savings of £200,000 per year. He insisted that he entered into the role of reformer reluctantly, and that his purpose was skillful pruning of the constitution, not radical change. He assured the Commons that his plan of reform would not affect the personal comfort of the monarch but would fall almost wholly on "those who hold office by a tenure, in which they are liable to be, and frequently are, removed for accommodating the arrangements of administration." To demonstrate his moderation Burke laid down limitations: patent offices, which he considered as property, would not be touched; compensation would be given to persons dependent for their livelihood on the offices to be suppressed; offices useful to the state would not be retrenched; adequate resources would remain to reward merit; "the crown shall be left an ample and liberal provision for personal satisfaction, and for as much of magnificence, as is suitable with the burthened state of this country." Public demand, and vaguely hinted fears of something more drastic if the public voice went unheard, were his justification.[11]

Burke's focus on the civil list was shrewdly calculated. Despite setbacks and mounting military expenditures, the war still commanded support in Parliament and the country. Independent members who would support the North ministry in other respects, might be persuaded that courtiers and ministers should bear part of the fiscal burden, especially since the civil list had been increased as recently as 1777. Although it was a modest part of the total expenditure of government, the civil list was important politically, for the places, pensions, and perquisites of the civil list were highly attractive to members of the political class. Since the Crown was not accountable to Parliament for civil list expenditure, suspicions concerning its use for political advantage were easily aroused. The civil list was one of those "country" issues which erupted sporadically during the eighteenth century, drawing upon popular resentment of courtiers and ministers, who lived in grandeur at public expense. Furthermore, an attack on "the influence of the crown" was an attractive alternative to the movement for parliamentary reform which the Rockinghams were determined to forestall. Finally, as George III recognized, the civil list was personal to the King and an important support of his independent political role. Reduction of the civil list would be seen as a personal rebuke to the monarch and a curtailment of the political resources of the ministry.[12]

While Burke announced his plan of reform in the House of Commons the Earl of Shelburne, heir of the mantle of Chatham, presented his own approach in the House of Lords. Shelburne was primarily concerned with waste and lack of control in the voting and management of parliamentary appropriations. He proposed reform of public offices: "to take into consideration what savings can be made consistent with the public dignity, justice, and gratitude, by an abolition of old or new created offices, or reversion of offices, the duties of which had either ceased, or shall on enquiry prove to be inadequate to the fees, or other emoluments arising therefrom." He launched his main attack on the military expenditure, especially the army extraordinaries. "If indeed," he exclaimed, "millions could be thus issued, and afterwards unaccounted for, he might say with justice, that the army extraordinaries was the minister's civil list reserve, and that it might answer him every purpose of secret service money." He proposed a committee of accounts, chosen from both houses of Parliament and comprised of men without place or pension, to examine "the public expenditure and the mode of accounting for the same."[13] With the speeches of Burke and Shelburne two major thrusts of the movement for economical reform had been presented. Burke, by attacking the civil list, aimed directly at the King himself, whose determination and patronage resources he identified as the political core of the North ministry. Shelburne left the King untouched; he launched his attack against the treasury and its management of pubic finance. Both were concerned with establishing more effective parliamentary control in areas of finance where it was weak or nonexistent: Burke the civil list; Shelburne the army extraordinaries. Both recognized that the key to success was to convince the independent members and the growing force of public opinion that financial reform would make the ministry more responsible to Parliament and Parliament more responsive to the country.

During the Christmas recess Burke busied himself preparing a series of bills embodying his proposals for economical reform. He acknowledged the complexity of the task he had undertaken and the administrative and legal problems which his proposal would entail, but his major goal was the reduction of political influence—the technical details he would leave to others. In a letter to Portland he was explicit on the need for the kind of professional advice not available in opposition:

> I have, in some sort of way, nearly got through two Bills; which will hold, what I proposed in the Sketch. They are very rough I confess, but they will serve for a dead colouring. . . . More masterly hands will add the finish and raise the lights.[14]

He was also well aware of the political difficulties involved in getting such legislation through Parliament. Although he recognized the importance of popular support, he questioned the goals and doubted the unity and steadiness of the county associations. He wrote to Richard Champion:

> First that it is not to be attempted if the minds of the people concerned are not perfectly ripe for it. If it does not come from them freely without much address or management, the want of a real concurrence in opinion may possibly be conceald; but the chief part of the delusion will be on ourselves—because we may be led to count upon a Strength, which may fail us when we have most reason to call for it.[15]

The sweeping plan which Burke presented to the House of Commons on 11 February 1780 included or suggested most of the objectives of the movement for economical reform.[16] Horace Walpole, no friend to Burke, wrote that the speech was "temperate, moderate, sprinkled with wit and humour" and so well received that "it was thought he could that day have carried any point he had proposed."[17] The core of the plan was reduction and reorganization of the civil list. Burke proposed abolishing offices which he claimed were used primarily for political purposes: the Colonial Secretary and Board of Trade (tacit admission that the empire was lost), a wide range of household offices, the Board of Works, and the Paymaster of the Pensions. He would preserve the great offices of the bedchamber, which brought the King into daily contact with the aristocracy, but he overreached himself with a proposal, almost universally deplored, to provide meals to the royal household by contract. The pension list was to be reduced to a fixed sum and all pensions paid publicly at the Exchequer; secret service was to be regulated and curtailed. A major goal was to make the Treasury responsible for all civil list expenditure by abolishing subordinate spending offices such as the Board of Green Cloth and Treasurer of the Chamber. To prevent accumulation of debt, which made a mockery of the principle of a fixed civil list, Burke proposed a strict budget ordered in classes: all payments would be made at the Exchequer in an invariable order, with the Lords of the Treasury paid last, if any money remained. Treasury responsibility for all civil list expenditure was the key to proper control: "A minister under whom expences can be made without his knowledge," Burke declared, "can never say what it is that he can spend, or what it is that he can save."[18]

Although Burke's civil list proposals received most of the attention in 1780, his plan of reform included other aspects of financial management, many of which became important later as the movement for economical reform developed. He recommended abolition of the subordinate jurisdictions of Wales, Cornwall, the duchy of Lancaster, and the county palatines of Lancaster and Chester on the grounds that they furnished "more matter of expense, more temptation to oppression, or more means and instruments of corrupt influence, than advantage to justice or political administration." He proposed selling the Crown lands and forests, thus removing from the Treasury the political influence which it exercised through fines and leases. Since the Mint and Ordnance were primarily engaged in manufacture, they should be abolished and their services performed by private business under contract. The patent offices in the Exchequer should be reformed (not abolished) to prevent inordinate profits while still providing refuges where "the weather-beaten vessels of the state ought to come into harbour." Balances of public money would be removed from the Paymaster of the Forces and Treasurer of the Navy. Delays in the Exchequer audit, which permitted balances to remain in private possession long after their holders had left office, should be eliminated. Burke added to the list "some thoughts, not yet fully ripened, relative to a reform in the customs and excise, as well as in some other branches of financial administration."[19] Only the eccentric Lord George Gordon dissented from Burke's request to bring in his bill, although Lord North argued that it would be more proper to obtain the consent of the King first.[20]

The debate on Burke's bill was conducted primarily on constitutional grounds and in a mood of high excitement. The North ministry opposed the bill as an unconstitutional infringement on the independence of monarchy and a weakening of its necessary political influence. The Rockinghamites argued that the independence of Parliament was at stake, threatened by the excessive influence of the Crown.[21] From the beginning North recognized the danger of trying to defeat Burke's bill frontally; the mood of the House and the nation was such that defeat of the ministry on the general principle of the bill was likely. Thus North did not oppose the bill on its first and second readings but adopted the tactic of deferring crucial decisions to the committee stage, at which time each of Burke's many clauses might be defeated separately. Opposition leaders, recognizing that delay would permit feelings to cool, pressed hard to move the bill along as rapidly as possible.[22] The first clause to be considered in committee was the clause to abolish the office of Colonial Secretary. Lord George Germain was not a popular figure in the House, and the results of the war, for which he held principal responsibility, had been disappointing. The ministry, having avoided a division on the general principle of the right of Parliament to regulate the civil list, now made use of the argument to influence waverers on specific clauses of Burke's bill. The opposition strenuously asserted the right of Parliament to regulate the civil list, and insisted that a third secretary of state had been needless when the empire was still intact and was obviously useless when the empire was dissolving. When the House divided at 2:45 A.M. the clause was defeated, 208–201.[23] George III was surprised and pleased with the outcome, considering "the disinclination that has in general existed against that Arrangement, and no small prejudice against the present Possessor."[24] Lord Fitzwilliam was probably expressing the general sentiments of the Rockingham group when he expressed deep discouragement. "Thus, my good Sir," he wrote to Chaloner, "you see nothing can be done in Parliament." He continued: "If the next Clause is thrown out, (relative to the Board of Trade) in my opinion the business is up, and the father should strangle his own child."[25]

The next clause, abolishing the Board of Trade, was clearly the point at which the ministry could give the final blow to Burke's bill. The House was again unusually full when it met on 13 March to consider the clause. William Eden came forward as the principal defender of the Board of Trade; Lord North and other principal ministerial speakers were silent. Eden's defense of the board fell flat, and his reference to their 2,300 volumes of reports left him wide open to Burke's sarcasm. Burke outdid himself in pouring ridicule upon the board. Despite its earlier value, Burke argued that it had become a collection of sinecures used primarily for parliamentary influence. In the course of the debates on America, he said, "not so much as a single scrap of paper had been laid by that board before parliament respecting the state, condition, or temper of the colonies." Noting the literary talents of some members of the board, among them Edward Gibbon and Soame Jenyns, he declared, "As an academy of Belles Lettres, he should hold them hallowed; as a board of trade he wished to abolish them." Referring to their 2,300 volumes of reports, Burke replied that he "revered literature, but he did not wish to be overwhelmed by it." When the House divided, the clause was passed by a margin of eight, 207–199.[26] Burke's bill had taken a new lease on life, but by the narrowest of margins.

The division on the Board of Trade proved to be a pyrrhic victory. The speaker, Sir Fletcher Norton, supported abolition of the board and his intervention undoubtedly carried weight with the independent members. But he supported the clause on grounds which did not augur well for the rest of Burke's bill. Returning to the constitutional question, he drew a distinction between that part of the civil list "appropriated to the special purposes of government, and that other part applicable to the expences or maintenance of the King's household." He supported those parts of Burke's bill which regulated the public parts of the civil list, but declared that "he could not think it proper to interfere in the arrangement or controul of the King's household or domestic expences."[27] The effects of Norton's doctrine were felt a week later (20 March), when the House went into committee on the clause which abolished the offices of the Treasurer of the Chamber and other subordinate paymasters in the royal household. Once again North and other principal ministerial speakers were silent, and this time independent members were more prominent in the debate. Sir Edward Dering and Sir John Wrottesley expressed the views of independent members when they objected to the clause "not, they said, from any regard to the office, but from a strong disapprobation of interfering with the management of any part of the King's household."[28] Burke insisted that the clause was intended to prevent fraud and corrupt political influence, and not to affect the personal comfort of the monarch, but his arguments were in vain. The clause was defeated, 211–158, a crushing blow, and Burke declared that he abandoned his bill.[29] He wrote to Joseph Harford: "by refusing to destroy the subordinate Treasuries, or to enter into the Household the House has in my opinion rejected the whole plan."[30]

The resistance of independent gentlemen to interference with the royal household was firm and thus the remaining divisions on Burke's bill were anti-climactic. On 28 April the Commons rejected, 210–162, the clause which abolished the offices of the Great Wardrobe, Removing Wardrobe, Robes, Jewel Office, and most of the housekeepers of palaces and houses.[31] The clause to abolish the Board of Works was defeated next, 203–118.[32] On 18 May the remaining clauses were rejected, and Burke declared that he would no longer divide the House on his bill.[33] Despite defeat of the bill, the House of Commons had demonstrated strong interest in the management of the civil list, and was reluctant to let the subject drop. Thomas Gilbert was more in harmony with the independent members when he declared that the House should not interfere with the management of the civil list, but suggested an address to the King urging that he "make the necessary reformations in all offices within his household, by his own authority."[34] Such a proposal might bring improved management of the civil list, but it could not be expected to produce the political results intended by Burke. "The influence of the crown," to the extent that it was derived from the civil list, remained intact.

Throughout the debates the Shelburne group had given Burke lukewarm support, proposing instead a committee of accounts to examine military expenditure.[35] With the defeat of Burke's bill, however, they took up the mantle of leadership, supported by Wyvill and the county movement.[36] They won a stunning victory on the night of 6 April when Dunning's motion "that the influence of the crown has increased, is increasing, and ought to be diminished" was passed by a full House of Commons, 233–215, after which the House approved by voice vote a resolution affirming the right of Parliament to regulate the civil list.[37] Four days later Dunning offered an alternative to the rejected household clauses of Burke's bill. Instead of abolishing offices, he proposed a favorite measure of eighteenth-century oppositions, a place bill, which would exclude from the House of Commons holders of the principal household offices. The resolution was passed in another close division, 215–213.[38] Another "popular" measure was Clerke's bill to exclude from the House of Commons holders of government contracts, a favorite measure of independent members who, as Burke remarked, "are more disposed to the censure of abuses among Trading people than of those among any other description of Men."[39] A new addition to the panoply of economical reform was Crewe's bill disqualifying revenue officers from voting in elections, which was defeated in another full House, 224–195.[40] On 24 April Dunning returned to the attack with what Sir George Savile called "the most uncourtly opposition question we have had this year," proposing that the Crown not dissolve Parliament until steps had been taken "to diminish the influence of the crown, and to correct other evils complained of in the petitions of the people." The resulting division was the largest of the session, Dunning's motion being defeated, 254–206.[41] Thus ended the exciting session of 1780, as the country members began returning home, leaving the North ministry battered but in control of the field.

Although public pressure applied by Wyvill and the county associations had been an important factor, throughout the session the relationship between Rockingham and the county movement had been a strained one. Rockingham opposed the growing interest of the petitioners in parliamentary reform, while Wyvill was consistently suspicious of party politicians.[42] In his post-mortem comments Rockingham blamed the supporters of parliamentary reform for destroying the unity which had developed behind economical reform.[43] Burke, more realistically, recognized the difficulty in trying to carry through an extensive reform "in defiance of all the official power of the Kingdom, assisted with very much of the personal Credit, family influence, and property, which are usually connected with the power of government."[44] He decided that substantial reform could be achieved only with the support of "the *executive* power of the Kingdom," a conclusion which required the overthrow of the North ministry.[45] In Burke's view, only massive public support could have overcome such obstacles. On 24 May he wrote to Richard Champion: "The people only remain and you know that I never expected much from the people."[46]

The reform proposals of Burke and Shelburne came from men in opposition. It was Lord North who added to the movement for economical reform the missing ingredient: professional expertise. During the debates on economical reform North conceded the justice of complaints about excessive emoluments of office, balances of public money held by spending officers, and the inadequate system of audit.[47] He charged that Burke's bill "neglected the ground which . . . he thought the most essential of all."[48] His approach to economical reform was the appointment of a commission of accounts which would be a nonpartisan body comprised of "respectable, intelligent, and independent gentlemen, who were members of neither house of parliament." Their purpose was to prepare and present to parliament a clear picture of the state of the finances, recommend improvements in the keeping of accounts, and take steps that "the various balances in hand be immediately brought forward, and applied to the service of the ensuing year."[49] Burke was outraged, seeing North's commission as a red herring to divert support from his own bill and an infringement on the rights of the House of Commons in finance.[50] Shelburne's group denounced it as a travesty of the traditional parliamentary commission of accounts and a distortion of their original idea.[51] North's proposal was accepted and the commission was established. Although the parliamentary basis of the commission was maintained by naming the commissioners in the bill, the persons proposed by North were men with whom the Treasury could work comfortably.[52] With the establishment of the commission of accounts, North began to reverse the tide which was flowing so strongly against him. He created the instrument which would put the Treasury in control of economical reform, and he turned economical reform in the direction which was least threatening politically and most useful to a hard-pressed minister of finance.

The political reverberations of Burke's attack on the civil list continued long after his defeat in 1780. In the summer of 1780 Lord North proposed a coalition with Rockingham, but the Marquis stood firm on his commitment to "Part if not the whole of Mr. Burke's Bill."[53] In a letter to the Duke of Richmond, Rockingham spelled out his essential conditions: peace with America, the revenue officers bill, the contractors bill, and "Great Parts of Mr. Burke's Bill," including abolition of the Colonial Secretary and Board of Trade, reforming the sinecures of the Exchequer, restricting balances of public money held by the Paymaster of the Forces and Treasurer of the Navy, and consideration of bills to reform the governments of Wales, Cornwall, and the duchy and county palatine of Lancaster. Notably absent were Burke's proposals for reform of the royal household, pensions, and secret service. George III's reaction, Rockingham reported, was to complain that "he had 900,000 l. pr annum given by way of Civil List & that these Regulations seemed to point at taking part back."[54] Since the opposition had "run so wild," the King insisted to North that they abandon their tenets, although he noted that Burke would be a valuable acquisition.[55] The negotiation confirmed the breach between Rockingham and Shelburne, the latter abandoning his lukewarm support of Burke's bill.[56] In the election of 1780 Burke lost his seat at Bristol and was returned to Parliament for one of Rockingham's boroughs, although his leadership in economical reform was not a factor in his defeat. He introduced his bill again in 1781, but the civil list had lost its effectiveness as an opposition issue and the country gentlemen made clear their unwillingness to support reform of the royal household.[57] Wyvill turned his back on Burke's *"palliative plan"* and in October 1781, the Yorkshire Association declared that economical reform was "inadequate."[58] As the North ministry tottered to its fall, Burke's plan of reform had become a liability to himself and his party.

Early in 1782 the North ministry lost its parliamentary support as a result of failure in the American War. As the Rockingham party faced the possibility of taking office, Burke's bill was a major obstacle, both in the Closet and the House of Commons. Rockingham wrote in January 1782: "if the Civil List &c. should be moved in Parlt—we shall again have great difficulties with many of our friends."[59] George III refused to deal directly with Rockingham, conducting negotiations through Shelburne, to whom he described Burke's bill as "this very unpleasant business" and "very personal subject," referring to some clauses as "more revolting than others."[60] Burke urged Rockingham to hold fast, insisting that the key point was "the *Principle* of oeconomy by the appropriation of the Civil List."[61] Meanwhile in Parliament followers of North reminded members of Burke's plan for civil list reform, which they presented as an unconstitutional infringement on the independence of the monarch and a violation of the undoubted right of any gentleman to regulate the affairs of his family and household.[62] Rockingham refused to form a government until the King had guaranteed that he would not oppose American independence and had agreed to the main points in the Rockinghamite attack on "the influence of the crown," including "Mr. Burke's Regulation of the Civil List."[63] Negotiations hung fire until North settled the matter on 20 March by announcing his resignation. George III had to accept a ministry headed by Lord Rockingham, but he showed his disapproval by conducting negotiations through Shelburne, who thus claimed joint leadership. Burke took office as Paymaster of the Forces. Since American independence was a foregone conclusion and other aspects of the Rockingham program were not objectionable to the King, it is evident that the stumbling block was Burke's bill. Rockingham tried to pacify the outraged monarch by assuring him that nothing would be retrenched which contributed to his personal dignity or the well-being of his family and domestic arrangements, but without success.[64]

Unlike many eighteenth-century oppositions, the Rockingham group seriously attempted to implement proposals made out of office. In addition to civil list reform, notes and drafts in Rockingham's papers include other ideas found in Burke's speech of 1780: reform of the vestigial governments of Wales, Cornwall, and the duchy of Lancaster; sale of Crown lands and forests; reform of patent offices in the Exchequer, including fixed salaries; elimination of balances held by the Paymaster of the Forces and Treasurer of the Navy; parliamentary regulation of the method of accounting in the Exchequer; abolition of the principal offices in the Mint and regulation of the Mint "for the Cheap & proper execution of the Work, and the security of the Public."[65] It was an ambitious program involving complex matters of detail, but the Rockinghams were not concerned with administrative details. They knew the King was hostile, the cabinet divided, and their parliamentary support likely to disappear once peace was made. The changes they desired to make were those which would make future politics more difficult for the Crown and easier for the opposition. Charles James Fox expressed a characteristic view when he wrote to his friend Fitzpatrick that he did not expect the ministry would last long, but that the principal goal should be to "stay in long enough to have given a good stout blow to the Crown."[66] The Rockinghams were determined to strike while the iron was hot and make changes which could not be easily undone. Early in the ministry Burke wrote Rockingham to beware of proposals

> to keep the reform wholly out of Parliament upon a Pretence that it may be done by the Crown. If it could it ought not. The house of Commons will give it both grace and permanence; and the Crown, by a Message, may make it, as effectually, its own free act, as if it were done out of Parliament; and in my opinion with infinitely more dignity. . . . If we let slip *Parliament* we let slip *all*. This is our only security against Cabal and intrigue; and if that Cabal and intrigue should force us out, you have spread the Carpet of a fair reputation to receive you in your fall.[67]

Shelburne, who had the ear of the King, followed his own course. George III accepted Sir Fletcher Norton's distinction between the public offices of the civil list, which Parliament would be permitted to reform or abolish, and those aspects of the civil list which were his personal concern, such as the household offices. The latter, he insisted, should be reformed by "Interior Regulations." Shelburne advised the King to mix as little as possible "in the *Publick Regulations* proposed, which go to the Reduction of Ministerial Influence in the two Houses, and may go their course, independent of these Interior arrangements."[68] George III followed this course, using tactics at which he excelled: delay and sowing dissension. He raised questions about the details of the household and the provision to be made for those whose offices were retrenched.[69] Shelburne and Thurlow disrupted cabinet meetings by haggling over every point.[70] On 28 April the King gave Rockingham his approval, accompanied by extensive comments.[71] In another note written later the same day the King confided to Shelburne his fear that something more was intended: "I owne I suspect," he wrote, "on the whole of the alteration of the Civil List there is still some secret that is not yet disclosed. I hope this is a groundless idea, but it constantly haunts me."[72] What was the King's unspoken fear? Probably he feared a reduction of the privy purse, from which he annually saved £12,000 for his election fund. Earlier he had written to Lord North: "I think it is most likely that on the reduction of the expences of the Civil List, I shall be obliged to see my Privy Purse diminished the £12,000 per annum."[73] George III's anxiety for the privy purse was groundless. No evidence has come to light that the Rockinghams knew or even suspected that the privy purse had been used for political purposes.[74]

The King's message announcing a plan of civil list reform was presented to both houses on 15 April. Burke praised the King effusively, calling it "the best of messages to the best of people from the best of kings." Shelburne insisted that the message came from the King, not the ministers, at the same time making it clear that it was not the kind of reform he would have proposed.[75] George III's attempt to maintain some control of Burke's reform was weakened by the characteristic problem of the civil list—accumulation of debt.[76] Although the civil list debts had been paid as recently as 1777, and the civil list increased by an additional £100,000 per annum, the Rockingham ministry found the civil list almost £300,000 in arrears. Reduction of civil list expenditure was now linked with payment of civil list debt. On 2 May the outlines of Burke's plan of reform were presented to the House of Commons, along with an account of the civil list debt. Lord John Cavendish, Chancellor of the Exchequer, stated that the debt could be paid without additional propriation from Parliament by using the savings to be made by Burke's reforms. Later in the session Cavendish proposed issuance of £300,000 in Exchequer bills, to be paid off at a rate of approximately £72,000 per year out of the civil list itself.[77] Constitutional doctrines or personal feelings notwithstanding, an influential argument in favor of Burke's bill was the fiscal predicament of the state.

In addition to preparing his civil list bill Burke was given responsibility for reform of the royal household. He was overwhelmed with accounts of household establishments and complaints of household officers, despite his plaintive protest that he did not wish to become involved in "an establishment of *detail*."[78] His problems were further complicated by quarrels concerning the appointment of a new Lord Steward. Rockingham was urged to appoint Lord Carlisle as an overture to the followers of North and a demonstration of Treasury control of the office. Shelburne, to display his coequal power, proposed the Duke of Marlborough. George III was determined to preserve his right to decide household appointments while welcoming the opportunity to set his two chief ministers by the ears.[79] Burke pleaded with Rockingham that the office not be given as "a mere *peace offering;* but will strengthen the *Cause* by it." He urged Rockingham to reserve the right to reform that department: "Otherwise patronage will step in between reformation and abuse."[80] For political reasons Rockingham appointed Carlisle, who described Burke's bill as "a mass of nonsense and absurdity" and a violation of "common sense and justice."[81] Burke found that the civil list was a political tarbaby which complicated relations with the King, created opportunities for Shelburne to intrigue in the Closet, reduced the ability of the ministry to reward its followers, made him unpopular with his own party, and upset the independent members. He was hoist with his own petard.

Burke's civil list bill was ready for presentation to Parliament early in June. George III, who had consulted with Shelburne, Dunning, and Thurlow about the bill, grumbled that it was "slovenly constructed," but he decided it was best "to let it go without much discussion which might render the sting worse."[82] Passage by the Commons was a foregone conclusion, and use of the savings to pay civil list debt made it a money bill not subject to amendment in the Lords. In presenting the bill Burke explained the omissions from his more extensive bill of 1780. Local resistance had led him to abandon his proposals to abolish the subordinate jurisdictions of Wales, Cornwall, Lancaster, and Chester, and reform of the pay office would come in a separate bill. Reform of the Mint had foundered, he admitted, and the Ordnance he felt could be left to the new master-general, the Duke of Richmond. The unpopular provision to supply the royal household by contract had been dropped. Several household offices formerly intended to be abolished were spared. Debate in the Commons was desultory and concerned mainly with compensation to individuals affected.[83]

The debate in the Lords was more to the point. Opponents of the bill expressed resentment that it came to them as a money bill and generally damned it as hasty and ill considered. Lord Stormont, in terms similar to those which Burke would later use against the leaders of revolutionary France, stated that the bill showed "the distinction between real knowledge, and the mere conjectures of a speculative reformer." Thurlow was severe on the bill, but following the line laid down by George III he agreed to it because it would "preserve his Majesty's Civil List undiminished." Shelburne, as usual, showed his disdain for the bill as a measure of economical reform: "he hoped to introduce a general system of oeconomy, not only in the offices mentioned in the Bill, but into every office whatever." Until the time for general reform arrived, he conceded "ministers were bound to proceed with lesser systems, and smaller plans of regulation and oeconomy, like the present Bill." Richmond was the principal defender of the bill, but even he admitted that it was "the first experiment" and could be made "more perfect and more extensive" in the future.[84] Burke, however, had achieved his purpose. The independent civil list, hitherto sacrosanct, had been brought under parliamentary control. At the same time Clerke's contractors bill and Crewe's revenue officers bill were passed with slight opposition.[85] With this legislation there was general agreement that the attack on "the influence of the crown" had gone far enough. Thereafter economical reform took on a new character: an emphasis upon economy and efficiency, carried out by responsible ministers and using the information and expertise provided by professional administrators.[86]

While carrying through measures to reduce "the influence of the crown," the Rockingham ministry was forced to come to grips with the vast problems of finance and administration resulting from the war. Burke's original plan of reform included proposals concerning excessive emoluments of office, balances of public money in private possession, and the inefficiency of the Exchequer audit, but these problems became the principal concern of the commissioners of accounts established by Lord North in 1780. The early reports of the commissioners dealt with the balances held by collectors of taxes, the Treasurer of the Navy, and the Paymaster of the Forces.[87] Shortly before North resigned, the commissioners revealed excessive incomes from fees in the Exchequer and the offices of the Paymaster and Treasurer, recommending that they be replaced by fixed salaries and that some Exchequer sinecures be abolished.[88] Lord John Cavendish took the lead in committing the Rockingham ministry to economical reform based on the reports of the commissioners. On 18 June Cavendish presented a string of resolutions which embraced most of the recommendations of their reports. These included improved collection of the land tax (1st Rep.), consolidation of minor revenue boards (2nd Rep.), regulation of balances in possession of the Paymaster of the Forces (4th, 5th Reps.), establishment of salaries rather than fees for employees in the pay office (6th Rep.), similar regulations in the office of the Treasurer of the Navy (3rd, 5th Reps.), and regulation of the profits of the great patent offices of the Exchequer after the deaths of the present holders or reversions (6th Rep.).[89] The Cavendish resolutions gave the Rockinghams a commitment to economical reform of a different kind, and gave a new direction to Burke's efforts in this respect.

As the movement for economical reform developed, the office of Paymaster of the Forces was identified as a major problem. When Burke was appointed paymaster he reported with satisfaction to William Burke: "The office to be reformed, according to the Bill."[90] He plunged into the task with his characteristic energy, and he now had access to information and clerical assistance not available in opposition. Furthermore, the reports of the commissioners provided him with specific proposals and a broad base of parliamentary support. When Lord John Cavendish presented his string of resolutions, Burke stated that he intended to bring in a bill to reform his office "but it was impossible to do everything at once." With the wisdom gained from three months in office he added: "time was necessary to gather information: he found that theory and practice were two things."[91] Nevertheless he quickly cobbled together a stopgap bill which was presented on 26 June and "read twice for the greater dispatch."[92] The bill was rushed through both Houses as the session drew to a close. The act reformed the paymaster's office along the lines recommended by the commissioners by removing balances from the personal possession of the paymaster and placing them in the Bank of England. The act also directed that fees taken in the office be paid into a fee fund from which fixed salaries would be paid to the paymaster and his clerks. The 5th report of the commissioners had noted the padding of regimental muster rolls and the lack of order in computing and paying the wages of the troops. The act tried to prevent this practice by ordering the Secretary at War to prepare pay lists of the actual strength of each regiment, but since no effective system of mustering was required, this part of the act was ineffectual.[93]

On 1 July the Rockingham ministry ended with the death of the Marquis. The King asked Shelburne to form a new ministry. Although Rockingham and his followers did not expect to remain in office more than a few months, they assumed their tenure would be terminated by the King or by political intrigues involving Shelburne and North. That the ministry would be ended by Rockingham's death does not seem to have been thought of until a few days before the event. The death of Rockingham and the appointment of Shelburne as principal minister were political and personal blows to Burke of major proportions. Burke's antagonism toward Shelburne was of long standing, and Shelburne had not concealed his distaste for Burke's reform of the civil list. Led by Charles James Fox, the core of the Rockingham group, including Burke, resigned with bitter recriminations. A flurry of political activity followed, involving Shelburne, Fox, North, and their respective supporters.[94] In addition to the great problems of peace and imperial reorganization, Shelburne's difficulties were increased by his commitment to parliamentary reform and extensive projects of economical reform. On the other hand, Burke's civil list act complicated relations between Fox and North. William Eden wrote: "Burke's foolish bill has made it a very difficult task for any set of men either to form or maintain an Administration."[95] Burke in turn was convinced that the main concern of North's party was "their hope of destroying this ministry first, and the Establishment bill next; and so securing to themselves the return of the old system of emoluments. The Bill is their grand enemy."[96]

Despite political uncertainties, the Shelburne ministry immediately got busy with plans for financial and administrative reform. William Pitt, who held his first office as Chancellor of the Exchequer, wrote to his mother in September: "We are labouring at all sorts of official reform, for which there is a very ample field, and in which I believe we shall have some success."[97] When Parliament met in December Shelburne announced an extensive program of reform, including fees and emoluments of office, merit system in appointments, investigation of Crown lands and forests, better control of the expenditure of the army, steps to reform the Mint, improvements in estimates and accounts, and actions to deal with the funded and unfunded debt, including a plan for debt reduction.[98] In February 1783, the coalition of Fox and North led Shelburne to resign, leaving his ambitious plans in doubt. William Pitt, however, held office for another month and put the administration on record by introducing legislation for reform of customs administration and public offices.

Burke's reactions to Shelburne's proposals were inveterate opposition. He found in Shelburne a rationalizing principle of efficiency for its own sake which he declared was inhumane in its effects and led to an undesirable concentration of power in the Treasury. The custom house bill was the first to come forward, which Burke opposed on the grounds that it would strengthen "the influence of the crown" by removing the patent places which made customs officers independent. Opposition from merchants told against the bill, and with the session far advanced Pitt decided to drop it.[99] The public offices bill, introduced late in the session, came with the blessing of the commissioners of accounts, whose popularity assured it a respectful hearing. It included such features as fixed salaries paid from fee funds, performance in person of all duties of office, restrictions on personal use of stationery and other office supplies, and a new structure of duties and salaries to be prepared by the commissioners. By this time economical reform had gained such momentum that Pitt's bill passed the House of Commons, although it was defeated in the Lords.[100] Burke outdid himself rhetorically, expressing his contempt for inquiries into stationery and whipcord. Shelburne's reform, he said, was "as mean and inhuman, as his was public and generous. He [Burke] had aimed only at the destruction of parliamentary influence, and of sinecures for parliamentary men, but they had aimed their blows at poor inferior officers of twenty, thirty, forty pounds a year." In terms suggestive of a political cartoon, he compared Pitt to "a large serpent, gliding along in the dirt and mire of reform, with a number of little diminutive officers in his belly."[101]

Other aggravations arose. Shelburne's implementation of Burke's civil list act was such as to curry favor with the King, outrage those who lost offices, and cast most of the odium on Burke. Thomas Gilbert was appointed to undertake a thorough review of the royal household and make recommendations to be carried out by the Treasury.[102] Shelburne was quite willing to use powers granted by the act to eliminate waste, especially since the civil list was still accumulating debt, but he found that the importunities of victims and their patrons were incessant. He wrote to Grafton, one of the complainers:

> But it is impossible to describe to you how provokingly my time is taken up with the nonsense of Mr. Burke's bill. It was both framed and carried through, without the least regard to *facts:* and penned so that every line required the opinion of the Attorney-General.[103]

Although Burke had left the pay office the duties of paymaster followed him, for his paymaster act did not take effect until 1 January 1783. When Shelburne's treasury board routinely asked for a statement of his balance before issuing more funds, Burke reacted violently: the reformer of the office needed no lessons on how to conduct it! The Treasury replied that no offense was intended, and thereafter Burke complied.[104] His paymaster act created other problems, for questions arose concerning the provisions regarding army pay. Burke began work on revision of the statute, but his testy nature made it difficult for him to work with Shelburne's paymaster, Isaac Barré.

In the meantime, the coalition of Fox and North which had driven Shelburne from office took office under the Duke of Portland.[105] A major obstacle to formation of the coalition was economical reform, especially Burke's civil list act, which was deeply resented by many followers of North. Richard Rigby complained that "if the hon. gentleman's act was to continue in force, in two or three years it would be impossible to carry on the business of government in that House."[106] Opponents of the coalition used the same argument: Thomas Pitt advised the King to accept the coalition ministry on the assumption that they would not have enough patronage to satisfy their followers and would offend the public with "projects of reform *defeated* and other cruel and almost impracticable reforms."[107] Burke admitted that his reduction of the civil list made it difficult to satisfy the claims of "a party of the most numerous, and some of the most weighty people in the Kingdom."[108] Burke's civil list act made him an unpopular figure with his own party and its new allies, and Fox agreed with North that economical reform would go no further than commitments already made.[109]

The Fox-North coalition ministry inherited an agenda of economical reform shaped by three years of parliamentary debate, the reports of the commissioners of accounts, and the commitments of previous ministries. The achievements of the ministry in its brief life were substantial. Lord John Cavendish, who had returned to the Exchequer, prepared legislation for exchequer reform based on his resolutions of 1782. Cavendish's exchequer act set fixed salaries for the sinecure offices on the Exchequer, to take effect after the deaths of the incumbents; abolished the use of wooden tallies after the deaths of the two chamberlains; and put fees into a fee fund, from which salaries were paid, with part of the surplus going to the civil list.[110] Vigorous efforts were make to bring in balances of public money and expedite the audit of public accounts, including support for a resolution offered by Pitt advocating "such measures as may, on full deliberation, appear to be proper, in order to prevent the like delays for the future."[111] The treasury board energetically pursued reform of public offices "with a View to the Establishment of a rational Oeconomy through the whole": replacement of fees by salaries; better control of stationery, coals, candles, and other office expenses; and improvement of collection of stamp duties, swollen by the new receipt tax.[112] Pitt's plan for reform of customs offices was revived.[113] Improvement of the revenue through reduction of smuggling was a major goal, resulting in the establishment of a committee led by William Eden.[114] Charles James Fox urged establishment of a sinking fund for "constant and sensible" debt reduction.[115] The Shelburne program had been taken over, virtually in full, and the groundwork had been laid for the reforms of Pitt.

Burke's major project during the coalition ministry was revision and expansion of his paymaster act of the previous year. The commissioners of accounts had since published two extensive reports on the deficiencies of army administration, which went far beyond the modest goals of Burke's act of 1782.[116] The Shelburne ministry took some abortive steps toward further reform and Charles Jenkinson, Secretary at War under North, continued to be informed of the problems in his former office, but it was left to Burke to complete the task which he had begun a year earlier.[117] Burke worked with the commissioners of accounts and various army officials in preparing his bill, which was introduced while the Shelburne ministry was still in office.[118] After the coalition ministry was formed, Burke's bill made its way through Parliament without difficulty. The reports of the commissioners had shown that the ordinary of the army (primarily pay) was corrupt and inordinately complex, and that the extraordinaries were virtually without control or limit. The system of account and audit was useless.[119] Burke's second paymaster act strengthened the reform of the office which had been made in his first act, replacing the clumsy fee fund with fixed salaries paid from army appropriations. The main thrust of the new act was to reform the system of army musters and pay, giving the Secretary at War broad authority, for which he was responsible to Parliament. The extraordinaries of the army remained the responsibility of the Treasury.[120] The act was the basis of army administration for the next half century.

In the meantime Burke was confronted with the problem of Powell and Bembridge, two pay office officials who had been dismissed under Shelburne for irregularities in the account of Lord Holland, then awaiting audit. Burke, who had depended greatly upon the two men during his first stint at the pay office, was appalled at the human consequences resulting from the rigid application of reform principles which he had put on the statute book. He restored them to their posts, stating that no malfeasance had been proven and insisting that "he had so regulated the pay-office, that there was no danger of the public money being embezzled by these gentlemen or himself."[121] When Burke's decision was criticized in the Commons he was defended by Fox, younger son of Lord Holland, who insisted that, at worst, Burke's action must be attributed to "mistaken humanity, and a desire not to think persons guilty before they really were found so." Two days later Burke narrowly escaped censure by the House for reinstating the two men, and he agreed to accept their resignations.[122] Burke's chagrin was so great he seriously considered retiring from politics, but he was dissuaded by Samuel Johnson.[123] Powell committed suicide and Bembridge was tried and found guilty. Burke's generosity had brought only grief and he concluded ruefully: "Benevolence and friendship require more guards and caution than Malice and injury."[124] A year later Bembridge, a broken man, asked Burke for financial assistance. Burke responded angrily:

> I scarcely remember a troublesome affair in my life which has not arisen from a single cause. That is the active part I have taken in other peoples concerns, where no advantage could possibly arise to myself, but where the business has subjected me to obloquy and misrepresentation.[125]

Much to his dismay Burke found that he could not avoid the obligations which fell upon him as the reformer of the civil list. He must have regretted that he had ever gotten involved in that Sisyphean task! He received the new household establishment prepared under Shelburne by Thomas Gilbert and was immediately informed by Whitshed Keene, Secretary to the Lord Chamberlain, that it was "incompatible with the service to be performed in that office."[126] For the next six months Burke was pestered with questions and problems arising from Gilbert's reforms.[127] Furthermore, Burke's civil list act had not produced the savings expected, and the coalition ministry, adhering to the requirement of the act, faced the embarrassment of asking the House of Commons to pay another installment of civil list debt.[128] When the coalition proposed a generous allowance for Fox's friend, the Prince of Wales, who came of age in 1783, they encountered not only the adamant resistance of the King but cries of dismay in Parliament when they hinted that an increase of the civil list might be required.[129] In August Lord Ashburton, chancellor of the duchy of Lancaster died, which brought renewed discussion of Burke's plan to abolish the duchy, an idea quickly quashed by Portland and Fox, who named Lord Derby for the post.[130] Whatever political assets Burke might have gained in 1780 by his attack on the civil list had long since been dissipated or converted into liabilities.

George III's dismissal of the coalition ministry in December 1783 brought Burke's role in economical reform to a close. Young William Pitt inherited the agenda of reform created in the previous four years of investigation and debate. Burke turned his intelligence and industry to other interests, especially India. From his experience as a reformer, Burke learned lessons which strengthened his conservative instincts. In 1780 he stood forth with an extensive but ill-digested plan of reform directed at broad constitutional and political goals; by

1783 he realized the importance of limited objectives. In 1780 he was a private member; in 1783 he knew the importance of an official position and expert assistance in effecting substantial reform. In 1780 he proposed wholesale abolition of offices; by 1783 he had seen the political and human problems which such steps created. His plan of 1780 was intensely partisan; by 1783 economical reform had developed a momentum and consensus of its own, within which Burke was content to act. His original plan of reform was based on a constitutional theory; his final effort was a matter of practical efficiency. Theory and practice, he stated wryly in 1783, were two different things: "The truth of this observation he had felt in the Payoffice."[131] Despite his frustrations and disappointments, Burke was proud of the role he had played in those three strenuous years when he was actively engaged in the movement for economical reform. In 1790 he stated:

> That he was no enemy to reformation. Almost every business in which he was much concerned, from the first day he sat in that House to this hour, was a business of reformation; and when he had not been employed in correcting, he had been employed in resisting abuses. Some traces of this spirit in him now stand on their statute book.[132]

By that time he was assuming a new political role. As the spokesman for conservatism in Britain and Europe, Burke drew important lessons from those years of intense activity when he held the responsibilities of office and was identified as a reformer. In his *Reflections on the Revolution in France* (1790) he identified reform with conservative principles: "A state without the means of some change," he wrote, "is without the means of its conservation."[133] He noted the qualities needed in a reformer: "a vigorous mind, steady, perserving attention, various powers of comparison and combination, and the resources of an understanding fruitful in expedients." He also recognized the value of discussion, debate, and expert advice: "I have never yet seen any plan which has not been mended by the observations of those who were much inferior in understanding to the person who took the lead in the business."[134] In his *Letter to a Noble Lord* (1796) Burke insisted that he was a reformer, not an innovator: parliamentary reform changed the substance of the constitution; economical reform removed abuses. "It was not then my love," he asserted, "but my hatred, to innovation, that produced my plan of reform."[135] His civil list act he defended as a constructive approach to a serious problem. His reform of the pay office, Burke added, "cost me, with every assistance which my then situation gave me, pains incredible." What he did, he said, was in response to serious grievances and popular unrest which had produced dangerous proposals for constitutional innovation. "I had a people to gratify," Burke said, "but not to inflame or mislead. I do not claim the credit for what I did, as for what I prevented from being done."[136]

Looking back a decade or more, Burke undoubtedly distorted the motivations which led him to propose his plan of economical reform in December 1779. His views in the 1790s were closer to those which he held when he left office in December 1783. In 1779 his conservatism was typical of mid-eighteenth century Englishmen; he justified his plan of reform in that its purpose was to preserve the constitution. Four years later he saw pitfalls in the best-intentioned reform. He had become wary of "enlightened" nobles like Shelburne and well-meaning meddlers like Wyvill. He had experienced in an intensely personal way the frustrating inertia of established institutions, the unsteadiness of political friends, the vindictiveness of political enemies, the cumulative effect of petty personal interests when threatened by broad structural change, the fickleness of popular favor, and the ingratitude of electors like those of Bristol. He had seen appeals to "the people" explode in the Gordon riots. The Burke of the *Reflections* was waiting in the wings.

NOTES

I wish to acknowledge my debt to the Earl Fitzwilliam and the Wentworth-Woodhouse Estate for use of the Rockingham and Burke papers in the Sheffield City Library. The Newberry Library and the William L. Clements Library supported my research with summer fellowships. Special thanks are due to Frank O'Gorman for his comments and suggestions.

1 Frank O'Gorman, *Edmund Burke: His Political Philosophy* (1973), mentions economical reform in various contexts. Burke's politics can best be followed in O'Gorman's *The Rise of Party in England: The Rockingham Whigs, 1760–82* (1975). J. E. D. Binney, *British Public Finance and Administration, 1774–92*, overwhelms the reader with detail and his attitude toward Burke is so negative that his judgments must be viewed with caution.
2 *The Works of the Right Honourable Edmund Burke*, 8 vols. (1871), 1:313, 359–65. Hereafter cited as *Works*.
3 Ibid., p. 368.
4 *Observations on a Late Publication, intituled "The Present State of the Nation,"* ibid., p. 257.

5 *Speech on a Motion . . . for Explaining the Powers of Jurors in Prosecutions for Libels,* ibid., 6:164.

6 *The Correspondence of Edmund Burke,* 10 vols. (1958–78), 3:192.

7 Ibid., 4:158, 163. As early as July, Burke suggested to Rockingham the need for financial reform, noting especially "the seats of men interested in abuses with regard to publick Money and publick contracts" and "some vigorous and effectual plan of economy, in almost every department." Rockingham Papers, R155-2, Sheffield City Library.

8 Rev. Christopher Wyvill, comp., *Political Papers, Chiefly Respecting the Attempt of the County of York . . . to Effect a Reformation of Parliament,* 6 vols. (1794–1802), 3:115–17.

9 Ian R. Christie, *Wilkes, Wyvill and Reform: The Parliamentary Reform Movement in British Politics, 1760–1785* (1962), ch. 3. See also Herbert Butterfield, *George III, Lord North, and the People, 1779–1780* (1949).

10 Speeches on 7 December 1779 by Rockingham and Richmond. *The Parliamentary History of England,* 36 vols. (1806–20), 20:1255–67. Rockingham wrote on 12 December that the civil list had united all elements of the opposition; "I do assure you," he stated to Stephen Crofts, "I never saw so *good a Day* in ye House of Lords since I sat there." Rockingham Papers, R1-1869.

11 *Parliamentary History,* 20:1293–1305. Ian Christie, "Economical Reform and 'The Influence of the Crown,' 1780," in *Myth and Reality* (1970), pp. 296–310.

12 For general background see E. A. Reitan, "The Civil List in Eighteenth-Century British Politics: Parliamentary Supremacy versus the Independence of the Crown," *Historical Journal* 9 (1966): 318–37.

13 *Parliamentary History,* 20:1285–93. See John Norris, *Shelburne and Reform* (1966), ch. 6.

14 *Burke Correspondence,* 4:198. Notes and drafts in the Burke Papers, no. 14 a,b. Fitzwilliam MSS., Sheffield City Library.

15 *Burke Correspondence,* 4:199.

16 *Works,* 2:55–126.

17 *The Last Journals of Horace Walpole during the Reign of George III, from 1771–1783,* ed. A. Francis Stewart, 2 vols. (1910), 2:367. Burke's speech aroused such public interest that many spectators failed to get into the gallery, among them the reporter, William Woodfall. A. Aspinall, "The Reporting and Publishing of the House of Commons Debates, 1771–1834," in *Essays Presented to Sir Lewis Namier,* ed. Richard Pares and A. J. P. Taylor (1956), p. 234.

18 *Works,* 2:70. See Henry Roseveare, *The Treasury, 1660–1870: The Foundations of Control* (1973), pp. 62–63.

19 *Works,* 2:69–81, 122.

20 *Parliamentary History,* 21:72–73. Text of bill, ibid., pp. 111–35. On 14 February Burke requested leave to introduce bills for sale of the Crown lands and forests and reform of the governments of Wales, Chester, and the duchy and county palatine of Lancaster. A bill for the duchy of Cornwall

was withdrawn by Burke out of respect for the rights of Prince of Wales. Ibid., pp. 73–74. Royal consent (not approval) was given to bringing in these bills. *Journals of the House of Commons*, 37:598.

21 The constitutional arguments are summarized in Reitan, "Civil List," pp. 330–34.

22 *Parliamentary History*, 21:135–37.

23 Ibid., pp. 193–217.

24 *The Correspondence of King George the Third*, ed. Sir John Fortescue, 6 vols. (1927–28), 5:30–31. For the demise of this office see Marion M. Spector, *The American Department of the British Government, 1768–1782* (1940), pp. 159–65.

25 Wyvill, comp., *Political Papers*, 4:129–30.

26 *Parliamentary History*, 21:233–78. Ironically, a year earlier Eden had asked to be appointed "to some less useless station than that which I now fill." Eden Correspondence, British Library Add. MSS. 34, 416, fol. 278. Arthur H. Basye, *The Lords Commissioners of Trade and Plantations . . . 1748–1792* (1925), pp. 209–16. See Dennis S. Klinge, "Edmund Burke, Economical Reform, and the Board of Trade, 1777–1780," *Journal of Modern History* 51 (Sept. 1979): vi–vii.

27 *Parliamentary History*, 21:262–64.

28 Ibid., p. 302.

29 Ibid., pp. 304–9.

30 *Burke Correspondence*, 4:220.

31 *Parliamentary History*, 21:538–51.

32 Ibid., pp. 551–52.

33 Ibid., pp. 616–17, 621, 714. Burke's bills on Wales, Chester, and the duchy and county palatine of Lancaster died when the session ended.

34 Ibid., pp. 539–40.

35 Ibid., pp. 74–77.

36 Shelburne became the favorite of the associations in March when he gave his support to parliamentary reform. Wyvill, comp., *Political Papers*, 4:131–36. See Norris, *Shelburne*, pp. 124–28.

37 *Parliamentary History*, 21:340–68. When North reiterated his desire to resign, George III replied that Dunning's motions were not aimed at the ministry. He added: "I wish I did not feel at whom they are *personally levelled*." *Correspondence of George III*, 5:40.

38 *Parliamentary History*, 21:379–86.

39 *Burke Correspondence*, 4:219. Referring to the contractors bill (11 Mar. 1779), George III remarked on "the strange scruples many of the Country Gentlemen have harboured on that subject." *Correspondence of George III*, 4:302.

40 *Parliamentary History*, 21:403–14.

41 Wyvill, comp., *Political Papers*, 3:210–11. *Parliamentary History*, 21:494–522.

42 Rockingham Papers, R1-1869, 1881, 1882, 1883. Burke vigorously opposed parliamentary reform in a letter to the Buckinghamshire committee. *Burke*

Correspondence, 4:226–29. Christie, *Wilkes, Wyvill, and Reform,* pp. 100–104.

43 Rockingham Papers, R1-1892, 1896, 1897.

44 *Burke Correspondence,* 4:259.

45 Ibid., 4:298.

46 Ibid., p. 240. N. C. Phillips, "Edmund Burke and the County Movement, 1779–1780," *English Historical Review* 76 (Apr. 1961).

47 Complaints concerning emoluments of office, *Parliamentary History,* 20:1260; balances of land tax collectors, ibid., pp. 1184–87; military expenditure, ibid., 21:179–80.

48 Ibid., p. 76.

49 Ibid., pp. 145–47, 278–85. Charles Jenkinson drew up the bill with assistance from a variety of persons. Liverpool Papers, British Library Add. MSS. 38, 567, fol. 32; 38,213, fol. 199; 38,346, fols. 258–63; 38, 307, fol. 153.

50 *Parliamentary History,* 21:280, 284. *Burke Correspondence,* 4:222.

51 *Parliamentary History,* 21:147–49, 279–80.

52 20 Geo. III, c. 54. See Binney, *Public Finance and Administration,* pp. 7–15, and J. Torrance, "Social Class and Bureaucratic Innovation: The Commissioners for Examining the Public Accounts, 1780–1787," *Past and Present,* no. 78 (Feb. 1978), pp. 56–81.

53 *Correspondence of George III,* 5:92–93, 96. Ian Christie, "The Marquis of Rockingham and Lord North's Offer of a Coalition, June–July, 1780," in *Myth and Reality* (1970), pp. 109–32.

54 Rockingham Papers, R1-1910.

55 *Correspondence of George III,* 5:96–97.

56 Norris, *Shelburne,* pp. 132–35, 143–44.

57 *Parliamentary History,* 21:1223–92. Shelburne opposed Burke's bill. See Ian R. Christie, *The End of North's Ministry, 1780–1782* (1958), pp. 252–57.

58 Wyvill, comp., *Political Papers,* 1:365, 315.

59 Rockingham Papers, R1-1976.

60 *Correspondence of George III,* 5:452.

61 *Burke Correspondence,*4:424.

62 *Parliamentary History,* 22:1137–42.

63 *Correspondence of George III,* 5:392–93.

64 Rockingham Papers, R1-2064. See also R119-8.

65 Abstract of Burke's plan of civil list reform, ibid., R19-28. Also ibid., R1-2019 b,c, and R119-3, 8, 9, 13, 14.

66 *Memorials and Correspondence of Charles James Fox,* 2 vols., (1853), 1:316.

67 *Burke Correspondence,* 4:433–34.

68 *Correspondence of George III,* 5:463, 464.

69 Ibid., 451, 452–55, 489–90, 491–92.

70 *Fox Correspondence,* 1:314–16.

71 *Correspondence of George III,* 5:496–502. Rockingham Papers, R1-2063.

72 Ibid., p. 494.

73 Ibid., pp. 473–74. See Ian R. Christie, "George III and the Debt on Lord North's Election Account, 1780–1784," in *Myth and Reality* (1970), pp. 183–95.

74 When preparing his plan of economical reform in early 1780, Burke did not propose to reduce the privy purse, accepting the view of George Dempster that it was needless to be concerned with "the little purchases of a prince of this country." Burke Papers, no. 858. Ironically, when the civil list was increased in 1777, the £12,000 per annum added to the privy purse became the purest example of "influence" in the entire civil list.

75 *Parliamentary History*, 22:1269–75.

76 See E. A. Reitan, "The Civil List, 1761–77: Problems of Finance and Administration," *Bulletin of the Institute of Historical Research* 47 (Nov. 1974): 186–210.

77 *Parliamentary History*, 22:1395–96, 1412–16; *Journals of the House of Commons*, 38:971, 972–73.

78 *Burke Correspondence*, 4:446. Rockingham Papers, R-18, R-98-6, R-218, R-219; Burke Papers, nos. 1096, 1097-1, 1097-2, 1098.

79 *Correspondence of George III*, 5:503–4; 6:1–2; Rockingham Papers, R1-2061, 2068; R-130, 132; *Fox Correspondence*, 1:317, 324; Historical Manuscripts Commission, *Reports*, ser. 42 (Carlisle), pp. 614, 621, 626.

80 *Burke Correspondence*, 4:446.

81 Historical Manuscripts Commission, *Reports*, ser. 42 (Carlisle), p. 631.

82 *Correspondence of George III*, 6:54.

83 *Parliamentary History*, 23:121–27. Offices to be abolished: Third Secretary of State; Board of Trade; Treasurer of the Chamber; Cofferer of the Household; Board of Green Cloth; Wardrobes, Jewel Office; Board of Works; Paymaster of the Pensions; Master of the Foxhounds, Harriers, Stag Hounds. Offices proposed for abolition in 1780 but preserved: Master of the Household; Treasurer of the Household; Comptroller of the Household, Master of the Robes; Master of the Buckhounds.

84 Ibid., pp. 139–47.

85 Burke's civil list act was 22 Geo. III, c. 82. Clerke's and Crewe's acts, ibid., c. 45, 51.

86 Norman Baker, "Changing Attitudes Toward Government in Eighteenth-Century Britain," in *Statesmen, Scholars, and Merchants*, ed. Anne Whiteman et al. (1973), pp. 212–19.

87 Reports published in the *Journals of the House of Commons:* First Report (27 Nov. 1780), 38:74–85; Second Report (31 Jan. 1781), ibid., pp. 141–54; Third Report (7 Mar. 1781), ibid., pp. 247–70; Fourth Report (9 Apr. 1781), ibid., pp. 379–94; Fifth Report (28 Nov. 1781), ibid., pp. 572–93. Reactions in *Parliamentary History*, 22: 204–18, 358–70, 421–35.

88 Sixth Report *Journals of the House of Commons*, 38:702–78.

89 *Parliamentary History*, 23:116–21. Draft proposal for reform of the Exchequer, Rockingham Papers, R1-2065. On 29 April Rockingham reported to the King that the proposal was ready. *Correspondence of George III*, 5:506.

90 *Burke Correspondence*, 4:430.

91 *Parliamentary History,* 23:118.

92 Ibid., p. 134.

93 22 Geo. III, c. 81.

94 Summarized in Norris, *Shelburne,* pp. 171–76, and John Cannon, *The Fox-North Coalition: Crisis of the Constitution, 1782–4* (1969), pp. 20–31.

95 *The Journal and Correspondence of William Eden, Lord Auckland,* ed. George Hogge, 4 vols. (1861–62), 1:12.

96 *Burke Correspondence,* 5:57.

97 Philip Stanhope, 5th Earl, *Life of the Right Honourable William Pitt,* 4 vols. (1861–62), 1:86.

98 King's speech, 5 December 1782. *Parliamentary History,* 23:208–10. Norris, *Shelburne,* chs. 11, 12. John Ehrman, *The Younger Pitt: The Years of Acclaim* (1969), pp. 89–93.

99 *The Parliamentary Register,* 45 vols. (J. Debrett, 1781–96), 9:385–86, 500. *Parliamentary History,* 23:926–31.

100 *Parliamentary History,* 23:945–59, 1106–14.

101 Ibid., pp. 263, 958.

102 Public Record Office, Treasury Minutes, T. 29/52, 297–98. Gilbert's report in Shelburne Papers, vol. 125, Clements Library. Norris, *Shelburne,* pp. 176–85. See J. Mordaunt Crook, "The Office of Works and Economical Reform, 1780–1782," in *The History of the King's Works, Vol. VI, 1782–1851* (1973).

103 *Autobiography and Political Correspondence of August Henry, Third Duke of Grafton,* ed. W. R. Anson (1898), p. 338.

104 Treasury Minutes, T. 29/52, 270–71.

105 Cannon, *The Fox-North Coalition,* ch. 3.

106 *Parliamentary History,* 23:598. The followers of North drew up a list of places suitable for members of Parliament "to restore the influence taken away by Burke's Bill." Christie, in *Myth and Reality,* p. 299.

107 *Correspondence of George III,* 6:319.

108 *Burke Correspondence,* 5-70.

109 *Fox Correspondence,* 2:37–38.

110 23 Geo. III, c. 82.

111 *Parliamentary History,* 23:1114–21. Treasury Minutes, T. 29/54, 210–11, 221, 298, 311–12, 361–62, 441–42.

112 Treasury Minutes, T. 29/54, 48–49, 115, 320–25, 451, 453, 292.

113 Ibid., 348–49, 422–24.

114 Ibid., 147, 323–24, 339, 348. Debrett, *Parliamentary Register,* 12:58, 92–94, 99.

115 *Parliamentary History,* 23:1152–53. William Beldam, a Treasury official, wrote to Lord Hardwicke in December 1783 that Fox stated "he has a plan in Embryo, that He thinks will establish a Sinking Fund able to liquidate the national Debt; Bold Men pursue bold Measures and if they be just ones I wish him success." Hardwicke Papers, British Library Add. MSS. 35,621, fol. 237.

116 Seventh Report (19 June 1782), *Journals of the House of Commons*, 38:1066–1114; Ninth Report (31 Mar. 1783), ibid., 39:325–46. The Tenth Report (2 July 1783), ibid., pp. 522–33, was not published prior to passage of Burke's bill, but the information was available to him.

117 Norris, *Shelburne*, pp. 224–25. Liverpool Papers, British Library Add. Mss. 38,309, fol 76; 38,218, fols. 152–53, 166, 174.

118 See Burke's draft proposal in the Rockingham Papers, R-132, where the statement is made that "This plan has been examined and approved by the Commissioners of Accts" and by some army officers, agents, and the Secretary at War. Burke's unwillingness to cooperate with Barré is clear in *Burke Correspondence*, 5:73–74. For his association with the commission, see ibid., p. 85.

119 Debrett, *Parliamentary Register*, 9:201–2, 384–85, 407 ff., 486, 509–10; 10:111–16.

120 23 Geo. III, c. 50. Burke's implementation of the act in Treasury Minutes, T. 29–54, 204–5.

121 *Burke Correspondence*, 5:87–89. *Parliamentary History*, 23:801–5.

122 *Parliamentary History*, 23:900–927.

123 Thomas W. Copeland, "Johnson and Burke," in *Statesmen, Scholars, and Merchants*, ed. Whiteman et al., p. 289.

124 *Burke Correspondence*, 5:170.

125 Ibid., p. 171. Richard Rigby employed Bembridge to make up his accounts, on which he labored faithfully until they were ready for audit in 1792. Rigby Papers, Essex Record Office, D/DHw 047.

126 Burke Papers, no. 1245.

127 Ibid., nos. 1248, 1264, 1285.

128 Fox Papers, British Library Add. Mss. 47,561, fol. 51. *Journals of the House of Commons*, 39:676–77, 680–81, 691–92.

129 Good general accounts of this matter are in John Brooke, *King George III* (1972), pp. 248–49, and Cannon, *The Fox-North Coalition*, pp. 95–100. *Parliamentary History*, 23:1030–41.

130 *Auckland Correspondence*, 1:60. Fox Papers, British Library Add. MSS. 47,568 fol. 181. Burke was again authorized to prepare legislation to sell the Crown lands and forests and reform the separate jurisdictions of Wales, Chester, and the duchy and county palatine of Lancaster, but nothing came of this. *Journals of the House of Commons*, 39:32, 128.

131 *Parliamentary History*, 23:916.

132 "Speech on the Army Estimates," *Works*, 3:274.

133 Ibid., 2:295.

134 Ibid., pp. 439–40.

135 Ibid., 5:121.

136 Ibid., pp. 115–21.

Robert Boyle on Language:
Some Considerations Touching the
Style of the Holy Scriptures

ROBERT MARKLEY

Of all the scientific theorists in or associated with the Royal Society during its formative years, Robert Boyle was probably the most keenly interested in the problems of language, style, and representation. His prefaces to *Occasional Reflections* (1665) and *The Christian Virtuoso* (1690) include long defenses of his use of figurative language; and in both works he argues strongly against the stylistic prescriptivism that dominates the rhetoric of later seventeenth-century linguistic theory.[1] Boyle's fullest exposition of his often complex views on language, however, occurs in his wide-ranging defense of biblical style, *Some Considerations Touching the Style of the Holy Scriptures* (1661).[2] In this important but little-known work, Boyle undertakes what he sees as a set of integrally related tasks: defending both the style and the authority of the Bible, justifying his own stylistic views, and trying to account for what in his mind is the paradoxical nature of language— its existence as both a temporal instrument and an atemporal ideal. In this respect, *Style of the Scriptures* is an extremely ambitious, if difficult, work—part defense of the Bible, part stylistic manifesto, and part testament to the author's own spiritual quest for salvation.[3]

For Boyle, the essential linguistic questions are always those of religious celebration: in what language should one worship? what language most fully demonstrates a sincere devotion to God? These

159

questions are as crucial to Boyle as they are to Isaac Newton; both men, as "natural philosophers," devote a good deal of energy to trying to develop an ideal method of representation that accurately describes the phenomena of nature and demonstrates, rather than simply alleges, the perfection of God's universe.[4] In *Style of the Scriptures*, however, Boyle goes beyond Newton and most of their contemporaries in recognizing that language may constitute, and not simply reflect, the reality it attempts to describe. This recognition defines Boyle's interest in language epistemologically as well as teleologically. Underlying his treatise is his belief that the problems of "style" and representation inhere in the nature of language itself and cannot be "solved," as Hobbes and Sprat believed, ideologically.[5] The questions of representation that Newton answers by his ideal mathematization of nature,[6] Boyle grapples with linguistically, trying to resolve what, for him, is the basic paradox of writing: one must use an imperfect language to try to describe perfection. It is precisely his willingness to confront this paradox—to argue for an essentially dialectical view of language—that makes *Style of the Scriptures* an intriguing personal as well as historical document.

In his early *Occasional Reflections*, a seminal work in his development as a philosopher, Boyle constructs what is, in effect, a semi-private mythology of language and thought. He justifies at length in the opening chapters his practice of "occasional meditations" as an ideal method of freeing the imagination to contemplate divine Grace and its operation throughout the universe. By carefully observing and meditating on the significance of even the most mundane objects and actions, the "Ingenious Man" is able "to pry into the innermost Recesses of mysterious Nature, and discover there so much of the Wisdom, Power, and Goodness, of the Authour, as are most fit to give the Discoverer a high and devout Veneration for those Excellencies" (p. 35). Reflection becomes a way of transcending the world by the very act of studying it: "the restless mind having div'd to the lower most parts of the Earth, can thence in a trice take such a Flight, that having travers'd all the corporeal Heavens, and scorn'd to suffer her self to be confin'd with the very Limits of the World, she roves about in the ultra-mundane spaces, and considers how farr they reach" (p. 35). This metaphysical process of contemplation, as J. R. Jacob argues, is crucial to Boyle's scientific and religious thought.[7] His "occasional reflections" allow him to perceive the discrete phenomena of "Nature" as evidence of God's "Excellencies"; they both promote and are promoted by his identification of "natural philosophy" with a belief in a divine, if mysterious, "Authour."

Yet if Boyle's meditations are, as he claims, the results of "meer chance," the uses to which he puts them are not. However "occasional" his reflections may be, the act of his putting them into writing is a deliberate, heuristic, and self-consciously literary process. His "occasional reflections" are, as he states, rhetorical pieces designed to "cherish piety . . . and help make the man *good*, whether or not they make his *style* be thought so" (pp. 26–27). They are meditations cast—and imaginatively recreated—in language; and, in an important sense, they are also meditations on the power of language to communicate the mystical experience of reflection: "rov[ing] about the ultra-mundane spaces" and "pry[ing] into the innermost Recesses of mysterious Nature." The language of his occasional meditations, then, is "like *Jacob's* Ladder, whereof though *the foot lean'd on the Earth, the top reach'd up to Heaven*" (p. 80). This image seems particularly revealing—language, for Boyle, is both mundane *and* mystical. Like Jacob's ladder, it is a form of metaphysical representation that mediates between the actual and the ideal.

In one respect, *Style of the Scriptures* is Boyle's attempt to work his way through much of what he leaves implicit in *Occasional Reflections*. In theory, at least, Boyle tries to resolve the paradoxes of representation by viewing language dialectically: everyday discourse is mundane, a necessary evil; the word of God, as manifested in the Bible, is perfect, as worthy of study as the Book of Nature. But this distinction—although it is an important one for Boyle—does not work out neatly in practice. It is undermined by his own ambivalence about writing and his wariness of language's deferred nature, its existence at one remove from the experiences of both the physical and "ultra-mundane" realms. He is impatient with the limitations of his medium, yet firm in his belief that, through a perfect faith, a writer's language can in fact transcend itself. Boyle's dilemma in *Style of the Scriptures*, then, is that he must try to demonstrate, as well as argue for, the ideal potential of language from within a system of representation that he recognizes is inadequate to his needs. If he writes, as he frequently says, to further the mysterious ends of divinity, he must do so in a language constrained by its own fallen nature.

Boyle's recognition of his dilemma—his emphasis on both the experiential and moral dimensions of "style"—distinguishes his treatise from the works of Wilkins, Sprat, Glanvill, and other progressive theorists associated with the Royal Society.[8] Implicitly and explicitly, Boyle challenges many of his contemporaries' assumptions about the social nature of language. Unlike his reformist counterparts, he is less concerned with promoting a synthetic "Real Character" or defending the stylistic fashions of his own era than with describing and championing the union of "Rhetorick and Mystery" that he sees as the basis of biblical language.[9] While his colleagues in the Royal Society perceive style as a social artifact that can be consciously improved, Boyle argues that it is an individual process of questioning and discovery, a reflection of one's moral nature. While they locate their ideal language in an unproblematic future, he seeks his in the mystery of the past made present, in the Christian reader's experiencing and recognizing the truth of the Scriptures. In these respects, Boyle seems closer to the Anti-Ciceronian prose stylists of the earlier seventeenth-century—particularly Bacon—than to the linguistic reformers of the Restoration. His stated aims in *Style of the Scriptures*—to defend the Bible against rationalist criticism of its stylistic "flaws" and "improprieties" and (as in *Occasional Reflections*) to justify his own rhetorical methods—reflect his vision of language and style as what amounts to an epistemology of faith.[10]

Boyle's definition of "style" in the opening pages of his treatise is characteristic of his often idiosyncratic approach to language; he is less concerned with delimiting an acceptable range of meanings than with conveying a sense of all the possibilities that "style" may include. His description is based on what he calls the "Complication . . . of Rhetorick and Mystery" that he finds operating throughout the Bible. This "Complication" both subsumes and transcends conventional notions of "style" as an expression of self. In examining the Old and New Testaments, Boyle states that he will not "consider the style . . . in the stricter acception, wherein an Authors style is wont to signify the choice and disposition of his words, but in that larger sense, wherein the word Style comprehends not only the Phraseology, the Tropes and Figures made use of by a Writer, but his Method, his lofty or humbler Character (as Orators speak) his Pathetical or languid, his close or incoherent way of writing . . . almost the whole manner of an Author expressing himself" (p. 2). In one respect, Boyle's emphasis on a writer's "whole manner" of expression is an outgrowth of both his own rhetorical needs and his perception of the Bible. By defining "style" as broadly as possible, he is able to avoid confining himself to arguments based narrowly on contemporary notions of linguistic propriety and to counter the arguments of the Bible's detractors: "some . . . say that Book is too obscure, others, that 'tis immethodical, others that it is contradictory to it self, others, that the neighbouring parts of it are incoherent, others, that 'tis unadorned, others, that it is flat and unaffecting, others, that it abounds with things that are either trivial or impertinent, and also with useless

Repetitions" (p. 4). Boyle's response to these objections is to challenge the stylistic assumptions on which they are based. His own argument in *Style of the Scriptures* depends on his stretching the idea of "decorum" to limits that can accommodate a variety of rhetorical strategies. In the course of his treatise, Boyle deplores poor translations of the Bible; emphasizes the differences between the rhetorical practices of the ancient "East" and contemporary "West"; attacks the rigidity of Ciceronian rhetoric and its elevation of manner over matter; parodies the style of "Wits" and other "Anti-Scripturists"; and offers a number of occasional observations on ethics, morality, ancient history, Christian humility, contemporary philosophy, and the art of rhetorical persuasion. The copiousness of Boyle's argument, in effect, precludes a narrow emphasis on "style" as merely a formal structuring of language.

Instead, "style" becomes less a precise linguistic construct than an abstraction derived from Boyle's perception of biblical "Eloquence." It comprehends both means and ends, both the individual's "choice and disposition of words" and the experiential—and moral—"Method" of the Scriptures. For Boyle, the ideal of biblical language underlies all human discourse; it is the standard against which all individual styles must be judged and, to varying degrees, found wanting. In this regard, his concept of style is essentially a measure of the distance between the individual's utterance and the ideal of scriptural language. As it does for Bacon and other Anti-Ciceronians of the earlier seventeenth century, "style" becomes an experiential rendering of one's moral identity, a necessarily incomplete progress towards an ideal discourse.[11] It is, in effect, an extension of the writer's faith.

Implicit in Boyle's definition is his rejection of the prescriptive approaches to style favored by Hobbes, Sprat, and other contemporary linguistic reformers. If Hobbes's "Perspicuous Words" and Sprat's "Mathematicall plainess"[12] exclude the metaphorical and insist on a one to one correspondence between words and things, Boyle's "Complication . . . of Rhetorick and Mystery" rejects all merely formal approaches to language, all systems of representation that neglect the spirit behind the words. For Boyle, "style" is affective, less a property of the text than of the writer's (or reader's) mind. As "a Collection of composures of very differing sorts, and written at different times" (p. 17), the Bible provides the exemplary ideal. To achieve His ends, says Boyle, God "varied the heavenly Doctrine into Ratiocinations, Mysteries, Promises, Threats, and Examples" to suit "the several abilities and dispositions of men" (p. 22). The Bible's enduring truths are therefore evident in its copious and timeless appeals to "the Generality of its Readers" (p. 151). Biblical style, then, transcends both the historical conditions of its ancient composition and the formal "Rules" of those "Anti-Scripturists" who would presume to judge it negatively. In this respect, Boyle's stylistic ideal of "Rhetorick and Mystery" subsumes "reason" and "progress" (the watchwords of Hobbes's, Sprat's, and Wilkins' programs for linguistic reform); it becomes a timeless representation of the majesty of God's creation.

The image of the Bible that emerges from Boyle's introductory remarks on style, in effect, structures the remainder of his treatise. The Scriptures are both literal texts to be read, studied, and interpreted and an ultimate mystery. Their logic is that of "Revelation" rather than reason. Each of the Bible's parts, Boyle argues, contributes to the design of the whole, "the least Text in it being as contributory to the Compleating of the Bible, as Every Loop or Pin was to the Perfection of the Tabernacle" (p. 79). His simile here is revealing; the "Perfection" that Boyle sees in the Scriptures is an article of his faith rather than simply a quality of the text. In what is perhaps the key passage in *Style of the Scriptures*, Boyle gives a relatively succinct account of the relationships he perceives among language, "Method," and faith:

> But when I remember how many things I once thought Incoherent [in the Bible], in which I now think I discern a Close (though Mystick) Connection; when I reflect on the Authour and the Ends of Scripture, and when I allow my self to Imagine how exquisite a Symmetry (though as yet undiscern'd by me) Omniscience Doth, and after-Ages (probably) Will discover in the Scripture's Method, in spite of those seeming Discomposures that now puzzle me: when I think upon all this, I say, I think it just to check my toward Thoughts, that would either presume to know all the Recluse Ends of Omniscience, or premptorily judge of the Fitnesse of Means to Ends unknown; and am reduc'd to think that Oeconomy the Wisest, that is chosen by a Wisdom so Boundlesse, that it can at once Survay all Expedients, and so Unbyass'd, that it hath no interest to choose any, but for it's being the Fittest. (pp. 73–74)

Boyle's faith in the "Recluse Ends of Omniscience" is his ultimate proof of the Bible's stylistic perfection. He allows himself to imagine and believe in "a Wisdom so Boundlesse" that it overcomes his admitted doubts about the Scriptures' coherence. In fact, the "seeming Discomposures" he finds in the Bible paradoxically convince him of God's omniscience and provide a check to human presumptions to "judge of the Fitnesse of Means to Ends unknown." Decorum, in this respect, becomes a matter of faith, of the individual's willingness to admit his limitations and to open his imagination to the "Mystick" connections that define the Bible's "exquisite . . . Symmetry." The Bible thus becomes an historical and narrative account not only of times past but, as this passage suggests, of the individual's own spiritual journey, his progressive, though necessarily incomplete, education in Christian morality and mystery.

Boyle's perception of biblical language is, in essence, part of his larger vision of the unity of God's works. The essential metaphor in *Style of the Scriptures*—and one that appears throughout his writings[13]— equates the Bible and the "Book of Nature." In Boyle's mind, studying the language of the former is analogous to investigating scientifically the phenomena of the latter. Both books display the mysterious unity of their "Author's . . . divine intelligence":

> . . . the Book of Grace doth herein resemble the Book of Nature wherein the Stars, (however Astronomers have been pleas'd to form their Constellations) are not more Nicely nor Methodically plac'd than the Passages of Scripture: That where there's nothing but Choice Flowers, in what Order soever you find them, they will make a good Poesie: That it became not the Majesty of God to suffer himself to be fetter'd to Humane Laws of Method . . . (p. 53)

Nature and the Bible are mutually reinforcing and mutually inclusive for Boyle; their mystical union comprehends all of God's creation. Yet his image itself underscores a basic paradox: although the two books may be equated (as they are in this passage) through the medium of language, they cannot be truly represented—or understood—by means of language. They are united in Boyle's mind by both their innate perfection and their limited accessibility to man; he can come to know them only through the imperfect processes of interpreting their languages. The Book of Nature and the Bible are both to be "read" and studied as evidence of "the Majesty of God," yet both remain unfettered by "Humane Laws of Method," whether scientific or linguistic.[14] In this respect, the processes of interpretation in both natural philosophy and biblical exegesis can illuminate only the possibility of glimpsing the "Order" that Boyle accepts as an article of faith. The "Recluse Ends" of omniscience remain unknowable, cast in the equally mysterious languages of Nature and the Bible.

The underside of Boyle's insistently idealistic conception of God's languages is his ambivalence—even downright hostility—to the imperfections of human discourse. A good portion of *Style of the Scriptures* is devoted to making implicit and explicit distinctions between the perfections of biblical language and the faults, inaccuracies, and

duplicities of everyday writing and speech. In a passage his eighteenth-century biographer Thomas Birch "extracted from some loose
sheets, intended as part of his *Essay on Scripture*," Boyle reveals his
contempt for the study of language as an end in itself. "My propen-
sity and value for real learning [natural philosophy]," he says, "gave
me so much aversion and contempt for the empty study of words,
that not only have I visited divers countries, whose languages I could
never vouchsafe to study, but I could never yet be induced to learn
the native tongue of the kingdome [Ireland] I was born and for some
years bred in."[15] Boyle's distinction between "real learning" and "the
empty study of words" suggests the extent to which he divorces the
languages of God's creation from the languages of a fallen, imperfect
world. But, he continues, "in spite of the greatness of these indispo-
sitions to the study of tongues, my veneration for the scripture made
one of the great despisers of verbal learning leave *Aristotle* and *Paracelsus* to turn grammarian . . . to learn as much Greek and Hebrew,
as suffered to read the old and new testament . . . and thereby free
himself from the necessity of relying on a translation" (1:30). For Boyle,
the study of language can be justified only as a means to a greater
end. Turning "grammarian," in this respect, is really another form of
Boyle's "aversion" for "the empty study of words," an attempt to escape from the constraints of language. Studying Greek and Hebrew
becomes his way of rejecting the essentially literary process of translation and of trying to return to the pristine languages in which the
Bible was first written.

Taken together, Boyle's disparaging remarks on linguistic study and
his insistence on the moral dimensions of language suggest something of his ideational debt to the Anti-Ciceronian movement of the
late sixteenth and early seventeenth centuries.[16] His arguments in
Style of the Scriptures often create the impression that one is reading a
contemporary of Bacon or Ben Jonson rather than Dryden. Significantly, Boyle reserves his most direct attacks on stylistic prescriptivism for the hoary bogeyman of Ciceronian rhetoric, inveighing against
its suffocating "Rules," elevation of form over substance, and implicit
assumption that style is inherently social and aesthetic rather than
individual and moral. For Boyle, the formal structuring of language
is at best decorative and at worst distracting, if not dangerous. "Our
strict Ciceronian Rules," he claims, "are Crutches that may be Helps
to Weak or Lame Phansies, but are Cloggs or Burdens to Sound and
Active Ones" (p. 168). Like Bacon, Boyle sees stylistic artifice for its
own sake as a trap, an exercise in perverse ingenuity that divorces
language from its proper moral ends. He finds "the Apothegms of

the Sages, the Placits of Philosophers, the Examples of Eminent Persons, the Pretty Similes, quaint Allegories, and quick Sentences of Fine wits . . . such two-edg'd Weapons, that they are as well applicable to the service of Falshood, as of Truth" (p. 126). In short, Boyle perceives rhetoric itself as "two-edg'd" and inherently susceptible to corruption. It can be redeemed only by the writer's recognition of language's fallen nature and his subsequent attempts to invest it with an ultimate moral and teleological purpose.

In this regard, *Style of the Scriptures* becomes a kind of anti-rhetoric; its underlying purpose is to reassert what are essentially Baconian stylistic values in the midst of the revolutionary turmoil of the late Commonwealth and early Restoration eras. "Our strict Ciceronian Rules" are not simply a convenient target for Boyle but are emblematic of much of what he finds dangerous or distasteful: amoral wit, anti-scriptural rationalism, the unthinking adherence to classical precedent. Ciceronian rhetoric, in his mind, is to language what unregenerate Aristotelianism is to mechanical philosophy. In effect, then, Boyle is responding to what we might call the ideology of language—its necessary and inevitable involvement with a socially, intellectually, politically, and theologically volatile world. By rejecting the formal, aesthetic, and social dimensions of language, Boyle is able to assert a linguistic idealism commensurate with his religious beliefs. As I have suggested, the goal he sets for himself is to redeem language, to demonstrate the biblical ideal of "Rhetorick and Mystery" anew. In this regard, *Style of the Scriptures* is a work born of Boyle's millenarian faith. His disdain of rhetorical forms for religious ends is thus apocalyptic as well as (in a conventional sense) stylistic.

Yet Boyle's attacks on those who concern themselves solely with the formal properties of language paradoxically reflect the tensions that characterize his ambivalence towards his own writing. In writing *Style of the Scriptures*, Boyle finds himself committed to using a medium he distrusts. He must describe his stylistic ideal and the imperfections of human language from within an imperfect system. The more he tries to redeem language, and the more he deplores its inevitable corruption in a fallen world, the more he is bound by its temporal constraints. In this regard, his idealizing the Bible's "Complication . . . of Rhetorick and Mystery" occasions another paradox. To demonstrate his faith, to continue what is, in effect, the ongoing process of his self-justification, Boyle must attack not only "Anti-Scripturists" and latter-day Ciceronians but also that within him which is seduced by the written word—the "two-edg'd Weapons" of rhetoric—as an end in itself.

Much of the latter third of Boyle's treatise is devoted to attacks on those "Wits" who pervert the Scriptures "to Abuse the Words, to Irreligious Senses, and perhaps passing to the Impudence of Perverting Inspir'd Expressions, to deliver Obscene Thoughts" (p. 178). Much of this assault takes the form of parody; Boyle goes to some lengths to appropriate the language of wit for his own purposes:

> Considering Persons will scarce think it a Demonstration of a Mans being a Wit, that he will Venture to be Damn'd to be Thought one . . . For Persons Really Knowing, can easily Distinguish betwixt that which Exacts the Title of Wit from our Judgments, and that which but Appears such to our Corruptions . . .[The wit] Prostitutes his Wit to Evince and Celebrate the Defeat of his Reason . . . and takes it for as high a Proof as Desirable a Fruit of Eloquence, to Perswade a Vain Mistresse that She is Handsome and Ador'd, to whom 'twere Eloquence indeed to be able to perswade the contrary. (pp. 179, 181, 182–83)

This is hardly Congreve, but Boyle seems to think enough of his parodic strategy to go on in the same vein for nearly six pages. His verbal wit in these passages becomes a two-edged weapon; he satirizes and succumbs to it at the same time. By parodying the language of profane wit, then, Boyle is also engaging in a subtle form of self-criticism, attacking that part of himself given to eloquence and to playing the rhetorician.[17] In this respect, his parodies imply a recognition of the inevitable secularization—or corruption—of biblical language in a fallen world. They represent both an attack on—and a demonstration of— the divergence of rhetoric and mystery, of language and faith, in temporal discourse.

In his preface to *Style of the Scriptures* (written, as he says, after he had completed the body of the text), Boyle duly notes his dilemma. His treatise begins, in one sense, with an apology for where it ends, with Boyle disparaging rhetoric and simultaneously justifying his use of its embellishments:

> Orators may not unjustly bear with some Rudenesses in the Style of a Person that Professes not Rhetorick, and Writes of a Subject that Needs Few of her Ornaments, and Rejects Many, as Indecencies misbecoming its Majesty: and that Severer Divines may safely Pardon some Smoothnesse in a Discourse Written Chiefly for Gentlemen, who would scarce be fond of Truth in every Dresse, by a Gentleman who fear'd it might misbecome a Person of his Youth and Quality Studiously to Decline a fashionable Style. (sig. A7r)

For all of his disclaimers about "Rhetorick," Boyle justifies his own style by claiming that it is consciously crafted and defers to social standards of "Quality" and gentlemanly decorum. "Truth" itself must appear in aristocratic "Dresse" to seem fashionable enough for "Gentlemen." "Style" in this passage is divested of the moral and experiential connotations it assumes in the body of the treatise. Here it is ideological, the product of an aristocratic culture that balances "Truth" against verbal "Smoothnesse." In this respect, Boyle's conventional apology for the rhetoric of "Youth and Quality" is, as he himself suggests, a measure of the compromises he must make to be able to write about biblical language at all.

Yet Boyle's accommodating preface and his parodies of profane wit seem less a retreat from the idealism of "Rhetorick and Mystery" than evidence of his sensitivity to the complex problems of language and representation. His struggle in *Style of the Scriptures* is to turn contradiction into dialectic. The crucial word for Boyle, in this regard, is "Complication"—it suggests that ultimately there is no clear distinction between "Rhetorick and Mystery," between the word on the page and the spirit that animates it. "Complication" defines an experience rather than a relationship;[18] it resists expression as a systematic philosophy of language. "Style," then, remains beyond "Humane Laws of Method." It offers itself finally as a dialectical transcription of Boyle's own religious and intellectual experiences as he pries into the "innermost Recesses" of language and its mysteries.

NOTES

1 *Occasional Reflections upon Several Subjects* (London, 1665); *The Christian Virtuoso* (London, 1691). All quotations from these editions will be noted parenthetically in the text. On Restoration linguistic theory see Murray Cohen, *Sensible Words: Linguistic Practice in England, 1640–1785* (Baltimore: Johns Hopkins University Press, 1976), and James Knowlson, *Universal Language Schemes in England and France 1600–1800* (Toronto: University of Toronto Press, 1975).
2 *Some Considerations Touching the Style of the Holy Scriptures* (London, 1661). All quotations from this edition will be noted parenthetically in the text.
3 See J. R. Jacob, *Robert Boyle and the English Revolution* (New York: Burt Franklin, 1977), pp. 118–21. My view of Boyle's linguistic thought is indebted to the broad outlines of Jacob's argument. See also, for important contextual information, Jacob, "Restoration Ideologies and the Royal Society," *History of Science* 17 (1980): 25–38; and Barbara Shapiro, *Probability*

and Certainty in Seventeenth-Century England (Princeton: Princeton University Press, 1983).

4 I treat this subject at greater length in "Objectivity as Ideology: Boyle, Newton, and the Languages of Science," *Genre* 16 (1983): 355–72.

5 See Thomas Hobbes, *Leviathan*, ed. C. B. MacPherson (London: Penguin, 1968), pp. 116–17, and Thomas Sprat, *The History of the Royal Society*, ed. Jackson Cope and Harold Whitmore Jones (St. Louis: Washington University Press, 1959), pp. 1–4, 113.

6 See Morris Kline, *Mathematics: The Loss of Certainty* (New York: Oxford University Press, 1980), pp. 55–58.

7 Jacob, *Boyle and the English Revolution*, pp. 29, 98–99.

8 See Sprat, *History of the Royal Society*, p. 113; John Wilkins, *An Essay Towards a Real Character and a Philosophical Language* (London, 1668); and Joseph Glanvill, *Plus Ultra* (London, 1684), pp. 84–85.

9 For Boyle's one reference to universal language schemes see his letter of 19 March 1646/7 to Samuel Hartlib, reprinted in *The Works of the Honourable Robert Boyle*, ed. Thomas Birch (London, 1744), 1:22.

10 On Bacon and Anti-Ciceronianism see particularly Stanley Fish, *Self-Consuming Artifacts: The Experience of Seventeenth Century Literature* (Berkeley: University of California Press, 1972), pp. 78–155. A word of caution, however: Fish, like most of his predecessors, sees seventeenth-century prose style as a binary opposition—in his case, self-consuming versus self-satisfying artifacts. His terminology, then, tends to suggest neat divisions where, in my opinion at least, there are none. I would argue that the moral, ideological, and religious implications of style in the later seventeenth century are more problematic than most critics have assumed. See the second chapter of my dissertation, "The Language of Comedy from Fletcher to Congreve, 1615–1700" (University of Pennsylvania, 1980), pp. 40–65, and Paul Arakelian, "The Myth of a Restoration Style Shift," *The Eighteenth Century: Theory and Interpretation* 20 (1979): 227–45.

11 See Fish, *Self-Consuming Artifacts*, for an effective defense of the view that style can be both a mirror of the writer's mind and a quest for a certainty that lies beyond language's ability to describe it.

12 Hobbes, *Leviathan*, p. 86; Sprat, *History*, p. 113.

13 On the metaphor of the two books see my "Objectivity as Ideology," and Frank Manuel, *The Religion of Isaac Newton* (Oxford: Clarendon Press, 1974), pp. 25–50.

14 This is Newton's view as well. For Boyle's view of the relationship of science and theology as disciplines, see his *The Excellency of Theology, compar'd with Natural Philosophy* (London, 1674).

15 *Works of Robert Boyle*, 1:30.

16 On the Anti-Ciceronian movement see *"Attic" and Baroque Prose: Essays by Morris W. Croll*, ed. J. Max Patrick et al. (Princeton: Princeton University Press, 1966).

17 See particularly pp. 158–72 in *Style* for Boyle's explication of his views on rhetoric.

18 Ironically, Boyle's views of the experiential nature of God's word bring him close to those of at least one prominent "Anti-Scripturist," Samuel Fisher. However, where Fisher elevates the inner light of faith over the Bible's written word, Boyle conflates the two. On Fisher and the anti-scriptural tradition in seventeenth-century England see Christopher Hill, *The World Turned Upside Down: Radical Ideas during the English Revolution* (London: Temple Smith, 1972), pp. 208–15.

Domesticating Minerva: Bathsua Makin's "Curious" Argument for Women's Education

MITZI MYERS

Bathsua Makin's modern-day reputation instances the fate of many "lesser" women writers, the "minor" authors of "minor" genres who occupy an occasional footnote. The *Dictionary of National Biography,* for example, rates Makin's *Essay to Revive the Antient Education of Gentlewomen, in Religion, Manners, Arts & Tongues: with an Answer to the Objections against this Way of Education* (1673) as a "curious" piece by an almost forgotten female worthy, a work which piques some merely antiquarian interest with its didactic energies and quaintly pro-woman polemic. Under the stimulus of twentieth-century feminism's first wave, female historians of women countered such a view. Myra Reynolds in her 1920 record of learned ladies and Dorothy Gardiner in her 1929 history of women's education rightly saw Makin not as an isolated oddity, but as part of a female continuum. And, though their work was less analysis than descriptive summary, they made large claims for her consequence. Reynolds, for instance, points to the "great historic interest" of the curriculum Makin describes for her Tottenham High Cross girls' school: "It is the first known attempt to organize a scheme of definite and solid study for girls," and Makin herself is "one of the most significant personages connected with the education of girls in the mid-seventeenth century." Attempts later in the century to "revive the more solid type of girls' education characteristic of Tudor times," Gardiner finds, operate "under the inspiration and by the initiative of Mrs. Makin." Moreover, Gardiner reminds us, our contemporary commonplaces were once the "great advance in educational theory" of such practising teachers as Makin, marking "a growth of the pedagogic conscience."[1]

Despite this promising beginning, for many years Makin received only passing paragraphs in the rare register of women's activity, like Doris Mary Stenton's *The English Woman in History* (1957), but she has recently begun to attract fresh attention as an early and generous exponent of women's advancement and as a pedagogic innovator. The Augustan Reprint Society has reissued her major work with an intelligent introduction, anthologies of and about early women of letters like Mary Mahl and Helene Koon's *Female Spectator* and J. R. Brink's *Female Scholars* include her, and she has been noticed in such feminist publications as the *International Journal of Women's Studies* and *Signs*.[2] In Brink's study, Makin figures as at once a reformist language instructor à la Milton and an anticipator of twentieth-century structural grammarians. For Brink, she "is not so much a feminist as an educator," a scholar, a linguist, and "an important, and possibly central, figure" in a tradition of learned ladies extending back to the daughters of Sir Thomas More and Sir Anthony Cook and forward to Elizabeth Elstob and Elizabeth Montagu, Queen of the Bluestockings. More lately yet, Hilda Smith's 1982 chronicle of seventeenth-century feminism takes a different view. Makin the defender of women plays a small supporting role in *Reason's Disciples*, where she comes off as a mild precursor of Smith's stellar example, Mary Astell, though Smith criticizes Makin's masculine persona, which, she argues, "tempered her work" and "gave a conservative tone to much of her essay." Validating Makin as a female scholar, Brink highlights one strand of her achievement; tracing the feminist lineage, Smith's study, along with Moira Ferguson's forthcoming anthology of *First Feminists*, documents Makin's credentials as a feminist foremother, important though inhibited.[3]

My intention here is less to adjudicate these rival interpretations than to suggest their inextricable interweave (for pro-education arguments and proto-feminism are the firmest of partners in women's writing) and, more important, to situate them within a more suggestive frame of reference, to propose a reorientation of vantage from which female didactic and polemic works like Makin's reveal women's relation to their culture and to the canon. I want to talk about power and anger and argumentative strategies, about the interplay of female or feminist ideology and textuality, the ways in which women's structures of feeling and perception—necessarily ambivalent vis-à-vis their culture—get embodied in characteristically female polemic. I am concerned with women's attitudes toward language and culture, with the strategem, indirection, contradiction—and inventive vigor—which inevitably accompany their attempts to carve out a place for themselves in relation to each, to speak with cultural authority. I want to take women's didactic genres seriously as a mode of female moral discourse, as complex cultural artifacts, introits to autonomy and public activity which have much to show about the social and historical development of the woman writer's role and the female literary tradition, and as a neglected literary mode which has much to tell about how ideology inheres in aesthetic form and how gender differentiation shapes textual configuration. I want to locate my subject within a model of female agency, rather than the more usual one of passivity, oppression, and victimization, and I want to speak from the interpretive perspective of discourse as power. If Michel Foucault reminds us that discourse is a locus of power and that certain forms of discourse correlate with certain sociocultural roles, recent work by feminist historians similarly suggests fresh ways to examine female power. Caroline Lougee remarks on "the need to recognize within the context of seemingly debilitating limitations placed upon women in European societies the persisting power of women; the integrity of their choices; and their participation in the definition of roles, values, and behavior." Natalie Zemon Davis alerts us to the multivalence of popular sexual symbolism, its susceptibility to manipulation for female leverage, the ways in which women's power lodges in unexpected "nooks and crannies."[4]

Such a perspective promises a way to make sense of such slippery rhetorical strategies and argumentative indirections as these: Makin's clever conversion of anti-woman bromides like Solomon's virtuous housewife of Proverbs 31 to her own purposes of educational reform (so clever a manager had obviously benefited from learning, she wittily demonstrates); her ringing indictment of oppressive custom and her biting attacks on male misogyny, vice, and intellectual pretension (not to mention the outmoded pedagogy of Lily's Latin grammar), a forthright feminism oddly coexisting with ritual invocations of masculine superiority—"God hath made Man the Head"—and resigned pragmatism—"To ask too much is the way to be denied all" (p. 4); or again, her earnest pleas for improved female access to arts, tongues, and culture and her astringent critique of that culture as the work of "debauched Sots," "inconsiderate and illiterate Men, that prize their own Lusts and Pleasure more than [women's] Profit and Content" (pp. 21, 4); her politic suturing of female improvement and social betterment—"We cannot expect otherwise to prevail against the Ignorance, Atheism, Prophaneness, Superstition, Idolatry, Lust, that reigns in the Nation, than by a Prudent, Sober, Pious, Vertuous Education of our Daughters" (p. 28); or finally, the piquant conjunction of her masculine personae, for she has more than one, with her jumbled and ahistorical catalogues of famous women, which range from the likes of Minerva and the Sybils to Esther and Deborah, to Lady Jane Grey and Queen Elizabeth, to Makin's correspondent and literary model, Anna Maria van Schurman, the famous scholar of Utretch, and Margaret, Duchess of Newcastle, epic roll calls which, most significantly, frankly privilege women as culture's inventors, conservators, and foremost promoters.

Alternating between assertion and qualification, sporadically lurching from conciliation to aggression, advancing a theoretical rehabilitation of woman fissured by hesitancy and indeterminacy, Makin's argument threads together female anger, education, and virtue, cultural renovation and female power. For power—indirectly expressed in a woman's way, defined according to a woman's lexicon, not legalistically from outside as control and dominance *over*, but from within as capacity, capability, competence, energy, influence—power is what Makin's text foregrounds. Once sensitized to her woman-power-text problematic—her opening address "To all Ingenious and Vertuous Ladies," for example, urges that "this discourse may be a Weapon in your hands to defend your selves," for the tongue, she continues, is woman's "only Weapon" (pp. 3–4, 11)—and once attentive to the filiations of such textual feminism over time, Makin's case emerges, not as an almost isolated utterance, but in relation to a rich mass of kindred writing, "curious" not because so rare, but because in many ways so representative of the female cultural and intellectual traditions embedded in didactic and polemic writings. Ranging from books for children and advice manuals for daughters, wives, and mothers to moral essays, educational tracts, and defenses of women, from rationales for female charity to anti-slavery, anti-war, and feminist polemic, this didactic discourse constitutes a canonically neglected but remarkably persistent woman's mode, hardy generic hybrids which perdure over centuries, from Christine de Pisan in the fifteenth to Mary Wollstonecraft at the turn of the eighteenth to Virginia Woolf's *Three Guineas* (1938) and on.

Like Makin's, such educative works typically link female improvement and cultural amendment, making the former a precondition to the latter. For in this progressive tradition of moralizing feminism, the seemingly restrictive topos of feminine influence can be turned to salutary uses, virtue can encode power, virtue and social good can function as the legitimating ideology for female advancement and achievement. Written mostly by that class Woolf terms educated men's daughters and sisters (Makin's brother John Pell, for example, was a noted mathematician), these pro-woman, pro-education writings offer a critical perspective on the dominant intellectual and cultural traditions of their times, a cultural critique from the viewpoint of the disadvantaged sex, real-life examples of the "Outsiders' Society" Woolf projects as a corrective to social ills.[5] Vigorously alive, if on the fringes of LITERATURE, women's didactic and defensive writings reveal a submerged tradition of female intellectual resistance to oppressive and repressive cultural givens, a disregarded "genre," if you will. Demonstrating both positively and negatively, both substantively and formally, women's oblique relation to power, they enact how a female cultural outgroup relates to, redefines, and grasps at power, achieves a social voice. Theirs are ambivalent strategies of carefully negotiated dissidence, of propitiation, of appropriation.

Take, for example, Makin's insistence on formal, classical learning, combined, to be sure, with a thorough grounding in woman's lore, the needle, neatness, genteel accomplishments—"all those things that do particularly belong to their sex" (p. 22). She opens her tract by sharply contrasting "the barbarous custom to breed Women low . . . grown general among us" with the days "when many did rise to a great height in Learning" (p. 3), when, as William Wotton observes, "It was so very modish, that the fair Sex seemed to believe that *Greek* and *Latin* added to their Charms. . . . One would think by the Effects, that it was a proper Way of Educating of them, since there are no Accounts in History of so many very great Women in any one Age, as are to be found between the Years 15 and 1600." If modern research more skeptically measures the limitations of the humanist educational program for women, this mythic golden age of the Tudor paragon nevertheless functioned as an imaginative ideal in an age of satiric hostility toward the learned lady, who was popularly viewed as vain and neglectful of domestic duties, socially dangerous and up to no sexual good, her wit, as Thomas Wright's *Female Vertuoso's* has it, "always a Pimp to her Pleasures."[6] Women themselves, like van Schurman or Makin or the heroine of Erasmus's colloquy between the abbot and the learned lady that Makin zestfully cites, counter male jealousy and fear by arguing for learning as an aid to the moral life, to women's usefulness and moral agency.

Language, such female educational reformers perceive, is a locus of power; they want entrée to it, but they also want to change it. Latin, as Walter Ong points out, was the symbolic property and tongue of a male educational elite; it was a sex-linked language, a badge of masculine identity acquired through elaborate initiation rites: "The Latin world was a man's world." Because learning Latin thus meant transgressing their society's gender codes, women's relationship with this traditional transit to cultural wisdom was an anxious one, hostile, envious, or ambivalent. Protesting against male socio-literary prerogatives, some, like Judith Drake, laughed at pompous pedants and schoolmasters: "so ignorant of the Domestick Affairs and manners of their own Country and Times, that they appear like the Ghosts of Old Romans rais'd by Magick." Some mastered Latin in secret and blushed to have it discovered, like the heroine of Hannah More's *Coelebs*, and some, like Fanny Burney, were scared to learn at all. A disgruntled wife in *Aubrey's Brief Lives* hurls her husband's Latin dictionary into the fire; Jane Austen playfully mocks herself as an "unlearned and uninformed female" who "knows only her own mother tongue"; Margaret, Duchess of Newcastle, proudly rejects the "Formal, or Worditive" for the "natural, plain style, without Latin sentences."[7]

If Latin language study served different functions for men and for women, it probably lured some women as a limited means of insinuating themselves into a closed system; for others, it signified access to a storehouse of knowledge to be plundered for their own purposes. Makin urges Latin as strongly as any pedantic pedagogue, but not for its symbolic artificiality and elitism. For her it is a strictly functional tool, one which will lose its clout when popular languages come further into play as vehicles for erudition. Paradoxically, the terms in which she appropriates Latin for women's uses ally her with a long-lived female tradition of language—vernacular, prosaic, anti-hegemonic, organized not by artificial rhetorical pattern but according to its own internal logic, steeped in the informal experiential details of women's family-sittingroom mentality. Demanding access to Latin and education and thence to "culture," Makin appropriates the language of the fathers for a woman's vernacular tradition of "Tongues . . . in order to Things" (p. 11) or "things, not words!" as Mary Wollstonecraft exclaims a century later, in the very same phrase as Mary Astell and Lady Mary Wortley Montagu before her, for the plain style has a symbolic value to women officially barred from classical rhetoric.[8]

Indeed, Makin's linguistic fixation and her extensive pedagogical strictures (she has a wonderful time revealing the absurdities of Lilyean grammar) can be read as an attack on male methodology and logocentrism. The curricular specifies she appends to her plea evince at once her educational reformism and the inevitable concessions to consumer expectation of a practising schoolmistress. Languages are where her heart lies, and she stands ready to teach Latin, French, Greek, Hebrew, Italian, and Spanish, but trying to include "all manner of Sober and Vertuous Education," she has to serve up "all things ordinarily taught in other Schools": "Works of all Sorts," dancing, music, singing, writing, and keeping accounts. Limning, preserving, pastry-making, and cookery are available, as are astronomy, geography, history, and experimental philosophy for those with more time to invest. (Boarding school provision resembles a buffet where students can sample "more, or fewer" dishes "as they incline" [p. 42].) And, because girls' school attendance was normally shorter than boys', Makin has to explain how they can be taught twice as many things in half the time, a recurrent objection to girls' higher training: where would the time come from if they were to add men's arcana to women's lore? Maria Edgeworth answered that, freed from blind subservience to Latin ritualism, girls really had more time for genuine mental cultivation and, unencumbered with "all the melancholy apparatus of learning," a better vernacular style, and Harriet Martineau, something like Makin, was still sturdily announcing in 1864 that if boys have two fields to master, girls must more efficiently manage three.[9]

Like these successors, Makin belongs to that woman's tradition of educational reform that touches so many didactic and educative works. Whether influenced by Comenius (as Makin obviously is) or another, women's linguistic concerns and the changes that they seek show a surprising continuity over time. Adapting method to pupil, to the pedagogically and psychologically sound "Rules of True Didacticks," Makin would commonsensically ground a girl in her mother tongue's observed grammar, rather than making her memorize Latin rules in Latin as a preface to academic study—"that wild-Goose-chase usually led" (pp. 37–38). She has shrewd tricks to identify nouns and the like, and she never forgets, in contrast to the abstract male scholarship she deplores, that concrete common life owns primacy and that words and tongues are but marks, always subservient to things. Like her Comenius-inspired repositories "for Visibles" which teach students about the natural world through eyeing the objects themselves, Makin's educational reforms bring traditional learning based on Latin into a closer approximation with domestic life that is characteristically (though not of course exclusively) female (pp. 36, 30, 43). As such, her pedagogical innovations belong to that call for women to develop their own linguistic powers and traditions—a female idiom to capture a "difference of view" and values—which stretches from the Duchess of Newcastle to Wollstonecraft and beyond.[10] Makin, then, has her linguistic cake and eats it too.

Similarly appropriative, Makin's choice of a male persona is less the conservative indicator that Hilda Smith sees than a canny stratagem—an argumentative ruse which objectifies women's oblique relation to their culture and embodies their covert seizure of power and cultural authority. Actually, Makin has not one male persona but several, each articulating a position paper on woman's nature and destiny. Much as she converts pedantic and patriarchal Latin discourse to serve women's "vernacular" uses, here she appropriates an "enlightened" male representative to refute the entrenched masculinist views of the Objector to women's education and partial enfranchisement who figures in her title. Actually, the male voice is always *there* in pro-woman writing, whether formally personified or not. Men's views and voices condition the ways that early feminist theory develops, for it arises in dialectical response to the misogynous squibs of a Joseph Swetnam (*The Arraignment of Lewde, Idle, Froward, and Inconstant Women*, 1615, reprinted for over a century) or the sentimental blandishments of a Rousseau. Pro-woman writers evolve their own arguments in confuting male charges and assertions; they often don or remodel male tones and strategies to suit their own argumentative purposes. Christine de Pisan borrows busily from Boccaccio on women; Wollstonecraft structures her argument as a quotation-laden refutation of Rousseau, Dr. Fordyce, and the like, as well as herself usurping the terminological voice of "masculine" rationality to rescue women from "feminine" feeling; Edgeworth's *Letters for Literary Ladies* negotiate her rationale for women's educational advance within the epistolary dialogue of warring male figures. Just so, between them, Makin's pro-woman "Champion" (p. 5) and her Objector work out the lines of her argument, which thus adapts and humanizes the bloodless syllogistic structure of her friend and anticipator van Schurman, whose *Learned Maid; or, Whether a Maid May Be a Scholar?* (1638; trans. 1659) is accurately subtitled a *Logick Exercise*.[11]

Makin is no strict logician; her argument ranges and rambles, is filled with idealistic valorizations of learning's pleasure and power and earthy jibes at sottish men and sluttish women who bestially rank body above mind and soul. Despite its argumentative disjunctions and obliquities of form, Makin's text nevertheless musters in small space an encyclopedic enablement of women and a blunt censure of their misogynous devaluation and its inevitable cultural consequences—the "Clouds of Ignorance . . . the Flouds of Debauchery," "not only Learning but Vertue itself . . . scorn'd and neglected, as pedantick things, fit only for the Vulgar" (pp. 4–5). Makin's defense follows the lines laid down by the Objector's letter, which is part of that complex prefatory apparatus situating the pamphlet as serious moral discourse, making it more than the mere blurb for Mrs. Makin's school which it also is and with which it frankly concludes. The "Education of Gentlewomen in Arts and Tongues," pronounces the Objector, is "so vain a thing" because women do not desire knowledge and have neither capacity nor leisure for it. Moreover, public employment and discourse are forbidden women by custom and biblical authority. "And that which is worst of all," he continues, "they are of such ill natures, they will abuse their Education, and be so intolerably Proud, there will be no living with them" (p. 6). The text scrupulously refutes these classic calumnies and more as its subtitle promises, but the argument expends its greatest force and space in appropriating and re-imagining yet another topos, the catalogue of luminaries. Had not van Schurman called for *"examples of illustrious Women,"* and had not the Countess of Winchilsea complained, "Nor are we told / Fables, of Women that excell'd of old"? [12]

Anticipating by some 250 years Virginia Woolf's provocative notion that women writers "think back through our mothers," Makin fills tracts of her text with lists of women mythological, legendary, biblical, historical, and contemporary, rulers, writers, artists, moral heroines, mothers who formed the minds of great men, women famous for their own public deeds. [13] So pervasive are Makin's lists of women worthies—they form a lengthy preface to her argument proper and weave throughout it as well—that their functions and effects merit careful scrutiny. First of all, they impressively validate the author's intellectual credentials. In fact, *because* she writes anonymously and wears a male guise, she can show off her learning with impunity. Full of neat little rhetorical touches, her catalogues do not proceed linearly and logically, but tumble out breathlessly, associationally, as if there were such legions of learned women in history and her head that she must rush to get them down: oh, yes, I almost forgot, or I barely have room to name. . . . More important, the lists conclusively substantiate her pro-learning argument. If a humanist believer in the efficacy of example seeks, as her title has it, *to Revive the Antient Education of Gentlewomen, in Religion, Manners, Arts & Tongues*, what better corroboration than the record of female successes in these fields and more? Let "proud ignorant men . . . but look into History, they will find Examples enow of illustrious Women to confute them" (p. 29). And what better encouragement to women systematically inhibited by their culture? Verifying women's capabilities, achievements, and virtues,

Makin groups her exemplars by field to support each proposition, "Women have been good Linguists" and the like, though some notables like her friend van Schurman figure in several categories. Oration, philosophy, mathematics, divinity, and above all poetry, for, ever attentive to language's power, Makin finds women's poetic merits alone enough to vindicate their claims. After all, Minerva, Goddess of Wisdom, was so reckoned for her "excellence and cunning in Poetry and other good Arts" she invented. And since women like Anne Bradstreet, Katherine Philips, and Anne Killigrew have been such fine poets, Makin observes, in the acidic aside that is her specialty, men therefore injure women "exceedingly, to account them giddy-headed Gossips, fit only to discourse of their Hens, Ducks, and Geese, and not by any means to be suffered to meddle with Arts and Sciences, lest by intollerable pride they should run mad" (p. 16).

Considered as historically verifiable data, Makin's catalogues of lettered ladies look thin. "Unchronological, uncritical. . . . a list too undiscriminating to be convincing, but certainly creditable to Mrs. Makin's industrious learning," so went Myra Reynolds's assessment; "although inventive and resourceful . . . not very convincing," so follows J. R. Brink's. Hilda Smith, who wants to argue for a seventeenth-century advance in the serious analysis of relations between the sexes as opposed to simply a listing of women's glories based on ancient and biblical examples, concurs.[14] Makin's inventories, however, are not meant to be examined with scientific rigor, though they implicitly enact a potent argument. Like many elements in this piece, Makin's enumeration is a commonplace subtly rethought and turned to progressive uses. Far from being the archaic medieval leftover that Smith slights to privilege more "modern" and rationally structured argument, the catalogue of worthies (sometimes poetical, as in Mary Scott's 1774 *Female Advocate*) or the collective biography of celebrated women is a remarkably adaptable and persistent female didactic mode, recurrently available for feminist purposes, as the radical Mary Hays makes very clear in her preface to *Female Biography; or, Memoirs of Illustrious and Celebrated Women, of All Ages and Countries* (1803). Like Makin, Hays writes "in the cause, and for the benefit, of my own sex," to secure "their advancement in the grand scale of rational and social existence . . . to excite a worthier emulation." Smith argues that catalogues unhelpfully highlight the exceptional woman, but pro-woman writers insist that readers can find here encouraging role models to reshape their own lives, and female educators repeatedly revamp the heroic tradition to the level of the one-shilling purchaser, the schoolgirl, as in Mary Pilkington's numerous late-eighteenth-

century biographies for English adolescents, or the American housewife, as in Sarah Josepha Hale's enormously popular *Woman's Record;
or, Sketches of Distinguished Women, from the Creation to A. D. 1854.*[15]
And, indeed, the pantheon-of-notables approach to women's history
structures much twentieth-century feminist inquiry; such early clas-
sics as Mary Beard's *Woman as Force in History* (1946), like the surveys
of Reynolds, Gardiner, and Stenton, certify women's competence or
ascendancy by way of historical exempla. If men like Boccaccio,
Chaucer, Vives, Sir Thomas Elyot, Cornelius Agrippa, Thomas Heywood, John Shirley, George Ballard, John Duncombe, or William
Alexander, as well as numerous lesser seventeenth- and eighteenth-
century male writers both English and French, pioneered and embel-
lished the gallery of women good or great, female writers vitalize
these conventional materials in their own distinctive ways. Three-
fourths of Christine de Pisan's exemplary beadroll derives from Boccaccio, one researcher finds, but the pitch of her polemic marks *Le
Livre de la cité des dames* a woman's educative text, encoding an outgroup's attempt to upgrade present status through recapture of a collective past.[16]

Makin's argumentative strategies, then, claim kin with a respectable and long-lived lineage of pro-woman writing, and her registers
serve very definite—and effective—polemic purposes; they constitute an enabling mythology strategically designed to empower women
and to redefine—really, to reinvent—their relation to a culture that
currently devalues and deprives them. If women stand in ambivalent
relation to the acculturating myths of Western intellectual tradition—
now seeing their culture as potentially fruitful and liberating, now
perceiving it as rejecting and alienating, then they must create their
own celebratory myths from the materials at hand. Gesturing toward
women's past cultural centrality, Makin would rescue them from their
contemporary marginality, would weave them into a collective wom-
en's tradition, a matrilineal continuum that flows into the networks
of seventeenth-century female intellectuals she records with satisfaction: van Schurman; Lucy, Countess of Huntington; Margaret, Duchess of Newcastle, who "by her own Genius . . . over-tops many grave
Gown-Men" (p. 10). Thus Makin reads the Bible, that repository of
misogynous staple, as a record of female agency (as would Mary Astell a bit later); Wisdom, Faith, Hope, and Charity, Makin further points
out, are feminine in designation.[17] Thus she discovers in the mists of
antiquity a female origin for culture itself; if the "Vertues, the Disciplines, the Nine Muses, the Devisers, and Patrons of all good Arts,
the Three Graces" always invest a female form, does not that em-

blemize how "Women were the Inventors of many of these Arts, and the promoters of them"? (p. 21).

This matriarchal mythology and the biographical compendia which supply the connective tissue of Makin's tract are of course *loci communes*, as available to male as to female polemicists, but women didacts typically individualize these commonplaces differently from their masculine contemporaries. Makin here may be usefully compared with two contemporary male renderings, the 1670 Englishing of Agrippa's 1529 work, *Female Pre-eminence; or, The Dignity and Excellency of that Sex, above the Male: An Ingenious Discourse,* and a typical hack compilation of the period (probably by James Norris), *The Accomplish'd Lady, or Deserving Gentlewoman: Being a Vindication of Innocent and Harmless Females from the Aspersions of Malicious Men: Wherein Are Contained Many Eminent Examples of the Constancy, Chastity, Prudence, Policy, Valour, Learning, &c. wherein They Have Not Only Equal'd, but Excell'd Many of the Contrary Sex* (1684). Makin, indeed, refers to Agrippa in her pamphlet, but, significantly, only to reject his playful rhetorical tour de force, what the translator calls his "innocent *Paradox,*" for a measured pragmatism: "What I have written is not out of humour to shew how much may be said of a trivial thing to little purpose. . . . I do not (as some have wittily done) plead for Female Preeminence" (pp. 3–4). Unlike her flashy male coevals, whose long-breathed titles illustrate their wide-ranging claims, she asks only for socially functional access to education, not the palm of sexual superiority. Tonally, Agrippa's lists are permeated with his mysticizing of female beauty; he dilates lovingly on women's "breasts which seem two sphears of *Snow,* or swelling *Mountainets* of Delight . . . and all parts of her body *plump, juicy,* and *attractive,*" and indicatively, his notable women, even his biblical heroines, achieve their "power and excellency" through "this divine Ornament, *Beauty*"—theirs the preeminence of delicacy and softness, of "Terrestial Angels." The vindication offered by *The Accomplish'd Lady* savors of the domestic martyr genre. Here women pluck out their eyes or hack off their noses and upper lips to preserve their chastity, carry their sick husbands on their backs for miles, or drink a husband's ashes to become his proper tomb.[18] The tactics of these men stand in sharp contrast to the tradition that, say, Heywood exemplifies, which values women for being *like* men, for their manly deeds and masculine spirits.

But neither seductive beauties and domestic martyrs nor viragoes tempt Makin, who nevertheless finds her own distinctive voice, her own models of womanly nature. However achronological, her catalogues of historic female power are thematically organized: "My design is not to say all that may be said in the praise of women" (p. 29), but to conjoin learning and female competence, learning and virtue, learning and cultural benefit, learning and enlightened motherhood. And this last "is sufficient (if there was nothing else) to turn the Scale"; were not the Gracchi timely taught by their mother Cornelia? (p. 27). Like many a later pro-woman writer, Makin advances the social advantage contingent on intellectually upgraded wife- and motherhood—from the formation of young citizens to the reformation of men—as a telling argument for female education. Her commemorative compendium is "herstory," a primitive variety of women's history, a gift that endows women with a collective genealogy, a culture, a legitimating ideology; her recital of female genius offers empowering images to efface internalized male notions of ineptitude and inutility. Domesticating Minerva, celebrating her distinctively female resonance, Makin calls upon women to recognize and live up to their hereditary traditions, to "set a right value upon themselves," to make their lives and learning proportionable "to their noble Souls, nothing inferior to those of Men," and with "generous resolution" and "noble revenge, reassume" the ancient "Vertues" of their sex (pp. 41–42). Like Wollstonecraft (and a host of other successors), she pleads for women to achieve power "over themselves" through education.[19]

Whatever the limitations of Makin's feminist analysis (that it is firmly classbound is one—she pleads only for the educational rights of the leisured, those whose "quality ties them at home" [p. 25]), however clipped and cabined by feminine circumspection, the central insights of her argument bear the hallmarks of later feminist discourse: the recognition of gender as a social construct, a status shaped by custom and therefore amenable to change; the recognition that female shortcomings derive from cultural marginality and exclusion; the recognition that the masculine elite has a vested interest in such exclusion, keeping women "ignorant to be tyrannized over"—"Let Women be Fools, and then you may easily make them slaves" (pp. 23, 34). Makin's astute grasp of social and sexual power relations issues in scornful anger at the selfish and stupid men who think "A Learned Woman . . . a Comet, that bodes Mischief when ever it appears," who think the "liberal Education of Women" will undermine hegemonical power, so defacing "the Image of God in Man, it will make Women so high, and men so low, like Fire in the House-top, it will set the whole world in a Flame" (p. 3). Toward women, her anger is sadder; her feminist litany of grievances lingers most over human waste; rather than "gaining Arts, and Tongues, and useful knowledge," socially conditioned women trifle life away "meerly to polish their Hands and Feet," spending "the over-plus time of their youth, in making Points for Bravery, in dressing and trimming themselves like *Bartholomew*-Babies, in Painting and Dancing, in making Flowers of Colored Straw, and building Houses of stained Paper, and such like vanities," a critique of female education shriveled to ornamental "accomplishments" which initiates a staple of women's advice genres (pp. 22, 30). Pained at this squandering of female potential, struggling towards ways to empower women with productive social roles, Makin makes explicit the manners-corrupt-morals, virtue-confers-power constellation endemic to early feminist thought (Wollstonecraft is only the most obvious example): "Meerly to teach Gentlewomen to Frisk and Dance, to paint their Faces, to curl their Hair, to put on a Whisk, to wear gay clothes" is to "adulterate their Bodies . . . defile their Souls," to turn them to "Beasts" (p. 22).

Nature gives women capabilities to "equalize, some-times excel men"; custom makes them "onely . . . a finer sort of Cattle"; education renders them profitable to themselves and their relations and "beneficial to the Nation" (pp. 23, 28). Makin cannot make up her mind—or is too politic to say—whether women are the full intellectual equals of men; she has it both ways (e.g., p. 29), just as, though most often concerned with educational furtherance of women's private and domestic roles, she will not fully dismiss notions of "publick Imployment" (p. 33). Nor, herself keenly alive to the delights of education, will she limit her proposed curriculum: "I cannot tell where to begin to admit women, nor from what part of Learning to exclude them in regard of their capacities. The whole *Encyclopedia* of Learning may be useful some way or another to them" (p. 24).[20] For all that her educational program fails to offer a complete realization of female potentiality and power, its rich sense of possibilities, its ardent purpose, and its argumentative vitality break ground for later feminist agendas. If by 1795 Edgeworth could observe that "public opinion is at present more favourable to the cultivation of the understanding of the female sex than it was some years ago" and that "something more is now required, even from ordinary talents, than what distinguished the accomplished lady of the seventeenth century," the shift in educational status and cultural significance owes much to the long tradition of female moral discourse in which Makin plays an honorable part—that domestication of discourse which permitted women to speak out publicly.[21] Quietly testifying to the "persisting power of women," the neglected genre of female didactic writing amply rewards attention to its characteristic rhythms, tensions, and tactics, to the ways in which women deploy cultural counters to foster their social leverage, to achieve their own distinctive voice, their own style of cultural engagement.

NOTES

1 The *DNB*'s "G. G." was Gordon Goodwin; Myra Reynolds, *The Learned Lady in England, 1650–1760* (1920; rpt. Gloucester, Mass.: Peter Smith, 1964), pp. 280, 276; Dorothy Gardiner, *English Girlhood at School: A Study of Women's Education through Twelve Centuries* (London: Oxford University Press, 1929), pp. 229, 257.

2 Doris Mary Stenton, *The English Woman in History* (1957; rpt. New York: Schocken, 1977), pp. 191–93; subsequent references to the *Essay* in the text refer to the ARS edition, introd. Paula L. Barbour (UCLA: William Andrews Clark Memorial Library, 1980); *The Female Spectator: English Women Writers before 1800*, ed. Mary R. Mahl and Helene Koon (Bloomington and London: Indiana University Press, 1977), pp. 115–35; *Female Scholars: A Tradition of Learned Women before 1800*, ed. J. R. Brink (Montreal: Eden Press, 1980), reprints almost unchanged J. R. Brink, "Bathsua Makin: Scholar and Educator of the Seventeenth Century," *International Journal of Women's Studies* 1, no. 4 (July–August 1978): 417–26, as "Bathsua Makin: Educator and Linguist (1608?–1675?)," pp. 86–100; Joan Kelly, "Early Feminist Theory and the *Querelle des Femmes*, 1400–1789," *Signs: Journal of Women in Culture and Society* 8, no. 1 (Autumn 1982): 4–28, mentions Makin only briefly, but provides a stimulating context for her tract.

3 Brink, *Female Scholars*, pp. 94, 87; Hilda Smith, *Reason's Disciples: Seventeenth-Century English Feminists* (Urbana: University of Illinois Press, 1982), pp. 102–3; *First Feminists: British Women Writers from 1578–1799*, ed. Moira Ferguson (Old Westbury, N.Y.: Feminist Press, forthcoming). Further testimony to increasing interest in late-seventeenth-century feminism includes Jean Elizabeth Gagen, *The New Woman: Her Emergence in English Drama, 1600–1730* (New York: Twayne, 1954); Michael A. Seidel, "Poulain de la Barre's *The Woman as Good as the Man*," *Journal of the History of Ideas* 35, no. 3 (July–September 1974): 499–508; Carolyn C. Lougee, *Le Paradis des Femmes: Women, Salons, and Social Stratification in Seventeenth-Century France* (Princeton: Princeton University Press, 1976); Robert H. Michel, "English Attitudes towards Women, 1640–1700," *Canadian Journal of History* 13, no. 1 (April 1978): 35–60; Joan K. Kinnaird, "Mary Astell and the Conservative Contribution to English Feminism," *Journal of British Studies* 19, no. 1 (Fall 1979): 53–75; Simon Shepherd, *Amazons and Warrior Women: Varieties of Feminism in Seventeenth-Century Drama* (Brighton, Sussex: Harvester, 1981); Jerome Nadelhaft, "The Englishwoman's Sexual Civil War: Feminist Attitudes towards Men, Women, and Marriage 1650–1740," *Jour-*

nal of the History of Ideas 43, no. 4 (October–December 1982): 555–79; and Ruth Perry's forthcoming study of Mary Astell.

4 See, for example, Michel Foucault, "The Discourse on Language," trans. Rupert Sawyer, in *The Archaeology of Knowledge*, trans. A. M. Sheridan Smith (New York: Harper and Row, 1976); and "Politics and the Study of Discourse," *Ideology and Consciousness* no. 3 (Spring 1978): 7–26; Carolyn C. Lougee, "Review Essay: Modern European History," *Signs* 2, no. 3 (Spring 1977): 630; Natalie Zemon Davis, "'Women's History' in Transition: The European Case," *Feminist Studies* 3, nos. 3–4 (Spring–Summer 1976): 90; other useful approaches to women and power include Berenice A. Carroll, "Peace Research: The Cult of Power," *Journal of Conflict Resolution* 16, no. 4 (December 1972): 585–616; Elizabeth Janeway, "On the Power of the Weak," and Barbara Bellow Watson, "On Power and the Literary Text," *Signs* 1, no. 1 (Autumn 1975): 103–18; David C. McClelland, *Power: The Inner Experience* (New York: Irvington, 1975); and Leila Rupp, "Women, Power, and History," *Women: A Journal of Liberation* 6, no. 1 [1978]: 4–9.

5 Virginia Woolf, *Three Guineas* (1938; rpt. New York: Harcourt, Brace and World, n.d.), pp. 146, 106.

6 William Wotton, *Reflections upon Ancient and Modern Learning* (London: Peter Buck, 1694), pp. 349–50; Thomas Wright, *The Female Vertuoso's: A Comedy* (London: R. Vincent, 1693), Act III, p. 26. The older view of Renaissance women's education, perhaps best represented by *Vives and the Renascence Education of Women*, ed. Foster Watson (London: Edward Arnold, 1912), is challenged by Diane Valeri Bayne, "*The Instruction of a Christian Woman*: Richard Hyrde and the More Circle," *Moreana* 12, no. 45 (February 1975): 13; Joan Kelly-Gadol, "Did Women Have a Renaissance?" *Becoming Visible: Women in European History*, ed. Renate Bridenthal and Claudia Koonz (Boston: Houghton Mifflin, 1977), pp. 137–64; Gloria Kaufman, "Juan Luis Vives on the Education of Women," *Signs* 3, no. 4 (Summer 1978): 891–96; and Smith, *Reason's Disciples*, pp. 39–53, among others. David Cressy notes that female literacy in London climbed sharply at the end of the seventeenth century, partly because of schools like Makin's, *Literacy and the Social Order: Reading and Writing in Tudor and Stuart England* (Cambridge: Cambridge University Press, 1980), pp. 145–57.

7 Walter J. Ong, *The Presence of the Word: Some Prolegomena for Cultural and Religious History* (New Haven and London: Yale University Press, 1967), p. 251; "Latin Language Study as a Renaissance Puberty Rite," *Studies in Philology* 56, no. 2 (April 1959): 103–24; "Latin and the Social Fabric," *The Barbarian Within and Other Fugitive Essays and Studies* (New York: Macmillan, 1962), pp. 206–19; A Lady [Judith Drake?], *An Essay in Defence of the Female Sex* (1696; rpt. New York: Source Book Press, 1970), p. 43; *Coelebs in Search of a Wife: Comprehending Observations on Domestic Habits and Manners, Religion and Morals* (1808), *The Complete Works of Hannah More* (New York: J. C. Derby, 1856), 2:404; *Diary and Letters of Madame D'Arblay*, ed. Charlotte Barrett (London: Macmillan, 1905), 4:223; *Thraliana: The Diary of Mrs. Hester Lynch Thrale*, ed. Katherine C. Balderston (Oxford: Clarendon

Press, 1942), p. 502, emphasizes Dr. Burney's negative rather than Fanny's fear—Mary Hays's "fevered desire" to learn Latin is, in contrast, an index of the radical woman's intellectual ambition, Gina M. Luria, "Mary Hays's Letters and Manuscripts," *Signs* 3, no. 2 (Winter 1977): 524; *Aubrey's Brief Lives*, ed. Oliver Lawson Dick (Ann Arbor: University of Michigan Press, 1957), p. 71 (see also p. 113); *Jane Austen's Letters*, ed. R. W. Chapman (London: Oxford University Press, 1959), p. 443; Margaret, Duchess of Newcastle, *CCXI Sociable Letters* (London: William Wilson, 1664), Preface; *The Life of the (1st) Duke of Newcastle and Other Writings*, ed. Ernest Rhys (New York: E. P. Dutton, [1916]), p. 9 (the same concern runs through much of Newcastle's work). Often cited to illustrate mid-seventeenth-century male notions on female education, Sir Ralph Verney's fears center vividly on languages: a young girl "guilty" of learning "threaten[s] Lattin, Greeke, and Hebrew too," Margaret M. Verney, *Memoirs of the Verney Family during the Commonwealth 1650 to 1660* (London: Longmans, Green, 1894), 3:73.

8 Mary Wollstonecraft, *A Vindication of the Rights of Woman* (1792), ed. Charles W. Hagelman, Jr. (New York: W.W. Norton, 1967), p. 35; Mary Astell, *A Serious Proposal to the Ladies*, Part 1 (4th ed., 1701; rpt. New York: Source Book Press, 1970), p. 18; *The Complete Letters of Lady Mary Wortley Montagu*, ed. Robert Halsband, 3 vols. (Oxford: Clarendon Press, 1965–67), 3:21; see Josephine Donovan, "The Silence Is Broken," in *Woman and Language in Literature and Society*, ed. Sally McConnell-Ginet, Ruth Borker, and Nelly Furman (New York: Praeger, 1980), pp. 205–18, for an overview of women's stylistic tradition.

9 Shakespeare, as S. Schoenbaum points out, has a similar laugh at Lilyean method in *The Merry Wives of Windsor*, Act IV, *William Shakespeare: A Compact Documentary Life* (Oxford: Oxford University Press, 1978), pp. 67–78; for a sample of what "Works" might include, see Hannah Wooley, *The Gentlewomans Companion; or, A Guide to the Female Sex* (London: Edward Thomas, 1675), pp. 10–11 (the conventional attribution to Wooley is being challenged in a forthcoming study by Elaine Hobby); Maria Edgeworth, "Letter from a Gentleman to his Friend upon the Birth of a Daughter; with the Answer" (*Letters for Literary Ladies*, 1795), *Tales and Novels* (New York: Harper, 1850), 7:211; Harriet Martineau, "Middle-Class Education in England: Girls," *Cornhill Magazine* 10 (1864): 564 (the three are "study, the domestic arts, and play").

10 Although Brink's discussion in *Female Scholars* of Makin's linguistic innovations focuses solely on Milton, Makin herself mentions only Comenius (*Essay*, pp. 36–37), and her approach and phraseology recall his. For Comenius, see John William Adamson, *Pioneers of Modern Education in the Seventeenth Century* (1905; rpt. New York: Teachers College Press, Columbia University, 1971), chs. 3–5; John Edward Sadler, *J. A. Comenius and the Concept of Universal Education* (New York: Barnes and Noble, 1966); Richard L. Greaves, *The Puritan Revolution and Educational Thought: Background for Reform* (New Brunswick: Rutgers University Press, 1969), ch. 5; Aubrey

agreed with Makin's assessment of contemporary methods as causing youth "perfectly to hate learning," *Brief Lives,* p. 1xxxvi; Virginia Woolf, "Women and Fiction," *Women and Writing,* ed. Michèle Barrett (New York: Harcourt Brace Jovanovich, 1980), p. 49.

11 Van Schurman's *Learned Maid* was translated by C[lement] B[arksdale] (London: John Redmayne, 1659); Barksdale himself planned a college for women (Stenton, *The English Woman,* pp. 183–88); for a comparison of van Schurman and Makin, see Foster Watson, "Mrs. Bathsua Makin and the Education of Gentlewomen," *Atalanta* 8 (July 1895): 637.

12 Van Schurman, *Learned Maid,* p. 32; Anne Finch, Countess of Winchilsea, "The Introduction," in *By a Woman Writt: Literature from Six Centuries by and about Women,* ed. Joan Goulianos (Baltimore: Penguin, 1974), p. 72. Men write the books and suppress women's stories, Judith Drake—*Essay,* p. 40—and Jane Austen—*Persuasion* (1818), ed. Andrew Wright (Boston: Houghton Mifflin, 1965), p. 185 ("the pen has been in their hands")— typically complain.

13 Virginia Woolf, *A Room of One's Own* (1929; rpt. New York: Harcourt, Brace and World, n.d.), p. 79.

14 Reynolds, *The Learned Lady,* p. 282; Brink, *Female Scholars,* p. 92; for Smith's hostility to catalogues, see *Reason's Disciples,* pp. xiii, 7, 116.

15 For women worthies, see Davis, "'Women's History,'" pp. 83–84; and Kelly, "Early Feminist Theory," pp. 20–28; Mary Scott's verse catalogue, *The Female Advocate: A Poem Occasioned by Reading Mr. Duncombe's Feminead* (London: Joseph Johnson, 1774), is paralleled by Elizabeth Ogilvy Benger, *The Female Geniad: A Poem* (London: Hookham and Carpenter, Kearsley, 1791). Hays's work (London: Richard Phillips, 1803) and Mathilda Betham's *A Biographical Dictionary of the Celebrated Women of Every Age and Country* (London: B. Crosby, Tegg and Castleman, and E. Lloyd, 1804) appeared almost simultaneously; reviewers noted their especial appeal to youth. Mary Pilkington's *A Mirror for the Female Sex: Historical Beauties for Young Ladies Intended to Lead the Female Mind to the Love and Practice of Moral Goodness: Designed Principally for the Use of Ladies' Schools* (London: Vernor and Hood, 1798), and *Memoirs of Celebrated Female Characters, Who Have Distinguished Themselves by their Talents and Virtues in Every Age and Nation* (London: Albion Press, 1804) signal the extraordinary nineteenth-century outpouring of exemplary celebrated women for a mass readership, a particular feminine specialty being the collective biography of literary women. By 1860, Hale's weighty volume was in its revised and enlarged second edition (New York: Harper and Brothers, 1860); Hale's prefatory matter strikingly demonstrates the centrality of historical examples to pro-woman writing's large moral claims.

16 Mary R. Beard's *Woman as Force in History: A Study in Traditions and Realities* (1946; rpt. New York: Collier, 1971) is analyzed as a certain mode of women's history by Berenice A. Carroll, "Mary Beard's *Woman as Force in History:* A Critique," in *Liberating Women's History: Theoretical and Critical Essays,* ed. Berenice A. Carroll (Urbana: University of Illinois Press, 1976),

pp. 26–41; Boccaccio, *De Claris Mulieribus* (c. 1355–59; cited by Makin, *Essay*, p. 10); Chaucer, *The Legend of Good Women* (c. 1380–86); for Vives (1529) and Sir Thomas Elyot (*The Defence of Good Women*, c. 1531–38), see *Vives and the Renascence Education of Women*, ed. Watson, p. 208, 231–32; for Agrippa, see n. 18; Thomas Heywood's *Gunaikeion; or, Nine Books of Various History Concerning Women* (1624), reprinted as *The Generall History of Women* (1657), and *The Exemplary Lives and Memorable Acts of Nine the Most Worthy Women of the World* (1640) are discussed in Eugene M. Waith, "Heywood's Women Worthies," in *Concepts of the Hero in the Middle Ages and the Renaissance*, ed. Norman T. Burns and Christopher J. Reagan (Albany: State University of New York Press, 1975), pp. 222–38. William Austin, *Haec Homo, wherein the Excellency of the Creation of Women Is Described by Way of an Essay* (1637); Charles Gerbier, *Elogium Heroinum; or, The Praise of Worthy Women* (1651); and John Shirley, *Illustrious History of Women* (1686) illustrate typical seventeenth-century male versions; for consideration of other early examples, see A. H. Upham, "English *Femmes Savantes* at the End of the Seventeenth Century," *Journal of English and Germanic Philology* 12 (1913): 262–76; S. A. Richards, *Feminist Writers of the Seventeenth Century, with Special Reference to François Poulain de la Barre* (London: David Nutt, 1914); Lula McDowell Richardson, *The Forerunners of Feminism in French Literature of the Renaissance from Christine of Pisa to Marie de Gournay* (Baltimore: Johns Hopkins Press, 1929); Marc Angenot, *Les Champions des femmes: Examen du discours sur la supériorité des femmes, 1400–1800* (Montreal: Les Presses de l'Université du Quebec, 1977); Ian Maclean, *Woman Trimphant: Feminism in French Literature, 1610–1652* (Oxford: Clarendon Press, 1977); and Kelly, "Early Feminist Theory." In the preface to his own sensitive collection of exemplary women, *Memoirs of Several Ladies of Great Britain, Who Have Been Celebrated for their Writings or Skills in the Learned Languages Arts and Sciences* (Oxford: W. Jackson, 1752), George Ballard notes his many foreign predecessors in women's history, such as Juncker (*Catalogue of Learned Women*, 1692). Unfortunately, Ballard couldn't find enough material on "Mrs. Makins" to include her, though he notes her correspondence with van Schurman (p. vii). John Duncombe, *The Feminiad: A Poem*, introd. Jocelyn Harris (1754; rpt. UCLA: William Andrews Clark Memorial Library, 1981), is a verse catalogue, and William Alexander, *The History of Women, from the Earliest Antiquity, to the Present Time* (London: W. Strahan and T. Cadell, 1779), is a lengthy early example of cultural anthropology. For Christine, see Kelly, "Early Feminist Theory"; Richardson, *The Forerunners of Feminism* (for the statistic, p. 26); Susan Groag Bell, "Christine de Pizan (1364–1430): Humanism and the Problem of a Studious Woman," *Feminist Studies* 3, nos. 3–4 (Spring–Summer 1976): 173–84; and, for other early women historians as well, Natalie Zemon Davis, "Gender and Genre: Women as Historical Writers, 1400–1820," in *Beyond Their Sex: Learned Women of the European Past*, ed. Patricia H. Labalme (New York and London: New York University Press, 1980), pp. 153–82. The 1521 translation of *The Boke of the Cyte of Ladyes* is reprinted in *Distaves and*

Dames: Renaissance Treatises For and About Women, introd. Diane Bornstein
(Delmar, N.Y.: Scholars' Facsimiles and Reprints, 1978); newly translated
by Earl Jeffrey Richards, *The Book of the City of Ladies,* introd. Marina Warner,
is now available in paperback (New York: Persea Books, 1982).

17 "Our very reformation of Religion," Makin also asserts, "seems to be begun and carried on by Women" (*Essay,* p. 28); Mary Astell, *Some Reflections
Upon Marriage: With Additions,* 4th ed. (1730); rpt. New York: Source Book
Press, 1970), pp. 113–22. *The Gentlewomans Companion* attributed to Wooley
likewise purveys classical and biblical examples in "The Gentlewoman's
Mirrour, or Patterns for their imitation, of such famous Women who have
been eminent in Piety and Learning," pp. 98–103.

18 The translation of Henry Cornelius Agrippa that Makin knew is that of
H[enry] C[are] (London: Henry Million, 1670); quotations are from the
translator's preface and pp. 16, 18–19. Written in 1509, but published twenty
years later to court Margaret of Austria's favor, the tract was clearly regarded by the translator as a jeu d'esprit for this "*giddy Age,*" though
Arlene Miller Guinsburg, "The Counterthrust to Sixteenth Century Misogyny: The Work of Agrippa and Paracelsus," *Historical Reflections* 8, no.
1 (Spring 1981): 3–28, argues for the significance of Agrippa's intellectual
argument. Upham, "English *Femmes Savantes,*" p. 266, takes *The Accomplish'd Lady* and *Haec & Hic; or, The Feminine Gender More Worthy than the
Masculine* to be different works, but p. 1 of the Huntington Library's *Lady*
(London: James Norris, 1684) gives the latter as subtitle.

19 Wollstonecraft, *Rights of Woman,* p. 107. By the 1790s, Makin's mother-
hood-education symbiosis is everywhere in pro-woman writing, from
Wollstonecraft to Edgeworth to More.

20 Here, again, Makin recalls van Schurman, who affirms the whole "Circle
and Crown of liberal Arts and Sciences . . . to be convenient for the *Head*
of our *Christian Maid,*" *Learned Maid,* p. 4.

21 Edgeworth, *Tales and Novels,* 7:204.

Nymphs and Satyrs: Poet, Readers, and Irony in Dryden's Ode to Anne Killigrew

C. ANDERSON SILBER

> Susanna's music touched the bawdy strings
> Of those white elders; but, escaping,
> Left only Death's ironic scraping.
> Now, in its immortality, it plays
> On the clear viol of her memory,
> And makes a constant sacrament of praise.
> Stevens, "Peter Quince at the Clavier"

> Ein Gott vermags. Wie aber, sag mir, soll
> ein Mann ihm folgen durch die schmale Leier?
> Sein Sinn ist Zwiespalt. An der Kreuzung zweier
> Herzwege steht kein Tempel für Apoll.
> Rilke, Sonnets to Orpheus, I, 3

A large portion of the sixth stanza of Dryden's celebrated ode "To the Pious Memory of the Accomplisht Young Lady Mrs Anne Killigrew"—which was written and almost certainly published near the end of 1685, when Dryden was fifty-four years old—is devoted to a description of the "*Sylvan* Scenes" of her pastoral paintings. There, by the poet's account,

> . . . Nymphs of brightest Form appear,
> And shaggy Satyrs standing neer,
> Which them at once admire and fear.[1]

The following pages amount to a gloss on these lines, which epitomize not only the poem in which they appear but also a feature of Dryden's work in the large, a strain in his career. "Strain" implies opposition or at least difference and tension as well as a characteristic tendency or a line of development, and two potentially antagonistic contrasts are immediately apparent in the triplet: bright nymphs vs. shaggy satyrs and admiration vs. fear.[2] These obvious oppositions are compounded by a certain syntactical ambiguity or strain: who

193

admires and fears whom? What are the antecedents of "Which" and "them"? Strictly constructed, the grammar suggests that the satyrs admire and fear the nymphs, and of all straightforward readings of the lines this is undoubtedly the one to be preferred. A satyr who fears a nymph might be thought somewhat unconventional but is not entirely so, as appears from a couplet in Killigrew's own poem "On a Picture Painted by her self, representing two Nimphs of Diana's, one in a posture to Hunt, the other Batheing": "We ["*Diana*'s Virgin-Train"] *Fawns* and Shaggy *Satyrs* awe; / To *Sylvan Pow'rs* we give the *Law.*"[3] (Johnson defines *awe* as "To strike with reverence, or fear.")

If, however, we do not readily de-equivocate Dryden's syntax and instead allow play to other conventional expectations and possible implications, we conceive that the nymphs might fear the satyrs. Do they then, rather surprisingly, also admire them? Or does the syntax by obscure ellipsis indicate, most conventionally, that the satyrs admire the nymphs while the nymphs fear them? Finally, the sentiments of admiration and fear might be attributed to both satyrs and nymphs with respect to each other. In the aggregate, these possibilities comprise less a reading of Dryden's lines than the options available in their reading. Few readers will entertain every possibility and even fewer would finally accept them all. On the other hand, the passage is obscure enough that most readers will hesitate in making sense of it to consider alternative construings, and the understanding at which a reader arrives may well allow more than one of the available options.

This interpretive hesitation, much more than any resolution of meaning, is what makes the triplet an epitome of the ode. In pausing to consider the relation between nymphs and satyrs, a relation characterized—but just how?—by both opposition and affinity, the reader is not only locally engaged with questions that Dryden pursues throughout the poem (and indeed confronted through most of his career), but also personally implicated in the questions and their pursuit. The particular readerly engagement with the question of how Dryden's nymphs and satyrs are related to each other in these few lines is important because it corresponds to a demand made by the poem as a whole that its reader seek, as did its author, to adjust to each other "nymphic" and "satyrish" values—values subject to widely various kinds of association. At the heart of the demand upon the reader lie certain equivocations or ironies in the ode signalling differences between (to put the matter bluntly) Anne Killigrew as she actually was and Anne Killigrew as she appears most favorably in the poem. These ironies work to entrap readers—both originally much by design and latterly more by accident as the design has been obscured by having partly outlived its occasions. The ensuing discussion is mostly offered for what it may contribute to understanding the ode. However, not least because the ode itself insists upon its connections with its author's other writings, even so focussed a study as this must throw some light upon Dryden's career as a whole, most generally by proving further the importance of his vocational preoccupations and the extent to which they find expression in his oeuvre not simply in the form of remarks quite explicitly concerned with the literary issues of a poet-dramatist's work but in less direct ways that reflect Dryden's experience of his profession. It may be also that showing the fullness of such reflections in the ode will encourage notice of their appearance even in poems less obviously concerned with art, for professional students of Dryden still too often privilege political, religious, and philosophical attitudes at the expense of literary ones—as if Dryden's having been a poet were an all but incidental circumstance rather than the ground of our attention to his thought.[4]

Returning to the ode, let us begin by attaching the figures of nymph and satyr respectively to Anne Killigrew and the poet whose poem this is. These attachments are largely established in the ode itself. Although Killigrew is nowhere called a nymph, she has a nymph's attributes of youth (1), beauty (36–37, II; 135, VII; 149–50, VIII), virginity (1; 67, IV), innocence (70, IV), and artlessness or naturalness (71–76, V). She is associated with Diana (87, V) and the nymph Arethusa (68, IV), pastoral associations that are confirmed by the pastoral character of several of her poems.[5] To one of these poems, the one already quoted, Dryden's nymphs-and-satyrs passage itself seems an allusion, and of course Killigrew's excellence in poetry's sister-art is first celebrated by lengthy reference to her pastoral landscape-painting. The possibility that her soul had passed in pre-existence "through all the Mighty Poets . . . / Who *Greek* or *Latine* Laurels wore" (29–30, II) assigns her a priority in poetry that is explicitly associated with Sapphic lyric (33, II); this earliness, however, along with her precocity, also implies—in keeping with the Virgilian paradigm of the poet's career—a disposition for pastoral.[6] The ode, then, approximates Anne Killigrew to a "nymph," but the significance of her being thus marked must await further observations.

The attachment of the ode's author to the figure of the satyr is effected by a self-implicating collocation of the "satyrish" and the "satiric" that is most prominent in the fourth stanza, although again

Dryden eschews full explicitness, never saying outright that he is or has been a satyr-like author.[7] Behind both the guiltiness and the reticence lies a complicated set of circumstances including: first, Dryden's reputation at the time as the author both of satires and, even more, of plays that pleased many but also provoked others to attack him for rudeness and lechery (to appropriate the terms of Johnson's definition of "satyr");[8] secondly, Dryden's all but irrecoverable private understanding of his purposes at the time he wrote any work that others found debased in one way or another; and, thirdly and most important, his need to find a way of representing—first to himself but also to others—his destiny as an artist. The urgency of this last circumstance arose from Dryden's finding himself divided in his obligations between what he owed to his art and what his public demanded of him, between—as Frost makes the distinction in "Two Tramps in Mud-Time"—"love" (i.e., the poet's own pleasure or aspiration) and "need" (i.e., the requirement of a poet who would live by his pen that he produce to the taste of a paying public).

Dryden's parenthetical confession in stanza IV that his own "fat Pollutions" have contributed to the general profanation of poetry in his time is enough to establish his link with the *satyr*, given his characterization of contemporary literature and its authors: they are not only profane but "prostitute," "profligate," "Debas'd," "obscene," "impious," "wretched," "lubrique," "adult'rate," fallen, soiled, mixed "with Forreign Filth," defiled. But the stanza's implication of *satire*, particularly of Dryden as satirist, is not quite so obvious, especially since its indictment is ostensibly directed only against writing for "the Stage." (There is one circumstantial detail outside the ode to suggest that Dryden associated his literary "Pollutions" specifically with satiric, rather than dramatic, excess: in *The Hind and the Panther*, written and published about a year after the ode, the Hind checks her "boiling indignation" so as not to "Pollute her satyr with ignoble bloud" [III, 261–64].) Even apart, however, from any extratextual knowledge—Dryden's, his nearest readers', ours—of him as a satirical author, satire appears in the passage. It does so simply because the stanza is satirical itself. Its accusatory force derives from Juvenal; its exaggerations of best and worst accord with Dryden's own poetics and practice of satire; and the design of the stanza might even, by only modest ingenuity, be aligned with the desiderata of formal verse satire—a two-part structure, the larger first part attacking a vice or folly and the conclusion commending its virtuous opposite.[9]

Still more to the point, Dryden's satiric verve leads him to commit here again the very offense he is rebuking, in keeping with a tendency Dryden recognized in himself: "satire will have room, where e'er I write" ("To Sir Godfrey Kneller" [1694], l. 94). The clearest instance of the satirist's thus lapsing into satyrism is the scatological grossness of the image Dryden finds to represent what he and his fellow playwrights have produced: "the steaming Ordures of the Stage" (65). Such domestic filthiness is far indeed from the "no[t] ignoble Verse" (17) the ode's first stanza promises will follow. There is, furthermore, a vague but unmistakable lasciviousness in the lines celebrating Anne Killigrew's chasteness:

> Her *Arethusian* Stream remains unsoil'd,
> Unmixt with Forreign Filth, and undefil'd.
> (68–69)

A bawdy insinuation occurs by the allusive translation of Anne's chasteness of mind and art into the context of Ovidian sexuality. And any reader familiar with Arethusa's story remembers that her own transformation into a spring did not save her from Alpheus, who resumed his riverhood to mingle his waters with hers.[10] The allusion to Ovid, although it leaves untouched the virtue of Dryden's heroine, encourages pornographic response and indifference to female virtue—at least in some male readers (a qualification to be taken up later). The allusive celebration of Anne Killigrew's chastity is a libertine reminder, implicit but strong, of woman's yielding or unavailing resistance to male desire, of past and prospective sexual conquests: *her* stream remains unsoiled, but as for other nymphs . . . !

Finally, the satiric agenda of stanza IV jeopardizes the satirist's moral standing, imposes upon him the lineaments of the satyr, by leading him toward blasphemy. Immediately after "the steaming Ordures," Dryden offers a metaphor of a strikingly different order to summarize the profanation of contemporary literature, which he extends by assigning a special role to Anne Killigrew:

> What can we say t'excuse our Second Fall?
> Let this thy *Vestal*, Heav'n, attone for all!
> (66–67)

Almost any modern reader will easily take the comparisons drawn in these lines—and there are others like them in the ode—to be allowable satiric and complimentary hyperboles rather than blasphemies.[11] They undoubtedly amount to something less than outright abuse of religion; however, the anachronism of our ready forgiveness of wit's slighting faith in such instances becomes at once apparent with the recollection that Donne was explicitly accused of blasphemy—by no less sophisticated a reader than Ben Jonson—on a comparable occasion: his celebration of Elizabeth Drury in the *Anniversaries*.[12] Donne's famous reply, "that he described the Idea of a Woman and not as she was," accords closely with the distinction Dryden effects between the idea of an artist and Anne Killigrew as she was, although (as will appear) Dryden found means of recognizing quite fully the actual Anne Killigrew still without compromising the idea(l) she represents.

The contrasting characterizations of Anne Killigrew and John Dryden as nymph and satyr deserve this full attention because any reading or interpretation of the ode proceeds at root by determining the relations between what the two figures represent. This is especially so because the figures, even as types, cannot be abstracted from the ode. Being poets, they represent ways of writing—call them the sublime way and the satirical way—both of which are manifest in the ode itself and each of which might in principle appear anywhere in it. Hence the most local determinations of sense a reader makes, even in passages not immediately concerned with either figure as poet, bear directly upon the larger enterprise of grasping the relations between "nymphic" and "satyrish" values. Equally, of course, a reader's general understanding of these relations in the poem will affect local interpretations. The pattern is the familiar one of the hermeneutic circle, with the difference of an unusual intimacy between whole and part arising from the whole's comprehending two contrary sets of generic and stylistic "rules" that may be realized variously in the parts. And, for better reasons than have yet been offered, readers of the ode might themselves be designated relatively "nymphic" or "satyrish" according to how they understand it, according to how in their readings they severally adjust the proportion of sublimity to satire.

So elaborate an account of what reading the ode entails would be at best superfluous if sublimity and satire distinctly kept their places in the ode—if, specifically, the satire were confined to the poem's fourth stanza. That satire—or something akin to it—is not, however, thus circumscribed or merely digressive, not largely incidental to the general tenor of the ode, has been shown most fully in two important, similar articles published independently by A. D. Hope and David M. Vieth about twenty years ago.[13] Both these readings discover widely in the poem ironies—"ambiguities in phrasing, imagery, and tone" taken to be deliberate—that gently but still tellingly qualify the perfections otherwise attributed to Mistress Killigrew, especially to her artistry. Collating Hope's and Vieth's accounts, which overlap but do

not coincide in all particulars, one finds that together they have discovered such irony in about one-fourth of the poem's lines and in
every stanza except II, VIII, and IX. To some such extent do satire
and satyrism bleed from the fourth stanza into many other parts of
the ode.

A few examples are in order, although they cannot fairly represent
Hope's and Vieth's expositions, let alone the variety in both kind and
intensity of Dryden's ironies themselves. Quite a number of the ironic
touches arise from the sudden appearance amidst the ode's sublimi-
ties of suspiciously colloquial, half-indecorous turns of phrase. The
beginning and conclusion of Dryden's survey of Killigrew's painting
provide two instances of praise thus alloyed:

> Born to the Spacious Empire of the Nine,
> One would have thought, she should have been content
> To manage well that Mighty Government;
>
> (88–91)

and

> What next she had design'd, Heaven only knows,
> To such Immod'rate Growth her Conquest rose.
>
> (146–47)

To any but a most "nymphic" ear, these lines have dubious overtones
of amazement less admiring than condescending and vexed; and, to
a reader familiar with Dryden's ways, they look typical not only of
his generally vigorous, idiomatic expression but also of a particular
way in which he met tricky situations in which persons whom the
poet would praise have defects embarrassing to his purpose. (The
opening lines of *Absalom and Achitophel*, while they are not otherwise
very comparable to instances in the ode, are the most familiar case of
such equivocation by jauntiness of idiom and tone.)

In the instances cited (and others), the insinuated uncomplimen-
tary meanings find some support in their immediate contexts; Dryden at some length (88–105), for example, wittily characterizes Killigrew's pursuit of a second vocation in painting as an overreaching,
predatory conquest, one analogous to—of all people's—Louis XIV's
territorial imperative. In other cases, the ironies lack such local rein-
forcement and may well depend for recognition upon some readiness
in the reader to notice them. This skeptical inclination is not only a
matter of temperament, however, for the more obvious of the ode's
own ironies strongly encourage it. Thus to a reader anywise prepared

for irony, the line "And to be read herself she need not fear" (80) suggests that Killigrew is so obscure a poet that nothing can threaten her tiny fame, since the public will never bother to read her and so will never discover her deficiencies. The surrounding lines force so satirical a reading to be revised: the book in which she might be read is, like "the best of Books, her Fathers Life" (79), the book not so much of her writing as of her life, and in fact now that her poems are published "Each Test, and ev'ry Light, her Muse will bear" (81). Still, the ambiguous line plants a seed of doubt, one that other ironies can nourish. Here, as in a few other instances, Dryden opens the way to irony as much by syntax as by idiom, beginning with an equivocal statement subject to satirical construction and then "correcting" it toward commendation in what follows; e.g., "Art she had none, yet wanted none: / For Nature did that Want supply" (71–72). The effect of a reader's premature closure is not wholly cancelled, however, by the "true" conclusion, not when the initial, apparently misconstrued sense accords with an undercurrent of like intimations running through the ode against its flow of tribute.

I want to argue that such ironies function and signify in ways beyond any that have been noticed. The argument emerges from one answer—necessarily somewhat hypothetical, because readers are not likely to be fully conscious of the relevant effects—to a question posed by the body of commentary on the ode, not to mention most students' responses to the poem: *Why are the ironies so difficult for readers to recognize, or at least to take account of as fully as they deserve?*[14] This is the proper form of what a thoroughly "nymphic" reader would put another way: Are the ironies "really there," or do they only appear in the eyes of some too ingenious or skeptical modern misreaders? For reasons that may be gathered from what follows, however, the aptest question is not whether the ironies exist but rather how poetic items that demand recognition can paradoxically be concealed, and to what ends.

The reason for the veiledness of the ode's ironies, for a reader's unreadiness to notice or accept them, that deserves advancement is not simply the interpretive but the *moral* discomfort or embarrassment their recognition can entail. How so? The ironies are so subtly disposed and, on the face of it, so much at odds with the encomiastic character of the poem that the reader may indeed doubt that they are really there; accordingly, to the degree that he does detect them, he attributes his response to something only in himself—to a wholly personal tendency to be skeptical of such high praise as Dryden offers Anne Killigrew. This experience—feeling oneself to be innately a debunker, ready without obvious cause to violate Killigrew's memory, and also finding oneself, it seems, either incapable of responding rightly to the ode or mistakenly doubtful of Dryden's ability to write a thoroughly noble poem—is likely to be distressing, even shameful. Such readerly self-abashment might be compared with what a complacently high-minded person would feel upon discerning in another's talk a double-entendre that the speaker apparently did not intend. No wonder, then, that readers are often reluctant to acknowledge the ironies. At first glance, such reluctance may look like commendable resistance to a temptation that might be overcome, but of course the betrayal of nymphic high-mindedness is essentially accomplished once the temptation itself is felt. As with the double-entendre, the significant occurrence is only to have found oneself satyrishly capable of entertaining a base possibility.

Any and all such guilty recriminations of the ode's readers against themselves, along with what in the poem occasions them, need to be understood as consequences of a specific rhetorical design of Dryden's *to lead certain readers to enact and possibly to confront their own satyrism.* The timeless readership that includes us is not the one for which the ode's ironies were primarily devised. They were meant most of all to entrap Dryden's contemporary readers, specifically the portion of his public whose demands upon him as a professional playwright and poet Dryden felt to be at once compelling and compromising. This is the same public with which Dryden conducted almost life-long negotiations in the prologues and epilogues of his plays, which clearly reflect his love/hate—or, better, ingratiation/resentment or flattery/contempt—relations with it. It is, most immediately, the public indicated in the ode's fourth stanza, the public that encourages and fully participates in the profanation of heavenly poesy, and so on. Dryden's thorough use of *plural* first-person pronouns in articulating the stanza's indictment establishes the tonic note. In refusing to say "I," he writes not simply with decorum and some self-exoneration; he also insists that the blame for what has gone wrong in literature must be shared between poet and public, implicating consumers as well as producers of poetry in its debasement. This insistence that *we*—we literary "satyrs," writers and readers (or dramatic spectators) alike—are collectively responsible is realized in the ode's ironies, is both made immediate and tested in their reading. The ode not only says that the taste of the times has fallen from the high standard of art Killigrew represents but also is made, by its ironies, to prove it. A knowing, worldly reader would discover the ironies and relish his complicity with the poet, whose evident skepticism about Mistress Killigrew he would take as shrewdly witty good sense. Meanwhile, as ever, a more innocent reader would miss the ironies and be equally content.

The looming question of what Dryden's purpose may have been in leading a portion of his nearest public to enact its characteristic satyrism as it read his poem remains to be considered, but something else about the ode's readership must be mentioned first. This is that there is a significant distinction to be drawn between its female and male readers. The record of the poem's readings is, regrettably if not unusually, too sketchy to confirm any suspicion that the ode has generally been read differently according to the sex of the reader. One may speculate more securely that Dryden himself was conscious that the nymphic and satyrish divisions of his contemporary public corresponded to a degree with sexual difference. That he could think of a readership divided according to sex appears in the masculinist remark he makes about Cowley's undiscriminating poetic excess: "There was plenty enough, but the dishes were ill-sorted; whole pyramids of sweetmeats for boys and women, but little of solid meat for men."[15] That Dryden also on occasion addressed a sexually identified audience anyone familiar with his work knows, anyone familiar especially with certain of his songs.[16]

Anne Killigrew's own immediate circle, which comprised the most "nymphic" portion of the ode's contemporary readership,[17] had a distinctly female character thanks not least to her having become attached, as a Maid of Honor, to the household of Mary, Duchess of York, before James ascended the throne; Dryden speaks in the ode (134–41, VII) of Killigrew's portrait of the Queen, "Before [whom] a Train of Heroins was seen."[18] The circumstance most relevant to the sexual aspect of the ode's reading is, of course, that its subject was herself not only a woman but a young female artist. This alone would all but ensure that the most satyrish portion of Dryden's contemporary male readership—although it may be allowed in passing that some women would doubtless have joined this band of satyrs—brought its ready skepticism at once into play, for what serious claim could anyone, let alone a Dryden, make that a woman had importance as a poet and painter? Moreover, Killigrew's youthful innocence, the very virtue for which she is commended without irony, would have been for such readers a further reason to dismiss her art, since it ensures that she can express nothing but ignorance of the world. The ironies only encourage and confirm this satyrish assumption: Anne Killigrew was hysterically pretentious and silly, and a poet who wrote of what she did not know.[19]

But why, finally, did Dryden design the ode to have the immediate effect on a satyrish reader of making it easy for "him" to discover beyond the poem's ostensible celebration of its subject a readiness in the poet to undermine her merits precisely akin to his own debunking tendencies? Was Dryden, at one extreme, playing a bitter private joke on the considerable portion of his public that he felt was beyond improvement in taste?: "I will give myself the secret satisfaction of celebrating what art should be even as I lead you to enjoy the illusion that I share your mocking indifference to this ideal, and so prove to myself that your depravity alone is what makes the ideal unrealizable." The bitterness of this purpose, needless to say, would be compounded by the poet's own frustration in finding no way to be a poet except by compromise with a contemptible public. He cannot rise to the occasion and, against his own aspiration, finds himself too much in company with his worst audience. Or did Dryden, at the other extreme, hope to reform the satyrish reader's taste by forcing him guiltily to recognize the errancy of his reading? This purpose, could it be accomplished, would happily prove that "The Way which [Killigrew] so well . . . learn'd below" (195) can be followed by others, both poets and readers; that "the New Morning" (192) of poesy need not—as the ode's last stanza says—entirely await the end of time but can begin to dawn even now.

These extremes are not the only possibilities, but they are already enough to suggest that to grasp the rhetorical design of the ironies would be to understand a good deal more than simply Dryden's particular intention with respect to a certain kind of reader as it appears in some local tropes. The question of the ironies' effect is necessarily a question also about every important aspect of the ode as it reflects Dryden's attitude toward his vocation. The question cannot finally be answered, because Dryden's attitude—toward himself as poet, toward his public, and most inclusively toward the interrelation of the nymphic ideal and satyrish actuality—is equivocal enough to find no simple, self-consistent resolution.[20] Dryden's attitude has the same complexity and uncertainty as do the relations between the ode's own nymphs and satyrs, indeed so much the same that those ambiguous relations—which we traced at the outset—might almost be read as an allegory of Dryden's incisive but indecisive examination of the values informing his career. In such a reading the "fear" of either nymph or satyr before the other indicates an opposition between them, or their mutual exclusiveness: each figure, with all her or his associations, calls into question, jeopardizes, or denies the other. The satyr, like everything "satyrish" in art, threatens to compromise the pure virtue of the nymph and the "nymphic," even as the latter stand as intimidating norms measured against which the satyrish appears paltry and debased. However, that the nymph-satyr relationship is also characterized by admiration represents an affinity between them, their possible reconciliation or happy accommodation. That the satyrs "admire" the nymphs might be taken, among other things, as the satiric poet's desire to pursue the ideal and make it his own, not by debauching it but by his own improvement. And if—*if*—the nymphs also admire the satyrs, the possibility of their accommodation is all the more likely, for a mutual regard allows a reconciliation without the satyr's entirely surrendering his original character. It suggests even that there is something in the satyrish that would improve the nymphic, and accordingly shifts the ideal's locus away from the nymphic pole toward an intermediate place of *concordia discors* where, say, innocence and knowledge, grace and energy, the heavenly and the earthly are harmonized.

Dryden surely wanted to believe in something like this last possibility. Moreover, certain features of the ode suggest that he there sought to realize this possibility, and with some success. The endeavor is reflected most of all in the special character of the poem's irony, which lies in its unmistakably indicating particular faults, or at least deficiencies, *without* thereby qualifying at all the general praise of Anne Killigrew. Although any of the ode's ironic implications becomes more or less satirical when it is explicitly stated, its satiric force is deflected or dissolved in and by its commendatory context.[21] Hope's and, still more, Vieth's readings interestingly confirm this desatirization of the irony. They may even, indeed, be taken as patterns of how a satyrish reader's reformation might proceed, for, in each, sharp would-be satiric observations of irony are interpretively subsumed—offered finally as enhancing additions—to an essentially nymphic reading. Both insist that the ironies more than anything else express tender, affectionate regard for Anne, a personal warmth that authenticates the ode's elegaic sentiment. In both readings the ode remains as "noble" as any nymphic reader would have it, although the character of its nobility is somewhat altered, not to say improved. Dryden's refinement or sublimation of satiric impulse, it might also be concluded, shows the power of an exemplary ideal to rescue a poet fallen into literary satyrism.

It is only apparently a puzzle that these comfortable understandings originate in Dryden's irony itself. The ironies signal a distinction between the actual Anne Killigrew and the figurative, between what she and her art actually were and the artistic ideals they are made to represent—artistic ideals only, for Anne's personal virtue is never called into question. As qualifications, therefore, what the ironies temper is not *praise* but *metaphor*, particularly the witty identification between the two Anne Killigrews—the actual woman and the saint of Art— that the poem otherwise encourages. Such ironic qualification ac- cords both with Dryden's abandonment of "metaphysical" wit and with his opinion that a poet's fancy should be subject to judgment. It is, yet again, an undoing of "mythical" or "symbolic" metaphor by "realistic" metonymy: the ironies, by their particular reminders that the poem's substitutions of one Anne for the other are really only figurative extravagances, insist that the two Annes are related not by similarity but only by contiguity.[22]

Dryden, however, was too satyrishly conscious of the anti-nymphic powers of satyrism to hold steadily to the belief that the two strains could be joined, or not to doubt that any such belief could be more than a wishful thought. If the ode gives evidence of the wish's strength, it also offers nearly equal evidence of a contrary suspicion that the satyrish poet and his public are beyond redemption. Even if his prayer that Anne "attone for all" is answered, the last stanza explicitly places the event beyond the end of time. The prayer, for that matter, may amount to little more than a wry observation that, thanks to Killi- grew's exceptional character as a poet, all the poets of the time are only just spared a blanket indictment and condemnation. In any case, she has now passed to another, better world, "never more [to] be seen by Mortal Eyes" (151,VIII), and that death divides her from all living poets leaves no middle ground where ideal and actual might harmoniously meet. Dryden's lament that "we" are "hurry'd down / This lubrique and adult'rate age" (62–63, IV) is a complaint not only against the times but against Time itself, in its proximate and inescap- able linearity. Even a poet who, like the author of the ode, recognizes earthly limitations to the extent of aspiring at the outset to write not noble but merely "no ignoble Verse" finds himself so much lapsing from his modest goal within the length of a poem that before its mid- point he must deal directly (in stanza IV) with his disability. As Dry- den represents it, the literary world is one certainly no more of har- monious reconciliations than of unmediated contraries and vicious circles. Any real power Killigrew has as an inspiring example is re- stricted, but she stands as a constant, painful reminder to the satyrish poet of his failing. He is caught in an unbreakable circuit in which satyrish error and guilty self-satire alternate. And he and his public seem likewise trapped in a perverse symbiosis, the depravity of each fostering the other's, which then becomes the reason for continuing in reprobate ways.

Certainly this darker view of the possibilities, or impossibilities, of his vocation informs Dryden's earlier and fullest treatment of the subject—in *All for Love* (1677), which he said was the only play he had written for himself.[23] Antony finds that his public role, his life in the world, cannot be reconciled with what he has come most to value— both the "perpetual spring" (III.i.25) of his love for Cleopatra and the "native spring" (III.i.132) of his own most private and authentic self. There is an affinity between the Romans' failure to see anything good in Antony's attachment to Cleopatra and the skepticism towards Anne Killigrew of the ode's satyrish public. Antony and the Dryden of the ode are even more closely akin, for neither simply sets himself against the world; each is also partly of the world ("Roman" or "satyrish") and is self-divided by having internalized an irreconcilable opposition. Antony must become a "Roman" satirist of himself as lover, much as Dryden must satyrishly conspire to deny himself the role of sublime poet. They are, of course, most alike in their ultimate if not unwavering devotion each to his "nymph"—Cleopatra and Anne— and in sadly finding that the promise of their dedication can be fulfilled only in a transcendental other world. The pathos of Dryden's later career lies in his never for long escaping a sense that he had pursued, and possibly still might be able to pursue, his vocation only by violating it. With a persistence we must admire and be grateful for, he bore this burden and—by repeatedly finding ways to inscribe the paradox he lived—kept writing.

NOTES

Earlier versions of this paper were delivered to the University of Toronto "Eighteenth-Century Group," in January 1983, and to the seminar on "Audience Entrapment in Literature and the Fine Arts" at the March 1983 meeting of the South Central Society for Eighteenth-Century Studies. I am grateful to both these audiences and to their convenors, Heather Jackson and David Vieth respectively.

1 John Dryden, *The Works of John Dryden* (Berkeley and Los Angeles: University of California Press, 1956—), vol. 3, *Poems 1685–1692*, ed. Earl Miner and Vinton A. Dearing (1969), p. 113, ll. 116–18. Subsequent references to this printing of the ode are given parenthetically in the text by line and, when it may be convenient, stanza numbers.

2 "Admiration" and "fear" are not, of course, entirely opposite. In the context of sublimity and religious feeling associated with odes, the sentiments are especially likely to overlap, the common ground being designated by "awe" (see the definition cited from Johnson below). Even in

this context, however, "admiration" generally excludes fear, indeed is often used precisely to refer to *un*intimidating awesomeness or sublimity, to wholly pleasurable wonder or adoration before high objects of regard; for example, Addison on greatness: "Our Admiration, which is a very pleasing Motion of the Mind, immediately rises at the Consideration of any Object that takes up a great deal of room in the Fancy" (*Spectator* No. 413). Not surprisingly, Burke provides a partial exception: "The sublime, which is the cause of . . .[admiration], always dwells on great objects, and terrible" (*A Philosophical Enquiry into the Origin of Our Ideas of the Sublime and Beautiful*, ed. J. T. Boulton [London: Routledge and Kegan Paul, 1958], 3.13, p. 113), but Burke's regular term for the effect of the sublime is "astonishment" and he elsewhere (2.1, p. 57) numbers admiration with reverence and respect among its "inferior effects."

3 *Poems by Mrs Anne Killigrew* (London, 1686 [1685]; facsim. rpt. Gainesville, Fla.: Scholars' Facsimiles & Reprints, 1967), p. 29. On the date of publication, see Richard Morton's Introduction to this edition, p. vi.

4 To cite but the most relevant instance, Thomas H. Fujimura, "The Personal Element in Dryden's Poetry," *PMLA* 89 (1974): 1012–15, argues that the "vital personal element" of the Killigrew ode, "the one element that makes the poetic statement moving," lies in its being "Dryden's first major Catholic work." The importance of Dryden's conversion may surely be allowed for without assuming that the poet's or his reader's interest in literature is necessarily "impersonal" and "abstract" to the extent that it is "secular."

5 On Arethusa's links with pastoral poetry, see the note to l. 68 in *Poems 1685–1692*, p. 320.

6 That Dryden, in fact, followed others in closely connecting lyric—that is, poetry as music—and pastoral appears in the exquisite moment in *All for Love* (I.230–44) when soft music induces a state of soothing pastoral consciousness in Antony. This is not the place to pursue the subject of Dryden's general attitude to pastoral. Of immediate relevance, however, is that some of the terms he uses to describe Anne Killigrew and her art reappear in the epistle prefixed to his later (1697) translation of Virgil's eclogues (*Of Dramatic Poesy and Other Critical Essays*, ed. George Watson, 2 vols. [London: Dent, 1962], 2:216 ff., esp. 217–19; hereafter cited as Watson). Both the pastoral Virgil and Anne Killigrew wrote youthful love poetry and both display a native character of sublimity. Both were not only young but much younger than Dryden at the time of his own writing; moreover, he outlived them and writes with a strong sense of the cost of his longevity. Both are associated with the lark (Ode, 192, X; Watson, 2:218—where, interestingly, the Virgil-lark association is not simply a compliment to the poet). Both have ambitions that lead them to invade provinces that less presumptuous young artists would not aspire to make their own (Ode, 88 ff., VI; Watson, 2:218–19). These coincidences, like the equivocations of the ode considered below, invite an adjustment between two ways of taking them: they enhance the stature of Anne Killigrew (she was a Virgil nipped in the bud) and/or they denigrate Virgil as a pastoral

poet (he wrote no better than Anne Killigrew). To be sure and as will become clearer, these stark options do not exhaust all the possible implications of a critical diction that brings together a Killigrew and a Virgil. What is at once apparent is that a reading of the ode has something to contribute to an understanding of Dryden's attitude toward pastoral and, conversely, that a thorough study of Dryden's attitude toward pastoral would enrich any reading of the ode.

7 Admittedly, Dryden himself rightly opposed any etymological grounds for this collocation in his "Discourse concerning . . . Satire" (1693): following Casaubon against Scaliger, he there rejects the derivation of "satire" from *satyrus* (Watson, 2:97–98). In the "Discourse" and elsewhere, also, Dryden wrote to establish the dignity of satire. Such *dis*collocations of "satyr" and "satire" are not at all beside the point, but should be understood as expressing (only) one of the directions the mature Dryden's second thoughts about his career took. Another direction appears even in the "Discourse," for in failing to distinguish orthographically between "satyr" and "satire"—and, still more, in making a point of this failure (Watson, 2:116)—he impishly qualifies or contradicts his own scholarly argument. If the earnest Dryden invites etymology to prove that a satirist cannot be a satyr, the witty Dryden allows something else—although just what remains a question (confession at one extreme, nose-thumbing at the other). The witty Dryden certainly realized at least that the satyr-satire connection, even as a pun, finds in literature all that it needs to sustain its meaningfulness. As late as the Prologue to *Amphitryon* (1690), Dryden wrote with obvious personal reference and unapologetic nostalgia of a satirical "Satyr." For an excellent general discussion of satire's "satyrism," see Michael Seidel, *Satiric Inheritance: Rabelais to Sterne* (Princeton: Princeton University Press, 1979), ch. 1.

8 See Hugh Macdonald, "The Attacks on Dryden," in *Essential Articles for the Study of John Dryden*, ed. H. T. Swedenberg, Jr. (Hamden, Conn.: Archon Books, 1966), pp. 22–53, and James Kinsley's Introduction to his and Helen Kinsley's *Dryden: The Critical Heritage* (New York: Barnes & Noble, 1971), which also includes (pp. 227–40) the passages concerning Dryden in Jeremy Collier's *A Short View of the Immorality and Profaneness of the English Stage* (1698).

9 On formal verse satire and Dryden's thorough familiarity with its pattern, see Howard D. Weinbrot, *The Formal Strain: Studies in Augustan Imitation and Satire* (Chicago and London: University of Chicago Press, 1969), ch. 3.

10 It should be remarked that Ovid's account (*Metamorphoses*, 5.574–641) allows for Arethusa's immediate escape from her pursuer. Ovid breaks off, however, before Arethusa's passage to Ortygia, where by other accounts no less familiar to Dryden and his audience, Alpheus caught up with her; in Dryden's own translation of the *Aeneid* (1697), for example,

> *Alpheus*, as Old Fame reports, has found
> From *Greece* a secret Passage under-ground:
> By Love to beauteous *Arethusa* led;

And, mingling here, they rowl in the same Sacred Bed.
(3.910–13)

That Dryden appears here to know and be taking some account of high-minded allegorical readings of the story, such as that Alpheus's pursuit of Arethusa represents the soul's aspiration to virtue, may complicate the ode's allusion but does not cancel its sexual innuendo.

11 For example, A. D. Hope, "Anne Killigrew, or the Art of Modulating," in *Dryden's Mind and Art*, ed. Bruce King (Edinburgh: Oliver and Boyd, 1969), p. 108.

12 "Ben Jonson's Conversations with William Drummond of Hawthornden," in *Ben Jonson*, ed. C. H. Hereford and Percy Simpson (Oxford: Clarendon Press, 1925), 1:133.

13 Hope's essay, cited here from *Dryden's Mind and Art*, ed. King, pp. 99–113, appeared earlier in *Southern Review: An Australian Journal of Literary Studies*, no. 1 (1963), pp. 4–14, reprinted in Hope's *The Cave and the Spring: Essays on Poetry* (Adelaide: Rigby, 1965; rpt. Chicago: University of Chicago Press, 1970), pp. 129–43. David M. Vieth, "Irony in Dryden's Ode to Anne Killigrew," *Studies in Philology* 62 (1965): 91–100; the phrase quoted in the following sentence appears on p. 92.

14 By "readers" the question designates primarily those who read the ode knowing neither Hope's nor Vieth's discussion of the poem, nor any of the few subsequent treatments acknowledging the strain of irony. Even among professional readers, however, these accounts have established less of a watershed in the history of the ode's reading than might be expected. Earl Miner, both in *Dryden's Poetry* (Bloomington: Indiana University Press, 1967), pp. 253–65, and in annotating the ode in *Poems 1685–1692*, acknowledges the strain of irony but treats it in rather gingerly fashion, as does Barbara Kiefer Lewalski; *Donne's "Anniversaries" and the Poetry of Praise: The Creation of a Symbolic Mode* (Princeton: Princeton University Press, 1973), pp. 345–48. Even the fullest other discussions of the ode, however early or late, are with rare exception all but uniformly "nymphic," although Vieth (p. 93) has acutely noticed signs in some of these that "critics have not been entirely unaware of the irony" even as they explain it away; in addition to accounts cited elsewhere here, see those listed by Vieth, p. 91n., and also Ruth Wallerstein, *Studies in Seventeenth-Century Poetic* (Madison: University of Wisconsin Press, 1950), pp. 136–41; Germaine Greer, *The Obstacle Race: The Fortunes of Women Painters and their Work* (New York: Farrar Straus Giroux, 1979), pp. 283–84; and Eric Rothstein, *Restoration and Eighteenth-Century Poetry 1660–1780* (Boston: Routledge & Kegan Paul, 1981), pp. 9–10.

Contrary, however, to most of these testimonies is the possibility that the ode's most famous reader felt its ironies even without the benefit of modern criticism. What Johnson—whose declaration in his life of Dryden that the poem "is undoubtedly the noblest ode that our language ever has produced" (*Lives of the English Poets*, ed. George Birkbeck Hill, 3 vols. [Oxford: Clarendon Press, 1905], 1:439) provides the nymphic readers' motto—

both says and fails to say about the ode is tantalizingly suggestive. Certainly he noticed in it an unevenness or inconsistency that the irregular mixture of "nymphic" and "satyrish" elements easily accounts for: "All the stanzas are not equal. An imperial crown cannot be one continued diamond; the gems must be held together by some less valuable matter" (1:439). Johnson also found a particular incongruity in the last stanza's account of Judgment Day—"When rattling bones together fly, / From the four quarters of the sky"—and commented that "It is indeed never in [Dryden's] power to resist the temptation of a jest" (1:463; and see Hope, "Anne Killigrew," pp. 102, 111–13). Perhaps more telling is that Johnson's sharp eye for insincerity, most famously exercised in his comments on *Lycidas*, was not aroused by reading the ode; did he, then, sense the ironic qualifications that make Dryden's praise of Killigrew more credible? Likewise, Johnson's impatience with Milton's pastoralism finds no echo in his response to the ode, although it provides him with strikingly similar occasions: "Passion . . . calls [not] upon Arethuse . . . nor tells of 'rough satyrs and fauns with cloven heel.' 'Where there is leisure for fiction there is little grief'" (1:163). Doubtless Dryden escapes censure largely because the pastoralism of the ode is not his but his subject's; even so, one cannot but suspect again that Johnson may have apprehended that the ode is especially ironical in its treatment of Anne's pastoral painting.

15 Preface to *Fables Ancient and Modern* (1700), in Watson, 2:280.

16 See especially the "Song for a Girl" in *Love Triumphant* (V.i; 1694), of which Earl Miner (*Dryden's Poetry*, pp. 240–42) provides a most perceptive account where anyone interested in the sexual agendas of Dryden's work will find even more than Miner finds space to explain fully. The song is teasingly directed just to the satyrish male portion of the audience and catches it between idealism and baser sexual motives. Elsewhere Miner suggests that Dryden's awareness in his later years that his audience had expanded to include "a larger component of women readers" led him to amend his poetics to allow more emphatic "moral import" ("The Poetics of the Critical Act: Dryden's Dealings with Rivals and Predecessors," in *Evidence in Literary Scholarship: Essays in Memory of James Marshall Osborn*, ed. René Wellek and Alvaro Ribeiro [Oxford: Clarendon Press, 1979], p. 59). Miner goes on to speak (p. 60), rather as I do, of a "discrepancy" in Dryden's later work "between the simple moral foreground and the more complex moral background" corresponding to the capacities and needs of unsophisticated readers (mostly women) and sophisticated readers (mostly men). In the ode, however, the "knowing audience" figures not as the faithful "saving remnant" of literati Miner describes, but in its darkest guise as an unexaggerated parody of Dryden's best audience, of what he desired but too little found in his actual public.

17 The ode's ironies may well partly have originated in the conflict between the expectations of this assuredly nymphic audience and those of Dryden's larger public, with respect especially to Dryden's treatment of Killigrew's artistry. Her family and courtly circle naturally expected sincere

praise, yet Dryden could hardly allow more disinterested readers to think that he really conceived *ne plus ultra* Killigrew's poetry and painting. Forced by these rhetorical circumstances toward an uncomfortable choice between tact and truth, between presenting himself as either an obliging fool or an ungracious expert, Dryden ingeniously escaped from his double bind by introducing ironic qualifications of Killigrew's merits as an artist subtle enough that any reader predisposed to think well of her—but, he might suppose, only such a reader—would not notice them!

By 1685, of course, Dryden's talent for compounding praise and more or less satiric fault-finding was very highly developed and had been exercised often in celebrating the merits of artists whose actual achievements were modest, i.e., "To John Hoddesdon, on His Divine Epigrams" (1650—Dryden's second published poem, written by one eighteen-year-old to another, in which already appear playful subversions of high compliment); "To My Honored Friend, Sir Robert Howard" (1660; see David M. Vieth, "Irony in Dryden's Verses to Sir Robert Howard," *Essays in Criticism* 22 [1972]: 239–43); "To Mr. Lee, on His *Alexander*" (1677); "To the Earl of Roscommon, on his Excellent Essay on Translated Verse" (1684); and "To the Memory of Mr. Oldham" (1684; see Dustin Griffin, "Dryden's 'Oldham' and the Perils of Writing," *Modern Language Quarterly* 37 [1976]: 133–50). The same talent continued to find occasions after the ode's composition, as "To Sir Godfrey Kneller" especially shows; see Cedric D. Reverand II, "Dryden on Dryden in 'To Sir Godfrey Kneller,'" *Papers on Language & Literature* 17 (1981): 164–80. Taken together, such genially ironic poems define a vocational milieu in which rivalry and fellow-feeling are compounded. Quite the same literary world is very differently represented in the extreme mockeries of *MacFlecknoe*, the work of Dryden's arguably nearest (allowing for inversions) to the ode; on the two poems' affinities, see Mother Mary Eleanor, "*Anne Killigrew* and *Mac Flecknoe*," *Philological Quarterly* 43 (1964): 47–54.

18 The passage is somewhat ambiguous: it may be that the "Train of Heroins" appeared only in the actual Coronation Day procession and does not appear in the painting (which I have had no success in tracing). By a happy coincidence, Anne Kingsmill (later Anne Finch) was likewise a Maid of Honor at the same time, although she was not then yet a poet, or at least not evidently known to be one. I thank Ann Messenger for—in keeping with her name—improving my knowledge of Kingsmill's early years.

19 Most relevantly, and as a last example of the ode's irony:

> Ev'n Love (for Love sometimes her Muse exprest)
> Was but a Lambent-flame which play'd about her Brest:
> Light as the Vapours of a Morning Dream,
> So cold herself, whilst she such Warmth exprest,
> 'Twas *Cupid* bathing in *Diana's* Stream.
>
> (83–87, V)

20 I here openly join others who eschew the procedures of New Criticism for establishing literary coherence or unity, procedures the strictness of which has kept an essential feature of Dryden's work—its radical contra-dictoriness—from being easily described; see especially the wide-ranging and important account of Dryden's "disjunctions" in Laura Brown, "The Ideology of Restoration Poetic Form: John Dryden," *PMLA* 97 (1982): 395–407 (pp. 400–401 on the ode), and also David M. Vieth, "Divided Con-sciousness: The Trauma and Triumph of Restoration Culture," *Tennessee Studies in Literature* 22 (1977): 46–62, where the ode's oppositions are de-scribed—in a significant revision of his earlier explication—as unme-diated (pp. 53–54). An early account, still nearly the best, of Dryden's "divided consciousness" is R. J. Kaufmann's Introduction to Dryden's *All for Love* (San Francisco: Chandler, 1962), reprinted with revisions as "On the Poetics of Terminal Tragedy: Dryden's *All for Love*," in *Dryden: A Col-lection of Critical Essays*, ed. Bernard N. Schilling (Englewood Cliffs, N.J.: Prentice-Hall, 1963), pp. 86–94.

21 Some modern nymphic readers would find less reason to resist the ode's ironies were they less inclined to take sarcasm as the model of negative irony and accordingly to suppose that an irony's covert meaning simply reverses and supersedes its explicit sense. Such unnecessary resistance appears, for example, in Robert Daly's otherwise valuable "Dryden's Ode to Anne Killigrew and the Communal Work of Poets," *Texas Studies in Literature and Language* 18 (1976): 184–97.

22 This last formulation derives from Roman Jakobson, "Two Aspects of Lan-guage and Two Types of Aphasic Disturbances," in Jakobson and Morris Halle, *Fundamentals of Language*, Janua Linguarum, Series Minor, 1 (The Hague: Mouton, 1956), pp. 69–96.

23 Preface to the translation of Fresnoy's *De arte graphica* (1695), in Watson, 2:207.

"More Strange than True": Sir Hans Sloane, King's Transactioneer, and the Deformation of English Prose

ROGER D. LUND

Of all those "abuses of human learning" arraigned by the members of the Scriblerus Circle, perhaps none was lampooned more consistently or more memorably than the antics of the modern scientific virtuosi.[1] That "tribe, with weeds and shells fantastic crown'd" not only frolics through the *Dunciad*,[2] it also appears in *Three Hours After Marriage*, assumes new life in the third book of *Gulliver's Travels* and finds its ultimate incarnation in *The Memoirs of Martinus Scriblerus*. Of course, the Scriblerians were not alone in their satirical assaults on the pretensions of the modern scientist. Shadwell and Butler had established the pattern in *The Virtuoso* and *The Elephant in the Moon*. But of all those early satirical portraits of the modern virtuoso, none was more sharply outlined or more garishly colored than *The Transactioneer* of William King, a work described by a contemporary observer as "one of the severest and merriest satires that ever was written in Prose,"[3] a work that exerted a significant influence upon later satirists of science, and one which deserves to be rediscovered by modern readers.[4] Perhaps more important, King's parody of modern scientific prose style, as revealed in the *Philosophical Transactions*, introduces a new element to satires on the modern virtuoso. To quote that great compiler of ephemera, Isaac Disraeli: [King] "took advantage of their [the *Philosophical Transactions*] perplexed and often unintelligible descriptions; of the meanness of their style . . . of their credulity that heaped up marvels, and their vanity that prided itself on petty discoveries, and invented a new species of satire."[5]

Published anonymously in 1700, *The Transactioneer with some of his Philosophical Fancies: In Two Dialogues* satirized the editorial competence and professional reputation of Sir Hans Sloane, secretary of the Royal Society and editor of the *Philosophical Transactions*. The work itself consists of two dialogues: the first between a Gentleman (King's spokesman) and a Virtuoso, who defends Sloan's accomplishments as a writer of scientific reports; the second between this same Gentleman and the Transactioneer (Sloane), who defends his own editorial practice in the *Philosophical Transactions*. The satirical logic here is much the same as that in King's earlier dialogue satires aimed at the pedantry of Richard Bentley: a naïve observer (the Gentleman) asks seemingly innocent and well-meaning questions of the satirical victims (the Virtuoso and the Transactioneer) eliciting from them a series of sincere, pompous, stupid, and damningly self-revelatory answers.[6] Apparently the satire did its work only too well, outraging such reputable scientists as John Ray, who condemned *The Transactioneer* as a "scurrilous pamphlet,"[7] and inspiring the Royal Society itself to attempt the discovery and prosecution of the anonymous author.[8] It is not entirely clear why King took such direct aim at Sir Hans Sloane, since there exists no evidence to suggest that Sloane had in any way injured or insulted King or his friends, as had Bentley in the Phalaris Controversy. What seems more likely is that as a staunch defender of the Ancients, King could have been expected to aim his satirical shafts at Moderns of every stripe. Sloane was certainly a conspicuous Modern, and as King observed in *The Transactioneer*, his "peculiar way of expressing himself," was a "modern style" (p. 45).[9] Moreover, as the secretary of the Royal Society and the editor of the *Philosophical Transactions* (roles he had assumed in 1693),[10] Sloane stood as the most visible embodiment of the Royal Society, its aims and methods. And as a scientist not universally admired by his colleagues, one whose "gambols had brought the study of nature much into ridicule,"[11] Sloane easily symbolized all that was most excessive, self-aggrandizing and ridiculous in the activities of the modern virtuoso.

Sloane was perhaps most notorious for his collections of natural and antiquarian curiosities, a prodigious aggregation of stuff that was eventually to form the basis for the collections of the British Museum.[12] As one might expect, King laughs at this passion for collecting, quoting copiously from the *Philosophical Transactions* regarding Sloane's acquisition of a great Chinese cabinet containing among its numerous treasures "Eight several instruments made for paring the nails, at which in China the people are very curious and dextrous . . . an instrument much like a horse curry-comb with which 'they curry the natives as we do horses'" (p. 16). As the Virtuoso triumphantly asserts, Sloane "hath not so much as neglected an ear-picker or a rusty razor; for he values any thing that comes from The Indies or China at a high rate; for, were it but a pebble or a cockleshell from thence, he would soon write a comment upon it, and perpetuate its memory upon a copper plate" (p. 14). The essence of the Gentleman's question, "But pray of what use are the China ear-pickers, in the way of knowledge?" (p. 14) suffuses the satirical argument of *The Transactioneer* as it does most Augustan satires on science. In this respect, King's implicit indictment of the virtuosi and the activities of the Royal Society seems familiar enough: that the Fellows of the Royal Society were primarily interested in those things which no one wanted to know; that their mania for collecting revealed less desire for real knowledge than an indulgence of some freakish private enthusiasm; that what they finally discovered (when they discovered anything at all) had no practical application; and that for all their protestations of seeking to advance human knowledge, the members of the Royal Society, by and large, had contributed little or nothing to the collective health, wisdom, or material comfort of mankind.

Such charges are unfair, to be sure, but then fairness was never a salient feature of any Augustan satire on modern science. Indeed, were the repetition of this familiar litany of complaints the sum of King's literary achievement in *The Transactioneer*, the present obscurity of that work might seem richly deserved. What sets this particular satire apart from other Augustan satires on science, however, and what makes it worthy of our notice, is its preoccupation with the language of scientific reporting, and its serious examination through irony and ridicule of the degree to which the Royal Society and Sloane as its public representative, had preserved those new standards of scientific style so boldly enunciated by Thomas Sprat in *The History of the Royal Society* (1667).

Sprat had established high standards, nothing less than a "constant Resolution to reject all the amplifications, digressions, and swellings of style; to return back to the primitive purity, and shortness, when men deliver'd so many *things*, almost in an equal number of *words*."[13] Indeed, according to Sprat, these were more than fervent hopes; they were accomplished fact. The Royal Society had "exacted from all their members, a close, naked, natural way of speaking; positive expressions; clear senses; a native easiness; bringing all things as near the Mathematical plainness, as they can; and preferring the language of Artizans, Countrymen, and Merchants before that of Wits, or Scholars."[14] Whatever else Sprat may have been suggesting with regard to the reformation of modern prose style in general, there can be no question that he *was* demanding a new set of stylistic standards specifically tailored to the requirements of empirical observation and the description of material phenomena.[15] It was to be a superior style, defined by its clarity, its referential precision, and one characterized by the absence of that rhetorical obfuscation so common to the Schoolmen and that self-consciousness and preciosity so characteristic of the modern Wit.

Such was the new standard by which scientific writing was to be judged, and such is the standard by which King ironically condemns the works of Sir Hans Sloane. While King nowhere explicitly mentions Sprat or the Royal Society's program of language reform, it is only within the context of those new stylistic standards established by the Royal Society that King's assault on the barbarous style of the *Philosophical Transactions* makes sense to the modern reader.[16] As the first modern satirist to turn his attention to the actual style of the *Philosophical Transactions* themselves, King not only ridicules the dubious achievement of their editor, Sir Hans Sloane, he also calls into question the success of the Royal Society's program for reforming scientific prose. Indeed King's unique achievement as a satirist of modern science, I would suggest, is his ability to isolate and ridicule precisely those stylistic excesses which the Royal Society had so proudly claimed to have rooted out of their own publications.

As the editor of the *Philosophical Transactions*, the most obvious and familiar specimen of modern scientific writing, Sloane was *de facto* the defender of those stylistic reforms outlined in the *History of the Royal Society*. Yet, according to King, Sloane had torpedoed the linguistic program of the Society and subjected both the *Philosophical Transactions* and the Royal Society to public ridicule:

> All who read his "Transactions," either in England or beyond the seas, cry out, "That the subjects which he writes on are generally so ridiculous and mean; and he treats of them so emptily, and in a style so confused and unintelligible, that it is plain he is so far from any useful knowledge, that he wants even common grammar." (p. 5)

Like the ironic spokesman of Swift's *Tale of a Tub*, King's narrator claims to be a sincere defender of the Royal Society, himself a virtuoso, who attacks only the individual—Sir Hans Sloane—and not modern science itself:

Perhaps it may seem strange, that I, who am no Member of the
Royal Society, should deal so freely with the person and some correspondents of one who is slipped into the post of Secretary to that
illustrious Body. But I am moved by the respect I have for Natural
Studies, and a fear least those men who have made such great advances in it, and thereby gained the applause of all the learned world,
should lose any part of it by the trifling and shallow management
of one who wants every qualification that is requisite for such a
post. (p. 5)

There is some logic to King's ironic disclaimer here, for the *Philosophical Transactions* were the personal responsibility of Sloane himself,
and did not become the "official" journal of the Royal Society until
1753.[17] Moreover, one senses the palpable disingenuousness of King's
defense of the Royal Society, since nowhere else in his writings does
King suggest anything but hostility toward modern virtuosi, Sloane
in particular.[18] Just as Pope draws attention to the political overtones
of his own works by vociferously claiming to be apolitical, so King
attracts our attention to the responsibility of the Royal Society itself
by so loudly defending its innocence.

   Like Pope's assault on the dunces, King's attack on Sloane and his
fellow correspondents grows out of a pattern of selective misquota-
tion. Although King claims that Sloane's "own words will be the best
proof" of his want of grammar, confusion and unintelligibility, and
claims as well that he has "been so careful in producing them, that I
defy him to show he is once misrepresented" (p. 5), a careful comparison of King's excerpts from the *Philosophical Transactions* with their
originals, reveals a consistent pattern of calculated (albeit minor) mis-
quotation and quotation out of context, all designed to magnify Sloan's
stylistic peccadillos into cardinal sins against language and against
that program of stylistic reform originally proposed by the Royal Society. While it is true that virtually every "word" King attributes to
Sloane is indeed lifted from the pages of the *Transactions,* at times he
conflates passages not closely linked in the text itself, or omits significant mitigating information as a way of highlighting (if not indeed
fabricating) solecisms not nearly so apparent in the original text.

   Yet, where King's misquotations ironically distort the arguments
and observations in the *Philosophical Transactions,* his consistently accurate annotation of the passages quoted suggests that he expects his
readers to consult the record for themselves in order to verify the
substantial validity of his charges concerning Sloane's trivial subjects,
mangled grammar and garbled syntax. In this respect, King's artful
synthesis of imaginary narrative, dialogue, and carefully annotated

quotations from his satirical target anticipates the practice of the Scriblerians in the *Dunciad Variorum* and *Memoirs of Martinus Scriblerus*. Just as Pope was to comb the works of his victims for salient examples of their dullness, so King sifts the *Philosophical Transactions* for specimens of incoherence which are meant to imply far graver forms of intellectual weakness on the part of modern scientists. One might argue that King's satirical anatomizing of scientific style and his hostility to Sloane's careless use of language are but extensions of that form of philological criticism so characteristic of his satirical evisceration of Bentley in the *Dialogues of the Dead* and so important in later Scriblerian satires on modern dullness.[19]

Whereas the Scriblerians were later to assert that failures of written style were outward signs of some greater moral and cultural betrayal, some impending "Universal Darkness," King argues only that Sloane's stylistic failures are a betrayal of the original mission of the Royal Society. Part of that mission, of course, was to draw careful distinctions between those rhetorical flourishes proper and necessary in imaginative writing and that leaner, less rhetorical style suitable for the description of natural phenomena. Yet, as King points out, Sloane's version of the *Philosophical Transactions* actually contained a wide range of materials of a literary rather than a purely scientific interest. For example, the Transactioneer cites No. 263 of the *Transactions* to the effect that in Lincolnshire they use strained hog's dung to wash clothes, hence the proverb "in Lincolnshire where the hogs sh-t Soap, and the cows sh-t Fire" (p. 41).[20] Surprised by this account, the Gentleman observes: "Truly we are much obliged to you and your Correspondent, for this proverb and its explication" (p. 41). Failing to recognize the implicit suggestion that perhaps it was not the business of the Royal Society to be retailing proverbs in the first place, the Transactioneer merely confirms the infelicity of his editorial choices: "I must needs say, a great many Philosophers would never have heard this proverb, had it not been published in my 'Transactions'" (p. 41). Where Sloane himself had proclaimed that the work of the Royal Society was the discovery and transmission of "real knowledge,"[21] the Transactioneer takes particular pride in having published "a copy of verses upon an Eel" (p. 42).[22] So it is that he also quotes proudly from No. 233 an account of a medicinal spring submitted by a Mr. Aubrey, a spring containing "a rill an ell broad; between two collines, covered with wood, about twelve yards from this spring; the rill, which falls from a rock eight or nine foot high, makes a very grateful noise" (p. 33). King's ironic spokesman is quick to detect the note of non-scientific aesthetic appreciation here, remarking "A very fine description of a medicinal spring; surely that 'grateful noise' will invite several curious persons to take a view of it. But is that the only medicinal quality?" (p. 33). Here, as he does throughout *The Transactioneer,* King draws our attention to the rhetorical "adornments" of the accounts in the *Philosophical Transactions.* Even though a close check of *Transactions* No. 233 indicates that Aubrey mentions the peculiar presence of a limestone deposit near the spring (apparently accounting for its medicinal properties), King's satirical point is well taken. For Aubrey's description of this spring does seem more the recollection of a poetical tourist than the considered report of a careful scientific observer.[23]

Sprat had vociferously denounced both modern wits and religious controversialists for their "trick of Metaphors" and "volubility of tongue,"[24] but King points out that Sloane himself was no stranger to the exploitation of figurative language, choosing for special notice a passage from one of Sloane's correspondents who had reported that "of late the poor people have set their wits as if it were on the tenterhooks, to make turnip-bread in Essex" (p. 37). While the Gentleman observes sardonically that the "world will be very much obliged to you, for teaching them to make turnip-bread" (p. 37), presumably not one of the primary goals of the new science, he is even more amazed by the "language of your Correspondent" (p. 37). Replies the Transactioneer: "I thought the novelty of the style would surprise you" (p. 37). To which the Gentleman answers: "Surprize me! I am amazed at it. 'Set their wits as if it were on the tenter-hooks!' The simile is very close and noble" (p. 37), an ironic encomium on Sloane's enthusiasm for figurative description which subtly undermines his credibility as an editor. Here, as throughout *The Transactioneer,* King suggests that Sloane and his confederates were as proud of embellishing their accounts as any Court Wit, and repeatedly the Transactioneer draws particular attention to the elegance of his own style and that of his fellows.[25]

Where Sprat had recommended the rejection of all "amplifications, digressions, and swellings of style,"[26] King's Virtuoso praises Sloane for writing in a language "most prodigiously sublime, and penned too in a wondrous manner: so that it is a hard matter for the generality of Virtuosi, who imitate Bacon, Boyle, or men of that character, to write in the language observable in most of those papers; for there the expressions are suitable to the sublimity of their subjects, and consequently mighty mysterious, and above the reach of those Gentlemen" (p. 8). The Royal Society had certainly not intended that scientific reports should ever be "mighty mysterious"; King implies, however, that so lofty and careless had Sloane's style become, that the remnant within the Society who still adhered to its original stylistic principles could neither copy nor even understand him.

The Virtuoso, of course, defends such obfuscation. To the Gentleman's remark, "This to a man of ordinary understanding is pretty odd! What would the drift of this be, did the Author put it into English?" the Virtuoso contemptuously replies: "I see, Sir, you are altogether a stranger to the language of our Author's writings, and the present 'Philosophical Transactions;' otherwise you would easily have known the meaning of all this" (p. 10). Consistently, both the Virtuoso and the Transactioneer alike speak of modern philosophic style as if it were a kind of private and hieratic language not meant to be revealed to vulgar eyes. Nowhere is this new grand style more proudly displayed than in *Philosophical Transactions* No. 192, an account of the *Arbor baccisera, laurisolia, aromatica fructu viridi calyculato ramoso,* a plant whose "bark consists of two parts, one outward, and another inward." When the Gentleman remarks that such a definition clarifies little since he knows "none but what hath an out-side and an in-side," the Virtuoso responds:

> But you misapprehend; this bark is different from all others, for it is two Barks; our Author uses *parts* and *barks* as synonymous terms. . . . This he does by dividing the word *bark* in two parts, and then calling each of those parts a bark; for, says he, "the outward bark is as thin as a milled shilling, the inward bark being as thick as a milled crown piece." Mark the aptness of the similies. But the excellence of our Author in describing plants will be much more evident if we look upon what follows: for a little after he adds, "The ends of the twigs are branched into bunches of flowers, standing something like Umbels, each of which hath a foot-stalk, on the top of which is a Calyx, made up of some Foliola, in which stand five purple Petala, within which is a large Stylus. (pp. 11–12)

Confused, the poor Gentleman asks, "Pray, where lies the excellence of all this? The style is so lofty, I am not able to discern it" (p. 12). To which the Virtuoso replies: "The excellence! Where should it lie, but in the Umbels, the Calyx, the Foliola, and the purple Petala; these are high-flowing words, and not common English" (p. 12). So much for the simple language of "Artizans, Countrymen, and Merchants." Where Sprat had pleaded for simplicity and clarity, Sloane offers instead only figurative language (those "apt similies") and hard words.[27]

When asked to explain the meaning of one of Sloane's terms—"calyculated berries"—the Virtuoso off-handedly replies, "It is only a term of our Author's." Observes the Gentleman, "Indeed he is a happy man, in forming of phrases and in coining new words" (p. 12). Bacon, Hobbes, and Sprat (among others) had all complained of the Ancients' predilection for inventing hard words (Hobbes condemns "incorporeal substance," for example) and for multiplying meaningless distinctions. Yet, as King suggests here, Sir Hans Sloane and his correspondents were as taken with the coining of new words and the creation of their own specialized nomenclature as any Schoolman. Indeed this "synonymyzing" tendency is one of the features of the new scientific style that King ridicules most sharply. He draws particular attention to the reports of one James Pettiver, a wit and "darling of the Temple coffee-house club" (p. 24), whose submissions to the *Philosophical Transactions* provided precisely those minute descriptions of caterpillars, spiders, thistles, and moss so gleefully ridiculed by Shadwell, Swift, and Pope. "Butterflies are his main delight. He gives them strange cramp names, and values himself for being the first catcher. 'Papilos Leucomelanos,' says he 'is not yet clearly described by any author'" (p. 25), an ambiguous statement carefully excerpted by King to suggest that perhaps Pettiver has not described the creature either. However, Pettiver does have the gift of elaborating and multiplying names for things: "he values nothing that has not as many titles and names as the King of Persia. He will find in one Author or other twenty names for the same thing; and thinks it impossible 'to enumerate the many advantages that will occur from this synonymizing of Authors'" (p. 25). Here King ridicules James Pettiver as a contributor to the *Philosophical Transactions*, but in the Transactioneer's fatal admission that Pettiver's style "is my style too exactly; only a little more clear" (p. 25), King also attacks Sloane as editor for encouraging this wild substitution of words for things, and as writer for having adopted this style himself.

At times King suggests that Sloane publishes such nonsense as Pettiver's catalogue of rarities (No. 224) out of political motives in order to enhance his own position or to reward his favorites, a suspicion actually shared by many of the Fellows of the Royal Society itself.[28] And King argues that there is something quite self-serving about Sloane's use of difficult and incomprehensible jargon. When the Gentleman asks why, for example, it is necessary to know that the fossilized tongue of a fish dug up in Maryland looked exactly like that "taken from the Pastinaca marina, frequent in the seas of Jamaica" (p. 16), the Virtuoso rather pompously replies:

> You mistake the design: it was never intended to advance Natural knowledge; for who is the wiser for knowing that the bones of a dead fish have been dug up, or where? No, the true use of the story is to amuse the ignorant; for, if they talk of things that are out of the

> way, we presently make an harangue about "the Mandibulum of a *Pastinaca Marina* found fossile in Maryland" and then they are "silenced in an instant." (p. 17)

Time and again, King complains that Sloane had offered his readers tautology in the place of definition, mere nomenclature and neologism where explanation and identification ought to stand. He suggests that for Sloane and his favorite correspondents, scientific reporting had become a kind of arcane game played by a small coterie for their own obscure purposes. As evidence King carefully selects the following excerpt from the *Philosophical Transactions*, No. 251, a description of an experiment concerning the anatomy of a child born without a brain. Writes Sloane's correspondent:

> I did take off the three upper *vertebrae* of the neck before I could find the *medulla spinalis*—the tongue was fresh, and doubtless had performed the deglutition, to make the child swallow the *colliquamentum*. The *larynx* and all the parts of the throat were, as the rest of the body were, in as good and natural a condition as can be. I leave to others to explain how the child could live without brains. (p. 49)

Noting the correspondent's careful avoidance of the only question that matters—how the child could survive without brains—the Gentleman observes: "Oh dear Sir, that should never have been omitted; it was the main thing in the relation. Besides, the *explaining* that would have solved a Problem at present much debated in the world; which is, how most of your Correspondents *can live* under the very same circumstances with that child" (p. 49). Still unsatisfied with the Virtuoso's account of the experiment, the Gentleman presses the case: "But, pray, if the child wanted brains, I understand not how the *larynx* and all the parts of the body could be in a good and natural condition" (p. 49). Having run out of answers, the Virtuoso finally responds; "That is, only, as I told you before, our way of expressing ourselves; for as, amongst the Beaux, a careless dress is the most admired, so we Philosophers signalize ourselves by a careless use of language" (pp. 49–50). It is precisely this careless if fashionable use of language, the linguistic equivalent of bag wigs and shoe buckles, that Sprat had warned against, and that King ridicules so frequently.

Sprat had counseled the Royal Society to "make faithful *Records* of all the Works of *Nature*, or *Art*, which can come within their reach"[29] in order both to avoid the promiscuous recapitulation of fabulous tales and to free mankind from the tyranny of premature hypotheses based upon insufficient evidence.

To accomplish this, they have indeavor'd to separate the knowledge of *Nature*, from the colours of *Rhetorick*, the devices of *Fancy*, or the delightful deceit of *Fables*. They have labor'd to enlarge, it from being confin'd to the custody of a few; or from servitude to private interests. They have striven to preserve it from being over-press'd by a confus'd heap of vain, and useless particulars; or from being straitned and bounded up too much by General Doctrines.[30]

As King would have it, Sloane had ignored all of Sprat's warnings concerning the arbitrary limitation of scientific knowledge to the "custody of a few." But King also ridicules Sloane's very method of collecting and publishing the reports in the *Transactions,* a miscellaneous compendium of isolated and unrelated reports thrown together in no discernible order, accounts which must have been intended to entertain since they certainly could not be said to instruct. Quite rightly, Sprat had warned about the dangers of premature hypotheses. King suggests in reply that given the miscellaneous and often trivial contents of the *Transactions,* one would be hard-pressed to form any hypotheses at all. The data simply do not arrange themselves and without some presiding intelligence to collate and integrate these reports (presumably the work of the editor), they must remain forever what they seem, a "heap of vain and useless particulars."

To substantiate this charge King gleefully quotes from the *Philosophical Transactions,* No. 242, an account of one Charles Worth, apothecary, who having made a pie out of a poppy plant, called *Papaver corniculatum,* "and eating of the said poppy-pie whilst hot, was presently taken with such a kind of delirium, as made him fancy that most that he saw was gold and, calling for a chamber-pot being a white earthen one, after having purged by stool into it, he broke it into pieces; and had the by-standers to save them for they were all gold" (p. 27). When questioned about the need for all of the trivial detail included here, the Transactioneer replies: "O dear Sir! there was an absolute necessity to be exact in particulars; for, had he only told us, that the herb purged, and caused a delirium, how must we have known that he had made use of an earthen chamber-pot, that he purged into it, and then broke it" (p. 27). The Gentleman wants to know what this kind of sordid detail can possibly add to the sum of natural knowledge, and the Transactioneer has a ready answer: "If it encreases knowledge, it certainly advances it. And pray, does not a man know more, that knows the chamber-pot was broken than he that hears of a delirium and purging?" (p. 28). The Transactioneer's logic is both unassailable and inane, blissfully ignoring the point of the Gentleman's question. Instead, he offers the Gentleman more of the same story, how "the man and the maid servants, having also eaten of the same pie, stripped themselves quite naked, so danced one against another a long time" (p. 28). The pattern is repeated throughout *The Transactioneer*, as the Gentleman seeks to know why certain reports have ever been included in the *Philosophical Transactions* and the Transactioneer responds with other stories equally inconsequential and bizarre. In an attempt to describe the effects of the herb popularly known as "Dog-mercury" the Transactioneer regales his guest with an account abstracted by the Gentleman as follows:

> A woman boiled herbs and bacon for supper; the children purged; the good man slept longer than ordinary; went to work at Mr. Newport's; filled his hat full of water, and was so discerning as to think his chin was all the day in the fire, though he dipped it often in water. (p. 29)

A comparison of this mad abstract with the *Philosophical Transactions*, No. 203, indicates that King exaggerates only slightly as he deftly parodies the trivial particularity and rampant parataxis of the original.[31] To quote the Gentleman, it is "a very Philosophical relation" and "very fine circumstances to be particular in" (p. 29). The Transactioneer defends his account on the grounds that "dog-mercury" is mentioned by several of his correspondents and therefore one ought to "take notice of 'its effects.'" "But pray, what inferences, or what consequential use do you make of this observation?" asks the Gentleman. "Why, from the effects of this plant, I draw this inference, 'That, whether the quantity or quality of this herb were the cause of its effects, I know not; but think that everybody will do well to be cautious and wary of the use of it, in such quantities after such a warning" (p. 29). The more the Gentleman (and the reader) learns of these scientific reports, the less he understands. Indeed King implies that like the Academicians of Lagado, who have quite literally substituted the thing for the word, Sloane's correspondents have created a perfectly factual and precise style of description which certainly focusses on things themselves, without providing the slightest clue as to why those particular things have been described, or how those descriptions are to be used. Where Sprat had recommended a linguistic transparency born of referential precision, the modern virtuosi have produced instead only confusion and opacity of thought as a result of the unrestrained circumstantiality (even garrulousness) of their accounts.

It is the frivolity of much that passes for serious science that King ridicules so often in *The Transactioneer*. In words that prefigure Swift's caustic evaluation of the practical achievements of the Academy of Lagado, King's Gentleman concludes that:

> One may learn how prettily you and your Correspondents are employed; but nothing that will make a man wiser, or more a Philosopher; for what am I the wiser, for knowing "the Mice creep into holes," [No. 251] or how "nastily the Moors pull their Meat?" [No. 254] Nor is what you have acquainted me with, of the generation of Fleas, any more than what a louzy beggar could have told many years ago [No. 249]. And as for your Coffee-story [No. 256], I take it to be a tale fit to be related only amongst old women and mechanicks. (53)

Here King suggests that what passed for scientific writing in the later seventeenth century frequently amounted to little more than glorified story telling. Sloane himself is ironically defended as "a great promoter of philosophical and innocent mirth; for there is scarce any thing that is comical and diverting, but he takes care to place it in the 'Philosophical Transactions'" (p. 16). One might argue that comedy and diversion did not figure prominently in the Royal Society's original plans for its own records, and Sprat himself had vigorously criticized the Ancients for the sheer fantasy that found its way into their natural histories, condemning the works of Pliny, Aristotle, Solinus, and Aelian for

> abounding more with pretty Tales, and fine monstrous Stories; than sober, and fruitful Relations. If they could gather together some extraordinary Qualities of *Stones*, or *Minerals*, some Rarities of the *Age*, the *food*, the *colour*, the *shapes* of *Beasts*, or some *vertues* of *Fountains* or *Rivers*; they thought they had perform'd the chiefest part of *Natural Historians*.[32]

Yet, the *Philosophical Transactions* of Sir Hans Sloane, particularly as they have been abstracted by William King, often seem little more than a vast collection of "romances" multiplying "varieties of extraordinary Events, and surprising circumstances."[33]

At the heart of King's second dialogue is a lengthy recapitulation of various marvels and monstrosities soberly chronicled by Sloane and his correspondents around the world. King pays special attention to a sensational list of obstetric anomalies, including excerpts from No. 229, an account of a fifty-one year old woman, who "after one year and a half being with child, was at the last delivered by the navel" (p. 35); from No. 221 "an account of a lady that was delivered of a child, 'with a wound in her breast above four fingers long— occasioned by the strength of imagination'" (p. 42); from No. 233, of yet another woman "seven years bringing forth a child, bone by bone, and all by the fundament" (p. 35). The list goes on. From No. 233 King abstracts an account of a woman who "bore an infant who had two heads; one head was a bag, resembling the hood of a Benedictine Monk" (p. 36). No. 226 provides yet another "account of a child born without a brain; which, had it lived long enough, would have made an excellent Publisher of 'Philosophical Transactions'" (p. 36), while No. 228 "gives an account of another, that had his brains in the nape of his neck" (p. 36). When assured by the Transactioneer that all of these wonders have indeed been witnessed by his correspondents in the field, the Gentleman archly observes: "Indeed, your Correspondents are as judicious in making observations, as you are in publishing them" (p. 36). Ignoring the Gentleman's irony, the Transactioneer offers to provide "an account of stranger things than these" (p. 38), and proceeds to do so, including among his various tales descriptions of "a shower of Fish," and a "shower of Butter" (p. 41) to baste them. The Transactioneer cites No. 214, where we are told of a lamb who sucked a wether, "and brought him to milk, and was maintained by him all this summer" (p. 42), and No. 235, a description of "one of the most unmannerly Dogs that ever you heard of" (p. 41). To paraphrase Shakespeare's Gloucester, here indeed is matter and impertinancy mixed, data of potential scientific interest, indiscriminately mingled with the most lurid and irrelevant stories, old wives' tales, and popular wonders of the day, all elegantly committed to paper and published with the semi-official blessing of the Royal Society.

Throughout *The Transactioneer* such epithets as "remarkable," "strange," and "amazing" are repeatedly used to describe the works of Sloane's correspondents, and King ridicules the editor of the *Transactions* for his own credulity. When pressed to explain his reasons for believing (let alone publishing) such strange and marvelous tales, the Transactioneer replies: "Reason! Pshaw! I do not trouble myself to inquire after the reason of everything that is told me; if I should, I should have work enough, to find reasons for everything that is communicated in the 'Transactions'" (p. 36). Of all the sins committed by Sloane and his correspondents, this predilection for the preposterous meets with King's sharpest irony. When the Transactioneer exclaims over a report of "Glow-worms-volant and Butterflies eggs that were testaceous, and near as big as Wrens, most gloriously bestudded with gold and silver; and they hatch in windows, and are a sport for children" (p. 43), the Gentleman replies, "Pray, how came your Correspondent to take notice of things only fit for children? What! did he think your genius lay the same way as childrens do?" (p. 43). King's answer seems obvious enough. Indeed, throughout *The Transactioneer*, King treats us to a satirical vision of the men of modern science observing the freaks, monsters, and anomalies in nature with all that crude avidity with which the Brobdingnagian peasants paid their shillings to watch a tiny Gulliver perform.[34] Presiding over this whole performance is Sir Hans Sloane, who if King is to be believed, was little more than a glorified carnival barker and mountebank exploiting his position as Secretary of the Royal Society and editor of the *Philosophical Transactions* to make a mockery of modern science: a writer and editor who subverted the stylistic aims of the Royal Society with prose marked by bombast and obscurity and withal more strange than true.

NOTES

This paper was originally presented at the thirteenth annual meeting of the East-Central American Society for Eighteenth-Century Studies, Bethany, West Virginia, October 1982. Support for research was provided by the Le Moyne Committee on Faculty Research and Development.

1 According to Warburton, "Mr. Pope, Dr. Arbuthnot, and Dr. Swift projected to write a satire, in conjunction, on the *abuses of human learning;* and to make it the better received, they proposed to do it in the manner of Cervantes (the original of this species of satire) under the history of some feigned adventures." Quoted in *The Memoirs of the Extraordinary Life, Works, and Discoveries of Martinus Scriblerus,* ed. Charles Kerby-Miller (1950; rpt. New York: Russell and Russell, 1966), p. 68.

2 Alexander Pope, *The Dunciad,* ed. James Sutherland (London: Methuen; New Haven: Yale University Press, 1963), bk. 4, l. 498.

3 Theophilus Cibber, *The Lives of the Poets of Great Britain and Ireland to the Time of Dean Swift* (London: 1753), 3:229.

4 Aside from the Scriblerians, other satirists who ridiculed the style of the *Philosophical Transactions* included Henry Fielding, *Some Papers Proper to be Read before the Royal Society Concerning the Terrestrial Chrysipus, Golden-Foot or Guinea* (1743) and John Hill, *A Review of the Works of the Royal Society of London: containing animadversions on such of the Papers as deserve Particular Observation* (1751). Although *The Transactioneer* almost certainly influenced the Scriblerian mode of satire, King's continuation of his satirical assault on the *Philosophical Transactions* in a work entitled *Useful Transactions in*

Philosophy And other sorts of Learning (London: 1708/9), had an even more direct effect on Scriblerian satire. See Kerby-Miller, ed., *Martinus Scriblerus*, p. 72.

5 Isaac Disraeli, *Calamities and Quarrels of Authors* (London: Frederick Warne, n.d.), pp. 358–59.

6 For an account of King's manner of proceeding in his earlier dialogue satires on Bentley see Frederick M. Keener, *English Dialogues of the Dead: A Critical History, An Anthology, and a Check List* (New York and London: Columbia University Press, 1973), pp. 33–48. See also Colin J. Horne, "The Phalaris Controversy: King *Versus* Bentley," *Review of English Studies* 22 (1946): 289–303.

7 Quoted in E. St. John Books, *Sir Hans Sloane: The Great Collector and his Circle* (London: The Batchworth Press, 1954), p. 109.

8 For the Royal Society's reaction to *The Transactioneer,* see Joseph M. Levine, *Dr. Woodward's Shield: History, Science, and Satire in Augustan England* (Berkeley, Los Angeles, and London: University of California Press, 1977), pp. 85–86.

9 All quotations from *The Transactioneer* are taken from *The Original Works of William King,* ed. John Nichols (London: 1776), 3:1–56, and are cited parenthetically by page number in the text.

10 See Brooks, *Sir Hans Sloane,* pp. 100–101.

11 Dr. Woodward, Sloane's archenemy, quoted in Levine, *Dr. Woodward's Shield,* p. 86.

12 On the fate of Sloane's collections, see Brooks, *Sir Hans Sloane,* pp. 176–201.

13 Thomas Sprat, *The History of the Royal Society,* ed. Jackson I. Cope and Harold Whitmore Jones (St. Louis: Washington University Studies, 1958), p. 113.

14 Ibid.

15 For a full sampling of the debate over the significance of the Royal Society's program of language reform, see Richard Foster Jones, "Science and English Prose Style in the Third Quarter of the Seventeenth Century," in *The Seventeenth Century: Studies in the History of English Thought and Literature from Bacon to Pope* (Stanford: Stanford University Press, 1951), pp. 75–110; and George Williamson, *The Senecan Amble: A Study in Prose from Bacon to Collier* (London: Faber and Faber, 1951), pp. 275–301. See also Jackson I. Cope and Harold Whitmore Jones, Introduction, *The History of the Royal Society,* p. xxvii; and Francis Christensen, "John Wilkins and the Royal Society's Reform of Prose Style," *Modern Language Quarterly* 7 (1946): 179–87, 279–90.

16 There can be little doubt that Sprat served only as the mouthpiece for the Royal Society, and that the program of stylistic reform was the work of John Wilkins and others. See Christensen, "John Wilkins and the Royal Society's Reform of Prose Style"; and Barbara J. Shapiro, *John Wilkins 1614–1672: An Intellectual Biography* (Berkeley and Los Angeles: University of California Press, 1969), pp. 203–4.

17 Sloane makes himself an easier target by absolving the Royal Society "(which is no way concerned therin) from all the Miscarriage he may possible [sic] commit," a confession whose garbled syntax seems to reinforce King's caricature of Sloane as an enemy of the English language (Royal Society of London, *Philosophical Transactions* [rpt. New York: Johnson Reprint and Kraus Reprint, 1963], 17 [1693]: 582). In his Preface to vol. 21 (1699), Sloane also apologizes for the haste with which the *Transactions* had been published and for "the mistakes" that "happen in the Press." On the question of editorial responsibility for the *Transactions*, see Dorothy Stimson, *Scientists and Amateurs: A History of the Royal Society* (1948; rpt. New York: Greenwood Press, 1968), p. 69; also Henry Lyons, *The Royal Society 1660–1940* (1944; rpt. New York: Greenwood Press, 1968), p. 85.

18 In *Useful Transactions in Philosophy and Other Sorts of Learning* (London: 1708/9), King burlesqued various numbers of the *Philosophical Transactions* and took particular aim at Sloane's *History of Jamaica*.

19 Isaac Disraeli describes King's ironic style as follows: "The new species of literary burlesque which King seems to have invented, consists in selecting the very expressions and absurd passages from the original he ridiculed, and framing out of them a droll dialogue or a grotesque narrative, he adroitly inserted his own remarks, replete with the keenest irony, or the driest sarcasm," *Calamities and Quarrels*, p. 359. Like Swift, King was a purist in style and ridiculed Sloane for many of the same sins presumably committed by Bentley. Frederick Keener points out that in the *Dialogues of the Dead*, King "assiduously twisted passages . . . making the scholar seem lascivious by telescoping several widely spaced remarks" (p. 40). See also Horne, "The Phalaris Controversy," p. 291.

20 Of all the passages quoted in *The Transactioneer*, this is the only one which is misidentified. There is no mention of "hogs that sh-t Soap, and cows that sh-t Fire" in No. 263.

21 See the Preface, *Philosophical Transactions*, vol. 17 (1693).

22 No. 233 includes the following two-line poem on eels: An *Ankham* Eel, and a *Witham* Pike, / All *England* cannot shew the like.

23 See No. 233, *Philosophical Transactions* 19 (1697): 727.

24 Sprat, *The History of the Royal Society*, p. 112.

25 See *The Transactioneer*, pp. 34, 38, 45, 47, 48.

26 Sprat, *The History of the Royal Society*, p. 113.

27 In "Early Parody of Scientic Jargon: Some Notes for *O.E.D.*," *Notes and Queries*, 30 January 1943, pp. 66–69, Colin J. Horne calls attention to King's parody of scientific jargon, in particular Sloane's use of "rare and uncouth words," the coining of new terms by the Virtuosi, the "embedding of Latin technical terms in the structure of the English sentences," and the use of colloquial terms out of context.

28 Joseph M. Levine points out that even within the Society there were doubts about Sloane's fitness as an editor, doubts which were not assuaged by the appearance of *The Transactioneer*. Levine remarks that "it was particularly distressing to discover that the Society had voluntarily relinquished

its control over the *Transactions* to the secretary, who had *carte blanche* to print what he liked—and reject the rest," *Dr. Woodward's Shield*, p. 86. This fact lends some validity to King's charge that Sloane used the *Transactions* to reward his friends.

29 Sprat, *The History of the Royal Society*, p. 61.

30 Ibid., p. 62.

31 An excerpt from No. 203, *Philosophical Transactions* 17 (September 1693): 875, proceeds as follows: "About Three Weeks ago, the Woman went into the Fields and gathered some Herbs, and (having first Boyled them) Fryed them with Bacon for her own her Families Supper: After they had been about Two Howrs in Bed, one of the Children (which is Dumb and about Seven Years Old) fell very Sick, and so did the other Two presently after; which obliged the Man and his Wife to Rise and take the Children to the Fire, where they Vomited and Purged, and within half an Hour fell fast asleep. . . ."

32 Sprat, *The History of the Royal Society*, pp. 90–91.

33 Ibid., p. 90.

34 The whole question of the Royal Society's preoccupation with monstrosities was one to which Sprat was particularly sensitive. "When my Reader shall behold this large number of *Relations;* perhaps he will think, that too many of them seem to be incredulous stories," ibid., p. 214. Sprat steers a middle course, hoping to avoid natural histories which consist of nothing but "strange, and delightful Tales," while allowing room "to consider the singular, and irregular *effects,* and to imitate the unexpected, and monstrous *excesses,* which *Nature* does sometimes practice in her *works*" (p. 215). In fact, a review of the *Philosophical Transactions* for that decade (1691–1700) covered by *The Transactioneer* reveals just how popular accounts of monstrosities were in the early reports of the Royal Society. In this respect, King exaggerates not at all.

"Thy Own Importance Know":
The Influence of Le Comte de Gabalis on
The Rape of the Lock

DONNA SCARBORO

The most striking difference between Pope's 1712 version of *The Rape of the Lock*, in two cantos, and the five-canto version of 1714 is of course the presence of the sylphs. In the letter prefaced to the 1714 edition, Pope names as his source for the "machinery" a "French Book call'd *Le Comte de Gabalis*" (1670), which he says is the "best account" he knows of the philosophy of the Rosicrucians.[1] Pope's tone is ironic, but his statement that the Rosicrucians are a people he "must bring" his reader "acquainted with" and his recommendation of *Gabalis* as the "best account" of them reflect the importance of Villars' book to the meaning of *The Rape of the Lock*. Pope's use of Villars' version of the Rosicrucian system was a choice which had a special meaning for contemporaries familiar—as Pope's dedication suggests Miss Fermor should become—with Villars' *Gabalis*. Pope's borrowings of detail and tone from Villars' satire are substantial, and many isolated parallels have been noted elsewhere; but in order to see the thematic unity of *Gabalis* and *The Rape* it is necessary to look at the similarities as a whole. Additionally, while there are many fine studies of the sylphs' role in Pope's poem, none has treated Pope's use of Villars' work as thoroughly or as seriously as it deserves. Ralph Cohen has perhaps gone furthest in making "Belinda's self-adoration . . . a religious rite."[2]

Cohen finds the theme of transformation and the related theme of self-deification crucial aspects of the poem and emphasizes the ritualistic tenor of Pope's treatment. The fact that these themes were adopted in the 1714 edition along with Villars' sylphs and their rituals, however, has gone unnoticed. The full influence of the original sylphs on Pope's poem needs closer attention.

The purpose of this essay is to reconstruct the significance of Rosicrucianism and Villars' satire of it in Pope's expansion of an occasional piece into the poem we now read. Once the verbal and visual parallels between *Gabalis* and *The Rape* are established, it is not surprising to find that aspects of the history of Rosicrucianism, which I will touch on in the last few pages, are specifically relevant to Pope's characterization of Belinda in *The Rape of the Lock*. The adaptation of Villars' sylphs to the revised poem is more than a happy accident; it is the result of a coincidence of theme which emerges from a shared concern with the trap of self-importance.

Villars' unnamed narrator in *Le Comte de Gabalis* is an urbane intellectual who poses as a novice in order to have fun at the expense of the Rosicrucian mystics. In the course of his comic investigations he keeps company with a variety of individuals, every one of whom, he says, "had so good an opinion of themselves in particular, as to believe they were of the number of the Elect."[3] He is approached by the Count of Gabalis, a sage who has determined through astrological charts that the narrator is "predestined" to be a leader of the order. Like Ariel who sees fated events in "the clear mirror" of Belinda's ruling star, the Count divines the future through astrology. The narrator's telling of the Count's terms is familiar to readers of *The Rape*: the elect "must satisfy a single condition in order to gain the knowledge promised by the inhabitants of the elements. . . . You must (he added very softly, laying his Mouth to my Ear) renounce all carnal dealing with women" (p. 17). The condition and the Count's motion as he reveals it are identical, with allowance for the change of sex, to Ariel's when he informs Belinda that she is the "distinguish'd care" of the sylphs. Ariel first appears to Belinda as "a youth more glittering than a birthnight beau" who "Seemed to her ear his winning lips to lay" (I, 25), and who whispers that "whoever fair and chaste / Rejects mankind is by some sylph embraced" (I, 67–68).

Pope artfully elaborates and transforms the material he found in Villars, yet the central ideas are the same: susceptibility to "revelation" is grandiose vanity, and reliance on self is the common trait of fools and sages. Ariel enjoins Belinda to trust her eager imagination:

Hear and believe! thy own Importance know,
Nor bound thy narrow views to things below.

(I, 35–36)

Similarly, Gabalis, preparing the narrator for the revelations to come, exclaims, "I adore thee, O great God! in that thou hast crowned Man with so much Glory and made him Monarch over all the works of thine Hands." Certainly, Pope's lines need not be explicated in the light of an inferior piece of satire. But Pope appears to share a laugh with Villars while making poetry out of an admonition very similar to that of Count Gabalis. The Count continues, "Do you feel, my Son, . . . do you feel that Heroic Ambition, which is a sure Character of the Children of Wisdom?" (p. 15). If the initiate has this "sure Character," says the Count, he can attain "that Pitch of Elevation for which [he was] born" (p. 17).

Aubrey Williams and others have noticed the parallel between "the dream of pride and vain-glory" whispered into Belinda's ear by Ariel and the dream Satan "insinuated into Eve's ear" in *Paradise Lost*.[4] Other parallels to this scene have been identified in Milton's *Comus* (1634–47) and in Boileau's *Le Lutrin* (1674). Tillotson notes in the Twickenham Edition that "the gods sometimes communicate with the epic hero by means of apparitions during sleep."[5] But since we know from Pope's own insistence that Villars was before him in his revision of the poem, the more immediate influence may be *Gabalis*.

Another Miltonic parallel that may be found in both *The Rape* and *Gabalis* is the scene which Williams calls the "parody of Mass at Belinda's dressing table." As Eve awakes to admire herself in a pool (*Paradise Lost*, IV, 460 ff.), so Belinda worships herself at the mirror of her dressing table. Although the resonances of Milton and Milton's epic predecessors are essential to Pope, the parallel with Villars is again more immediate. Belinda's toilet, in which she sees "keener Lightenings quicken in her eyes," parodies the rituals of Villars' alchemical sages, who use looking glasses, water glasses, and basins to effect a transformation similar to that which Belinda works with her cosmetics. Gabalis explains that the adept who wishes to call on the elemental powers must "exalt the element of Fire" that is in him (p. 30). Ingredients are distilled by the use of mirrors and a bowl of glass into a "Solary Powder" which becomes "a Sovereign Remedy to exalt the Fire that is in us; and [makes] us . . . become of an igneous Nature" (p. 31). These rituals in *Gabalis* also help to explain the importance of the glass imagery which Aubrey Williams has already explored.[6]

In Pope's description of the toilet, Belinda "calls forth all the Wonders of her Face" and "Sees by Degrees a purer Blush arise, / And keener Lightenings quicken in her Eyes" (I, 142–44). The appearance of lines like these in the revisions suggested to Pope by his reading of *Gabalis* infer that they parody Villars' parody of the sages. The idea of having Belinda mystically "exalt the element of Fire" may have encouraged Pope's decision to change the lines

> Sol thro' white Curtains did his Beams display
> And op'd those Eyes that brighter shine than they

to

> Sol thro' white Curtains shot a tim'rous Ray
> And op'd those Eyes that must eclipse the Day.
> (I, 13–14; 1712 and 1714)

This revision, along with the placement of phrases like "Bright as the Sun," "like the Sun," and "the Rival of his Beams" (II, 13–14, 3) after the ritual of the toilet, emphasizes the increasing intensity of Belinda's "igneous Nature." Not until after she has invoked her own fire does she shine like the sun. More generally, Belinda's "rite of pride" resembles the rites of Villars' occultists in that the intent of both is to transform the human into the divine. Pope appropriates this emphasis on transformation along with Villars' system, in which the sage becomes like a god to the denizens of the elements: "they have . . . for us," the Count says, "all the respect which they owe to their creator" (p. 31). Belinda's mystical transformation from self-centered female to cosmetically self-created deity is of the same prideful order.

Since Villars' occultists are attempting not only to gain knowledge of the mysteries but also to secure the love of a nymph or sylph, their rituals are laced with sexual innuendo. Gabalis says that the mortal honored with such a liaison not only gains superhuman knowledge but also immortalizes the sylph, who otherwise must die and "return again into the abyss of nothing" (p. 21). The prerequisite for the sage, of course, is to "renounce all carnal dealings" with humans. The idea of such an extreme sacrifice is "so far from scandalizing the Philosophers" and appears to them "so just" that the wise men "have all with one consent resolved to give [themselves] to no other Pleasure but the immortalizing of Nymphs and Sylphides" (p. 24). In Pope's 1714 edition similar implications abound. Of the line "Sol thro' white Curtains shot a tim'rous Ray" (I, 13), Robin Grove observes that "only in the later version does the sun himself offer the masculine compliment of 'shooting' his ray through [Belinda's] Curtains."[7] Grove is right to conclude from this that some of Pope's revisions were intended to highlight sexual innuendo in the poem. Villars' joke of having the sages seduced by beautiful nymphs, sylphs, and salamanders may have helped to add this new dimension to the poem. Both satirists found the double of intellectual narcissism in the sexual narcissism suggested by the pleasures of "conversation" with sylphs.

Once Pope made the decision to emphasize the sexuality of the story, many episodes in *Gabalis* would have offered hints to Pope's comic genius. Belinda's alliance—one might say "liaison"—with Shock resembles a story related by Villars which capitalizes on the suggestion of dalliance between mortal and elemental beings. Gabalis tells of a race of people in the Indies who are "begotten by a Dog upon a Woman" (p. 108), explaining earnestly:

> The sylphs perceiving that they are taken for Devils when they appear in Humane shape, that they may lessen the aversion which people have to them take the shape of those Animals, and so accomodate themselves to the whimsical weakness of Women, who would have a lovely Sylph in Horrour, and are not startled at a Dog or a Monkey. I could tell you many fine stories of the Ladies Lapdogs, with some virgins in the world . . . (p. 109)

Like Belinda, these young ladies sleep with their dogs little suspecting the possibility of compromise: "A maid would swear when she awakes that she is a Virgin, who in her sleep hath had the honour she dreamt not of . . ." (p. 110). In the 1714 version Shock wakes Belinda just as Ariel has said his last words: "Beware of all, but most beware of Man!" (I, 114). Sexuality is subtly transferred from Ariel to his special charge, Shock, who "wak'd his Mistress with his Tongue" (I, 116). The equation of animal and beloved carries over in the lines from Canto III, "Not louder shrieks to pitying heaven are cast, / When Husbands or when Lapdogs breathe their last" (157–58), and in Belinda's exclamation, "Men, monkeys, lapdogs, parrots perish all!" (IV, 120).

Visitations may also take place in forms other than animal and human. Something like Pope's "Virgins visited by Angel-pow'rs" (I, 33) is present in *Gabalis* in tales such as that of Magdalene of the Cross who, wooed by a gnome, began to "make him happy" when she was twelve, and "continued their commerce for the Space of thirty Years" (p. 85). Tales like this one and others from *Gabalis* would be included in "all the Nurse and all the Priest have taught," the Catholic lore which is the common heritage of Pope and Villars. Gabalis, however, faced with a pupil who is a Catholic and a believer, gravely opposes the traditional tales because they attribute the activities of the sylphs to evil forces. When the narrator asserts his belief in goblins, Gabalis is outraged that an intelligent man will "still give credit to his nurse" (p. 27). Later the Count complains that this credulity in forces of evil is

> one of the strangest effects of Ignorance and perverse Education; because one has heard his Nurse tell Tales of Sorcerers, what-ever comes to pass extraordinarily, must have the devil for Author. It is in vain for our greatest Doctors to talk, we will never believe them, unless they say as our Nurses say. (p. 92)[8]

Belinda's voyage on the Thames is present in the 1712 edition, but in the 1714 edition it is more than three times as long and claims an entire canto. The expanded version of the voyage results from the presence of the sylphs, and is attributable to Villars' influence on that account only. However, episodes in *Gabalis* may have actually suggested the fantastic elaboration of the voyage. A sylph, according to the Count, once visited his mortal mistress "in a miraculous Ship, drawn by a Swan that was yok'd to it by a Silver Chain . . . and departed one day at Noon in his Aerial Ship in the sight of all the People" (p. 94). In another episode recounted by Gabalis, the sylphs appear "in a Fleet of Aerial Ships of an admirable Build, which sailed with gentle Zephyrs" (p. 121). Description of this sort suggests Pope's images of Ariel's "lucid squadrons" (II, 56) and the military pomp of the game of Ombre. As Gabalis describes them, the sylphs at times "shew themselves publickly in the Air . . . with great Pomp and Magnificence . . . sometimes in Battle Array, marching in good Order, standing to their Arms, or encamped under rich Pavillions" (p. 121).

The Cave of Spleen episode in *The Rape of the Lock* has no precise parallel in *Gabalis*. It may be Pope's way of fulfilling one of Le Bossu's minor requirements of mock epic, a visit to the underworld. Or it may, as Robin Grove proposes, suggest "the realm of the Uterus, and of what etymology proclaims is its 'hysteric' power."[9] Grove argues that the Cave of Spleen represents the neurosis that underlies the art, the discontent that underlies the civilization, of the poem. As such it balances the climactic "art" scene—Belinda's toilet.[10] But the description also draws on alchemical material—the object of Villars' satire—for some of its effect. Rosicrucian tradition included images of the "cave of the Illuminati,"[11] which became to eighteenth-century humanists a symbol of the withdrawal of the mystic into his esoteric studies. In eighteenth-century satire the cave was often interchangeable with the alchemist's oven; both were retreats for the excessively

serious and self-absorbed. Villars makes humorlessness a requirement for would-be adepts, and his narrator is concerned that he may
be denied an initiation into the secret sciences because of his readiness to laugh, "for without Melancholy no progress can be made in
them." Gabalis, however, insists that the stars show the jovial narrator to be the potential equal of the greatest previous sage, even though
"it is not known that ever he laughed in his life time" (p. 3). The
following excerpt from *The Spectator* of 1714 demonstrates the cur-
rency of similar notions for Pope's audience. Pope and Villars are not
alone in their attacks on the mystics as self-important and ill-humored
reprobates:

> Trophinius's Cave was made in the Form of a huge Oven, and had
> many particular Circumstances, which disposed the Person who was
> in it to be more pensive and thoughtful than ordinary; insomuch
> that no Man was ever observed to laugh all his life after, who had
> once made his Entry into this Cave. It was usual in those Times,
> when any one carried a more than ordinary Gloominess in his Fea-
> tures, to tell him that he looked like one just come out of Trophin-
> ius's Cave.[12]

Ariel's visit to the Cave of Spleen brings about just such a change in
Belinda's countenance, and for contemporary readers the allusion of
mysticism must have been fairly plain. The accoutrements that sur-
round Spleen—vapours, phantoms, mists, fiends, crystal domes,
teapots, a pipkin, a tripod, a jar, bottles and corks, all reminiscent of
the alchemist's workshop—would have confirmed any suspicions that
Belinda was somehow akin to the occultists.[13]

In *Gabalis* the adept is led not to a cave but to a labyrinth, which
symbolizes contortions of thought as the cave symbolizes extreme
gravity. One of the interviews between Gabalis and his protégé takes
place in the city of Ruel, where "the Count disdaining to admire the
beauties of the place, marched straight to the Labyrinth" (p. 14). In
this appropriate setting Gabalis' mystical lucubrations commence. In
the revised first canto of *The Rape of the Lock* Pope added the lines,
"Oft when the World imagine Women stray, / The Sylphs thro' mystic
Mazes guide their way" (I, 91–92). Kent Beyette, with good cause,
ascribes the metaphor of mazes to Milton,[14] but a more immediate
precedent is again Villars, who like Pope uses the figure to enjoin the
reader to laugh at those who let themselves be led down the twisted
paths of solipsism.

The success of Villars' book, which was reprinted in French in 1700
and widely enjoyed in two English translations of 1680, implies that

his readers were familiar with the occult studies of the serious-minded religious and scientific enthusiasts of the previous generation, some of whom were the fathers of Rosicrucianism. Commentators like Sir William Temple have associated the Rosicrucians with mildly exotic foreign centers of study, particularly Germany and Bohemia.[15] But the origins of the movement were actually closer to England and to Pope's interests than that association would imply. The background of the Rosicrucians shows why Pope may have been particularly interested in them and thoroughly unsympathetic to their beliefs, and why Villars' ironic treatment of them fit so well with Pope's plan to satirize pride in Belinda.

Pope's satire does not draw on specific historical events surrounding the rise of Rosicrucianism, but they were undoubtedly common knowledge to Pope, Villars, and even to the Fermors, the Catholic family for whom Caryll asked Pope to write the poem. Rosicrucianism was one result of the struggle between Catholic and Protestant powers, and the outcome of that struggle would have important implications for a Catholic like Pope living in Protestant England. Modern readers, having lost the connection between alchemical satire and Catholic humanism, generally overlook the importance of Pope's Catholic background to this aspect of the poem's satire. Rosicrucianism and other mystical orders like it were specifically and stridently anti-Catholic in their inceptions. For instance, one of the early prophetic books related to such cults is the *Naometria*, published in Wüttemburg in 1604, which prophesied that by 1620 the anti-Christ, embodied in the Pope and Mohamet, would be overcome by an evangelical army formed by a coalition of Protestant sympathizers in England, France, and Germany.[16] Later tracts combining militant Protestant politics with mystical prophecies included the Rosicrucian manifestos and were in part the work of prominent English reformers who traveled to Bohemia to help form esoteric sects. John Dee, Edward Kelley, and Robert Fludd were some of the Englishmen who joined Giordano Bruno and Johannes Kepler in esoteric and scientific studies which nurtured ideals of radical religious, scientific, educational, and political activity. They believed their efforts "promised a new dawn for mankind." The pursuit of esoteric studies "through which the adept believed that he could achieve both a profound insight into nature and a vision of a divine world beyond nature," was propagated in England for decades by men who taught "universal reformation, advancement of learning, and other utopist ideals,"[17] and was a favorite target of humanist satire.

In 1670 the Abbé Nicholas de Montfaucon de Villars wrote a satire of Rosicrucian philosophy for some of the same reasons Pope and Swift satirized mysticism some years later. The point of Villars' satire is to undercut the "learned pride" of occultists, religious fanatics, and radical social reformers who, like the Rosicrucians, promote their own versions of Renaissance confidence in man's knowledge and power. Extreme faith in individual revelation and achievement was perpetuated in Pope's time by religious zealots like the millenarists, whose prophets continued the tradition of militant anti-Catholicism.[18] Given the instability of the English church and government in 1714, such sympathies would have been alarming not only to Catholics but to moderates of all persuasions. Opposition to such beliefs had come earlier from distinguished humanists like Erasmus and Bacon, and Ben Jonson was among the first to object through satire. Jonson's *The Alchemist* (1610) may present the prototype in English of the egotistically demented sage, although unlike Gabalis, Jonson's alchemist is aware of the sham in his own presumptions. When Pope appropriates the characteristics of the sages in creating Ariel and of the novice in creating Belinda, he intentionally carries over the implied criticism of enthusiastic religion and radical social reform.[19]

The most important contribution of *The Count of Gabalis* to *The Rape of the Lock* is the emphasis, only tacitly present in the poem of 1712, on Belinda's elaborate self-absorption, prompted or played upon by Ariel's command: "Thy own Importance know!" (I, 35). Ariel and his legions encourage as well as symbolize Belinda's almost megalomaniacal self-importance. The sylphs represent not only "honor," the "supernatural," or the "imagination,"[20] but also the underlying evil that thwarts the function of these and all abstractions of thought— worship of the isolated self. The sylphs personify the psychology not only of a coquette but of all single-minded enthusiasts, including religious fanatics and social idealists. Pope's poem and Villars' "novel" both take their inspiration from objections to the extremes of philosophical speculation that resulted in the deification of the individual. "Thy own Importance know" could serve as a motto for a vain, petty woman and also for a solipsistic mystic and reformer.

Pope was said to be delighted with the fact that the sylphs "fit so well" with "what was published before," and considered it "one of the greatest proofs of judgment of anything I ever did" to have managed to make the first version of the poem so perfectly adaptable to the machinery of the second.[21] In fact, it is not surprising that Villars' variation on the Rosicrucian system fit into Pope's work, since both set out to satirize extremes of self-importance. Warburton did not exaggerate when he claimed that "There was but one system in all nature which was to Pope's purpose, the Rosicrucian Philosophy."[22] Of course, Pope does not adopt Villars' sylphs without significant changes. Their size, for instance, is not the same. And the influences of Shakespeare, Pope's own imagination, his newly developed painter's eye, and his recent acquaintance with the microscope have been examined elsewhere.[23] But *Gabalis* provided the inspiration for their sexuality and to an unacknowledged extent for many of the graces and ironies they bring to the poem. Most important, Villars stands behind Pope's use of the sylphs as expressions of the worship of self—that dangerous "sure Character" common to the celebrated beauty, the magus, and the enlightened divine.

NOTES

1 Alexander Pope, *The Twickenham Edition of the Poems of Alexander Pope*, ed. John Butt (New Haven: Yale University Press; London: Methuen, 1939–67), vol. 2, *The Rape of the Lock and Other Poems*, ed. Geoffrey Tillotson (1954), p. 142. All future references will be from this edition and be noted parenthetically in the text.
2 Ralph Cohen, "Transformation in *The Rape of the Lock*," *Eighteenth Century Studies* 2 (1968–69): 213.
3 Abbé Nicholas de Montfaucon de Villars, *The Count of Gabalis*, trans. A. Lovell (London, 1680), p. 6. All future references to *Gabalis* will be from this edition and will be noted parenthetically in the text.
4 Aubrey Williams, "The 'Fall' of China and *The Rape of the Lock*," *Philological Quarterly* 41 (1962): 412–25, reprinted in *Essential Articles for the Study of Alexander Pope*, ed. Maynard Mack (Hamden, Conn.: Archon Books, 1968), p. 293.
5 Tillotson, ed., *The Rape of the Lock*, p. 146.
6 Williams, "The 'Fall' of China," in Mack, ed., *Essential Articles*, p. 284. For the uses of glass by mystics and sixteenth-century scientists see Marjorie Hope Nicholson, *Science and Imagination* (Ithaca, N.Y.: Great Seal Books, 1962), p. 31. The association of glasses and mirrors with celestial observation may have suggested to Pope the inclusion of astronomical terms such as the "eclipses" of I, 14, and the "sudden star" of V, 127, both in the 1714 version.
7 Robin Grove, "Uniting Airy Substance," in *The Art of Alexander Pope*, ed. Howard Erskine-Hill and Anne Smith (New York: Barnes and Noble, 1979), p. 54.
8 Minor White Latham (*The Elizabethan Fairies* [New York: Columbia University Press, 1930], p. 2) suggests that the Catholic priests were responsible for keeping the belief in fairies and goblins alive.

9 Grove, "Uniting Airy Substance," p 81.

10 See Tillotson, ed., *The Rape of the Lock*, p. 155n.

11 Frances Yates, *The Rosicrucian Enlightenment* (Boston: Routledge and Kegan Paul, 1972), pp. 38–39.

12 *Spectator* no. 589. See also Michael R. G. Spiller, "The Idol of the Stove: The Background to Swift's Criticism of Descartes," *Review of English Studies* 25, No. 97 (1974): 15–24.

13 *The Rape of the Lock*, IV, 39–54. See also Tillotson, ed., *The Rape of the Lock*, p. 184n., in which he observes that the scene brings to mind epic Hades and the Italian opera as well as the activities of the pseudoscientists. Aubrey Williams ("The 'Fall' of China," in Mack, ed., *Essential Articles*, p. 290) sees these as Freudian female symbols, a view that squares with Robin Grove's notion of the Cave as the "realm of the Uterus" ("Uniting Airy Substance," p. 81). Compare also the items Ariel mentions in his speech to the ranks in Canto II, 126–31: washes, vials, gums, pomatums, and alom-stypticks.

14 Kent Beyette, "Milton and Pope's *The Rape of the Lock*," *Studies in English Literature* 16 (1976): 429.

15 *Sir William Temple's Essays*, ed. J. E. Spingarn (Oxford: Clarendon Press, 1909), p. 88n.; quoted in Tillotson, ed., *The Rape of the Lock*, p. 356.

16 Yates, *The Rosicrucian Enlightenment*, pp. 33–34.

17 Ibid., pp. xxii, 30, 37, 39, 176, and 237.

18 See Margaret C. Jacob, *The Newtonians and the English Revolution, 1689–1720* (Ithaca, N.Y.: Cornell University Press, 1976), p. 251.

19 I am indebted for the recognition of the similarities between *The Rape of the Lock* and Johson's *The Alchemist* to Dr. Robert Silliman and to J. S. Mebane, "Art and Magic in Marlowe, Jonson, and Shakespeare: The Occult Tradition in *Dr. Faustus*, *The Alchemist*, and *The Tempest*," (Ph.D. diss., Emory University, 1974).

20 For the sylphs as "honor" and the "supernatural" see Cleanth Brooks, "The Case of Miss Arabella Fermor: A Re-examination," in Mack, ed., *Essential Articles*, p. 254. For the sylphs as representative of the imagination see David Fairier, "Imagination in *Rape of the Lock*," *Essays in Criticism* 29 (1979): 53–75.

21 Pope quoted by Spence in Tillotson, ed., *The Rape of the Lock*, p. 121.

22 Warburton, note on I, 20, quoted ibid., p. 356.

23 For the various influences on Pope's sylphs, see Pat Rogers, "Faery Lore and *The Rape of the Lock*," *Review of English Studies* 25, no. 97 (1974): 25–38; Marjorie Nicholson and G. S. Rosseau, *'This Long Disease My Life': Alexander Pope and the Sciences* (Princeton: Princeton University Press, 1968); and Norman Ault, *New Light on Pope* (London: Methuen, 1949), ch. 5.

Smollett's Briton *and the Art of Political Cartooning*

BYRON W. GASSMAN

"The most shocking exhibitions of infamous scandal and stupid obscenity, are publicly vended in the shops of this metropolis, to the reproach of government, and the disgrace of the nation." Thus did the 1 January 1763 issue of Tobias Smollett's *The Briton* pay tribute in its own way to the success and notoriety of the scores of political prints—cartoons in twentieth-century terminology[1]—that had been satirizing and caricaturing the government of Lord Bute for the preceding several months. Since its first number, published in the preceding May, the *Briton* had pugnaciously sought to promote popular favor for the recently crowned George III, for his chief minister, and for their policy of quickly ending the Seven Years' War. But the opposition, using the popularity of the discarded William Pitt as a rallying point, had been increasingly vocal and visible in papers and prints poured forth by the presses of London to belittle Bute and those about him. The *Briton* of 1 January gave further evidence of the bothersomeness of the prints to Bute's ministry by calling their purveyors "those audacious wretches who, by dint of nauseous obscene sketches, or rather scratches, which they denominate political prints, have endeavoured to debauch the morals, loyalty, and taste of their fellow-creatures." Smollett was obviously acutely aware at the midterm of his editorship of the potency of graphic satire.

Smollett was naturally dismayed by the spate of political prints in the early 1760s, probably not so much by their methods and tactics

243

per se—as we will see they were often similar to his own—but by the fact that practically all of the prints now known to have been struck off during the short period when Bute was a central figure in the administration were directed against Bute's person and his policies. M. Dorothy George has established the amazing ratio of some four hundred prints against Bute as compared to only four in support of him.[2] Many of those against Bute played on the most simple-minded prejudice against the Scots, their reputed poverty, barbarity, clannishness, and treachery. Many others pointed at the alleged scandalous intimacy between Bute and the Dowager Princess of Wales, the King's mother. Verbal and visual double entendres blatantly intimated that Bute's chief prowess and entry to influence was his performance in the dowager princess's bed. They give considerable warrant to Smollett's charge of obscenity.

Although Smollett resented the indignities that his own political favorites—and he himself as a Scotsman and editor of the *Briton*—suffered at the hands of the print "scratchers," the pages of the *Briton* demonstrate that he was something of a printmaker himself, that often the bent of his imagination and writing skills was towards a kind of expression that strikes the reader as a political print or cartoon might. Our understanding of what was going on in the *Briton* (which, along with the *Auditor*, a similar weekly journal, was Bute's chief propaganda vehicle) and more generally in the propaganda war waged in England during the final months of the Seven Years' War may be enriched by noting the ways in which Smollett, as editor and writer of the *Briton*,[3] was a kind of political cartoonist.

A metaphor such as "fanning the flames of dissension" (to be looked at shortly) is a rather obvious figure of speech, and the transformation of such fairly obvious figures into literal visual forms has always been basic to the political cartoonist's art. But one can also look at the situation the other way around and observe that when the propagandist fills up his prose with such visual metaphors and pictorial allegories, he is cartooning. This is not to suggest that Smollett equated his editorial role with that of verbal printmaker or cartoonist, but rather to suggest that the impulses of imagination that gave rise to political prints such as *John Bull's House sett in Flames* (BM 3890),[4] picturing Bute as an incendiary, and to polemical essays adorned with visual metaphor and allegory such as the *Briton's* often have much in common as weapons in the battle for popular favor. A number of techniques and motifs, figures and images (often rather naturally suggested by the issues, personalities, and tactics of the fray and by emblematic and rhetorical tradition) were shared by Smollett and the makers of political prints during 1762–63.

Smollett was already well-experienced in the exercise of the graphic imagination when he undertook the *Briton*.[5] We know virtually nothing about how or why Smollett was chosen by the Bute ministry to undertake its counterattack against the papers and prints that were vilifying the minister and his policies. His being a Scot may have been helpful—certainly the opposition thought so. More helpful was probably the fact that he had already questioned in print the merits of continuing Pitt's victorious war and seemed to understand the high-minded principles that George III and Bute believed they were establishing to replace the factionalism and corruption of the old Walpole and Pelham administrations and their successors. Clearly part of Smollett's commission was to counteract the popular furor being aggravated by the prints, but it is unlikely that in any particular way the sponsors of the *Briton* saw that one potentially valuable skill of Smollett's was an already developed ability to create verbal equivalents and responses to the objects and scenes and notions that crowded the productions of the printmakers. Nonetheless, this ability turned out to be one of Smollett's most effective qualities as he sought to counter the barrage of anti-Bute abuse in the papers and prints of the day. Indeed for the modern reader, who may find himself rapidly wearied by much of the reiterative argumentation in the *Briton*, this is the quality most likely to attract positive response and prove valuable in measuring Smollett's particular achievements as a voice of his age.

It was an ability that his literary experience had frequently nurtured. In his earlier novels Smollett had of course exhibited a marked talent for creating picturesque grotesques, the kinds of images particularly effective in visual satire. One may recall the figures of Captain Trunnion and his bizarre crew or the misanthrope and trickster Cadwallader Crabtree in *Peregrine Pickle* as support for this observation. A talent for creating grotesques, buffoons, charlatans, gulls, and brutes put Smollett on ground familiar to the printmakers and their customers. An anti-Bute print entitled *The Mountebank* (BM 3853; see fig. 1) brings before the viewer the world of the greedy, the gullible, the voracious, and those who prey upon them, a world also imaged in many of the vivid figures of Smollett's novels. In the print itself Lord Bute stands on an itinerant stage as a mountebank offering to relieve his audience, the English people, from the golden itch with which they are troubled. Smollett stands beside him as his zany with a scroll labeled "The Briton" tucked under his arm; at his feet are torn copies of the *Monitor* and the *North Briton*, the two most prominent anti-ministerial papers; the latter of course was the voice of John Wilkes. Peering out of the curtains behind Bute and Smollett is the Princess

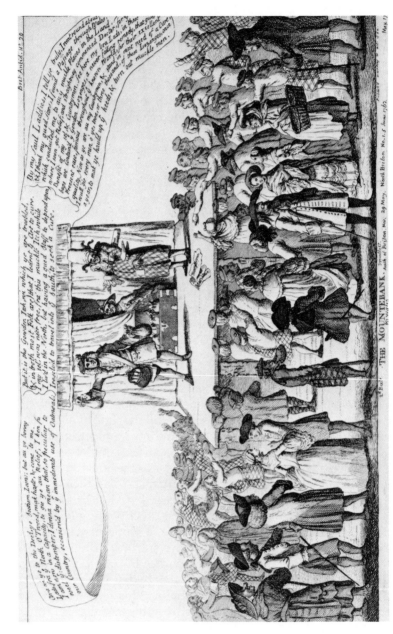

Figure 1: *The Mountebank.* The British Museum; BM 3853. Photo courtesy of the British Library.

of Wales. The curtains suggest those of a bedstead, thus making the common scandalous suggestion that Bute shares the princess's bed. Since the scurrility is directed against himself and his patron, Smollett would have resented the *dramatis personae* in the scene, but the scene itself is one that he thoroughly understood, *Ferdinand Count Fathom* (1753) of a decade earlier being the most thoroughgoing of his looks at the seamy world of the confidence man and his gulls.

A second significant element of Smollett's fiction akin to many of the prints of the age is his creation of what one might call his over-stuffed scenes, pictures brimful of busy details, the kind of thing that George Kahrl described when he observed that "both painters and writers, Hogarth and Smollett especially, were tempted to crowd the moment, the episode, with 'realistic' violent action rather than to select and develop one action."[6] The following from Smollett's *Sir Launcelot Greaves,* published only the year before Smollett undertook the *Briton,* could readily serve as a description in a catalog of satirical prints or as instructions to the inventor of a satirical print.[7] The passage starts off with noise rather than visual stuffing, but quickly becomes crowded with graphic detail:

> . . . The rumbling of carriages, and the rattling of horses feet on the pavement, was intermingled with loud shouts, and the noise of fiddle, french-horn, and bagpipe. A loud peal was heard ringing in the church-tower, at some distance, while the inn resounded with clamour, confusion, and uproar.
>
> Sir Launcelot being thus alarmed, started from his bed, and running to the window, beheld a cavalcade of persons well mounted, and distinguished by blue cockades. They were generally attired like jockies, with gold-laced hats and buckskin breeches, and one of them bore a standard of blue silk, inscribed in white letters, Liberty and the Landed Interest. He who rode at their head was a jolly figure, of a florid complexion and round belly, seemingly turned of fifty, and, in all appearance, of a choleric disposition. As they approached the market-place they waved their hats, huzza'd, and cried aloud, No foreign Connections,—Old England for ever. This acclamation, however, was not so loud or universal, but that our adventurer could distinctly hear a counter-cry from the populace of No Slavery,—No Popish Pretender. [Such exclamations would have fitted very neatly in balloons above the heads of the figures.] An insinuation so ill relished by the cavaliers, that they began to ply their horse-whips among the multitude, and were, in their turn, saluted with a discharge or volley of stones, dirt, and dead cats; in consequence of which some teeth were demolished, and many surtouts defiled.[8]

And this lengthy, graphically detailed passage is only the Tory half of the scene; when the Whigs enter, as they presently do, the picture does not become any larger, nor is there any propulsion of the narrative action, but the picture certainly gets denser, one may say Hogarthian. This then was a characteristic of Smollett's descriptive prose that served him well when he undertook the *Briton*.

The significance of this Hogarthian characteristic as an element in the *Briton* will become clearer if, before looking at some specific passages of that journal, we review William Hogarth's *The Times*, one of the most famous political prints of the period, one of the four that is clearly on Bute's side, and one that touches upon many of the themes that engaged Smollett and other ministerial writers.[9] *The Times* was published on 7 September 1762, some three months after the *Briton* had first launched its attack against the anti-ministerial *Monitor*, only in turn to be counterattacked by John Wilkes's *North Briton*. Hogarth's engraving pictures the flames of war threatening buildings which represent the continental powers and Great Britain. William Pitt, raised on stilts and surrounded by an adoring mob, is encouraging the flames with a bellows. George III (or his representative) stands on a fire wagon directing a stream of water at the flames, assisted by several Scotsmen. None of these is specifically identifiable, but Bute is surely one and quite possibly Smollett is another. Their efforts are hampered by two persons leaning out of garret windows, John Wilkes and his associate on the *North Briton*, the satirist and former curate Charles Churchill; in another window a faceless person, Earl Temple, Pitt's brother-in-law and a sponsor of the *North Briton*, joins them in squirting streams from clyster pipes at the fireman. On the left a grotesque figure, possibly the Duke of Newcastle, wheels a wheelbarrowful of *Monitors* and *North Britons* into the legs of one of the hurrying firemen, further impeding rescue efforts.

Although many graphic motifs are at work in *The Times* (hence the "overstuffed" effect), the central metaphor is that of a Great Britain in danger of being engulfed by flames. A few days before *The Times* was published, *John Bull's House sett in Flames* had been published, apparently anticipating Hogarth's basic conception, although in it roles are reversed: Bute, not Pitt and his allies, is the incendiary, and Pitt, not the King and his supporters, is the fireman. It appears that Hogarth was picking up an idea already worked on, although the maker of the earlier print may have picked up his idea from prepublication descriptions of the print Hogarth was known to be doing. Or of course, since the metaphor is a rather obvious one, they could have been independently conceived (although the close conjunction in time would make that a rather remarkable coincidence). However, if some kind of priority is to be awarded, it should go to Smollett, who was using the image of the incendiary in his prose months before either Hogarth or the unknown engraver of *John Bull's House sett in Flames* published their prints. (Ronald Paulson thinks the creator of *John Bull's House* may be Paul Sandby, who in September 1762 published another print with the same theme entitled *The Fire of Faction*, BM 3955.)[10]

In the very first *Briton*, Smollett uses the figure of the King's enemies as incendiaries setting England aflame. He announces the *Briton's* purpose as being "not to puzzle, but explain; not to inflame, but to allay. . . . to pluck the mask of patriotism from the front of faction, and the torch of discord from the hand of sedition." After this bit of allegory, he directly accuses the *Monitor* of undertaking "the vilest work of the worst incendiary: he has scattered his fire-arrows with a rash and desperate hand; he has not only directed them against a M[inistr]y without blame, but even dared to aim them at the bosom of a Sovereign that never knew dishonour." Any hack printmaker could easily have used these words as instructions for a print typical of the day. In fact there exists a print of the early 1760s quite similar to Smollett's basic picture, although the arrows in it are not fire-arrows and the print is anti-Bute rather than pro-Bute. The print is *The Scotch Butt* (pun on Bute of course), *Or the English Archers* (BM 3956; see fig. 2). In it five English archers—from left to right, Wilkes, Churchill, Cumberland, Temple, and Pitt—are launching their arrows at a boot raised to eminence and holding a Scotch thistle. The boot is another obvious pun on Bute, who indeed was represented in numerous prints by a jackboot. Smollett and Arthur Murphy stand between the boot and the archers with shields labeled "The Briton" and "The Auditor." (A few weeks after Smollett began the *Briton*, a second ministerial paper called the *Auditor*, edited by the Irish playwright Arthur Murphy, had joined him in defending Bute.) An arrow labeled "Monitor" has hit Smollett's shield, and one labeled "N. Briton" has made a direct hit on the boot. Behind the pedestal holding the boot stands the King's mother, whose overhead balloon contains a double entendre typical once more of the innuendos circulated about her and Bute: "I'll present my Shield while thou canst Stand and raise thee up when thou art fallen."

In later issues of the *Briton*, the image of inflammatory attack occurs frequently: ". . . blow the scorching furnace of discord and sedition" (No. 2); ". . . the vilest stubble of faction, supplying fuel to every incendiary" (No. 6); ". . . industriously blow the coals of discord" (No. 17); "blow the flame of discord under the mask of mod-

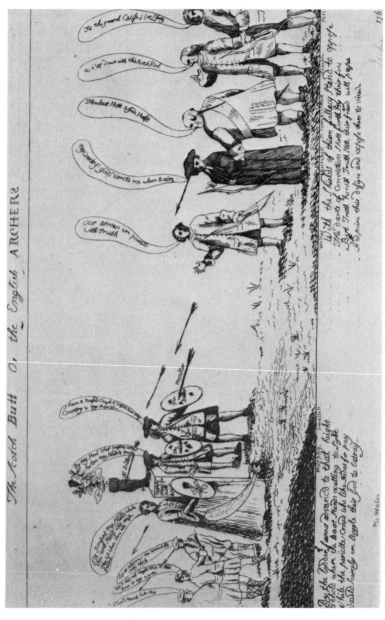

Figure 2: *The Scotch Butt, Or the English Archers*. The British Museum; BM 3956. Photo courtesy of the British Library.

eration" (No. 38). Many other brief passages present pictorial allegories with visual images of other kinds of assault: "the hounds of faction began to mangle the reputation of a M[iniste]r" (No. 10); "the abuse and censure of the multitude is a kind of artillery, which hath been levelled at all ministers; and . . . the management of this artillery, is one of the dearest privileges of the English people" (No. 24); an anti-ministerial writer "lifts the murderous quill to stab the reputation of innocence, to sully the fair fame of the most shining merit" (No. 32). And a correspondent to the *Briton*, discussing a pamphlet that predicted that the preliminaries to the peace would blow the English up in a trice, ironically queries, "What then does that minister deserve who has charged the mine, and now stands with his dark lanthorn and match, ready to kindle the train, which is to send us all up in the air in a moment!" (No. 24). The image of Guy Fawkes, his explosives, and his dark lantern had been, as M. Dorothy George indicates, used by political printmakers for more than a century to accuse others of treason.[11]

In a somewhat more developed passage, Smollett creates a turbulent scene of merit and virtue under attack that suggests the detailing craft of a Hogarth:

> I no sooner brandished my weapon, like a political knight-errant, in defence of innocence traduced, than the whole caitiff crew exalted their throats with redoubled clamour; the monsters, the giants, and the dwarfs of falshood, malice and misrepresentation. New sluices of slander were opened; new defamers retained: your Lordship was bespattered from every dark alley of scandalous insinuation; while the poor Briton was reproached as a fool, a dunce, and the venal prostitute of a minister. (No. 6)

Another passage where the *Briton*'s words are even more clearly conceived in terms of an emblematic scene occurs in No. 8, in which Smollett suggests that Temple, patron of Wilkes and Churchill in undertaking the *North Briton*, might create a gallery in which his friends would be properly emblemized:

> After all these pains taken to light the torch of national discord, he may repair to his villa, and from his temple warehouse, select a new structure to be dedicated to the *concordia civium*. There it is to be hoped he will find a place for the head of the writer who calls himself *North Briton*, (I do not mean his real head, as that and his body may be destined to another fate) I mean a bust of him, to represent the united virtues of decency and candour.

Within the same gallery, Smollett also ironically proposes statuary that would acknowledge the support of the wealthy alderman William Beckford in the anti-ministerial cause:

> I would . . . humbly propose to the right honourable personage, who admits his friends into the temple of immortality; that in his new *Aedes concordiae*, he would represent the coalition of the sugar and malt distillery [Beckford and Wilkes; Beckford owned plantations in Jamaica, Wilkes's father was a wealthy distiller], under the figures of the *Monitor* and the *North Briton*, mixing up a drench of rum and geneva, to animate their understrappers to a more inflammatory pitch of defamation; and this union may be distinguished by an inscription to the following effect; . . . Cocamus pro Bono Publico.

Complete with ironic inscription ("Let us brew for the public good"), the *Briton's* tableau could readily be turned into a print, perhaps similar to one of a decade and a half earlier entitled *A Collection of Modern Statues and Caracters* (BM 2829). This showed an array of statues in modern dress standing on pedestals engraved with such classic names as Proteus, Cicero, Clodius, Curio, and others. Half the print is text with characterizations of the figures that make it clear that Proteus is Bolingbroke, Cicero is Walpole, Curio is the Earl of Bath, and so on.

A Collection of Modern Statues reminds us also of one of the most common tactics of the printmakers—and of eighteenth-century political propagandists such as Smollett. That tactic is to comment on a figure of national importance by picturing him in the guise of some well-known, usually notorious, historical or literary figure.[12] In a print of around 1762 entitled *The Fishermen* (BM 3876), a figure representing the *Monitor* has a collection of baits, among which is one entitled "Parallels unlike," apparently referring to this tactic of comparing current persons and events to historical and literary ones. Thus a print entitled *The Scotch Colossus* (BM 3939) connected Bute with the well-known figure of antiquity, depending for its derogation of Bute on the viewer's memory of the characterization by Shakespeare's Cassius of Caesar as a Colossus. In other prints Bute was identified with such other figures as Macbeth and Roger Mortimer, who had been the illicit lover of Edward II's Queen Isabella. Bute was also pictured as Sejanus, the Roman minister supposed to have had the Emperor Tiberius under his sinister control.[13] (Sir Robert Walpole too, in the preceding generation, had been pictured by printmakers as, among other figures, a Colossus and a Sejanus.)

The immediate occasion for *Briton* No. 1 was an allusion to Bute as a Sejanus in the *Monitor,* a comparison that Smollett went on at rather tiring length to refute. But, while rejecting that particular parallel, Smollett also used the tactic of historical pictorialization to make points of his own. In No. 16, for example, he likens the rebellious mobs of London to the Peasants' Revolt of 1381 and dresses up John Wilkes and Charles Churchill in the form of Jack Straw and John Bull, two of the leaders of the earlier uprising (the modern identity of Wat Tyler in the following passage is not certain, probably Pitt or Temple):

> . . . the present Reformers pique themselves upon being free-born Englishmen: but, like their predecessors, they are headed by their Wat Tyler and Jack Straw, and animated by a reverend apostle of equal virtue and capacity with the celebrated John Bull, the honest priest of those days, who acted as principal incendiary, spiriting up the multitude to mischief and rebellion by inflammatory sermons, quaint rhimes, and treasonable papers, dispersed among the leaders of the people. . . . Jacky Straw assures them, it is their privilege to be insolent and refractory; and Bull the parson declares, that *Vox populi est vox Dei:* the voice of the people is the voice of God.

An even more developed allusion that includes also both a detailed drawing of a figure and a typical visual metaphor of dirty attack appears in *Briton* No. 14. This claims to describe a character drawn from the *Arabian Nights,* a wretched troublemaker by the name of Jahia Ben Israil Ginn, who plagues the reign of the Caliph Haroun Rachid. The identification of Jahia Ben Israil Ginn is clear: John Wilkes's father was named Israel, and his family fortune came from a profitable gin distillery. The *Briton* gives an elaborate physical description that takes note of Wilkes's two best-known facial features, features well suited to cartooning, his notorious squint and his prominent teeth:

> His external form was such as happily expressed the deformity of his mind. His face was meagre, sallow, and forbidding, as if he looked pale and haggard from the consciousness of guilt. His eyes were distorted, with such an hideous obliquity of vision, that the sight of him alone had frightened some matrons into miscarriage. . . . His chin was long and incurvated, like the moon in her first quarter. His jaw was furnished with large irregular tushes; and when he spoke, his mouth overflowed with a plentiful discharge of slaver.

The account then goes on with an illustration of Jahia's activities:

> . . . he made a large collection of filth, and chusing his station near the precints of the palace, began to pelt the Vizir as he passed and repassed to and from the court of the Caliph: but, whether he was

too blind to take a proper aim at his object, or too unskilful to throw his dirt with any effect, certain it is, he never once hit the mark. . . . The Genii that protected this district, taking compassion on the inhabitants, exerted his power for their relief. *Jahia Ginn* going to the common sewer of the city, for a supply of soil, was suddenly petrified in the very act of stooping, and converted into a grotesque image, his mouth standing wide open as a spout for the discharge of filth.

The last image is one particularly apt for a typically scatological political cartoon of the period. Wilkes himself reacted to the *Briton's* description of Jahia Ginn in terms recognizing its graphic force and the parallel between political journalism and printmaking when he wrote goodnaturedly to Churchill, "I am excellently portrayed in Saturday's Briton. Why do not the printshops take me? I am an incomparable subject for a print."[14] Perhaps William Hogarth picked up the hint, for his famous print of Wilkes was published some months later in May 1763.

There may also be connections between the *Briton's* satire and *The Bruiser,* Hogarth's portrayal of Wilkes's companion-in-arms, Charles Churchill, a print almost equally famous with that of Wilkes.[15] The depiction of Churchill as a bear in Hogarth's print published in August 1763 may be prefigured by a passage in *Briton* No. 13, published a year earlier. The passage complains of the "tides of scurrility and treason" flowing from "a fourth estate distinguished by the name of *Rabble.*" The rabble's leaders are Jacky-Dandy (Wilkes), Paedagogus Latro (Robert Lloyd, an obscure writer and friend of Churchill), and Bruin (Churchill): "Jacky is what the world calls a *buck* and a *smart.* . . . Sometimes [Paedagogus] feeds on Bruin's offal, whom he frequently follows, and helps out with scraps of blasphemy, ribaldry and treason. As to Bruin himself, *O Dii boni!* What language can do him justice!" The circulation of the image of Churchill as Bruin may have influenced Hogarth's choice of the bear figure for his *Bruiser* attack on his and Smollett's common enemy.

The *Briton* also used a variety of devices akin to those of the printmaker to mock William Pitt. He too is called the "Great Colussus" (No. 8), a "modern Demosthenes" (No. 25), and "our modern Gracchus" (No. 37). He is a "political alchymist" (No. 8) and has mounted "the pontifical chair of politics" to become "infallibility itself" (No. 30). The popularity of Pitt with the London populace was especially obnoxious to the ministerial writers and accounts for such pictorial accusations as one that Pitt "had raised himself into a colossal idol of popularity" (No. 5). Another passage, reminiscent again of motifs of *The Times,* asks, "Shall he, anointed with the dregs of popularity, believe himself invulnerable, and direct his emissaries to squirt their poison at the T[hro]ne, secure against censure and rebuke?" (No. 37).

One of the more extended attacks on Pitt describes the career of a famous Florentine demagogue, Luca Pitti, "who had appeared like a comet in politics, now set, never to rise again" (No. 11). The fortunate coinciding of *Pitt* with *Pitti* helped Smollett make allegorical points with the alleged historical parallels. Pitt's appearance in the House of Commons, despite his suffering a severe attack of gout, to attack the preliminaries to the peace, gave the *Briton* the occasion for one of its best cartoon scenes: "the great methodist of mock patriotism mounted the rostrum, like a candidate of ancient Rome, solliciting the mob, in a flannel gown, the frowzy badge of courted popularity." And the failure of Pitt's efforts is thus pictured: "the once worshipped idol is fallen to rise no more" (No. 32).

Usually prints were published and sold individually for around six pence. (The *Briton* sold for less than half that, two pence halfpenny for a six-page issue.) But often a number of prints were collected and crudely reprinted in small volumes. During the early years of George III's reign, collections were published with titles such as *Political & Satirical History Displaying the Unhappy Influence of Scotch Prevalency* and *British Antidote to Caledonian Poison*. A small compilation of prose pieces, published in 1763, suggests a kind of parallel again between what the printmakers were doing and what political journalists like Smollett and Murphy and Wilkes had undertaken. This work was *The True Flower of Brimstone: Extracted from the Briton, North Briton, and Auditor*, an anthology of some of the more striking satiric depictions and scenes from the three papers and a few others, arranged under the names of the chief political figures of the day. The little volume would seem to have been promoted by a desire to appeal to the customers who bought the collections of prints, to those who found satisfaction in seeing prominent men displayed in demeaning images or satiric rep-resentations. One of the passages from the *Briton* reprinted in *The True Flower of Brimstone* is a lampoon of that very lampoonable figure, the aging, officious Duke of Newcastle. Mocking Newcastle's part in the parliamentary debate on the preliminaries to the peace in Decem-ber 1762, the passage effectively epitomizes that element in the *Briton* that parallels the satiric and political prints of the age (the original is in *Briton* No. 32):

One superannuated original, a quondam St[atesma]n floundered on as usual in a sea of absurdity, and was saved from sinking by nothing but his want of weight. His folly had formerly been produc-tive of laughter, but now it was heard with silent disdain. Since that

period, he is said to have been incessantly haunted . . . with the
ghost of his departed greatness. Sometimes it appears in Motley
with a cap and bells; sometimes in the shape of a borough-elector
hanging upon a gibbet, with a purse of money about his neck; sometimes it multiplies itself into a whole Mughouse-mob, drinking
d[amnatio]n to the Tories; sometimes it assumes the form of a West-
phalian rat with long whiskers; and sometimes it takes the figure of
public credit, with a consumptive look, sailing down the wind on
blown bags of paper.

A little further on in the passage, Newcastle "begins to wag his head
and shake his heels, to utter incoherent jargon, while he dances himself into a profuse sweat." These last touches particularly may remind
readers of the satiric passages in *Humphry Clinker* (written of course
after Smollett's experience with the *Briton*), where Newcastle appears
again as a kind of cartoon figure, an addled busybody.

The *Briton* was thus both a continuation of some of the graphic
skills that Smollett had found useful in his earlier fiction and a work-
basket of pictorial tactics from which he could draw in his two final
works, *The History and Adventures of an Atom* and *The Expedition of
Humphry Clinker*.

Numerous other passages could be cited from the *Briton* to demonstrate that when Smollett moved into the field of partisan political
journalism, his gifts of verbal grotesquerie, of pictorial allusion, of
overstuffed scene and emblematic detail stood him in good stead,
indeed were given new force. Truth to tell, the *Briton* was not noticeably successful in quieting the clamor of the pro-Pitt populace or in
answering the more serious arguments of Bute's opponents. But as
he raised his shield to defend George III and Lord Bute against the
incendiary shafts of the satiric writers and printmakers of the opposition, he usually proved their equal—admittedly the standard was
often not high—in provocative image making, in the dramatic and
emblematic tactics characteristic of the political prints of the early 1760s.
Examination of the *Briton* makes clearer the extent to which Smollett
was a caricaturist—a cartoonist if one will—and the extent to which,
in the give-and-take of the political propaganda that hoped to move
the tides of popular sentiment, both tracts and prints were the products of similar traditions and impulses of the imagination.

NOTES

1 The age had no single term that conveniently expressed what we today would generally understand by *cartoon*, a meaning that in general use goes back only to the middle of the nineteenth century. It nonetheless now seems the appropriate term to designate the kind of visual political comment or propaganda here considered. M. Dorothy George (see n. 2) in her introduction and George Kahrl (see n. 5) touch on the problems of shifting nomenclature and denotations.

2 M. Dorothy George, *English Political Caricature to 1792* (Oxford: Clarendon Press, 1959), p. 121.

3 Many issues of the *Briton* contain material presented in the form of a letter. Smollett as editor quite certainly wrote some of these, but some may be *bona fide* letters to the editor. Thus one cannot safely attribute everything in the *Briton* to Smollett's own pen. But one can be reasonably sure that everything met with his approval, was congruent with his way of thinking, and reflected his approach to propaganda warfare.

4 Numbers in parentheses refer to the British Museum *Catalogue of Political and Personal Satires*, vols. 1–4 (1870–83). A reproduction of *John Bull's House* may be found as illustration no. 108 in Herbert M. Atherton, *Political Prints in the Age of Hogarth* (Oxford: Clarendon Press, 1974).

5 See George Kahrl, "Smollett as a Caricaturist," in *Tobias Smollett: Bicentennial Essays Presented to Lewis M. Knapp*, ed. G. S. Rousseau and P.-G. Boucé (New York: Oxford University Press, 1971), pp. 169–200; also Robert Adams Day, "Ut Pictura Poesis: Smollett, Satire, and the Graphic Arts," *Studies in Eighteenth-Century Culture*, 10 (Madison: University of Wisconsin Press, 1981): 297–312. The latter is particularly concerned with graphic satire and Smollett's *The History and Adventures of an Atom* which followed the *Briton* by about six or seven years.

6 Kahrl, "Smollett as Caricaturist," p. 185.

7 Day, "Ut Pictura Poesis" (pp. 297–98) stresses how the recognized genre of "instructions to the painter" often seems discoverable in Smollett's fiction.

8 *The Life and Adventures of Sir Launcelot Greaves*, ed. David Evans (London: Oxford University Press, 1973), pp. 71–72. Evans recognizes the printlike quality of the scene by suggesting in his introduction (p. xi) that Hogarth's *Four Prints of an Election* (1755–58) "offer possible visual sources for the conception and details of chapter ix."

9 Two states of this are reproduced as pls. 233 and 234 in vol. 2 of Ronald Paulson, *Hogarth's Graphic Works* (New Haven: Yale University Press, 1965). The description here is of the one identified by Paulson as the third state.

10 *Hogarth: His Life, Art, and Times*, abr. Anne Wilde (New Haven: Yale University Press, 1974), p. 415. *The Fire of Faction* is illustration no. 114 in Atherton, *Political Prints*.

11 See George, *English Political Caricature*, Index under "Fawkes, Guy."

12 Atherton (*Political Prints*, p. 192) points out how, following the lead of the *Craftsman*, the opposition pamphleteers and printmakers of Walpole's day found English history to be "a storehouse of apt parallels" for attacking supposed criminal ministers.
13 George, *English Political Caricature*, pp. 122–23.
14 Quoted in John Wardroper, *Kings, Lords and Wicked Libellers* (London: John Murray, 1973), p. 38.
15 The Wilkes print is pl. no. 237 and the Churchill print nos. 238 and 239 in Paulson, *Hogarth's Graphic Works*.

The Musical Quality of Goldsmith's The Deserted Village

WILLIAM BOWMAN PIPER

There are four formal aspects of any musical setting of an English poem: number; stress; duration; and pitch. Since the audible pitch of poetic developments is formalized only in actual songs and, perhaps, chants; and since both number and stress have been traditionally formalized in English discursive poetry at least since the Renaissance: the measuring of duration is the one formal concern of anyone who would consider the musical quality of such a discursive poem as Oliver Goldsmith's *The Deserted Village*. I posit a thesis, then, that such a poem is musical to the extent that the durations of its syllables, feet, and lines are or seem to be formally measured. A discursive English poem approximates song, that is to say, to the degree that its elements are felt to constitute a system of temporal ratios and equivalents. By way of prophesy, I suggest that *The Deserted Village* can be proven to be the most musical of any extensive heroic-couplet or, indeed, iambic-pentameter poem in our language ("Lycidas" being, in such a survey as I have made,[1] its only close rival for this distinction).[2]

The unstressed syllables of English poems, broadly speaking, have been traditionally rendered in song settings one-half as long as the stressed syllables—and thus worked into systems of durational ratio—or exactly as long—and thus worked into systems of durational equivalence. In the first of these cases, as Elise Jorgens has recently explained, temporal discrimination was being used in music to represent stress determination in verse; in the second case, musical accent was adjusted to do so.[3] Professor Jorgens has quoted a setting by Campion to exemplify the first of these two musical practices (fig. 1). The measuring of the verse syllables in this song, "I care not for these ladies,"[4] is not mechanically exact, of course; but, generally speaking, the unstressed syllables are set to half-notes and the stressed to whole. Professor Jorgens has quoted the following song by Campion, "Tune thy Music,"[5] to illustrate the second kind of musical adjustment (fig. 2). Here, as Professor Jorgens has pointed out, both stressed and unstressed syllables are set to half-notes and "stress [is] correlated with musical accent."[6]

Such musical practices, which Professor Jorgens has recognized in

Figure 1: Thomas Campion, "I care not for these ladies," from *The Songs from Rosseter's Book of Airs* (1601); *The English Lute-Songs*, Series 1, Vol. 4/13, ed. Edmund H. Fellowes, rev. Thurston Dart (London, and New York: Stainer and Bell, Ltd., and Galaxy Music Corp, 1969), pp. 6–7.

Figure 2: Thomas Campion, "Tune thy Music," from *The Works of Thomas Campion*, ed. and with Introduction by Walter R. Davis (Garden City, N.Y.: Doubleday and Co., Inc., 1967), p. 67.

English songs composed between 1597 and 1651, persisted undiminished up to and through the time of Goldsmith. In this quotation from that remarkable eighteenth-century smash, *The Beggar's Opera* (1728), for example (fig. 3), the iambic verse is accommodated to music in a virtually invariable durational ratio of 1 to 2. In this song from Thomas D'Urfey's popular *Pills to Purge Melancholy* (1719–20), again (fig. 4), it is anapests that are durationally adjusted, being set in a ratio of 1 to 1 to 2. There is a powerful tendency in these and, indeed, in all songs to regularize, not only the metrical feet, but the longer spans of poetry as well. In "The first time at the looking glass" above, for instance, each of the four lines we have quoted has been fit into two musical measures.

The first time at___ the look - ing glass The moth-er sets her

daugh - ter, The i - mage strikes the smi - ling lass With

self - love ev - er af - ter.

Figure 3: John Gay, "The sun had loosed his weary teams," from *The Beggar's Opera*, ed. Edgar V. Roberts and Edward Smith (Lincoln: University of Nebraska Press, 1969), p. 148.

The MOHOCKS. *A* SONG.

THERE's a new set of Rakes,
Entitled Mohocks,
Who infest Her Majesties Subjects ;
He who meets 'em at Night,
Must be ready for flight,
Or withstanding he many a Drub gets.

Figure 4: Thomas D'Urfey, "The Mohocks," from *Pills to Purge Melancholy* (1719–20); facsimile reproduction of the 1876 reprint of the original edition (New York: Folklore Library Pub., Inc., 1959), 6:336.

Songs in which verse syllables, as well as feet and lines, have been made equal in duration are just as common as those in which the syllables have been discriminated. In this song from D'Urfey's *Pills* (fig. 5), every one of the syllables (except those at the ends of lines 2 and 4, by the exaggeration of which the larger elements of the song have been emphasized and regularized) has been given an eighth-note, and the stress system of the verse has been realized, as in Campion's "Tune thy Music," by musical accent. Similarly, in this beautiful Restoration song by Dryden and Purcell,[7] which was also published and thus broadcast by D'Urfey in *Pills* (fig. 6), the stresses of the dactyllic verse have been set in accordance with musical accent, the separate syllables having been made equivalent in duration. Consider, finally, this song from *The Beggar's Opera* (fig. 7). The syllables of the first and third lines, which are iambic in verse, have been set into a system of durational ratio, 1 to 2; whereas the syllables of the second and fourth lines have been made equivalent in duration, their anapestic system of verse stresses having been accommodated to the musical accent. Such examples, although sixteenth- to eighteenth-century songs are various in their handling of verse—and Dowland at the turn of the sixteenth century often quite reconstituted the verses he set[8]—are typical of the songs Goldsmith must have known, and himself often performed, throughout his life.[9] A seventeenth- or

A New Song, *upon the* Robin-red-breast's *attending Queen* Mary's *Hearse in* Westminster Abby.

A LL you that lov'd our Queen alive,
    Now Dead lament Her fate ;
And take a walk to *Westminster*,
    To see Her lie in State.

Figure 5: Thomas D'Urfey, "A New Song . . ." from *Pills to Purge Melancholy,* 3:76.

Bright Nymphs of *Britain*, with Graces attended,
    Let not your days without Pleasure expire ;
Honour's but empty, and when Youth is ended,
    All Men will praise you, but none will desire :
Let not Youth fly away without Contenting,
Age will come time enough, for your Repenting.
    Let not Youth, &c.

Figure 6: John Dryden and Henry Purcell, "How blest are shepherds," from *King Arthur* (1691); D'Urfey, *Pills to Purge Melancholy,* 3:290–91.

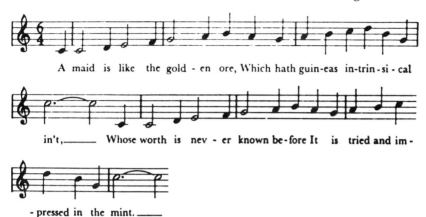

A maid is like the gold-en ore, Which hath guin-eas in-trin-si-cal

in't,_____ Whose worth is nev-er known be-fore It is tried and im-

-pressed in the mint._____

Figure 7: John Gay, "Of all the simple things we do," from *The Beggar's Opera,* ed. Roberts and Smith, p. 102.

eighteenth-century English songwriter, to generalize, could easily establish verbal systems of durational ratio or equivalence—or of the two combined, as in "A maid is like the golden ore"—and thus compose larger systems of formally measured duration.

In his own way, as I must now argue, Goldsmith has done just this sort of thing, without the benefit of pitch or any musical notation, to the syllables, feet, and lines of *The Deserted Village.* Sometimes he has composed patterns or, more accurately, suggested optional patterns of durationally equal syllables, sometimes of syllables in a 1 to 2 durational ratio; and with the extensive if incidental introduction of such patterns—of such options—he has infused his poem with this one musical quality, that is, the formalization of duration, thus drawing it into a significant approximation with song.

By the use of close-coupled assonance, first off, he has provided many options for quantitative spondees, that is, for feet of two durationally equal syllables.[10] He has used many spondaic words: not only such showy proper names as *Pambamarca* and *Altama,* but such terms as *murmur, mingling, sedges, cumbrous, feebly, maintained, wretched* and *relieve,* each of which, having two adjoining syllables with the same or virtually the same vowel sound, more or less strongly suggests a pair of durational equivalents. By using such words he has composed lines with spondaic options such as these:

> Unwieldly wealth, and cumbrous pomp repose (66);
>
> The mingling notes came softened from below (116);

Up yonder hill the village murmur rose (114).[11]

Every one of these lines presents sounds beyond the coupled assonance that I have mentioned which intensify and extend its effects. In line 116, for example, "notes," which immediately follows "mingling," is strongly echoed by the line's last syllable, "-low"; it is immediately followed, moreover, by the obviously long syllable "came," so that the spondaic option focussed in "mingling" reaches virtually throughout the line.

The mingling notes came softened from below.

In this line, again,

Thus to relieve the wretched was his pride (163),

there are two spondaic words, the one with a rising the other with a falling stress pattern. The inverted first foot of this line dignifies the first syllable of "relieve," enforcing the optional equivalence in duration between its syllables; and the alliterating *r* in "wretched" and "pride" provides a kind of linkage the other way, so that, once again, a possible quantitative measure has been spread across the whole line:

Thus to relieve the wretched was his pride.

Such closely linked assonance is sometimes extended, as in this line,

And still as each repeated pleasure tired (23),

in which, first, three like syllables, "each repeat-," are yoked together and, then, immediately afterwards, another pair, "-ted plea-." The first three syllables of this line, moreover—since the second one, "still," has naturally some temporal scope and since the first and third, both of them schwas, chime together—further support the formal measurement of syllabic duration:

And still as each repeated pleasure tired.

The spondaic effect is rendered both more pervasively and more subtly in *The Deserted Village* with assonantally paired syllables that occur in different words. The last line above reveals two cases of this; or consider now:

And fools, who came to scoff, remained to pray (180).

The effect of the spondaic option offered here by "fools, who" is continued, if with diffused force, by the remote assonance, "came . . . -mained . . . pray" and by the balancing infinitives, "to scoff . . . to pray." The fact that the recurrent "to" chimes with "fools, who" strengthens the spondaic quality of these phrases and of the whole line:

And fools, who came to scoff, remained to pray.

Please notice, I am not denying the persistence of stress and number in Goldsmith's poetic formula; but, rather, arguing for the enrichment of these normal elements of English discursive verse by a third, an incidental but nevertheless widely evident, formal element. It may be worthwhile to notice an oddity about this tendency toward the formalization of duration in *The Village*. Normally the details of verse, the immediate words and rhythms, draw *away* from the form: this is as true in Virgilian quantitative poetry as in Milton's blank verse compositions. But in *The Village* certain details in words and rhythms, although they no doubt draw *away* from the normally English formal system of stress and number, creatively draw *toward* a system of measured duration, indicating a new form even as they modify the old.

In a subtle case of this formal enrichment,

The sober herd that lowed to meet their young (118),

the assonantal pair, "-ber herd," is strengthened by the obvious assonantal bracket, "so- . . . lowed," and, perhaps, by the balancing spondaic pair, "that lowed . . . their young."

The sober herd that lowed to meet their young.

In other cases Goldsmith's practices are more evident, more insistent. In this line, for instance,

Farewell, and O where'er thy voice be tried (417),

the immediately joined pairs, "where'er" and "thy voice," extend in their effect to "tried," which echoes the second of them, and reach back to the naturally long "O" and to the naturally spondaic "Farewell":

> Farewell, and O where'er thy voice be tried.

This line thus rivals in apparent musicality such obvious quantitative systems as Tennyson's famous line,

> On thy cold gray stones, O sea,

and Jonson's still more finely measured line,

> Slow, slow, fresh fount, keep time with my salt tears.

In this line, again,

> Silent went next, neglectful of her charms (377),

the five successive short *e* sounds, especially as these are alliteratively reinforced, suggest an equalling of syllables that can hardly be ignored, but Goldsmith's practices are often both impressive and subtle at once. In this line,

> The robe that wraps his limbs in silken sloth (279),

although a first assonantal pair, "that wraps," is immediately followed by a doubled pair, "his limbs in silk-," there is sufficient variety in the consonants to make the movement fluent and easy. The flow of the line is augmented, moreover, by the remote chime, "robe . . . sloth," which brackets the interior spondees, so that one enjoys the measured sweep of the line without being troubled by its machinery:

> The robe that wraps his limbs in silken sloth.

In this line, likewise,

> Yes! let the rich deride, the proud disdain (251),

the effect of the emphatic opening spondee is diffused by a variety of sound patterns none obtrusive but all contributing to a system of finely delineated spondaic pairs:

> Yes! let the rich deride, the proud disdain.

There are well over one hundred lines (among the four hundred and thirty that make up *The Village*) containing such close-coupled assonance as I have been describing, virtually all of which are strengthened as durational measures by bracketing assonance, alliterative def-

inition, or some other sound effects. This number of lines, more than
a fourth of all those in *The Village,* might almost by itself prompt a
reader, it seems to me, to conceive of a formal measuring of duration
throughout the poem.

An equally considerable category of incidents, one that suggests
primarily durational ratios rather than equivalents, further encourages such a conception. This category, the anapestic option, comprehends incidents of two elided syllables, which, as the elision itself
strongly suggests, must wedge into a time span equal to that filled
by one long syllable, and of one long syllable. Such an incident presents a ratio of a half to a half to a whole, but it resolves into a verse
foot of two equal durational spans and thus harmonizes with the optional spondee, the many cases of which we have already surveyed.
More than a hundred lines of *The Village*—almost as many lines as
those offering assonantal spondees—present the reader with this option, which is dramatized by occurring in every one of the first seven
lines of the poem. In line 3, for example,

> Where smiling spring its earliest visit paid,

one faces not only a virtually inescapable anapest, but two cases of
close-coupled assonance as well, "-ing spring" and "visit," and the
definitive alliteration of "spring" and "paid." "Its," moreover, to touch
a further point, is echoed especially by the second syllable of "visit":
so that the line reverberates with optional patterns of durational ratio
and equivalence:

> Where smiling spring its earliest visit paid.

Consider another clustered system, one that seems to me, for all its
effective elements, to work quite subtly:

> Unfit in these degenerate times of shame (409).

The paired "-fit in" and "these de-" are variously disguised: the second of them by the rapid progress to the naturally stressed "-gen-"
and on to the artificially speeded movement through "-erate times."
The bracketing echoes of *n* and *m* both extend and diffuse the interior
movement and fill out a line which, although significantly musical,
also remains safely within the English discursive tradition:

> Unfit in these degenerate times of shame.

I am not at all sure how Goldsmith rationalized his many elisions—
or, indeed, that he did so.[12] As Professor Friedman's authoritative
edition makes clear, the poet clipped very few of his extra syllables

with apostrophes. And the interior *er* (or *ur*) syllable, which often figures in his elisions, he sometimes preserved in full force: "intolerable," "venerable," and "luxuries," for instance, must be reeled out at full length to make lines 348, 178, and 284 (respectively) satisfy the principle of number. And Goldsmith could hardly have insisted on this syllable at these points and simply cancelled it elsewhere. There are, interestingly, several cases—"lingering" (line 4), "whispering" (line 14), and "shivering" (line 326), for instance—in which a strict cancellation of each elided syllable would transform an optinal anapest into the close-coupled assonance wherein I have found an optional spondee. The hard insistence on narrowing such words as "labouring," "wandering" and "ponderous" would surely transform them into optional spondees too. It seems better to me, however, to think of all these cases of elision—as we must think of terms like "loveliest" and "influence"—as strong promptings toward an elided lilt, an anapestic ratio, that is, of a half to a half to a whole and along this track to the resolved equivalence between two shortened syllables and one long. Thus lines like

> Sweet smiling village, loveliest of the lawn (35),
>
> Ill fares the land, to hastening ills a prey (51),
>
> In all my wanderings round this world of care (83),

all strike my ear with an anapestic lilt, that is, with a quantitative lilt; and, being usually enriched, like the spondaic options, with supportive sound effects, they emerge as systems of formalized stress and number and duration—all the more apparent since in these cases number and duration are at dynamic odds.

The lines in *The Deserted Village* that reveal either a spondaic or an anapestic option, of which there are over two hundred, are augmented as quantitative or musical events by many others that individually present special and diverse sound systems. In this line,

> Amazed the gazing rustics ranged around (214),

the effect of the long *a* in syllables 2, 4, and 8 is variously enriched and extended: early on by the alliterating *z* and, perhaps, by the recurring schwa in syllables 1 and 3; later by the alliterating *r*, by the near equivalence of "ranged" and "round" and, more distantly, by the possible echoing of "Amazed" and "around":

> Amazed the gazing rustics ranged around.

These effects suggest a primary durational equivalence rather between feet, or so I hear it, than between syllables within feet. Another such measuring of feet occurs in this line,

> These far departing seek a kinder shore (73),

in which echoing heavy syllables 2 and 4 are interspersed by echoing light syllables 1 and 3—and by the chiming of the light syllables, perhaps, with heavy syllable 6:

> These far departing seek a kinder shore.

A more dramatic emphasis of light syllables, which provides a more apparent equalizing of the quantities of different metrical feet, occurs in this line,

> He tried each art, reproved each dull delay (169),

in which every light foot has the same vowel sound. This effect is disguised by orthographic differences, perhaps, but strengthened by the close similarity of syllables 1, 5, and 9 and the exact repetition of 3 and 7:

> He tried each art, reproved each dull delay.

Such incidental suggestions of durational measure, which variously imply equivalencies between feet, half-lines, and lines, are common, not to say pervasive, throughout *The Deserted Village*

We might now begin to organize and test a full system of quantitative categories and establish a grid or table of varying musical suggestiveness, reaching from the spondaic and anapestic options I have enumerated toward more and more fugitive and peculiar effects. We could distinguish, perhaps with the aid of machines, between the durational implications of spondees stressed on the first syllable ("mingling"; "fools, who") and those stressed on the last ("that wraps"; "-ber herd"); between those coming early in a line ("-lent went"; "Yes! let") and those coming later ("-deared each"; "thy voice"); and calculate the special value of such bunched assonance as "seats beneath." I must in fact acknowledge a development in this essay, however, away from statistically verifiable and hence technically substantial effects toward others more individual and, partly because of this, more impressionistic. This turn toward mere impressions I must pursue a step or two further in order to represent adequately the musical quality of *The Deserted Village*.

Its many repeated phrases, for one thing, recall more or less strongly the refrains in songs, adjust one's ear accordingly to musical effects, and thus intensify a reader's susceptibility to the quantitative suggestions I have been describing. Surely everyone is struck by such repetitions as "How often" (lines 7, 9, 15); "I still had hopes" (lines 85, 89, 95); "Sweet Auburn" (lines 1, 31, 35, 75, 337); and "No more" (lines 241, 243, 244, 245, 247). The poem is, moreover, as songs prevailingly have always been, a tissue of repeated terms, the very repetitiveness of which should, once again, infuse the reader with musical susceptibilities.[13] More than two hundred terms occur at least twice each in the poem's four hundred and thirty lines; more than ninety occur at least four times each; more than thirty-five, seven. Many of these repeated terms, moreover, like the diction of the poem in general, seem to have been transported from the world of song. Among them are *lovely* (repeated 15 times), *play* (3), *murmur* (3), *sweet* (11), *pain* (5), *cheer* (3), *mirth* (3), *smile* (8), *bower* (6), *swain* (5), *sport* (8), *charm* (13), *bloom* (4), *toil* (5), *fond* (4), *heart* (6), *train* (5), *solitary* (5), and *woe* (6). I cannot catalogue or enumerate the entire diction of sixteenth- to eighteenth-century English songs, but I feel pretty confident, nevertheless, in describing the diction of *The Village* as conveying the flavor of this musical literature and thus strengthening its own musical quality. The prominence throughout its course of intensifiers like *loveliest, last, brightest, best, earliest*, of emphatic terms like *even, still, often* and *many a*, and of comprehensive terms like *all* (which occurs thirty-seven times), *each, every*, and *no*: all these further enforce the kinship of *The Deserted Village* to the literature of song.

Such interwoven effects, these primarily impressionistic ones and those I have perhaps been able to encumber with statistical dignity, infuse the discursive qualities of *The Deserted Village* with a distinctive musical quality.

NOTES

1 I have examined several likely poems for the effects that will be described herein in *The Village*: besides "Lycidas," sections of *Paradise Lost;* "The Traveller"; *The Dunciad;* Keats's odes; sections of *The Seasons* and *The Pre-*

lude; "Tithonus"; and "Sunday Morning"—among others. None of these poems revealed the density of durational suggestiveness that I found in *The Village;* "The Traveller" had barely half its number of quantitative elements.

2 This essay is in part a response to the review of my book, *The Heroic Couplet,* by W. K. Wimsatt, Jr., *Journal of English and Germanic Philology* 70 (1971): 312–15. In that review Wimsatt complained, quite justly, as I have come to see, about the vagueness with which I explained "the 'lyric' quality" of *The Village.*

3 Elise Jorgens, *The Well-Tun'd Word* (Minneapolis: University of Minnesota Press, 1982), pp. 97, 122, and especially 134–35.

4 Ibid., p. 123.

5 Ibid., p. 96.

6 Ibid., p. 97.

7 This song comes originally from *King Arthur* (1691); I have printed Dryden's second verse, which reveals the metrical quality of the piece somewhat more vividly.

8 See especially "In darkness let me dwell," from *A Pilgrimes Solace* (1612), which has been extensively discussed by Jorgens, *The Well-Tun'd Word,* pp. 231–37.

9 Goldsmith's intense and variously creative concern with music and with song is widely attested in both his works and his biography. He himself acknowledged the persistent popularity of *The Beggar's Opera,* by the way, with some annoyance (see Oliver Goldsmith, *The Collected Works,* ed. Arthur Friedman, 5 vols. [Oxford: Clarendon Press, 1966], 2:345–46).

10 I realize that quantity, especially in English verse, has come under some skeptical scrutiny: recently by Derek Attridge, *Well-Weighed Syllables* (Cambridge: Cambridge University Press, 1975); earlier by G. L. Hendrickson, "Elizabethan Quantitative Hexameters," *Philological Quarterly* 28 (1949): 237–60. Hendrickson argued persuasively that Elizabethan quantitative poetry was composed in observance of artificial syllabic lengths and read in observance of natural English accents—a point Attridge has extensively confirmed. I nevertheless use the term *quantity* in this essay quite simply as the formal observance of syllabic duration. My argument does not, however, depend on this usage.

11 All my quotations of *The Deserted Village* are from Friedman's authoritative edition in *The Collected Works,* 4:283–304.

12 On verbal contraction, see Paul Fussell's excellent *Theory of Prosody in Eighteenth-Century England,* Connecticut College Monograph, no. 5 (New London: Connecticut College, 1954); and, perhaps, the rigid pronouncements in the introduction of his anthology, *English Augustan Poetry* (Garden City, N.Y.: Doubleday, 1972), pp. 13–17. In opposition to the latter, note the consistently sparse use of apostrophes in Friedman's edition; and Fussell's own sense of the complexity and the fluidity of the prosodic situation in the late eighteenth century in his *Theory.*

13 To consider the expressive effect of the musicality of *The Village*, one might consult Mark Booth, *The Experience of Songs* (New Haven: Yale University Press, 1981). Especially interesting in this connection are Booth's suggestions: that song enforces a "degree of identification between singer and audience," a "fusion" between the two, so that a song's words are uttered "somehow in extension *by* us" (p. 15); and that song constitutes a "constructive and healthful . . . regression into infancy" (pp. 202–6).

Dr. Johnson's Practice: The Medical Context for Rasselas

GLORIA SYBIL GROSS

> *He nursed whole nests of people in his house, where the lame, the blind, the sick, and the sorrowful found a sure retreat . . .*
>
> Piozzi, Anecdotes

Samuel Johnson's interest in medicine, and particularly medical psychology, deeply influenced his life and his writing. Mrs. Thrale notes: "He had studied medicine diligently in all its branches, but had given particular attention to the diseases of the imagination,"[1] and Boswell mentions a case history Johnson wrote of his own melancholy, which Dr. Samuel Swinfen, physician in Lichfield and Johnson's godfather, admired for its "extraordinary acuteness, research, and eloquence."[2] Johnson's library contained a respectable collection of ancient and modern medical volumes, including some on psychiatry,[3] and he maintained close friendships with several physicians, including the noted Dr. Robert James—Johnson studied "physick" with him and contributed the Dedication and the "Life of Boerhaave," revised from an earlier form in the *Gentleman's Magazine* (1739), to James's *Medicinal Dictionary* (1745).[4]

Johnson's own writing is marked by keen psychological insights, by sensitive investigation of problems of personal identity and human relationships. Perhaps in this respect, he received one of his greatest tributes from physicians who were his contemporaries: from Thomas Arnold, Robert Anderson, William Perfect, and John Haslam, who admired his accurate descriptions of mentally disturbed patients whom they found in their own clinical practices.[5] The account of how he prepared to write the *Dictionary* applies in large part to his preparation in medical psychology:

275

> I extracted from philosophers principles of science; from historians remarkable facts; from chymists complete processes; from divines striking exhortations; and from poets beautiful descriptions.[6]

The carrier of this rich intellectual tradition, Johnson developed—as only a few individuals have—a fully humanistic, scientifically rigorous theory of human psychology.

In this essay I wish to explore some examples—from clearly a much larger body of material—of Johnson's contributions to medical psychology in the eighteenth century. Knowledge of the medical context for *Rasselas* (1759) enhances the understanding of that work as a valuable document in the evolution of psychiatric thought. I believe that Johnson's close attention to mental states in *Rasselas* relates to his perception of important medical issues of the time, particularly a famous dispute in the 1750s between two eminent psychiatrists, John Monro and William Battie. Johnson's work, in this regard, contains some of his most sophisticated and innovative contributions to the state of the art. While W. K. Wimsatt, in his pioneering studies of Johnson's prose, has pointed out themes of medicine and disease, which run deep in Johnson's writing, he also suggests that these themes are pervaded by "melancholy" and "certain lugubrious shades of Johnson's moral temper."[7] I see, however, no reason to interpret Johnson's analyses of mental dysfunction as any more sorrowful or depressing than those which appear in the *Journal of Nervous and Mental Disorders* or the *Psychoanalytic Review*. Certainly Johnson had not the established methods and language for discussing psychological principles as these do, so that he had to invent his own, borrowing from other disciplines. If his style on psychological topics seems influenced by theologians and moral philosophers, as well as by scientists and physicians, this stresses even more Johnson's conveying of an ongoing intellectual tradition.

Apparently, Johnson labored under strong cultural prejudices with his work in medical psychology. Medical historians point out that the eighteenth century, though notably advanced in social and scientific areas, was still hampered by superstition and authoritarian error when it came to understanding mental processes.[8] Medical psychology in the eighteenth century, when not one of the last strongholds for the scholastic dogma of Hippocrates and Galen about organic imbalances, or a casebook for so-called Christian exempla, became one of the favorite agents for promoting sentimentalism[9] and its own peculiar brand of abstruse reasoning and moral propaganda. These have in common a casuistry and evasion of the very problems they were supposed to explore. Johnson resisted these popular modes chiefly by his thoroughgoing empiricism, based on careful observation and involvement in the world, on knowledge gained through experience. He distrusted rationalism which was based on knowledge gained through the isolated activity of theorizing and abstraction, having little connection with the outside world, and ending, in the Cartesian system, with a view of human beings as little more than complex pieces of machinery. Johnson disparaged this inhuman, mechanical approach to human behavior so prevalent in the eighteenth century. He distrusted those fashionable cults of Deism, Stoicism, and the like for their smug rhetoric and sheer obliviousness to the nature of human suffering. "Life must be seen before it can be known,"[10] he wrote in a scathing denunciation of Soame Jenyns' *A Free Inquiry into the Nature and Origin of Evil* (1757), a popular Deist tract. Devoting his studies to the analysis of complex human emotions, to the discovery of psychodynamic principles and profound sources of feeling, Johnson formed his theories with a scrupulous eye to the thoughts and actions of real people. He was one of the guardians and transmitters of devout humanism in an age of amazing social and scientific growth.

Medical historians note that incarceration in madhouses during the seventeenth and eighteenth centuries was not unusual. The "mad-business," in fact, seemed to be booming by the mid-1700s, and gave rise to some fascinating, well-publicized controversies. Of these, the famous psychiatric dispute between two eminent rival "mad-doctors," John Monro of Bethlem Hospital and William Battie of St. Luke's, provides an important focus in an investigation of the medical context for *Rasselas*. It is worth looking into the historical background in some detail to see more clearly Johnson's remarkable contributions.

John Monro, chief physician to Bethlem Hospital from 1751 to 1791, was the second of five generations of Monros who achieved eminence as "mad-doctors," of whom four held this office in succession, and he advocated the standard eighteenth-century approach to madness. This was imprisonment under harsh coercion and restraint, and a variety of physical punishments, including vomits, purges, blows, stripes, surprise baths, copious bleedings, electric shock, and meager diet. Such outright cruelty was justified by the attitude that madness was caused by "vitiated judgment," where, Monro states, "every quality which distinguishes a man from a brute, except a few unconnected, incoherent words, seems totally obliterated."[11]

As "vitiated judgment," madness was traditionally associated with sin or departure from God-given reason. Even in the eighteenth century, these concepts were not entirely undifferentiated from the medieval Christian notion of demonic possession. Indeed, the notorious *Malleus Malificarum,* much of which contained painstaking pictures of so-called madness and was devoted to the thesis that mental illness was the devil's inspiration, went through ten editions before 1669 and nine more before the mid-eighteenth century.[12] Like the cure for heresy, the cure for insanity lay in a "moral physick," a treatment aimed at scourging the body as well as the soul. The madder the patient, the more severe the punishment. Johann Christian Reil (1759–1813), one of the more advanced psychiatrists of the period, remarks on the dreadful lot of the insane in Europe:

> We incarcerate these miserable creatures as if they were criminals in abandoned jails, near to the lairs of owls in barren canyons beyond the city gates, or in damp dungeons of prisons, where never a pitying look of a humanitarian penetrates; and we let them, in chains, rot in their own excrement.[13]

As a lapse in reason, mental illness became the symbol of a fall from grace, and its portrayal in literature a polemic against sin and evil. The satirist, in particular, represented the torture and punishment associated with madhouses through his satiric victims.[14] These are base, vice-ridden creatures, physically as well as mentally repulsive, who are condemned to a symbolic hell to suffer the disfiguring symptoms of their Pride, Envy, Lust, etc. Thus Pope and Swift, for example, are not content merely to expose their enemies' wrongdoing, but must besmear them with excrement and curse them with disease, particularly venereal disease, as well as perversion. The scurrilous reports in *The Dunciad, A Tale of a Tub, Gulliver's Travels,* and other pamphlets of abuse imitate in various ways the horrendous procedures, the physical agents and techniques, used to punish people in madhouses.

The eighteenth-century novelist, likewise, used madness as a form of moral propaganda to show the detestable effects of deviating from the great Christian virtue, Reason. Stock characters and stock situations in, for example, Fielding and Smollett, derive in part from paradigms of good and evil, according to prevalent notions of physiognomy, organic imbalance, and symptom-formation. Much like the old Renaissance "humor" characters, these characters in novels were assigned grotesque punishments to fit their mental aberrations—as they would be in madhouses. Just as psychiatric practice during the eighteenth century made superfluous the study of the patient's mind, so many writers made superfluous the need for real character analysis. To treat mental problems was to recover reason through a variety of severe physical trials, and for doctors and writers alike, the individual's mind entered into this only for an *ad hoc* assessment of symptoms before, during, and after treatment.

Medical treatises of the period noted in careful detail the latest refinements of physical agents and techniques. One such notorious method is described in the following excerpt from a case history by Patrick Blair, physician in Lincolnshire. It shows the physician's standard lack of psychological insight. But more important, this strange narrative of the refractory housewife forced to undergo her doctor's abhorrent torture machine seems to be reflected in the moral-punitive ordeals, the punishments and forms of physical abuse, undergone by fictional characters in many eighteenth-century literary works before they recover—if indeed they ever do—their proper reason.

> A married Woman . . . became mad, neglected every thing, would not own her husband nor any of the Family, kept her room, would converse with nobody but kept spitting continually, turning from any that turn'd from her and chiding any who put their hand in their sides, telling them she was not a whore.

After prescribing the usual "frequent bleedings, violent Emeticks, strong purgatives and potent Sudorificks and Narcoticks," Blair reports:

> She began to enquire more seriously into the state of domestic affairs at the servants who came to see her, spoke more kindly to them, shew'd a desire to be at home, quitted much of her former gestures, speeches and behavior, was obedient when reprov'd because of them and gave all signs of recovery except that of the dislike to her husband.

At this lattermost obstinacy and sure sign of lingering madness (!) Blair resigns her to the ordeal of his "cold bathing engine," a sort of shower with the double shock of surprise plus quantities of cold water poured on the patient's head from measured heights.

> I ordered her to be blindfolded. Her nurse and other women stript her. She was lifted up by force, plac'd in and fixt to the Chair in the bathing Tub. All this put her in an unexpressable terrour especially when the water was let down. I kept her under the fall 30 minutes, stopping the pipe now and then and enquiring whether she would take to her husband but she still obstinately deny'd till at last being

much fatigu'd with the pressure of the water she promised she would do what I desired on which I desisted.

But the next day she became "obstinate" again, so that the entire treatment had to be repeated the next week, in fact, over a period of weeks, during which she would "promise to take to her husband," to "love him as before," but she would renege the next day. Finally, explains Blair,

> I gave her the 3rd Tryal of the fall and continued her 90 minutes under it, [she] promised obedience as before but she was as sullen and obstinate as ever the next day. Being upon resentment why I should treat her so, after 2 or 3 days I threatened her with the fourth Tryal, took her out of bed, had her stript, blindfolded and ready to be put in the Chair, when being terrify'd with what she was to undergo she kneeld submissively that I would spare her and she would become a Loving obedient and dutiful Wife for ever thereafter. I granted her request provided she would go to bed with her husband that night, which she did with great chearfullness.[15]

In contrast to the violent therapies of Blair, Monro, and others, based upon madness as "vitiated judgment," William Battie, who helped found St. Luke's Hospital, the only other public asylum in London, believed that "deluded imagination" was the essential disturbance: "That man [is mad] who is fully and unalterably persuaded of the existence or of the appearance of any thing, which either does not exist or does not actually appear to him, and who behaves according to such erroneous persuasion."[16] This progressive view took its focus from refinements of physical agents, religious superstition, and moral propaganda and opened the door to psychological investigation. Battie taught (he was the first psychiatrist to take on students) more humane methods of "Management" and "Regimen," and he censured the standard physical treatment as "shocking" and "destructive," even calling madhouses "loathesome prisons."

Battie's opposition to Monro's regime at Bedlam seems to have been something of a *cause célèbre* during the mid-century. After the publication of Battie's *Treatise on Madness* in 1758, Monro was stung into an immediate reply with his *Remarks on Dr. Battie's Treatise on Madness,* the first publication on insanity to come out of Bedlam, where there had been physicians for over two hundred years. On the title page, Monro took as his motto a quote from Horace, "*O Major, tandem parcas, Insane, minore*" [O greater madman, pray have mercy on a lesser one], and he proceeded to justify his standard procedures. Defending himself against Battie's charges of backwardness and secrecy, Monro emphatically states, "Madness is a distemper of such a nature, that very little of real use can be said concerning it. . . ."[17] The rest of the book follows this unfortunate dictum: madness is too difficult to understand, too unpleasant to go into deeply, and after all, purging, bleeding, and vomiting are the most effective treatments. So widespread was the Monro gospel that Battie was covered with ridicule as a result of the *Remarks*, and henceforth known as "Major Battie." Nevertheless, Battie's pioneering example seems to have inspired a different, if less popular attitude toward mental illness in eighteenth-century culture, one clearly adopted and developed by Johnson in his writing.

Rasselas was published in 1759, one year following the appearance of Battie's and Monro's treatises in 1758, when their conflict became public. I assume that Johnson was quite familiar with the issues, as the controversy was widely publicized, with Tobias Smollett, for one, analyzing both books in *The Critical Review*.[18] With his strong interest in the "diseases of the imagination," Johnson would have followed closely and discussed with his friends—particularly those who were practicing physicians—ideas about medical psychology so relevant to his previous work in, for example, the periodical essays and the *Life of Savage*. Moreover, when Johnson's young friend, the poet Christopher Smart, suffered a mental breakdown, he was fortunate to be admitted to St. Luke's Hospital rather than Bedlam, from May 1757 to May 1758,[19] under Dr. Battie's enlightened care. Surely Johnson would have been aware of the difference. The theme of the "dangerous prevalence of imagination," a basic concept in *Rasselas*, takes on a more comprehensive meaning in this medical context. Discarding Monro's moral-punitive views of mental illness, Johnson upholds Battie's views. In doing so, he helps create a modern, discursive structure for understanding mental illness, which leads the way to psychological inquiry.

In *Rasselas*, Johnson portrays abnormal mental states in several characters, whose symptoms include bizarre fantasies, depression, and paranoid hallucinations. But while Johnson's characters share some of the dangerous delusions of the characters in satire and novels mentioned earlier, it is important to realize that Johnson's people are not subjected to physical torture and vicious reproach. Their mental problems seem, in fact, as unaffected by external punishment and the stigma of sin and evil as can be found during this period. G. B. Hill notes the difference when he comments that whereas Johnson allows the deluded aeronaut in *Rasselas* to be saved after he jumps from the cliff, Voltaire, for example, would have had him plunge instantly to the bottom of the lake and be drowned.[20] And one can only speculate on the excruciation and mayhem in store for him at the hands of Pope, Swift, or Fielding. These writers were sure to have their characters severely punished for their mental defects: in *Candide* (1759) Voltaire has the hero beaten, enslaved, and narrowly escape death many times, and the heroine see her parents butchered and herself suffer all kinds of physical torture. In contrast, Johnson never allows the characters in *Rasselas* to be physically abused: even the kidnapping of Pekuah ultimately proves non-threatening. His interest is more with internal than external states. I suggest that under the influence of Dr. Battie and other enlightened medical men, Johnson breaks with the past by seeking the solution to mental problems in the "deluded imagination," not in moral-punitive ordeals. Mental problems were treatable by uncovering their delusional bases, the "erroneous persuasion," as Battie put it, and this is a dramatic moment in the evolution of psychiatric thought.

Johnson avoids the bitter disgust with human nature held by many eighteenth-century satirists, by cultivating a compassionate, if shrewd, understanding of the struggle for personal identity and intimate relationships. He explores these with clinical accuracy, particularly in three major episodes in *Rasselas*, where descriptions of characters' mental states seem amazingly modern. In Rasselas' condition before he leaves the happy valley, Nekayah's depression over the loss of Pekuah, and the astronomer's madness, he provides comprehensive analyses of the loss of contact with reality and consequent impairment of the personality. Never does Johnson judge these problems as evil, nor does he punish or befoul these individuals in the traditional way for their aberrations. Instead, their ordeals are entirely psychological ones, and deep-seated emotional processes, not mere surface symptoms, are the subject for further inquiry.

The plight of Rasselas in the "happy valley" is a penetrating look at the stultifying effects of narcissism. In a setting where wishes are immediately gratified, whims or impulses seem to shift erratically and are never supported by continuous aims or interests. Thus desires become "short-circuited": they are never sustained in an object, but only in some form of self-indulgence. As Imlac observes, the inhabitants, "whose minds have no impression but of the present moment, are either corroded by malignant passions or sit stupid in the gloom of perpetual vacancy."[21] Even more specific on this discontinuous lifestyle, dominated by fragmented impressions and shifting attention, is Pekuah's later account of the female "happy valley", the Arab's harem, where the inmates' activities mark the emptiness of their thoughts:

> They ran from room to room, as a bird hops from wire to wire in his cage. They danced for the sake of motion, as lambs frisk in a meadow. . . . Part of their time passed in watching the progress of light bodies that floated on the river, and part in marking the various forms into which clouds broke in the sky.[22]

Johnson describes a state of pathological narcissism with Rasselas' mental crisis, when the prince finds himself helpless, immobile, and unable to direct his energies toward the outside world. From the onset of illness, Rasselas mostly languishes alone, experiencing radical mood swings, ranging from self-admiration to self-reproach. He indulges in grandiose fantasies, a "secret stock of happiness," which further isolates him from society, and a vicious circle is established: the more he fantasizes, the less fit he becomes to associate with others. In Chapter 4, "The Prince Continues to Grieve and Muse," Johnson goes into the syndrome with descriptions of the fantasies themselves, and he notes:

> Thus passed twenty months of the life of Rasselas. He busied himself so intensely in visionary bustle that he forgot his real solitude, and, amidst hourly preparations for the various incidents of human affairs, neglected to consider by what means he should mingle with mankind.[23]

Rasselas is lucky to change his condition, and during his initial insight, Johnson emphasizes how Rasselas "looked around him" and "examined" minutely the environment where he was held:

> He discerned the various instincts of animals and properties of plants, and found the place replete with wonders of which he purposed to solace himself with the contemplation, if he should never be able to accomplish his flight; rejoicing that his endeavors, though yet unsuccessful, had supplied him with a source of inexhaustible inquiry.[24]

Through contact with reality and receptivity to life's rich sources of delight and knowledge, Rasselas now gives up the narcissistic delusions induced by the happy valley: he is roused to discover the outside world. His "captivity" and the resulting psychological damage to him foreshadow the mad astronomer, whose malady Johnson attributes to an even more severe emotional crisis.

The incident of the loss of Pekuah is another sophisticated analysis of mental trauma, here neurotic depression. When the princess, Nekayah, falls desperately ill at the separation from her beloved companion, Johnson describes with scrupulous detail the various stages of depressive illness, from hostility toward the self and the lost object, to powerful feelings of guilt, identification with the lost object, and gradual withdrawal from the world. Nekayah "sunk down in hopeless dejection" and endlessly reproaches herself for imagined wrongdoing, and Pekuah for imagined weakness. This sudden release of hostile impulses produces a profound sense of guilt, which is soon followed by strange idealization and taking on the attributes of the abandoned Pekuah: Nekayah seems to feel a need to imitate or become the image of what she has lost:

> She sat from morning to evening, recollecting all that had been done or said by her Pekuah, treasured up with care every trifle on which Pekuah had set an accidental value and which might recall to mind any little incident or careless conversation. The sentiments of her whom she now expected to see no more were treasured in her memory as rules of life, and she deliberated to no other end than to conjecture, on any occasion, what would have been the opinion and counsel of Pekuah.[25]

Johnson shows how the individual treats herself as the abandoned person, a common occurrence with depressed patients. Withdrawing more and more from society, Nekayah vows, in a veiled suicidal threat, to retire altogether from the world, but Imlac brings her back among the living by helping her develop more contact with reality:

> Do not suffer life to stagnate; it will grow muddy for want of motion. Commit yourself again to the current of the world; Pekuah will vanish by degrees. You will meet in your way some other favorite, or learn to diffuse yourself in general conversation.[26]

And most interestingly, Nekayah gets better by establishing a kind of "regimen," perhaps not unlike that recommended by William Battie to his psychiatric patients. She returns to "common cares" and "common pleasures," still taking one hour each day to think about Pekuah. At last her depression is gone, with its false beliefs and self-inflicted misery. But powerful feelings remain, as Johnson wisely adds, "her real love for Pekuah was yet not diminished." She somberly states, but this time with a realistic appraisal, "I shall henceforward fear to yield my heart to excellence, however bright, or to fondness, however tender, lest I should lose again what I have lost in Pekuah.[27]

The case of the mad astronomer provides some extraordinary insights into the dynamics of paranoid schizophrenia, and Johnson's observations here were much celebrated by eighteenth-century physicians. The astronomer reveals himself to Imlac, who first notices symptoms of acute anxiety, of disorientation and vacillation, which are common problems with psychotic patients. With grim earnestness and with the typical obstinacy of a mental patient indulging in his favorite fantasy, the astronomer tells of his supernatural powers over the universe. He has "drawn out his soul in endless calculations," explains Imlac, and his so-called powers are attempts to compensate for this crushing loss of himself. Images of imprisonment and constraint, far more menacing than those in the happy valley, indicate the severe impairment of personality: for forty years he has sat in his tower, his "thoughts have been long fixed upon a single point," with the "images of other things stealing away."[28] In the famous chapter, "The Dangerous Prevalence of Imagination," Johnson analyzes the "reign of fancy" over "truth," for which might be substituted the words *fantasy* over *reality*. Here is one of Johnson's most refined developments of Dr. Battie's theory of "deluded imagination":

> In time some particular train of ideas fixes the attention. . . . The mind . . . feasts on the luscious falsehood whenever she is offended with the bitterness of truth. By degrees the reign of fancy is confirmed; she grows first imperious and, in time, despotic. Then fictions begin to operate as realities, false opinions fasten upon the mind, and life passes in dreams of rapture or of anguish.[29]

With a brilliant understanding of paranoid hallucination, Johnson notes the delusive threats of the conscience projected upon external reality: as the astronomer complains that his "thoughts are chained down by irresistible violence," Imlac explains:

> No disease of the imagination is so difficult of cure as that which is complicated with the dread of guilt; fancy and conscience then act interchangeably upon us and so often shift their places that the illusions of one are not distinguished from the dictates of the other.[30]

Johnson explores the nature of guilt, in a startlingly modern vein, as a projection of the "deluded imagination," not simply a mechanistic or supernatural abstraction, or a cause for vicious retribution or

profuse sentimentalism, opinions variously held by many of his contemporaries. And just as other characters were advised to end their
self-imposed exiles and seek happiness in the outside world and the
company of others, so the mad astronomer learns:

> Open your heart to the influence of the light which from time to
> time breaks in upon you; when scruples importune you, which you
> in your lucid moments know to be vain, do not stand to parley, but
> fly to business, or to Pekuah.[31]

The unusual quality of Johnson's contribution to medical psychology was his ability to combine the precise observation and clinical
probing of the scientist with the compassion of the humanist. Much
has been made of Johnson's melancholy temperament, his serious
spells of depression, and it is probably true that he analyzed his own
suffering to create the structure from which his theories developed.[32]
In this light, I believe these lines from the "Life of Boerhaave" (1739),
the great Dutch physician, lines composed early in Johnson's career,
help to explain his ardent pursuit of a discipline just then beginning
to take form:

> Then it was that his own pain taught him to compassionate others,
> and his experience of the inefficacy of the methods then in use in-
> cited him to attempt the discovery of others more certain.[33]

NOTES

1 George Birkbeck Hill, ed., *Johnsonian Miscellanies*, 2 vols. (1897; rpt. New
   York: Barnes and Noble, 1966), 1:199.
2 James Boswell, *The Life of Samuel Johnson*, ed. George Birkbeck Hill, rev.
   L. F. Powell, 6 vols. (Oxford: Clarendon Press, 1934–50), 1:64.
3 Donald J. Greene, *Samuel Johnson's Library: An Annotated Guide*, English
   Literary Studies, no. 1 (Victoria, B. C.: University of Victoria, 1975), p. 20.
4 For information on Johnson's medical acquaintances, see Richard B.
   Schwartz, *Samuel Johnson and the New Science* (Madison: University of Wisconsin Press, 1971), pp. 35–38. For Johnson's contributions to James's *Medicinal Dictionary*, see O M Brack, Jr., and Thomas Kaminski, "Dr. Johnson, Robert James, and the *Medicinal Dictionary*," *Modern Philology* 81 (1984):
   378–400.
5 For example, Thomas Arnold, M.D., in *Observations on the Nature, Kinds,
   Causes and Prevention of Insanity* (1782; 2nd ed., London: R. Phillips, 1806),

1:136–37, illustrated cases of megalomaniac patients with Johnson's astronomer in *Rasselas,* praising the accurate description and insight, while Robert Anderson, M.D., in *The Life of Samuel Johnson, with critical observations on his works* (London: J. and A. Arch, 1795) believed Johnson was a "master of all the recesses of the human mind . . . possessed of a corrosive to eradicate, or a lenitive to assuage the follies and sorrows of the heart" (p. 209). William Perfect, M.D., began his Preface to *Annals of Insanity, Comprising a selection of Curious and Interesting Cases* (1787; 5th ed., London: Chalmers, 1800) with a quotation from *Rasselas,* and John Haslam, M.D., used the same quotation on the title page of his *Observations on Madness and Melancholy* (London: J. Callow, 1809). For more details on Johnson's recognition by eighteenth-century physicians, see Kathleen M. Grange, "Dr. Johnson's Account of a Schizophrenic Illness in *Rasselas,*" *Medical History* 4 (1962): 162–69.

6 *The Works of Samuel Johnson, LL.D.,* 9 vols. (Oxford: William Pickering, 1825), 5:38. Hereafter cited as *Works.*

7 W. K. Wimsatt, *Philosophic Words: A Study of Style and Meaning in the Rambler and Dictionary of Samuel Johnson* (New Haven: Yale University Press, 1948), ch. 3.

8 See, for example, Michael De Porte, *Nightmares and Hobbyhorses: Swift, Sterne, and Augustan Ideas of Madness* (San Marino: The Huntington Library, 1974), ch. 1; and George S. Rousseau and Roy Porter, ed., *The Ferment of Knowledge: Studies in the Historiography of Eighteenth-Century Science* (Cambridge: Cambridge University Press, 1980), ch. 4, "Psychology."

9 See R. F. Brissenden, *Virtue in Distress: Studies in the Novel of Sentiment from Richardson to Sade* (New York: Barnes and Noble, 1974), ch. 2, "'Sentimentalism': An Attempt at Definition."

10 *Works,* 6:54.

11 John Monro, *Remarks on Dr. Battie's Treatise on Madness* (London: Clarke, 1758), p. 6.

12 Gregory Zilboorg, *A History of Medical Psychology* (New York: Norton, 1941), pp. 151–52.

13 Johann Christian Reil, quoted in Franz Alexander, *The History of Psychiatry* (New York: Harper and Row, 1966), pp. 115–16, from E. Kraeplin, *Hundert Jahre der Psychiatrie* (1918).

14 See, for example, the discussions in Mary Claire Randolph, "The Structural Design of the Formal Verse Satire," *Philological Quarterly* 21 (1942): 368–84; and Lillian Feder, *Madness in Literature* (Princeton: Princeton University Press, 1980), ch. 4, "The Spleen, the Vapors, and the God Within."

15 Patrick Blair, *Some Observations on the cure of mad persons by the fall of water,* 1725: rpt. in Richard Hunter and Ida Macalpine, *Three Hundred Years of Psychiatry 1535–1860* (London: Oxford University Press, 1963), pp. 325–29.

16 William Battie, *A Treatise on Madness* (London: J. Whiston, 1758), p. 6.

17 Monro, *Remarks,* "Advertisement."

18 Tobias Smollett, *Critical Review* 4 (1757): 509; 5 (1758): 224.
19 Christopher Devlin, *Poor Kit Smart* (London: Rupert Hart-Davis, 1961), p. 129. See also Boswell, *Life*, 1: 397.
20 As quoted in Donald J. Greene, *Samuel Johnson* (New York: Twayne, 1970), p. 133.
21 Samuel Johnson, *Rasselas*, ed. Warren Fleischauer (New York: Barron's Educational Series, 1962), p. 59 (ch. 12).
22 Ibid., p. 149 (ch. 39).
23 Ibid., pp. 25–26 (ch. 4).
24 Ibid., p. 30 (ch. 5).
25 Ibid., p. 131 (ch. 35).
26 Ibid., p. 134 (ch. 35).
27 Ibid., p. 137 (ch. 36).
28 Ibid., pp. 153–54 (ch. 40).
29 Ibid., p. 164 (ch. 44).
30 Ibid., p. 176 (ch. 46).
31 Ibid., p. 177 (ch. 46).
32 See, for example, George Irwin's account of Johnson's mental problems in the excellent psychological biography, *Samuel Johnson: A Personality in Conflict* (Auckland, New Zealand: Auckland University Press, 1971). Of particular interest is the section on his mother's illness and death during the composition of *Rasselas*, pp. 108–12.
33 *Works*, 6:271.

From Early Anthropology to the Literature of the Savage: The Naturalization of the Primitive

CHRISTIAN MAROUBY

Why this sudden interest in various forms of "Otherness"? Beyond the obvious exotic or even escapist appeal of such explorations—perhaps itself a sign of the times—it seems to me that several assumptions of a more theoretical nature, even if not always explicitly formulated, have recently contributed to making the Other a particular focus of attention. One critical factor, perhaps the most evident, is the importance attributed by various disciplines to what can be defined as the specular mode: the Other functions as a locus of projections; it reflects, if only indirectly, the imaginary perceptions of a given culture. The discourse on the Other has thus become, for us, a privileged source of information on its elusive subject, be that subject a historical one. Another of those productive assumptions, more directly Foucaldian this time, is the idea that a culture defines itself as much by what it excludes from its dominant discourse, or rejects from its consciousness, as by what it admits into it; hence our interest in the marginal, the repressed, in those cultural objects which at a given time seem to elicit a kind of denegation. The Other, in this very different sense, is that which cannot be represented. There would of course be other ways of accounting for our present interest in Otherness. The reason I have chosen to emphasize these two particular and complementary modes of operation is that in our period of concern they can be seen to illuminate in an exemplary manner the fate of what is undoubtedly the most significant Other: the savage.

In the long history of our relation to the primitive, the eighteenth century, and perhaps most strikingly the second half of that period, stands out as an exceptional time. In a strangely belated aftershock of the discovery, the mass of documentation and missionary relations which had for over two centuries been accumulated by explorers of the New World, and so largely ignored, seems finally to break through the defenses of Europe and elicit the kind of large-scale reaction one might have expected much earlier. The disquieting and even slightly threatening presence of an Other on the new Western horizons, which had for so long failed to have a significant impact on European consciousness, suddenly captures its imagination and provokes, at least indirectly, an unprecedented wave of speculations on the origin and the nature of man. In a spectacular *après-coup* that I am tempted to interpret as a return of the repressed, Europe is discovering America.

Of that phenomenon, the most visible and celebrated manifestation, at once symptom and primary vehicle of a profound displacement of representations, is the coming of the savage into literature. More precisely, it is a process of translation, or to pursue a certain analogy, a secondary elaboration, which allows the observations of early anthropology to pass into the mainstream of literature, and thereby to become accessible and acceptable to European consciousness. From Lahontan's "sauvage philosophique" to Diderot's *Supplément au voyage de Bougainville* and the melancholy waning of the tradition in Chateaubriand's Chactas and Atala, the triumph of the savage is a literary promotion.

What I would like to suggest, and as much as possible to exemplify in some detail, is that in this process of translation something essential—something which in original relations takes the form of an unresolved and immensely productive interrogation—is lost, or perhaps more accurately, erased. While ensuring, and even celebrating, the admission of the primitive into the dominant discourse, the literary promotion of the savage is also the very operation by which the trauma of a true recognition is averted. Or to put it somewhat more explicitly, the literary representation of the primitive, and most perversely that particular version we have come to know as the "good" savage, can be seen to function as a strategy, however unconscious, through which Europe succeeds in protecting itself from the most radical implications of the discovery.

What, then, is at stake in a recognition of the primitive? Nothing less, I would submit, than a crisis of representation, a crisis which is at least implicit in the best examples of classical anthropology. I propose to illustrate this by looking at a few passages from one of the most remarkable French representatives in the eighteenth century: Charlevoix. But first we have to go back to the beginning, to the figure that has ever since the Renaissance been the obligatory framework of the discourse on the primitive, and will until the end of our period constitute its absolute limit. This figure, which has been aptly described as a rhetoric of negativity, has found its almost archetypal expression in this famous passage by Montaigne:

> C'est une nation, dirais-je à Platon, en laquelle il n'y a aucune es-
> pèce de trafic; nulle connaissance de lettres, nulle science de nombres;
> nul nom de magistrat, ni de supériorité politique; nuls usages de
> service, de richesse ou de pauvreté; nuls contrats; nulles succes-
> sions; nuls partages; nulles occupations qu'oisives; nul respect de
> parenté que commun, nuls vêtements; nulle agriculture; nul métal;
> nul usage de vin ou de blé.[1]

Nothing would seem more simple, more naïve even. The figure has become so familiar that we have ceased to wonder at its devastating implications. Nothing, in fact, could be less innocent. It isn't simply that savage society is represented in a fundamentally ethnocentric mode, as an inverted reflection of Western civilization, but that it is defined by a series of negations, as absence or loss of those attributes which for Europe constitute the very condition of civilized—and eventually, of human—existence. With each turn of the rhetoric the savage, deprived of yet another privilege of humanity, moves one step closer to the condition of beasts. What one expects to find, at the end of this series of negations, is a creature reduced to the lowest level of human life, a zero degree of humanity, or worse. This will become clearer with the next example, a much later but equally famous version:

> In such a condition there is no place for Industry, because the fruit
> thereof is uncertain; and consequently no Culture of the Earth; no
> Navigation, nor use of the commodities that may be imported by
> sea; no commodious Building; no Instruments of moving, and re-
> moving such things as require much force; no knowledge of the face
> of the Earth; no account of Time; no Arts; no Letters; no Society; and
> which is worst of all, continuall feare, and danger of violent death;
> and the life of man, solitary, poor, nasty, brutish, and short.[2]

This is of course the state of nature according to Hobbes. The form is the same, but here there is no doubt that each step of the rhetoric is a loss, a regression through all the major accomplishments of humanity, from industry to "culture" to science and the arts, and finally to the point of no return: "no Society." At the end of this regressive journey the savage has lost all but his nature; he is closer to brutes than to man. Such a verdict might seem rather harsh; it is, however, the logical outcome of a certain mode of representation, the necessary consequence of the vision of man which is almost unanimously that of the classical period, and even, I would add, of the Enlightenment itself. One need only think of Buffon. What is valued in man is his ability to change the face of the earth, to forge the new instruments of his mastery over the natural elements, and to produce the social institutions that will triumph over his own nature.

If we are to understand the missionary relations which constitute our first anthropological documents, and their potential impact on European representations, it is against this background that they must be situated. Not that those texts initiate any fundamental break with the dominant discourse, or even that they take a different form. In their observations, the missionaries do not alter the terms of the rhetoric; rather, and more radically, they ruin its logic. What they have discovered is that at the end of the series of negations, when the savage has been deprived of all the institutions that were for Europe the guarantee of humanity, he is not, as had been expected, less human than his civilized counterparts, but in many respects, more. The whole problematics of classical anthropology lies in this paradox, and in the missionaries' desperate attempts to rescue the savage from its logical impossibility.

Now it is true, and all too well known, that the paradox admits of a very tempting solution: a simple reversal of the rhetoric, which, instead of the state of nature according to Hobbes, posits as the original condition of man an equally hypothetical "good" nature. This is the solution that will triumph in the primitivism of the eighteenth century, and whatever its theoretical weakness, we have to recognize its importance for the evolution of our culture. The perception of an original "goodness" in man, however imaginary, can with some justification be seen as a momentous shift in the sensibility of Europe. It is, at least indirectly, one of the determining factors of that rehabilitation of human nature which is perhaps the most significant undercurrent of the Enlightenment. In that sense, the assumption of a "good" nature is a positive contribution of the discovery. It is also, however, what obscures and renders ineffective the essential lesson of early anthropology. For as I have been suggesting, there is in the original texts something else, something much more problematic than a simple inversion, which takes in the moments of revelation the form of an interpretive hesitation. This is what we see with a first example from Charlevoix's *Histoire de la Nouvelle France.*

The subject is education, or in keeping with the terms of the rhetoric, the absence of education. Charlevoix starts out with a "just reproach": "On peut encore leur reprocher avec justice la manière dont ils élèvent leurs enfants," and he immediately makes it clear why the savages are to blame: "Ils ne savent ce que c'est, que de les châtier." What is lacking from their practices is the indispensable attribute of a proper education: punishment. Until now there is nothing surprising, and Charlevoix acknowledges frankly what is to be expected from such a lack: "Il semble . . . qu'une enfance si mal disciplinée doive être suivie d'une jeunesse bien turbulente et bien corrompue." The problem is that the missionary, like so many others before him, is confronted with baffling evidence. Among these children, there is no more "turbulence" and "corruption" than among those of Europe. The paradox has to be explained, and it is at this point, in Charlevoix's rather troubled attempt to explain away the fact, that something interesting appears:

> mais d'une part les Sauvages sont naturellement tranquilles, et de bonne heure maîtres d'eux-mêmes, la raison les guide aussi bien que les autres hommes; et de l'autre, leur tempérament, surtout dans les Nations du Nord, ne les porte point à la débauche.[3]

There is something oddly circular in this answer. Two different arguments seem to be proposed, which turn out to be the same, but with a difference. On the one hand, the savages are calm and self-controlled; "reason guides them as well as other men." This would seem to be a particularly strong recommendation of their educational principles. They value moderation, control, putting into practice the human ideal of the Enlightenment, and invalidating the need for punishment. Charlevoix could be on the verge of a crucial recognition—but in fact, he has already protected himself from the implications of his discovery. They do all this, he has warned us, "naturally," and when he comes back with the second argument on the same idea, it is to restrict it even further. The whole problem of the difference between savage and civilized education has been reduced to a question of temperament; "especially among the Northern Nations" echoes Montesquieu and the prevalent theory of climates. In the end, what is potentially a universal observation—one that questions the very necessity of a repressive education—is dismissed in the name of a natural difference. And yet Charlevoix has come very close to an altogether dif-

ferent interpretation, an interpretation which cannot quite be acknowledged, but keeps reappearing with a stubborn insistence, for
instance in the following passage:

> tant qu'ils sont petits, on dit qu'ils n'ont point de raison, et les sau-
> vages ne sont point dans le principe, que la punition fait venir le
> jugement; quand ils sont dans un âge à pouvoir raisonner, on pré-
> tend qu'ils sont maîtres de leurs actions, et qu'ils n'en doivent ré-
> pondre à personne.[4]

What is being described here has nothing to do with nature. It is,
rather, a question of "principle," of ethos. The deliberate refusal to
practice punishment is being justified in terms of a psychology whose
wisdom Charlevoix, perhaps unknowingly, cannot help recognizing.
This will become even clearer as we move to another crucial articu-
lation of the rhetoric: no government. The first statement of the problem is again a classic example of negative representation:

> On croirait d'abord qu'ils n'ont aucune forme de gouvernement, qu'ils
> ne connaissent ni lois, ni subordination, et que vivant dans une in-
> dépendance entière, ils se laissent entièrement conduire au hasard
> et au caprice le plus indompté.[5]

Again the absence of a political structure, of laws and hierarchy, suggests a lack of restraint, and a society that would be given to disorder,
unruly impulses, and chance. And yet Charlevoix continues: "cepen-
dant ils jouissent de presque tous les avantages, qu'une autorité bien
réglée peut procurer aux Nations les plus policées." In the political
realm, therefore, savage society presents the same paradox as in its
educational practises—and the same interpretive problem. Here again
what we could call the naturalistic temptation tends to neutralize the
meaning of the discovery; but never so completely that another possibility cannot gradually appear. In the absence of a visible form of
government, savage society seems to be founded on a principle, a
kind of political model, but one that is the negation of the political
conceptions known to Europe. This ruling principle is the refusal of
power:

> Nés libres et indépendants, ils ont en horreur jusqu'à l'ombre du
> pouvoir despotique, mais ils s'écartent rarement de certains usages,
> fondés sur le bon sens, qui leurs tiennent lieu de Lois et suppléent
> en quelque façon à l'autorité légitime. Toute contrainte les revolte,
> mais la raison seule les retient dans une espèce de subordination,

qui pour être volontaire, n'en atteint pas moins au but qu'ils se sont proposés.

What is of crucial importance in this passage is the recognition of an equivalence, at the same time as of a radical difference, between the institutions of savage society and those of civilization. The savages have no laws and no authority, but it is the very rejection of those forms of coercion—that is to say, their "principles" and "customs"— which "makes up for" and "takes the place of" political institutions. In comparing two modes of social functioning which are radically different from each other, Charlevoix is nevertheless granting that of the other the same status as his own. Otherness, here, is not explained away in terms of a difference of nature, of temperament, but rather of institutions, of moral and social conceptions, and in a way which, if taken seriously, calls into question the universality of European representations. What I am of course suggesting is that Charlevoix, in a moment such as this, is on the verge of discovering what we have come to know, much later, as the concept of culture.

Now it is true, and hardly surprising, that neither he nor any of his most perceptive contemporaries ever come close to an explicit formulation of that concept. Their ethnological practice is in that sense far in advance of their theory. It might therefore seem rather naïve to wonder why they remain short of a full discovery. I think, however, that one last example of Charlevoix's interpretive dilemma could provide the beginning of an answer. The subject, this time, is the absence of property. The missionary first confesses to being "infinitely surprised" to find among savages demonstrations of generosity unparalleled in civilized nations:

> ce qui surprend infiniment dans des Hommes, dont tout l'extérieur n'annonce rien que de barbare, c'est de les voir se traiter entre eux avec une douceur et des égards, qu'on ne trouve point parmi le Peuple dans les Nations les plus civilisées.[6]

His explanation goes straight to the point:

> Cela vient sans doute en partie de ce que le mien et le tien, ces paroles froides, comme les appelle Saint Grégoire Pape, mais qui en éteignant dans nos coeurs le feu de la charité, y allument celui de la convoitise, ne sont point connus de ces Sauvages.

The cause of their surprising behavior would then be, if we are to believe this first formulation, the absence of an institution, "le mien et le tien," something, in any case, which is on the side of culture.

However, things are not so simple; any relation of causality runs the risk of being reversed, and this is precisely what happens in Charlevoix's second formulation:

> Le plus grand défaut de ce Gouvernement, c'est qu'il n'y a presque point de Justice Criminelle parmi ces Peuples; à la vérité, ce défaut n'a point dans ce Pays les mêmes suites qu'il aurait parmi nous. . . .

Indeed, this "greatest fault" turns out to be a moral advantage:

> le grand ressort de nos passions, et la source principale de nos des- ordres, qui troublent le plus la Société Civile, c'est à dire, l'intérêt, n'ayant presque point de force sur ces gens, qui ne songent point à thésauriser, et s'embarassent fort peu du lendemain.[7]

What need would they have of property, and therefore of "criminal justice," when they are virtually immune to what is the main "source of our disorders," self-interest? The logic has remained the same as in the first observation, only this time it has been inverted, turned inward. The cause of the difference is no longer to be found in an institution, but at the root of our passions, of what constitutes our personality: in a difference of nature. Again we seem to have a prime example of the kind of relapse into the natural which is the charac- teristic weakness and limitation of the dominant discourse on the primitive. This, however, is not Charlevoix's last word. In an almost dialectical progression, he comes back a third time on the same prob- lem, to give us his most interesting formulation:

> amitié, compassion, reconnaissance, attache, ils ont quelque chose de tout cela, mais ce n'est point dans le coeur, et c'est moins en eux l'effet d'un bon naturel, que de la réflexion, ou de l'instinct. Le soin, qu'ils prennent des Orphelins, des Veuves, et des Infirmes; l'hospi- talité, qu'ils exercent d'une maière si admirable, ne sont en eux qu'une suite de la persuasion, où ils sont, que tout doit être commun entre les hommes.[8]

We are apparently back to the first position. Primitive communism is the result of a moral conviction, "of the persuasion," Charlevoix writes, "that everything must be held in common." The qualities that had first been observed: compassion, generosity, etc., cannot be attrib- uted to nature; they do not come from "the heart" or a "good natural disposition," but from reflection. Until this point, everything is clear, but it is then, in the surprising alternative that follows, that the op- position so firmly established between conviction and nature is suddenly called into question. All of this results "from reflection, or from instinct." How are we to understand this? "Instinct," which we would have expected to find on the side of "the heart," of nature, suddenly reappears where we least expect it, associated with reflection. Not that it is the same thing; we obviously cannot understand this "or" as expressing an equivalence, it must then be interpreted as an alternative: the behavior of the savages results either from reflection, or from instinct, or both—and the opposition collapses. Without charging with meaning what is only a detail, if not a lapsus, I think we can see this "or" as the confirmation and ultimate outcome of that hesitation whose vicissitudes we have followed in the work of Charlevoix. In attempting to account, within the conceptual limits of classical representation, for institutions that can only be perceived as differences of character, of personality, the best representatives of early anthropology are caught in an interpretive bind. They are unable to formulate the concept of culture, and because they cannot do so, their reflection remains confined within the realm of the natural, but in a manner that within that realm renders infinitely problematic the idea of nature itself. Far from reinforcing, as will the literary tradition of the "good" savage, the notion of an original human nature, their paradoxical observations lead them to a restless and inconclusive questioning of what is essential and universal in man, and to displacing ever further the limits of what constitutes the core of our nature— until they reach what was then, as now, the last stronghold of the natural, the notion of character. What their reflection ultimately suggests, contrary to its almost literal translation in the dominant discourse, is not a strengthening of human nature, whether conceived as "good" or "bad," but rather a dissemination of the natural into the social, and perhaps even the possibility that the human personality, in the last analysis, is itself nothing but a social representation.

It is precisely this questioning, this doubt as to the status of the difference between civilized man and his primitive counterpart, which the literary representation of the savage manages to erase, or perhaps more properly, to cover up by the reassuring reaffirmation of a universal referent. In explaining away the "goodness" of the savage in terms of a "better" nature, the literary tradition that triumphs in the eighteenth century may well give the primitive a moral advantage, and even present an eager European audience with the seduction of an imaginary model; it also succeeds in creating a myth—in an operation strikingly similar to that described by Roland Barthes in his famous book *Mythologies*—thereby excluding the original observations from the realm of human possibilities. In naturalizing the primitive, Europe manages to deflect—I would even be tempted to say that it exorcizes—what was perhaps the most threatening and promising implication of the discovery: the collapse of its own representations of human nature.

NOTES

1 Montaigne, "Des cannibales," in *Essais* (Paris: Gallimard, 1958).
2 Thomas Hobbes, *Leviathan* (London, 1651), p. 97.
3 Pierre François Xavier Charlevoix, *Histoire et description générale de la Nouvelle France* (Paris, 1744), 3:272.
4 Ibid., p. 272.
5 Ibid., p. 341.
6 Ibid., p. 308.
7 Ibid., p. 272.
8 Ibid., p. 309.

The Novels of Isabelle de Charrière, or, A Woman's Work Is Never Done

SUSAN K. JACKSON

If, as popular wisdom would have it, a woman's work is never done, then the eighteenth century witnessed no more womanly works than the novels of Isabelle de Charrière. In his *Portrait of Zélide*, Geoffrey Scott singles out *Caliste*, where the heroine dies, as "the only one of her tales that can be said to have a conclusion."[1] Caliste aside, Charrière's protagonists are routinely abandoned, whether at a crossroads or simply en route, before their fates can be decided once and for all. The typical Charrière novel eschews comic and tragic denouements alike, in favor of a murky middle ground between death and the happily ever after. A particularly telling example is provided by the *Lettres de Mistriss Henley*, Charrière's recasting from the woman's point of view of Samuel de Constant's *Le Mari sentimental*. Whereas Constant's henpecked husband had been made to "end it all," Charrière's equally desperate wife declares herself incapable of suicide, and wonders whether she will have changed "dans un an, dans deux ans." As if to symbolize her own uncertain future, she alludes in her last letter to the baby which, contrary to conventional novelistic wisdom, she has *not* yet miscarried, though the perfect opportunity has just presented itself, and may again.[2] More inconclusive still are the several later novels: *Lettres écrites de Lausanne, Lettres trouvées dans des porte-feuilles d'émigrés, Trois femmes,* and *Sir Walter Finch et son fils William,* for which Charrière provided sequels, only to thicken her plots with new characters and complications.

Feeling themselves to have been left in the lurch, contemporary readers, from her own sisters-in-law to erstwhile rival Germaine de Staël, repeatedly cajoled and challenged Charrière to produce what Christabel Braunrot has called a "dénouement en bonne et due forme."³ But it was to no avail that Staël declared "rien de plus pénible que votre manière de commencer sans finir," and likened withdrawal pains suffered by readers of the *Lettres neuchâteloises* to those occasioned by the interruption of actual mail service from Paris. And it was only a matter of time before Charrière's alleged hard-heartedness would work to the detriment of her reputation as a writer of novels other than *Caliste*, that perennial favorite and, not incidentally, anomaly of completeness. At the hands of the critical establishment, she who *would* not became she who *could* not finish; the corpus became easy to dismiss as technically flawed, and seemingly impossible to rehabilitate without serious attention to the by now inevitable "charge of incompleteness often cast upon these novels."⁴

In her own defense, Charrière offers increasingly little direct testimony. Her purported reasons for failure to follow through are most often circumstantial and valid only for the particular novel in question, rather than suggestive of an overall philosophy or strategy. One early novel must be abandoned because, the author's identity having been discovered, she can no longer hide behind her fictional correspondents; another, because events in her own life have so soured her on men and marriage that she can summon no enthusiasm to write about them, even in negative terms. Or so she confesses to Benjamin Constant. For Chambrier d'Oleyres, she reserves the more impersonal claim that there can be no thought whatsoever of novels at a time when *le romanesque* pales in comparison with the reality of Revolution.⁵ Three novels of Revolution and emigration later, she would seem to have changed her mind.

However sincerely proffered at the moment, these excuses are finally less intriguing than one which comes closer to endowing Charrière's chronic incompleteness with an underlying purposiveness. Writing near the outset of her career on denouements in general, she confides: "j'aurois peut-être encore moins de talent pour les dénouemens que pour le reste. Les tristes sont tristes et les heureux sont fort sujets à être plats."⁶ Made under cover of modesty, the rhetorical attack on endings is nonetheless sudden, swift, and incisive. One, the tautological formulation "les tristes sont tristes" magically condemns the tragic denouement to absolute and absolutely sterile finality. Two, with the refusal to balance the period rhythmically or semantically, *les heureux* trail off appropriately into terminal insipidity. Three, by assuming the right to classify all possible endings as either *tristes* or *heureux*, a practice taken over from that most conventional of all genres, the classical theater, Charrière places a curse of conventionality on the ending per se. Nowhere is the theoretical irony more cleverly translated into practice than in the one novel, *Saint Anne*, whose loose ends would seem to have been tied up as neatly as those of any Corneille comedy or Gilbert and Sullivan operetta. Having duly unmixed and matched her young lovers, Charrière then undermines their happy ending by dispatching the title character and his new bride in search of two nameless friends whose only prior function in this novel has been to discourse on the implausibility of novels in general.[7] Rather than work within the system to refurbish old denouements or even invent new ones, Charrière has chosen, once and for all, to concentrate on *le reste*.

For want of imagination? So saying, the critical chorus has neglected, I think, to recognize that Charrière's unfinished novels perform an important illustrative function. I would suggest here that, through their very form or formlessness, these novels ultimately show what their content has been telling all along: namely, that a woman's work is unique in nature, and more precisely, never done.

By women's work, I mean not only the generalized business of living as a woman, but the specific womanly activities encompassed by the dictionary term *ouvrages de dames:* sewing, embroidery, knitting, and weaving. The latter *ouvrages* can be counted on to figure in each of Charrière's novels; linked to a female subject, the verb *travailler* invariably means nothing more than "to work with a needle." The corpus abounds in accomplished seamstresses, beginning with Julianne, the *Lettres neuchâteloises'* professional *tailleuse*, whose dressmaking assignments provide the sole occasion of her coming into contact with the two more socially prominent members of the novel's central triangle. Hers, though, turns out to be an isolated case, insofar as *les ouvrages de dames* gradually retreat, in the ensuing novels, from the actual and plot economies. Amateurs all, Cécile works in her mother's drawing room; Geneviève, in the solitude of her own apartment; groups of women, in the latter-day gynecea of both *La Nature et l'art* and *Le Roman de Charles Cecil.*[8]

This increasing isolation of the female workplace parallels Charrière's growing skepticism about the possibility of true interaction and intuitive understanding between the sexes. Whatever steps are undertaken to bridge the gender gap become the sole responsibility of her ever more enterprising heroines, who, for example, almost always initiate correspondence with their absent lovers. For their part,

Charrière's men take no interest in the world or work of women. Time and again, Charrière peoples her drawing rooms with a symbolic dyad, the woman with her *ouvrage*, the man absorbed in his book.[9] Even when treated to the spectacle of women's work, men do not see it. Sir Walter Finch promotes the invisibility of women's work to the status of an ideal, by repeated allegorical reference to the single scrawny cat who works behind the scenes to rid the household of rats so that her brother fat cats may thrive. Women's work is a sight fit only for the downcast eyes of the worker, as when Cécile hides her embarrassment at untoward advances in the *ouvrage* at hand.[10]

For Charrière's heroines, their *ouvrage* is, in fact, always at hand, ready at a moment's notice to serve as a diversion from what male-dominated society would call the real business of living. No need to mention Cécile's sewing prior to her availing herself thereof if, as Charrière suggests, sewing is less an economic activity than a natural biological function, less an autonomous piece of work than an always available appendage of the female body. Only an unnatural woman like the Marquise of *Trois femmes* would, by her perverse preoccupation with *toilette* and *vapeurs*, neglect the one end to which her hands were created.[11] Is it any wonder that Caliste and Bianca, the novels' two quintessential *femmes fatales*, are *said* to possess extraordinary aptitude for "tous les ouvrages de femme," Bianca to the exclusion of all other talents? Or that neither is ever *shown* in the act of sewing?[12] Women's work is always there, but never done. There is no credit given for women's work; it is certainly not the stuff of which lives—or novels—are made. Charrière thus exposes the assumption on which her predecessors had merely proceeded.

Nor is women's work ever done in the sense of "finished." What ever became of the purse in progress by which Henriette intended to spin a web of communication between herself and the absent Richard? No sooner has it served one evening as a receptacle for her tears than the purse disappears from the reader's sight once and for all.[13] In keeping with the dictates of French grammar, what women do—not "ouvrages" (works), but "de l'ouvrage" (*some work*)—remains a single, interminable process, devoid of product. It cannot count in part because it cannot be counted.

There is, of course, a sense in which the unfinished nature of *les ouvrages de dames* provides a safe and comforting alternative to forays into the domain of real life. The inaction of sewing serves Julie d'Arnonville well as a mirror and pretext for the inaction of relatively harmless reverie. Likewise, when tempted to unleash her tart tongue in after-dinner conversation, Henriette turns to her work as a defense against saying something she might always regret.[14] What Charrière's heroines fear more than anything else is the irrevocable word or deed by which their fate would be sealed once and for all. They recognize, as does their creator, that attempting to act would involve a trade-off: more *lauriers* perhaps, but more *souffrance* as well.[15] In this respect, they hardly differ from their counterparts throughout the eighteenth-century corpus, all those Julies and Clarissas whose missteps had proven fatal. Except that Charrière would dispense with the prevailing notion of female destiny as absolutely grounded in biology. Even in *Caliste,* death is no longer the inevitable long-term result of sexual relations per se. Rather, the heroine's mortal despair emanates from a series of trifling incidents which to her make all the difference: a door slammed and not reopened, a letter never sent, an apology tendered too late, and so forth. Even here, the infamous fatal moment is displaced and disseminated throughout the life.

In fact, Caliste long outlives her unworthy lover's first assumption that she must be dead by now. Has he read too many novels? Charrière suggests as much when she recasts heroines from novels past in the role of survivors. Where Rousseau's Baronne d'Etange had taken to her deathbed on discovering evidence of Julie's fall, Cécile's mother vows that, should history repeat itself, *she* would not die of chagrin. "Non," she continues, "je vivrois, je tâcherois de vivre, de prolonger ma vie pour adoucir les malheurs de la vôtre."[16] No longer, in Charrière's hands, is female life possessed of but a single shape. Rather, it is rendered shapeless, open-ended, subject to change for better or worse, perhaps tedious, even trivial, but at least not necessarily or uniformly tragic, in close conformity with the model provided by female *ouvrage*. Survivors all, Charrière's heroines are, like her heroes, entitled to contend, each in her own way, with the never finished business of living. In the process, the female novelist's work has been made to consist, not so much in doing, as in *un*doing, stitch by careful stitch, the ever-so-tightly woven tapestry of novelistic convention.

But if her own labor derives less from Hercules' than from Penelope's, so too, implies Charrière, does every woman's. It is fitting that Charrière should have given voice in the lyric opera *Pénélope* to the mythological figure who presides in silence over the whole of the novelistic production. Though only a brief opening fragment of the opera remains, the extant text makes clear the librettist's intention to focus on Penelope the weaver, rather than on Penelope the much-maligned mother or even on Penelope the faithful and long-suffering wife. Charrière's heroine is immediately shown in the act of unweaving which the Homeric material had relegated to flashback, albeit on three separate occasions.[17] A devotee of Fénelon's *Télémaque*, Charrière nonetheless confesses in her correspondence never to have read the original *Odyssey* because of deep-seated antipathy for *le prudent*, that is, *le trop prudent Ulysse*.[18] No wonder that, in her opera, the goal of fidelity to Ulysses is all but forgotten in favor of Penelope's chosen stratagem, unweaving by night what she has woven by day, so as never to complete Laertes' burial shroud.

Fashioning a coherent narrative out of the novels' scattered strands, the seven-page operatic fragment succeeds in telling the whole truth and nothing but the truth about women's work. An initial chorus for drunken suitors, supposed rivals now united in their adoration of Bacchus, dramatizes the solitude of the working woman in a world where real work is defined in masculine terms.[19] Though Telemachus does not figure in Charrière's scenario, one can almost hear his Homeric counterpart dispatching his mother to her room, commanding as follows: "Look to your own province, distaff and loom, and tell your women to ply their own task; public speech shall be men's concern, and my concern most of all; authority in this house is mine."[20] Meanwhile, addressed to no one but herself, Pénélope's own repeated imperatives: "Défaisons . . . Défaisons . . . Défaisons . . . Défaisons . . . Travaillons, . . ." eloquently declare the incompatibility, even the antonymy for her sex of "working" and "doing." Turning process into a finished product is likewise out of the question: "c'est un si long ouvrage."[21]

Suddenly caught in the act of unweaving by apparently sympathetic suitor Eurimaque, who here replaces Homer's traitorous handmaidens, Pénélope insists that she cannot work with someone watching.[22] Has it not already been written that women's work must remain, if not literally nocturnal, at least invisible to men? Pénélope is drawn to Eurimaque, so *séduisant* and *attendrissant* in his protestations of undying love, so different from the other suitors and, by implication, from Ulysse, whose *billets-doux* all date from *before* their marriage.[23] Yet she dares not speak, nor even avert her gaze from the fragile *ouvrage* which alone stands between her and total vulnerability. His advances, her retreat, are resumed in the counterpoint of their respective refrains: "Regardez-moi" and "Ah laissez-moi."[24] Pénélope feels her defenses to be weakening. If only, having seen her work, Eurimaque could read her mind and thus, embody the heretofore unattainable ideal of intuitive manhood. Alas! It only remains for the drunken chorus to thrust Pénélope's loom aside, with the mocking announcement that, prior bargains to the contrary, they will *play* for her hand, with dice no less. The opera itself may not be complete;

its dismissal of women's work as "ce chien d'ouvrage" most certainly is.[25]

But Penelope's story need not end on such a gloomy note. In the *Odyssey's* third, possibly apochryphal version, the burial robe is, for the first time, presented as a finished product: "With the weaving over, she washed the great web and then displayed it; it shone out like the sun and moon."[26] Likewise, Isabelle de Charrière finished— at least, according to her own lights—carefully edited, and published the majority of her novels. And yet, in making her escape into the literary world of discrete *ouvrages* (masculine plural), Charrière never failed to look back with subtle intelligence and subversive charm on the gyneceum of endless female *ouvrage*. Granted, she did not invent the possibility of interchanging needles and pens; the metaphor was already moribund, if not dead on arrival. Nor did she lack for models of incompleteness in an age which celebrated the open book as a passport to reflection, debate, and social change. In her hands, however, the metaphor lends new and particular meaning to the structure, which, in turn, rescues the metaphor from innocuous banality, and makes it a useful tool for understanding Everywoman's experience of everyday life. Forever undoing the complete novels of her fellow writers, Charrière provides a shining example of feminist revisionism already at work in the eighteenth century.

NOTES

1 Geoffrey Scott, *The Portrait of Zélide* (New York: Charles Scribner's Sons, 1926), p. 94.

2 Isabelle de Charrière, *Lettres de Mistriss Henley*, in *Oeuvres complètes*, ed. Jean-Daniel Candaux et al. (Amsterdam: G. A. van Oorschot, 1979—), 8:122. All references to Charrière's works are to this edition.

3 Christabel Braunrot's Introduction to *Lettres neuchâteloises*, in *Oeuvres*, 8:43. Braunrot cites Staël on the same page. For the sisters-in-law's entreaties, see Charrière's *Correspondance*, specifically, "De son frère Vincent," seconde quinzaine d'août 1784, Letter 533, in *Oeuvres*, 2:636. See also: "De sa belle-soeur Johanna Catharina van Tuyll van Serooskerken-Fagel," 24 juillet 1787, Letter 590; and "De sa belle-soeur Johanna Catharina van Tuyll van Serooskerken-Fagel," entre mi-juin et mi-juillet 1790, Letter 720, both in *Oeuvres*, 3:27, 226.

4 Sigyn C. Minier-Birk, "L'Oeuvre romanesque de Madame de Charrière: Réflexion systématique et création dans les *Lettres neuchâteloises, Mistriss Henley,* et les *Lettres écrites de Lausanne," Dissertation Abstracts International* 38 (1978): 4871A.

5 "A Jean-Pierre de Chambrier d'Oleyres," 1 février 1785, Letter 549, in *Oeuvres*, 2:454; "A Benjamin Constant," 31 août 1790, Letter 726, in *Oeuvres*, 3:231; "A Jean-Pierre de Chambrier d'Oleyres," 17 avril 1790, Letter 703, in *Oeuvres*, 3:200–201.

6 Charrière, Letter 549, in *Oeuvres*, 2:454.

7 Charrière, *Saint Anne*, in *Oeuvres*, 9:310.

8 Charrière, *Lettres écrites de Lausanne*, in *Oeuvres*, 8:164, 192; *Henriette et Richard*, in *Oeuvres*, 8:321; *La Nature et l'art*, in *Oeuvres*, 8:601; *Le Roman de Charles Cecil*, in *Oeuvres*, 9:642.

9 See, for example: Charrière, *Henriette et Richard*, p. 320; *Louise et Albert, ou Le Danger d'être trop exigeant*, in *Oeuvres*, 9:425.

10 Charrière, *Sir Walter Finch et son fils William*, in *Oeuvres*, 9:533, 535–36, 592; *Lettres écrites de Lausanne*, p. 169.

11 Charrière, *Trois femmes*, in *Oeuvres*, 9:47.

12 Charrière, *Lettres écrites de Lausanne*, p. 192; *Trois femmes*, p. 147.

13 Charrière, *Henriette et Richard*, pp. 325, 336.

14 Charrière, *Le Noble*, in *Oeuvres*, 8:25; *Henriette et Richard*, p. 335.

15 "Au baron Constant d'Hermenches," 22 novembre 1768, Letter 326, in *Oeuvres*, 2:133.

16 Charrière, *Lettres écrites de Lausanne*, p. 164.

17 Charrière, *Pénélope*, in *Oeuvres*, 7:103; Homer, *The Odyssey*, trans. Walter Shewring (Oxford: Oxford University Press, 1980), pp. 14, 231, 288–89.

18 "A Jean-Pierre de Chambrier d'Oleyres," 30 mars 1789, Letter 645, in *Oeuvres*, 3:133.

19 Charrière, *Pénélope*, p. 103.

20 Homer, *Odyssey*, trans. Shewring, p. 9.

21 Charrière, *Pénélope*, p. 106.

22 Ibid., p. 103.

23 Ibid., pp. 105–6.

24 Ibid., pp. 106–7.

25 Ibid., p. 108.

26 Homer, *Odyssey*, trans. Shewring, pp. 288–89.

The Philosophes and Popular Ritual:
Turgot, Voltaire, Rousseau

HARRY PAYNE

The question of the nature and future of popular ritual came up only in passing among the eighteenth-century philosophes. Though the history of popular culture and ritual is of central concern to twentieth-century historians, it was but one of scores of subjects which philosophes, as social observers, happened to note and worry about. That in itself is a historical problem—how popular culture came to be recognized and appreciated as a concern. And it is a story in which the Enlightenment of philosophes played a part, albeit a somewhat ungracious one. They recognized the separateness of popular attitudes from the elite culture they were trying to reform without, however, often suspending elite scorn in the name of broader understanding. Such separation ultimately bore multiple fruits—curiosity, hostility, intrusion, and nostalgia.[1] The question of popular ritual, then, can be seen as a brief footnote in the story of Enlightenment social thought, as the basis of some larger reflections on the nature of the Enlightenment's confrontation with *le peuple,* and as a "forecast" of the way the eighteenth century opened up such questions for subsequent eras.

Three texts can serve as the basis of this commentary. The first is a letter from the intendant Ann-Robert-Jacques Turgot in 1762 to his controller-general. Having dealt with some issues surrounding the Société d'agriculture in the region of Limousin, he brought up, almost as an afterthought, another small but vexing problem related to the fate of agriculture. He noted that for five years the Bishop of Angoulême had suspended several church fêtes in the interest of public order and efficiency—since the miscellaneous local fêtes of the Church had been associated with mandatory stoppage of work (*chômage*) and popular license. This suspension had the support of the Archbishop of Paris and other bishops. "But the Bishop of Angoulême," Turgot noted, "who had first given his support to the point of view of public utility, for whatever motive of misdirected zeal, has just reestablished [the fêtes] for next year. . . ." Turgot foresaw damage to the region in this decision and, since no "motive of conscience" was involved, he asked the controller-general to write directly to the bishop to help change his mind.[2]

The second text comes from Voltaire's *Dictionnaire philosophique* of 1764, in the entry "Catéchisme du curé." The conversation between a priest Théotime and his friend Ariston wanders over many favorite Voltairean subjects. In his new vocation Théotime intends to be a model Voltairean curé—virtually oblivious to matters of doctrine and dogma; scrupulously concerned about educating peasants in law, medicine, agriculture, and morality; and devotedly committed to work with the seigneur and his wife for public improvement. At the end of the conversation, Ariston asks how his friend is going to prevent his parishioners from getting drunk on fête days, describing in detail the brutalization of peasants through drink. "You have to admit," he cautions, "the state loses more subjects through drink during fêtes than from battles. . . ." Théotime has, in fact, thought the matter through. He will permit and encourage his charges to ignore the tradition of idleness on days of fêtes and to return to their fields after an early service. Not prayer but idleness leads to drunkenness, he concludes. Hence one must make fêtes into working days. He then calculates the loss to gross national product from the existing tradition of fêtes and their idleness (at least 1,500,000,000 sous) and ventures that God never intended for prayer to cost so much to the national wealth. Ariston is much pleased with this response.[3]

The third text comes from Rousseau's *La Nouvelle Héloïse* of 1761. Here Rousseau describes a fête as it ought to be, the harvest festival (*vendanges*) at the estate of Julie and Baron de Wolmar at Clarens. He offers a vision of a purified saturnalia, unlike those of the ancients. Julie works alongside her harvesters in the day and serves them in the evening; worker and mistress each experience the pleasures of change of station. Each day she rewards that person who harvested most. Work and fête slide easily into one another. The days are filled with hard labor and harmony, the nights with lively pleasures, bonfires, amusement, and songs of romance of old. The celebrations reflect "liberté" within the bounds of "honnêteté"; Julie superintends the fête while participating in it, exercising her "despotic empire of wisdom and good deeds." The evening ends in absolute harmony, with the victorious harvester casting the torch which ignites the bonfire of vinestalks—"a veritable fire of joy around which one jumps and laughs." There follows the toast to the victor and then sleep, "content from a day passed in work, gaiety, innocence, and which one would not mind beginning again the next day, the day after, or for a lifetime."[4]

To anyone who knows these writers—without necessarily knowing these particular texts—interpretation seems fairly straightforward. Indeed these texts easily fit what we know of the French Enlightenment and of Rousseau's particular variant of it. In the reflections of Turgot and Voltaire we see some of the paradigmatic attitudes of the French philosophes: they are non- or anti-religious, as matters of doctrine and tradition seem to matter hardly at all. They are elitist; they approach the problem of festivity as outsiders viewing a strange and distasteful object. They associate popular ritual with that license, drunkenness, and unreason foreign to their enlightened culture. And they are concerned above all with utility, what changes in society, within the boundaries of practicality, might make life more fruitful for all. Here they see an apparent abuse: too much time devoted to destructive and unproductive amusement, sanctioned by a Church whose main business ought to be popular instruction and morality. Hence they see no reason not to intrude and tinker.[5] For Turgot these concerns were marginal—a slight distraction in a world of taxes, agricultural improvements, *corvées*, and grain regulations. For Voltaire the problem of popular license and festivity was a theme which reappeared occasionally in his work, part of the broader assault on *l'infâme*. The two philosophes' values are substantially similar, though their métiers differed.

Rousseau also seems to operate in an identifiable mode: as Peter Gay has written, "of" the Enlightenment but not wholly "in" it.[6] Like the philosophes, Rousseau is clearly interested in popular ritual, and like them his purposes are arguably didactic and elitist. He is also secularist. His vision of good popular festivity, here and elsewhere, is not formally related to the doctrines or traditions of the Church. And he is utilitarian. The festivity at Clarens, however idyllic, serves the purposes of social function and economic production. Ultimately, though, his concerns are not wholly in the usual Enlightenment vein. His festival at Clarens—like those he proposed for Geneva in his *Lettre à d'Alembert* (1758) and Poland in his *Considérations sur le gouvernement de Pologne* (1772)—has a utopian air.[7] He is always the Enlightenment's Diogenes, proposing the dreamer's vision of virtuous order rather than pragmatic reforms. He demands more than the philosophes, and, with his contempt for elite sociability and his greater empathy for popular ritual, he perhaps sees more deeply into the essence of ritual. He uses festivals in his utopian visions both to reinforce the reformed social order and temporarily to release people from its burdens. The fête at Clarens provides relief from labor and an inversion of roles; it also motivates common people to more labor and deeper respect for those above their station. The festivals Rousseau earlier proposed for Geneva both allowed an outlet for youthful passion and a channel for those passions back into the values of the state and the social order. His proposed public festivals for Poland suspend everyday life and give vent to passions, yet they also celebrate values of physical strength, social hierarchy, and national pride.

For Rousseau the power of festivity had a peculiarly important attraction. He was caught in a bind between his deepest dreams and his desire to speak to the real world; between his love of equality and his acceptance of the necessity for inequality; and between his celebration of passion and his inherent rationalism and moralism. Rituals—with their suspension of everyday rules and their rich symbols—allowed him visions of utopian occasions experienced and remembered in the course of everyday life. They might allow societies to celebrate human equality through common experience while enforcing a concern for deference and order. They allowed him to reaffirm his love of *le peuple* while accepting their incapacity for abstract reason and their susceptibility to the senses.[8] Because of his uniquely moralistic concerns, Rousseau saw more deeply than most philosophes into the rich potential of ritual; the philosophes were ritually unmusical, unaccustomed to paradoxical, symbol-laden meanings which ritual could hide and nurture.[9]

In some ways this commentary might seem satisfactory and complete. But ought it to be? As one studies the history of popular ritual over a longer period one discovers other and broader contexts which resonate even in these slight documents. Looking back into the past, these texts bear witness to a process that the historian Peter Burke calls "the triumph of Lent."[10] Looking forward beyond the mid-eighteenth century, they reflect the anxieties which led to a century or more of evaluation and creation of new festive forms. In other words, these texts reflect not just the Enlightenment's disposition toward a minor problem but rather the Enlightenment's place in a much longer history of elite intrusion into the world of popular ritual.

There is, first of all, something startling in Turgot's proposed alliance with the Church in his minor skirmish about popular fêtes. We tend to assume a sharp cleavage between the interests of philosophe and Church. A wider perspective, however, reveals that Turgot's skirmish is part of a much longer conflict initiated in France by Church and state in the seventeenth century. Motives of mercantile economics had, in fact, worked relatively comfortably with motives of clerical reform in a prolonged war against local usages. Mercantile motives were clear. Colbert and his successors in royal financial power saw the numerous local fêtes as a blight on the national economy. They looked enviously toward Protestant England and the Netherlands, and they encouraged all initiatives to decrease the number of fêtes.[11] Moreover, fêtes had traditionally been associated with violence, drunkenness, and even revolt; hence concerns for *police* underscored concerns for productivity.

The alliance of state with Church on this issue proved fairly natural. Though we tend to associate "Baroque piety" with an efflorescent, ritual-laden Church, there was also a strong "puritanical" and reforming element to it. Many Roman Catholic localities were eager to imitate those reformed cities which used the religious revolution to attack many popular festivals. As early as 1627, Pope Urban VIII had tried to bring under control a good deal of local initiatives tending to decrease the number of fêtes and abolish those most offensive to public order and decency. Urban's motives were two-sided—both to prevent massive diminution of fêtes but also to reinforce, within the minimal number of fêtes required, the need for decorum and decency. His goal appears to have been an adequate number of festivals, reflecting the best moral and didactic values of a Church putting itself in order the better to counteract reform. In this case, the Church imitated within limits the much more virulent hostility to popular rituals and magical usages in the various reformed churches. In later years Jansenist bishops were eager to use the liberty given by Rome toward these ends. We see, then, pulses of reforming initiatives against popular fêtes in France—especially in the 1660s, 1720s to 1740s, and again in the 1770s. The emphasis rested both on quantitative and qualitative change—fewer festivals more scrupulously observed. Here motives of piety could part company from strict motives of economics. The Church wanted *chômage* to be less frequent but more complete. And for those rituals which were to survive, the Church received the help of the state's power of police. Royal statutes several times between 1650 and 1750 attempted to reinforce the strict observance of abstinence from work.[12]

The remarks of Turgot and Voltaire, therefore, reflect this administrative and clerical movement. And for both—though here Voltaire alone could be overt about the matter—the issue was no longer really encumbered by anxieties about past traditions or pieties. They lived in a world where the elite detachment from tradition and the administrative urge to control put festive life up for grabs. For instance, the cult of Saint Genevieve, known as an intercessor to end scarcity of food, was manipulated by civic authorities according to the needs of monarchical police. In the decades after 1766, priests and seigneurs created a whole new genre of popular ritual—the ceremony of the *rosières* to reward feminine virtue—as a way of reinforcing popular morality in a way so different from traditional fêtes. The royal coronation ceremony could be questioned and redesigned for Louis XVI according to the tastes of a more genteel and skeptical age.[13] Turgot and Voltaire prove to be, therefore, part of a larger early-modern agenda—lenten and didactic, mirrored in these activities and similar initiatives in England and the Germanies.[14]

This disdain for popular festive excess and this lack of concern for the past seem to link Rousseau to Turgot and Voltaire as well. But his attitude is laced with a heavy measure of anxiety for the future. Turgot and Voltaire are enmeshed in the present and the near future, worrying about changing present realities in view of the need for public order and productivity. They represent, as it were, the utilitarian face of Lent. Rousseau worked in a kind of timeless space, a mythical classical past and a vaguely defined utopian future, the better to underscore the bankruptcy of the present. In this way, he was better able to express the anxieties of the future.

In Rousseau we see the sense that festivity is a fundamental resource, a necessary part of the rhythm of social life. Through his festivals he wants to overcome certain anxieties—the social differences between seigneur and peasant or magistrate and citizen; the desire for play and the necessity of work. Hence his prescriptions on festivity seem to sense the power of rituals—both for cultivation of virtue and subversion of everyday social order. Ultimately, however, he remains committed to the didacticism of the lenten imperative and, to a lesser extent, the need to encourage productivity. In this way Rousseau prefigures much of the often crude manufacture of public ritual in ensuing decades and centuries.

To be sure, there continued substantial activity in the manner of simple reforming efforts of Counter-Reformation Church and mercantile economists. Napoleonic France saw renewed efforts at suppression and purification, and that remained a theme through the mid-nineteenth century.[15] We see, however, another growing field of ritual activity—new creations, real and fictive. Most dramatic, of course, were the revolutionary festivals so much in the Rousseauian vein, trying to create a new symbolic order adequate to the needs of the new political order. These attempts were echoed, albeit less dramatically, in the recreation of the Bastille Day in the 1870s; in the debates over a festival for Joan of Arc; and in the festivals of Vichy France.[16] Moreover, for every festival created, many more were dreamed—by social reformers such as Auguste Comte and the Comte de Saint-Simon; by romantic liberals such as Hector Berlioz; by royalist reactionaries such as Charles Maurras; by sport enthusiasts such as Pierre Coubertin; and even by make-believe elephants such as King Babar.[17] French attempts and dreams mirrored similar efforts across Europe. The century and a half after 1789 was a great age of manufacture of national rituals, anthems, and symbols, in turn mirrored in clubs, regions, and cities.[18]

The dream of new festivals which might work reflects, implicitly and explicitly, the assumption that the old forms could no longer hold. By the late Enlightenment much of European elite culture had moved to the side of Lent, and insofar as there remained—and even grew— a theoretical and literary appreciation of popular ritual, it was usually fraught with a mixture of antiquarianism and nostalgia—what the Germans call "Folklorismus," the experience of popular culture at second hand.[19] Turgot and Voltaire were willing participants in this aspect of a broader separation of the past from future, of populace from elite. For philosophes *le peuple* usually represented atavism in historical time, social space, and psychological capacity; the urge to reform and cure was paramount. Dreamers of new festivals thought, perhaps, they could accept this verdict of history, yet reassert the place of popular ritual, albeit purged of license, hostile to inversions, and controlled by the elite for good purposes. The anxieties were real and probably justified; the question remains whether the attempt was—and remains—fated to fail from the beginning.[20]

NOTES

1 On this process of separation—and attendant attitudes—see especially Harry Payne, "Elite Versus Popular Mentality in the Eighteenth Century," *Studies in Eighteenth-Century Culture* 8 (Madison: University of Wisconsin

Press, 1979): 3–32; Peter Burke, *Popular Culture in Early Modern Europe* (London, 1978); and E. P. Thompson, "Patrician Society, Plebeian Culture," *Journal of Social History* 7 (Summer 1974): 382–405.

2 Ann-Robert-Jacques Turgot, *Oeuvres de Turgot et documents le concernant*, ed. G. Schelle, 5 vols. (Paris, 1912–13), 2:226.

3 Voltaire, *Dictionnaire philosophique*, ed. R. Naves, J. Benda (Paris, 1967), pp. 88–89.

4 Jean-Jacques Rousseau, *Oeuvres complètes*, ed. B. Gagnebin et al. 4 vols. to date (Paris, 1959—), 2:607–11.

5 On the French Enlightenment's attitude toward *le peuple*, see especially Harry Payne, *The Philosophes and the People* (New Haven, 1976), and Harvey Chisick, *The Limits of Reform in the Enlightenment; Attitudes toward the Education of the Lower Classes in Eighteenth-Century France* (Princeton, 1981). (Both have extensive bibliographies on the subject.) Payne, pp. 121–22, has examples of other similar attitudes about rituals among the wider circle of French philosophes.

6 Peter Gay, *The Enlightenment, An Interpretation*, 2 vols. (New York, 1969), 2:529.

7 On Poland, see Rousseau, *Oeuvres complètes*, 3:962–64. On Geneva, see Allan Bloom, trans., *On Politics and the Arts; Letter to M. D'Alembert on the Theater* (Ithaca, 1960), pp. 126–31.

8 For a more extended, earlier version of this argument, see Harry Payne, "Rousseau and the Festive Process," *Proceedings of the Western Society for French Historical Studies* 2 (1975): 83–89. For other analyses of Rousseau's use of festivity, see Jean Starobinski, *J.-J. Rousseau; La Transparence et l'obstacle* (1957, rpt. Paris, 1971), 120–29, on the illusory quality of the *vendanges*; Christie Vance McDonald, *The Extravagant Shepherd*, Studies on Voltaire and the Eighteenth Century, Vol. 105 (Banbury, Ox.: Voltaire Foundation, 1973), pp. 133–44, on its utopian qualities; Jacques Proust, "La Fête chez Rousseau et Diderot," *Annales Jean-Jacques Rousseau* 37 (1968): 175–96, on Rousseau's use of rustic versus urbane festivity; and Paule-Monique Vernes, *La Ville, la fête, la democratie; Rousseau et les illusions de la communauté* (Paris, 1978), on the place of fête in Rousseau's larger social project.

9 Compare, for instance, their attitudes to the ritual elements in Greek tragedy to those of theorists a century later: Harry Payne, "Modernizing the Ancients; The Reconstruction of Ritual Drama 1870–1920," *Proceedings of the American Philosophical Society* 122, no. 3 (June 1978): 182–92.

10 Burke, *Popular Culture*, ch. 8.

11 J. Maarten Ultee, "The Suppression of *Fêtes* in France, 1666," *Catholic Historical Review* 62, no. 2 (1976): 181–99.

12 On Reformation proposals, see Steven Ozment, *The Reformation in the Cities* (New Haven, 1975), pp. 97–98, 117, 157. On French initiatives, see Michel Peronnet, "Police et religion à la fin du xviiie siècle," *Annales historiques de la Révolution Française* (1970), pp. 375–97; Yves Bercé, *Fête et revolte; Des Mentalités populaires due xvie au xviiie siècle* (Paris, 1976), 127–87;

and Michel Vovelle, *Les Métamorphoses de la fête en Provence* (Paris, 1976), chs. 4–9.

13 See, respectively, Stephen Kaplan, "Religion, Subsistence, and Social Control: The Uses of Saint Genevieve," *Eighteenth-Century Studies* 13, no. 2 (Winter 1979/80): 142–68; Jeffrey Willson Merrick, "From Sun King to Citizen Capet: The Desacralization of the French Monarchy in the Eighteenth Century" (Ph.D. diss., Yale University, 1979); and William Everdell, "The Rosières Movement, 1766–1789: A Clerical Precursor of the Revolutionary Cults," *French Historical Studies* 9, no. 1 (1975): 23–36.

14 On England, see especially Robert Malcolmson, *Popular Recreations in English Society 1700–1850* (Cambridge, 1973), chs. 6–8, and Peter Borsay, "The Urban Theatre; Popular Culture, Ritual and Ceremony 1660–1800," paper delivered to annual meeting, 1982, of the American Society for Eighteenth-Century Studies. On the Germanies—Protestant and Catholic—see Henri Brunschwig, *Enlightenment and Romanticism in Eighteenth-Century Prussia*, trans. F. Jellinek (1947; rpt. Chicago, 1974), p. 69; Dieter Narr, "Fest und Feier im Kulturprogram der Aufklärung," *Zeitschrift für Volkskunde* 62 (1966): 184–203; Fintan Michael Phayer, *Religion und das Gewöhnliche Volk in Bayern in der Zeit von 1750–1850* (Munich, 1970).

15 See Peronnet, "Police et religion," and Vovelle, *Les Métamorphoses* (cited above in n. 12). Also H. Forrestier, "La Loi du 18 novembre 1814 sur l'observation des dimanches et fêtes et son application dans l'Yonne," *Annales de Bourgogne* 28 (1956): 195–203.

16 E. G. Rosemond Sanson, "La Fête de Jeanne d'Arc en 1894; controverse et célébration," *Revue d'histoire moderne et contemporaine* 20 (July–September 1973): 444–63, and *Les 14 juillet, fête et conscience nationale, 1879–1975* (Paris, 1976).

17 See, inter alia, Frank Manuel, *The Prophets of Paris* (Cambridge, 1962), chs. 3, 4, 6; Conrad Donakowski, *A Muse for the Masses; Ritual and Music in an Age of Democratic Revolution 1770–1879* (Chicago, 1977); Ernst Nolte, *The Three Faces of Fascism* (New York, 1965), Part 2; Richard D. Mandell, *The First Modern Olympics* (Berkeley, 1976), chs. 1–3; Jean de Brunhoff, *Roi Babar* (Paris, 1933); and Harry C. Payne, "The Reign of King Babar," *Children's Literature* 11 (1983): 96–108.

18 The German case is the most dramatic and best documented because of the Nazi phenomenon. See especially George Mosse, *The Nationalization of the Masses; Political Symbolism and Mass Movements in Germany from the Napoleonic Wars through the Third Reich* (New York, 1975). For the European context, see Robert Bocock, *Ritual in Industrial Society* (London, 1974); George Mosse, "Caesarism, Circuses, and Monuments," *Journal of Contemporary History* 6, no. 2 (1971): 167–82; and Elizabeth Fehrenbach, "Über die Bedeutung der Politische Symbole im Nationalstaat," *Historische Zeitschrift* 203, no. 2 (1966): 296–357.

19 As an introduction to the problem, see Hermann Bausinger, "Folklorismus in Europa," *Zeitschrift fur Volkskunde* 65 (1969): 1–8.

20 That there is a "festive crisis" of sorts under modern conditions -a con-

spiracy against coherent, life-enhancing rite in conditions of rapid change and materialist values—has been argued by many observers, most notably Johann Huizinga, *Homo ludens* (Boston, 1955), and Harvey Cox, *The Feast of Fools* (Cambridge, 1969).

The Dialogues *as Autobiographical Truth*

JAMES F. JONES, JR.

FOR GITA MAY

> *Writing can never dispense with orality.*
> Walter J. Ong, S.J., Orality and Literacy

> *Pour qu'il y ait autobiographie . . . il faut qu'il*
> *y ait identité de l'auteur, du narrateur, et du personnage.*
> Philippe Lejeune, Le Pacte autobiographique

Two distinct and opposing forms of silence unceasingly perplexed Jean-Jacques Rousseau throughout the 1760s and 1770s. On one hand he was haunted by that Kafkaesque silence imposed upon him, or so he imagined the case to be, by his detractors.[1] As does the protagonist of *Der Process*, Rousseau asks time and again, "I know I have been found guilty, but will someone please tell me the nature of the crime?" Yet, no one would. His enemies would in his view never speak openly, would never show their true identities. (It is indeed something of a cruel irony that the *Sentiments des citoyens* which came to plague him in the mid-1760s was written by an anonymous Voltaire whose authorship of this work Rousseau never realized.) In 1772 or shortly thereafter, Rousseau writes of that enveloping nightmare about him as:

> Le silence profond, universel, non moins inconcevable que le mistére qu'il couvre, mistére que depuis quinze ans on me cache avec un soin que je m'abstiens de qualifier, et avec un succès qui tient du prodige; ce silence effrayant et terrible ne m'a pas laissé saisir la moindre idée qui peut m'éclairer sur ces étranges dispositions.[2]

Precisely this same silence had already appeared one year before in the last paragraph of the *Confessions* where, having finished this long and tortured account of his life and having painfully revealed his inner self, Rousseau states:

317

> J'achevai ainsi ma lecture et tout le monde se tut. Mad^e d'Egmont
> fut la seule qui me parut émue; elle tressaillit visiblement; mais elle
> se remit bien vite, et garda le silence ainsi que toute la compagnie.
> Tel fut le fruit que je tirai de cette lecture et de ma déclaration. (1:656)

Characterized by the deliberate absence of discourse on the part of
"toute la compagnie," "ces messieurs," or of "tout le monde," this
silence is frighteningly real for Rousseau. To this negative silence,
however, we may contrast an ideal form, one which is also marked
by the utter absence of discourse as described in the fifth part of *La
Nouvelle Héloïse*. In this instance, the "société des coeurs" inhabiting
the utopia of Clarens spends silent mornings in the "salle d'Apollon":

> . . . nous avons passé aujourd'hui une matinée à l'anglaise, réunis
> et dans le silence, goûtant à la fois le plaisir d'être ensemble et la
> douceur du recueillement. Que les delices de cet état sont connues
> de peu de gens! . . . Il est vrai, la langue fournit un babil facile aux
> attachmens médiocres. Mais l'amitié . . . l'amitié! Sentiment vif et
> céleste, quels discours sont dignes de toi? Quelle langue ose être ton
> interprète? . . . C'est dans ces dispositions qu'a commencé le silence
> dont je vous parlois . . . Que de choses se sont dites sans ouvrir la
> bouche! Que d'ardens sentimens se sont communiqués sans la froide
> entremise de la parole. (2:557–60)[3]

This silence is as therapeutic and redemptive as its antithesis is destructive and malevolent.

Of all the major works in the Rousseau canon, the text peculiarly
entitled *Dialogues ou Rousseau juge de Jean-Jacques* has traditionally been
the one work most often ignored.[4] Current scholarly interest in autobiography, especially on the part of those critics concerned with the
theoretical problems attendant to all autobiographical writing, may
now however bring to this neglected work the attention it rightfully
deserves. Labelled a decade ago by one prominent critic "this interminable work of a tortured mind . . .[t]urgid and repetitious . . .[and
not having] a wide appeal to the modern reader,"[5] the *Dialogues* bring
into full play a host of issues that touch on the essence of all autobiographical inquiry.

These *Dialogues* may be viewed, first of all, as positioned between
and responding directly to the two polar silences which haunted
Rousseau at that moment when he began the work's composition in
1772. The *Confessions*, destined to vindicate their author, had failed
abjectly and had been greeted by calls on the authorities to have their

oral reading forbidden and by utter silence on the part of those whom the *Confessions* were supposed to convince. Over against this harsh reality, Rousseau had more than ten years earlier constructed for himself in *La Nouvelle Héloïse* that perfect society where words are no longer necessary in order to communicate, this idealized construct characterized by a fictional "recueillement universel" which may be said to stand in stark contrast to the "silence universel" imposed upon him by his invisible detractors. But just what is one to do with a text whose frontispiece reads "Rousseau juge de Jean-Jacques, Dialogues, par Jean-Jacques Rousseau"?

Unlike his "frère ennemi" Diderot, Rousseau was not often wont to use dialogue—by definition the antipode of silence—as a rhetorical strategy. Yet in this particular instance the very fact that he chooses dialogue is telling indeed. Here, as is the case with many facets of this work, his choice of rhetorical procedure parallels Rousseau's theoretical musings on the nature of language. From his *Essai sur l'origine des langues* and from the analyses of Jacques Derrida, Paul de Man, Christie McDonald, and others, we know that Rousseau firmly believed that spoken words are far less arbitrary than their written counterparts.[6] Printed words may lie: ". . . l'écriture, qui semble devoir fixer la langue, est précisément ce qui l'altère."[7] Printed words can be plagiarized or even erased, as he thought had certainly been the case with many of his printed works at the outset of the 1770s. But for him orality is emphatically more pure. In the pre-Saussurian *Essai sur l'origine des langues* and elsewhere in Rousseau's writings, spoken words are given utter primacy over written words precisely because, like prayers, the signifiers of these signs are unquestionably rooted in their respective signifieds.[8] Walter Ong's latest study conclusively points to the critically important rôle that orality plays in literature, and Rousseau's *Dialogues* would furnish far more than merely adequate proof of Father Ong's timely thesis.[9]

Intricately related to Rousseau's choice of dialogue as a fictional strategy is the assigning of his own name—"Rousseau"—to one of his interlocutors and "Jean-Jacques" to the stated subject of the work's inquiry. Yet here too, Rousseau is being completely consistent with his own theories of language and language development. In the *Second Discourse,* he says that of all substantives (the word *substantive* connoting the very substitution of essence by word about which he is writing), proper names had to be created before all other nouns: "Si donc les premiers inventeurs n'ont pu donner des noms qu'aux idées qu'ils avoient déjà, il s'ensuit que les premiers substantifs n'ont pu jamais être que des noms propres" (3:150). Proper nouns are in his view the only words which can hope to remain constantly faithful to what they are supposed to represent. In his own life, and during a century in which anonymous authorship was commonplace, Rousseau had always made it a zealous and proud point to acknowledge publicly everything he wrote. Five or so years before he began to write the *Dialogues*, he had had great difficulty assuming the pseudonym Jean-Joseph Renou after returning from his ill-fated trip to England when he was specifically advised by the Prince de Conti not to use Jean-Jacques Rousseau any longer. Once he had given up calling himself Jean-Joseph Renou and once he had stopped signing his letters in such a fashion, on 26 December 1769, he was overjoyed in Grenoble to find that he was welcomed as himself, as Jean-Jacques Rousseau, and no longer as someone whose *false* identity he had had to feign.[10]

The authenticity of his name, the fact that proper names best exemplify the non-arbitrariness of the linguistic sign, and his choice of dialogue as a rhetorical strategy thus all converge in the seemingly bizarre title that Rousseau chooses for this work which is expressly destined to counter the silence in which he finds himself enveloped. *Jean-Jacques Rousseau* will thus *speak* in his own name. In fact, he will speak in several names, all of which are in one way or another his own. "Rousseau" the interlocutor will speak to "Le Français" about "Jean-Jacques," whom we never actually see within the fictional construct of this work but who is nonetheless the stated subject of the other two characters' discourse. And here too, Rousseau the author remains faithful to his theories as described elsewhere in his oeuvre. Only those who have the courage to *speak* in their own names are "true." All others are "false," as false as are the *comédiens* so decried in the *Lettre à d'Alembert sur les spectacles:*

> Qu'est-ce que le talent du comédien? L'art de se contrefaire, de revêtir un autre caractère que le sien, de paroître différent de ce qu'on est, . . . de dire autre chose que ce qu'on pense, aussi naturellement que si l'on pensoit réellement, et d'oublier enfin sa propre place à force de prendre celle d'autrui. . . .[11]

Opposed to these "false" *comédiens* are the "true" orators who represent the Rousseauean ideal:

> Quand l'orateur se montre, c'est pour parler, et non pour se donner en spectacle; il ne représente que lui-même, il ne fait que son propre rôle, ne dit ou ne doit dire que ce qu'il pense: l'homme et le personnage étant le même être, il est à sa place. . . .[12]

As its title page sets it forth, the *Dialogues, ou Rousseau juge de Jean-Jacques* formally and structurally will claim utter authenticity, making an even stronger appeal to this basic concept of autobiography than the very work, the *Confessions*, that is said to be the *Urtexte* in the modern phenomenon of autobiography from the eighteenth century to our own time. The *Dialogues* seek to establish the "truth" about the man and the writer whose name is Jean-Jacques Rousseau, and the text attempts to do so by crossing the spoken word, the conversation in the three dialogues, with the use of personae whose names are best able to demonstrate that "truth" since in Rousseau's view proper names best exemplify the untarnished and non-arbitrary linguistic sign in the latter's purest form. The *Dialogues* as literary work thus may serve as a model for the most recent theories of autobiography, namely those of Philippe Lejeune, Gadamer, who draws heavily upon Dilthey, Georges Gusdorf, and Janet Varner Gunn. When Lejeune writes tersely that the "sujet profond de l'autobiographie, c'est le nom propre,"[13] he would be hard pressed indeed to cite one work that more expressly illustrates this notion than the *Dialogues ou Rousseau, juge de Jean-Jacques*. In Rousseau's text, to speak and to speak in one's own name is to counter in the most resolute fashion conceivable the silence of those who anonymously refuse to speak at all. On the most elemental level, then, one speaks here in this work not only about but also to and with one's self.[14]

Over the past two hundred years, much has been written on Rousseau and the plot, on whether a conspiracy against him actually existed or whether it was some figment of Rousseau's tortured mind depicted within the pages of the *Confessions*, the *Dialogues*, and elsewhere. But to concentrate—as many previous commentators have—on the historical accuracy of Rousseau's various accounts of the story is to mistake one of the most intriguing aspects presented by the *Dialogues*, one whose importance Michel Foucault suggests in his Introduction to the 1962 Colin edition.[15] Rousseau's autobiographical text well demonstrates how dialogue and dialectic are here one and the same, precisely as they are in Plato's oeuvre where the philosophical presuppositions of dialogue as rhetorical strategy cannot be divorced from those of dialectic as the *a priori* basis of understanding. Plato's dialogues, the *Phaedrus* for one prominent example, prove that dialogue and dialectic share more than a common Greek *seme*. As far as Rousseau's *Dialogues* are concerned, the given subject of the two interlocutors' discourse is "Jean-Jacques" the character; the discourse itself sketches a paradigmatic search for the autobiographical "truth" that this "Jean-Jacques" embodies.

Furthermore, this "truth" about "Jean-Jacques" has been hidden. The intrinsic problem becomes that of a hermeneutic quest: how to discover the "truth," how to "know." At the end of the first dialogue, "Rousseau" goes to see this "Jean-Jacques" in order to "know" him, and Le Français sets out to "know" "Jean-Jacques" by systematically reading the latter's writings. Their ensuing dialogue evolves to become a masterfully wrought dialectic. Curiously enough, the inseparable link between dialogue and dialectic in this work was recognized but a few years after Rousseau's death by Louis Petit de Bachaumont who remarked: "Enfin suit le Dialogue fort long, où il y a peu de faits, où l'on remarque une imagination noire, exaltée jusqu'au délire, et en même temps une dialectique de la tête la mieux organisée et la plus froide."[16] Despite his pronounced antipathy towards Rousseau the man, Bachaumont had realized how intricately dialogue is related in this specific context to dialectic.

This dialogue-dialectic functions on at least two levels within this text. On one hand, the hermeneutic inquiry in evidence concerns *how* the two interlocutors may come to "know" "Jean-Jacques." On the other, the inquiry concerns the larger and more encompassing issue of how anyone may ever "know" the "truth" about anyone else. The search for the real "Jean-Jacques" becomes an inquiry into the very nature of autobiographical "truth" itself. To borrow from Gadamer, the "truth" that is sought cannot be differentiated in this instance from the "method" that seeks to find that same "truth." In his study appropriately entitled *Truth and Method*, Gadamer makes the following telling proposition:

> We say that we "conduct" a conversation, but the more fundamental a conversation is, the less its conduct lies within the will of either partner . . . it is generally more correct to say that we fall into conversation. . . . The way in which one word follows another, with the conversation taking its own turnings and reaching its own conclusion may well be conducted in some way, but the people conversing are far less the leaders of it than the led. . . . It is not for nothing that the actual problems of understanding and the attempt to master it as an art—the concern of hermeneutics—belongs traditionally to the sphere of grammar and rhetoric. Language is the middle ground in which understanding and agreement concerning the object takes place between two people.[17]

Gadamer's assertion that the "people conversing are far less the leaders [of the conversation] than the led" and that language is indeed the middle ground for understanding any object may perhaps best be witnessed in the hermeneutic quest that is the *Dialogues* by the concurrence of two pivotal images. These images—that of being buried alive and that of a labyrinth—are used portentously at the outset of the work. Le Français carefully explains to "Rousseau" that the detractors of "Jean-Jacques" have constructed an elaborate abyss into which the hapless victim has fallen after having lost his way in a labyrinth:

> Ils ont fait en sorte que, libre en apparence au milieu des hommes, il n'eut avec eux aucune société réelle, qu'il vécut seul dans la foule, qu'il ne sut rien de ce qui se fait, rien de ce qui se dit autour de lui, rien surtout de ce qui le regarde et l'intéresse le plus. . . . Ils ont élevé autour de lui des murs de tenebres impenetrables à ses regards; ils l'ont enterré vif parmi les vivans. . . . On a trouvé l'art de lui faire de Paris une solitude plus affreuse que les cavernes et les bois, où il ne trouve au milieu des hommes ni communication, ni consolation, ni conseil, ni lumière, ni rien de tout ce qui pourroit lui aider à se conduire, un labyrinthe immense où l'on ne lui laisse appercevoir dans les ténébres que de fausses routes qui l'égarent de plus en plus. (1:706, 713)

These images of being buried alive and of an immense labyrinth occur only at the beginning of the work, adroitly positioned, as it were, to announce the double-pointed thrust of the hermeneutic inquiry defined by Rousseau's text. The *Dialogues* as hermeneutic quest will thus seek to extricate "Jean-Jacques," and thus autobiographical "truth," from being forever lost in the labyrinth and from being buried alive.[18]

Two possibilities present themselves as means to the end of extricating "Jean-Jacques" from this labyrinth and from the abyss into which he has fallen. As stated above, one interlocutor will read without prejudice everything that "Jean-Jacques" has ever written while the other interlocutor will see "Jean-Jacques" himself. One action is dependent upon the other, and the two interlocutors' decisions resemble a formal *quid pro quo*. The "truth" the characters seek will by definition have to be an amalgam of what each discovers independently of the other. Le Français states:

> Si je fais pour vous cet effort [i.e., to read all that "Jean-Jacques" has written], n'espérez pas du moins que ce soit gratuitement. Pour m'engager à lire ces livres malgré ma répugnance, il faut malgré la vôtre, vous engager vous-même à voir l'Auteur, ou selon vous celui qui se donne pour tel, à l'examiner avec soin, et à démêler à travers son hypocrisie le fourbe adroit qu'elle a masqué si longtems. (1:699)

That the difficulty inherent in "knowing" "Jean-Jacques" points to the larger question of "knowing" the "truth" about anyone is emphatically borne out towards the conclusion of the first of the three conversations, at which time "Rousseau" begins a long and complicated discussion of the ontological status of "truth." "Rousseau" views himself as incapable of finding any ultimate resolution at this juncture and therefore leaves his argument with "Que puis-je faire dans une pareille situation pour parvenir, s'il est possible, à démêler la vérité" (1:769). The two dialogues which follow attempt to ferret out the answer to this question in regard to the individual who is the object of the interlocutors' inquiry. In so doing, the second and third dialogue respond to the more general question posed at the end of the first by "Rousseau"'s rhetorical question. As Gadamer observed, those conversing are less the leaders of the conversation than the led; in this case the hermeneutic quest for the essence of the "truth" on both levels becomes the overwhelming concern of the text.

At the end of the work, however, after several hundred pages of complex discussion and debate, we must ask ourselves what the final understanding has been, what "truth" about "Jean-Jacques" has been discovered. Le Français is now convinced that "Jean-Jacques" is not the incarnation of evil as he was once led to believe. He does realize that those unnamed conspirators have succeeded in altering in print what "Jean-Jacques" had written by hand. This interlocutor recognizes full well that printed words do indeed lie. But as for a total awareness of "Jean-Jacques," Le Français is far from capable of rendering any lasting and sure judgment. Despite "Rousseau"'s impressive rhetorical powers of persuasion, Le Français cannot make a definitive statement about the individual whose character has been so carefully analyzed and dissected over the course of this long and often tortuous dialectical maneuvering. The complete and absolute "truth" about "Jean-Jacques" never has been fully revealed to Le Français— either by what he has gleaned on his own from his reading or from what "Rousseau" has recounted to him.

This "truth" is to be revealed to Le Français only at some future time, only after *he* has seen "Jean-Jacques" for himself. Le Français refuses to relate what he senses to be true because he does not know the entire "truth." He, "Rousseau," and "Jean-Jacques" are to form a rarefied group, limited to themselves and shut off from the rest of the world:

> Si nous nous unissons pour former avec lui une société sincère et
> sans fraude, une fois sûr de notre droiture et d'être estimé de nous,
> il nous ouvrira son coeur sans peine, et recevant dans les nôtres les

épanchemens auxquels ils est naturellement si disposé, nous en pourrons tirer de quoi former de précieux mémoires dont d'autres générations sentiront la valeur, et qui du moins les mettront à portée de discuter contradictoirement des questions aujourd'hui décidées sur le seul rapport de ses ennemis. (1:974)

Thus the *Dialogues,* destined to counter the silence of Jean-Jacques Rousseau's innumerable detractors, curiously end themselves in silence—Le Français, convinced though he may be that "Jean-Jacques" is not evil, refuses resolutely to declare to others that this is indeed the case. Le Français, "Rousseau," and "Jean-Jacques" are together going to found this "société sincère et sans fraude," remarkably similar to the "société des coeurs" of *La Nouvelle Héloïse* in which communication is to be so perfect that mere words are no longer necessary. This "société sincère" with which the *Dialogues* end will have as its guiding purpose "le service de la vérité" (1:975), the last words spoken by Le Français. The *Dialogues* then close in on themselves and abruptly stop. The "truth" they were to reveal, the "Jean-Jacques" who was to be made manifestly understood, is a future promise that cannot be fulfilled in the present.

Janet Varner Gunn has recently argued that the epistomological supposition of all autobiography is not the Cartesian *Cogito ergo sum* but rather the Augustinian *Credo ut intelligam.* For Gunn all autobiography has therefore a pseudoreligious ontology.[19] Is this not precisely what is borne out by the conclusion of the *Dialogues?* While Le Français seems to have become a convert to some ineffable "truth" whose revelation will perforce have to occur at some future time, he is nonetheless a convert who "believes" first as a requisite to "knowing" later.

And what are we to do then with Jean-Jacques Rousseau, who tried to write, even using the ploy of the supposedly purer guise of dialogue, a story of his self and who introduced a distinct note of failure into the construct of his own work and who then likewise failed in his attempt to give his text over to the protective hands of Providence at the Cathedral of Notre Dame, when he found the gates to the high altar locked on that February afternoon in 1776? We are led in the *Dialogues* to Rousseau's own understanding of the ultimate autobiographical dilemma, that defined a century later by Rimbaud's "Je est un autre" and later still by Cocteau's observation that "Je est un mensonge qui dit toujours la vérité."[20] That the self exists is not at issue. What is at stake, as Rousseau the author came to realize, is that all autobiographical discourse is at one and the same time both the expression of the self and the failure of the self to be able to express itself conclusively. It is not just that printed words may lie. All words lie in autobiography. The individual who adopted as his life's motto *Vitam impendere vero* came to understand that the "truth" of the self can never be authoritatively shared.

NOTES

1 Jean Guéhenno writes of this period in Rousseau's existence in the following terms: "His life had begun in humiliation and outrage as if it had been part of a novel by Dostoyevsky; it was continuing as if it were a novel by Kafka" and later "In the last half-century Kafka, who was also overwhelmed by the fact that man seems to play the part of an accused prisoner at the centre of the universe, has described the trial of man in his novels. Jean-Jacques, being more conscious of his destiny than any other man has ever been, believed himself to be that prisoner at the bar." *Jean-Jacques Rousseau*, trans. John and Doreen Weightman (New York: Columbia University Press, 1966), 2:203, 243.

2 Jean-Jacques Rousseau, "Sujet et forme de cet écrit," in *Oeuvres complètes*, ed. Bernard Gagnebin and Marcel Raymond (Paris: Gallimard, Bibliothèque de la Pléiade, 1969), 1:662. All further quotations from Rousseau's works will be taken, where possible, from the Pléiade edition, and references will be given parenthetically in the text. The eighteenth-century spelling as reproduced in this edition has been retained throughout unaltered.

3 This scene, taking its title from the "matinée à l'anglaise" found in this passage, became the subject of the most celebrated of the prints which decorated the more expensive eighteenth-century editions of this novel. See the Garnier edition edited by René Pomeau (Paris: Editions Garnier Frères, 1960), pp. LXIV–LXXVI and commentary on pp. LIII–LXIII.

4 Christie Vance McDonald has cogently remarked that "critics have tended to shun this work which is 'autobiographical' as either marginal or simply the product of a sick mind, perhaps due to the belabored anguish which it manifests towards the problem of the reader, perhaps due also to the obsessive concern with meaning and authenticity. Whatever the reason, the work entitled the *Dialogues* has been considered Jean-Jacques Rousseau's most eccentric and least approachable text." "The Model of Reading in Rousseau's *Dialogues*," *Modern Language Notes*, 93 (May 1978): 723.

5 Lester G. Crocker, *Jean-Jacques Rousseau* (New York: Macmillan, 1973), 2:343–44.

6 "L'art d'écrire ne tient point à celui de parler." *Essai sur l'origine des langues*, in *Oeuvres complètes de Jean-Jacques Rousseau*, ed. V. C. Musset-Pathay (Paris: Dupont, 1823), 2:432. See also Paul de Man, "Theory of Metaphor in Rousseau's *Second Discourse*," *Studies in Romanticism* 12 (Spring 1973): 475–

98; Christie V. McDonald, "Rousseau's Autobiographical Venture: A Process of Negation," *Genre* 6 (March 1973): 98–113, and her excellent article, "The Model of Reading in Rousseau's *Dialogues*," cited above in n. 4. Derrida's most extensive analysis of Rousseau's linguistic theory is that found, of course, in the second half of *De la Grammatologie;* see also his "La Linguistique de Rousseau," *Revue Internationale de Philosophie* 82 (1967): 443–62.

7 *Essai sur l'origine des langues*, in *Oeuvres*, ed. Musset-Pathay, p. 435.
8 See especially ch. 5 of the *Essai sur l'origine des langues*, ibid., pp. 428–36. Cf. *Emile*, bk. 1, "Les prémiéres pleurs des enfans sont des priéres" and later "Le plus grand mal de la précipitation avec laquelle on fait parler les enfans avant l'age n'est pas que les prémiers discours qu'on leur tient et les prémiers mots qu'ils disent n'aient aucun sens pour eux, mais qu'ils aient un autre sens que le nôtre sans que nous sachions nous en appercevoir, en sorte que paroissant nous répondre fort exactement ils nous parlent sans nous entendre et sans que nous les entendions. C'est pour l'ordinaire à de pareilles équivoques qu'est düe la surprise où nous jettent quelquefois leurs propos auxquels nous prêtons des idées qu'ils n'y ont point jointes. Cette inattention de nôtre part au véritable sens que les mots ont pour les enfans me paroit être la cause de leurs prémiéres erreurs" (4:287, 298).
9 See Walter J. Ong, S.J., *Orality and Literacy, The Technologizing of the Word* (London and New York: Methuen, 1982), ch. 1, "The Orality of Language," pp. 5–15, and, in particular, ch. 5, "Print, Space, and Closure," pp. 117–38.
10 See Rousseau's remarks added to his "Note mémorative sur la maladie et la mort de M. Deschamps," in *Oeuvres*, 1:1180. On Rousseau's refusal to continue using Jean-Joseph Renou, see Gaspard Bovier, *Journal de Séjour à Grenoble de Jean-Jacques Rousseau sous le nom de Renou* (Grenoble: Roissard, 1964), pp. 64 ff., and Guéhenno, *Jean-Jacques Rousseau*, 2:223.
11 *Lettre à d'Alembert sur les spectacles*, in *Du Contrat social* [and other works] (Paris: Editions Garnier Frères, 1962), p. 186.
12 Ibid., p. 187.
13 Philippe Lejeune, *Le Pacte autobiographique* (Paris: Editions du Seuil, 1975), p. 33.
14 Michel Foucault has observed that in the *Dialogues* "le sujet qui parle . . . couvre une surface de langage qui n'est jamais close, et où les autres vont pouvoir intervenir par leur acharnement, leur méchanceté, leur décision obstinée de tout altérer." See Foucault's Introduction to the 1962 edition of the *Dialogues* (Paris: Librairie Armand Colin), p. XII.
15 Ibid., pp. XIX–XXI.
16 Louis Petit de Bachaumont, *Mémoires secrets pour servir à l'histoire de la République des Lettres en France, Depuis MDCCLXII jusqu'à nos jours; ou Journal d'un Observateur* (London: John Adamson, 1781), 15:315. The entry is dated 9 September 1780. See Crocker, *Jean-Jacques Rousseau*, 2:344.

17 Hans-Georg Gadamer, *Truth and Method* (New York: Seabury Press, 1975), pp. 345–46.
18 For a generally thorough analysis of the many recurring images in this work, see Timothy M. Scanlan, "Aspects of Figurative Language in Rousseau's *Dialogues*," *Essays in French Literature* 13 (November 1976): 13–27.
19 Janet Varner Gunn, *Autobiography, Toward A Poetics of Experience* (Philadelphia: University of Pennsylvania Press, 1982), see especially p. 24 and pp. 121–26.
20 The Rimbaud quotation, which serves as part of the title of Philippe Lejeune's *Autobiographie de la littérature au médias* (Paris: Editions du Seuil, 1980), is from Rimbaud's famous letter of 15 May 1871 to Paul Demeny; see the Bernard edition of Rimbaud's *Oeuvres* (Paris: Editions Garnier Frères, 1960), p. 345. The Cocteau quotation is from "Le Paquet rouge," *Opéra*, in *Oeuvres complètes* (Geneva: Marguerat, 1951), 4:152.

Executive Board, 1983–84

Institutional Members

of the American Society

for Eighteenth-Century Studies

Appalachian State University
Arizona State University
National Library of Australia
Brooklyn College
Bryn Mawr College
University of Calgary
University of California, Davis
University of California, Irvine
University of California, Los Angeles/William Andrews Clark Memorial Library
University of California, San Diego
California State University, Long Beach
Carleton University
Case Western Reserve University
The Catholic University of America
Art Institute of Chicago
University of Cincinnati
City College, CUNY
Claremont Graduate School
Cleveland State University
Colonial Williamsburg Foundation
University of Colorado, Denver Center
University of Connecticut
Dalhousie University
Delta State University
Detroit Institute of Arts, Founders Society
Institute of Early American History and Culture
Emory University
University of Evansville
Folger Shakespeare Library
Fordham University
Franklin and Marshall College

Georgia Institute of Technology
Georgia State University
University of Georgia
Gettysburg College
Herzog August Bibliothek, Wolfenbüttel
University of Illinois, Chicago Circle
The Johns Hopkins University
University of Kansas
University of Kentucky
Kimbell Art Museum, Fort Worth
Lehigh University
Lehman College, CUNY
The Lewis Walpole Library of Yale University
Los Angeles County Museum of Art
University of Massachusetts, Boston
McMaster University/Association for 18th Century Studies
The Metropolitan Museum of Art
University of Michigan, Ann Arbor
Michigan State University
The Minneapolis Institute of Fine Arts
University of Minnesota
Mount Saint Vincent University
State University of New York, Fredonia
Noel Foundation
University of North Carolina, Chapel Hill
North Georgia College
Northern Illinois University
Northwestern University
The Ohio State University
University of Pennsylvania
University of Pittsburgh
Princeton University

331

Purdue University
Rice University
University of Rochester
Rockford College
Rutgers University
Smith College
Smithsonian Institution
University of South Carolina
University of Southern Mississippi
Swarthmore College
Sweet Briar College
University of Tennessee
University of Texas at Austin
Texas A&M University
Toledo Museum of Art
Tulane University
University of Tulsa

University of Utrecht, Institute for
   Comparative and General Literature
University of Victoria
University of Virginia
Virginia Commonwealth University
The Voltaire Foundation
Washington University, St. Louis
Washington and Lee University
Westfälische Wilhelms-Universität,
   Münster
West Chester State College
The Henry Francis du Pont Winterthur
   Museum
University of Wisconsin, Milwaukee
Yale Center for British Art and British
   Studies
Yale University

Sponsoring Members

of the American Society

for Eighteenth-Century Studies

G. L. Anderson
Mary-Margaret H. Barr
Pamela Bennett
Edward & Lilian Bloom
Timothy R. Bovy
T. E. D. Braun
Patricia Brückmann
Max Byrd
Joseph A. Byrnes
Rosemary M. Canfield
W. B. Carnochan
David W. Carrithers
Ronald Cere
Ellmore A. Champie
Henry S. Commager
Brian Corman
Philip Daghlian
Robert A. Day
John Dowling
Lee A. Elioseff
Charles N. Fifer
Panthea Reid Broughton &
    John Irwin Fischer
William H. Flake
Frank J. Garosi
Morris Golden
Walter Grossmann
Leon M. Guilhamet
Basil Guy
H. George Hahn
Roger Hahn
Phillip Harth
Donald M. Hassler
Alfred W. Hesse

Stephen Holliday
Robert H. Hopkins
Adrienne Hytier
Margaret Jacob
Annibel Jenkins
Shirley Strum Kenny
Gwin J. Kolb
Carl R. Kropf
Colby H. Kullman
J. Patrick Lee
I. Leonard Leeb
J. A. Levine
Herbert Livingston
Robert Loy
Albert M. Lyles
David Macaree
Roger Mandle
H. W. Matalene III
Helen L. McGuffie
Sven Eric Molin
Nicolas H. Nelson
Melvyn New
Hal N. Opperman
Harry Payne
Jean Perkins
Leland Peterson
J. G. A. Pocock
John V. Price
Clifford Earl Ramsey
Thomas J. Regan
Walter E. Rex
Jack Richtman
Edgar V. Roberts
Ronald C. Rosbottom

333

Constance Rowe
E. L. Ruhe
Ambrose Saricks
Robert Shackleton
English Showalter
Henry Snyder
Robert Spector
Mary M. Stewart
J. E. Stockwell

E. J. Thomas, Jr.
Robert W. Uphaus
David M. Vieth
Morris Wachs
Renée Waldinger
Charles G.S. Williams
Raymond Whitley
Calhoun Winton

Patrons

of the American Society

for Eighteenth-Century Studies

Chester Chapin
Louis & Sara Cornell
Judith Keig
Earl Miner
R. G. Peterson